SOCIAL WORK
WITH FAMILIES

Related books of interest

Child and Family Practice: A Relational Perspective
Shelley Cohen Konrad

Social Work Practice with Families: A Resiliency-Based Approach, Second Edition
Mary Patricia Van Hook

Therapeutic Games and Guided Imagery, Volumes I and II
Monit Cheung

School Social Work: Practice, Policy, and Research, Seventh Edition
Carol Rippey Massat, Robert Constable, Shirley McDonald, and
John P. Flynn

Interviewing for the Helping Professions: A Relational Approach
Fred McKenzie

**Evidence-Based Practices for Social Workers:
An Interdisciplinary Approach, Second Edition**
Thomas O'Hare

**Essential Skills of Social Work Practice:
Assessment, Intervention, Evaluation, Second Edition**
Thomas O'Hare

**Clinical Assessment for Social Workers:
Qualitative and Quantitative Methods, Third Edition**
Catheleen Jordan and Cynthia Franklin

**Case Management: An Introduction to Concepts and Skills,
Third Edition**
Arthur J. Frankel and Sheldon R. Gelman

Understanding and Managing the Therapeutic Relationship
Fred R. McKenzie

SOCIAL WORK WITH FAMILIES

Content and Process

Second Edition

Robert Constable
Loyola University Chicago

Daniel B. Lee
Loyola University Chicago

LYCEUM
BOOKS, INC.
Chicago, Illinois

© Lyceum Books, Inc., 2015

Published by

LYCEUM BOOKS, INC.
5758 S. Blackstone Ave.
Chicago, Illinois 60637
773+643-1903 (Fax)
773+643-1902 (Phone)
lyceum@lyceumbooks.com
http://www.lyceumbooks.com

10 9 8 7 6 5 4 3 2

ISBN 978-1-935871-71-2

Printed in the United States of America.

Library of Congress Cataloging-in-Publication Data

Constable, Robert T.
    Social work with families : content and process / Robert Constable, Daniel B. Lee,. —
Second edition.
        pages cm
    Includes bibliographical references and index.
    ISBN 978-1-935871-71-2
    1. Family social work. I. Lee, Daniel B., 1939– II. Title.
    HV697.C665   2015
    362.82'53—dc23
2014023734

Dedication

To our many mentors and teachers
whose ideas and friendship have become parts of us,
whom we acknowledge
with profound gratitude
and to those
of whom space prevents recognition
we ask forgiveness
for debts unpaid.

Harriett Bartlett	Sarah Austin
Felix Biestek SJ	Man Keung Ho
Richard Schwartz	David Mace
Mollie Utkoff	Virginia Satir

Our clients
Our families

Contents

List of Tables and Figures

Preface to the Second Edition

Families have been a primary focus of social work for more than a century. This book takes its inspiration from the same relational paradigm that has governed social work throughout these years. Family is the society in which human solidarity and flourishing is first made possible. Family members interact at family life cycle stages to create a relational structure for the next generation and for themselves. Human needs, which can best be fulfilled in family membership, bring with them a demand for relational justice and human solidarity. Society, through its social institutions, supports what families are uniquely able to do. Social workers have long worked with families, as well as with social institutions, to help them in their tasks.

When this book first appeared, rather than focusing on multiple, competing methods of family intervention, it was more important to integrate methods by focusing on family interaction itself, family resilience, and social work intervention. With the focus on the strengths of families, social workers intervened to develop family solidarity and relational justice. It was clear that this focus brought together the best of the different methodologies of assisting families into a consistent picture. Over the past decade, as the field itself has moved toward synthesis, our approach has strengthened and is even more relevant today.

First of all, family therapy theories and family therapists, including social workers, are coming together into a common picture of the family, of its complexity, and of intervention into the different parts of that complexity that theories address. Intervention is less a question of competing methodologies and more a focus on building the strengths of families and their capacities. Most practitioners of family therapy or of couple therapy are doing this already, either integrating theories or assimilating other methods' approaches into a dominant, organizing, and central "home theory" (Gurman, 2011, p. 287). Second, the research is clear: Much of couples' intervention and family intervention, done well, is also effective. In the case of family intervention, family *systemic therapy*, identified and measured across nations and cultures, would commonly

1. Perceive behavior and mental symptoms within the context of the social systems in which people live
2. Focus on interpersonal relations and interactions, social constructions of realities, and the recursive causality between symptoms and interactions

3. Include family members and other important persons (e.g., teachers, friends, professional helpers), both directly and indirectly
4. Appreciate and use the client's perspectives on problems, resources and preferred solutions (Sydow, Beher, Schweitzer, & Retzlaff, 2010; Sydow, Retzlaff, Beher, Haun, & Schweitzer, 2013; Retzlaff, Sydow, Beher, Haun, & Schweitzer, 2013)

The move toward synthesis shifts the primary focus from a review of competing family therapy methods' approaches to a focus on social work family intervention. We ought to claim a century of our own practice and the theory that has generated this intervention. It shifts the focus from discrete and competing intervention methods to the family system itself as the family seeks to cope with its internal and external necessities. A decade has helped the entire field achieve some clarity on this. We are clearer as well. Our reflection has brought us to add family education components at family life cycle stages to our treatment of social work with families. We have developed further our discussion of social work, social institutions and the family, now into two chapters dealing with schools, child welfare, juvenile courts, health, and mental health. The framework for working between social institution and family is a unique contribution of social work to work with families. Finally, we have added a section of questions for discussion that provides a conceptual outline of the book as well as guiding class discussion.

The book relies heavily on cases for a number of reasons. We conceive of the case as the clearest way to integrate theory into practice. Cases in this book represent the actual practice of many social workers. They have been individually altered to be unrecognizable in an individual sense. These cases reflect the content and process of situations that social workers encounter every day in family work. The reader may recognize the outlines of a wide variety of case situations. None of the situations is esoteric. They are meant to represent practice in different situations with people from different cultures, seeking both connections and the support for action that families can uniquely provide.

Part of an introduction to this book is an acknowledgment of credits and debits. In the cover leaf, we acknowledged some of our mentors and teachers. We have both been very fortunate in our life narratives to have been influenced by a large number of people, and we apologize to those whom space has prevented our mentioning. Perhaps our greatest teachers and mentors have been our own clients. Their untold stories of resilience, courage, and creativity in the art of living have somehow been blended into every case. These stories, their greatest living lessons, validate the book's perspective and methodology. It is not an accident that in the cases cited, things have turned out not always as the client or family wanted, but not badly, and sometimes much better than expected. This has been our general experience. Rather than any triumph of methodology and perspective, the credit goes to human will and intelligence, galvanized by a helping process. It is our clients' success, not ours—a success best explained by no other expertise than human collaborative process.

Finally, we must credit our own families, those closest to us at our life stage, those who have left us legacies—some going back deep into our family histories—and, looking forward, those coming and still to come. We dedicate this book to the students who will use it. You are also part of our family. In particular, we remember our best and closest friends, Pauline Constable and Grace Lee, friends for fifty-one and fifty years, respectively, and the transcultural and multiracial families of our children and grandchildren, who have taught us the many meanings and shades of love.

Robert Constable   Daniel Booduck Lee

REFERENCES

Gurman, A. S. (2011). Couple therapy research and the practice of couple therapy: Can we talk? *Family Process, 50*(3), 287.

Retzlaff, R., Sydow, K. v., Beher, S., Haun, M. W., & Schweitzer, J. (2013). The efficacy of systemic therapy for internalizing and other disorders of childhood and adolescence: A systematic review of 38 randomized trials. *Family Process, 52*(4), 619–652.

Sydow, K. v., Beher, S., Schweitzer, J., & Retzlaff, R. (2010) The efficacy of systemic therapy with adult patients: A meta-content analysis in 38 randomized controlled trials. *Family Process, 49*(4), 457–485.

Sydow, K. v., Retzlaff, R., Beher, S., Haun, M. W., & Schweitzer, J. (2013). The efficacy of systemic therapy for child and adolescent externalizing disorders: A systematic review of 47 RCT. *Family Process, 52*(4), 576–618.

CHAPTER 1

The Strengths of Families and the Practice of Social Work

KEY TOPICS

Strengths-Based Family Intervention
The Scope of Social Work
Evolving Concepts of Social Work with Families
Fields of Social Work Practice with Families
A Social Work Frame of Reference for Working with Families
Basic Human Needs and Family Intervention
Family Resilience
Relational Justice
The Transcultural Perspective
Family Education

The fabric of our lives is woven from the people closest to us: our families and our friends, as well as our memories of both. Family mediates most of our fundamental relations with our environment. We are all part of a family of some sort, and families are a part of us, whether they are the families of our actual, current experience or the families of our memories. There are many ways in which we can establish associations to satisfy our deepest needs for permanency of relationships and for a secure base for action. An understanding of family relationships is essential for understanding every person's relational situation, even persons who are isolated and alone, living outside of a family framework. Each of us, whether living in a family or not, houses a set of relations — an interior family, perhaps a family of hurt and anger, of regrets, of experiences, perhaps a family of conflicting memories. These are the known patterns with which each day we face the world anew. They become the joys and sorrows of memory and lived experience. They become the models we use to construct and interpret experiences. They become fuel for our reflections. This is the bitter and the sweet poetry of our lives. These are the rivers we all travel toward the sea.

STRENGTHS-BASED FAMILY INTERVENTION — AN OUTLINE

Strengths-based social work practice (Weick, Rapp, Sullivan, & Kisthardt, 1989) with families builds on a family's own inherent resilience, its ability to compose itself into a functional unit and to be a source of human relational good. Such practice seeks to identify, use, build, and reinforce the unique strengths of families. At the heart of this resilience, families are adaptable relational structures. They have capacities to respond to the life cycle needs of their members as well as to changing environments. Families can provide a secure relational base and a sense of belonging for their developing members. They provide a set of relationships that uniquely permit growth and development. There is no good substitute for what families can provide. Social work practice seeks to help families be more effective and more just in the face of internal and external challenges. In a diverse, changing, multicultural world, social workers have long helped families of different sorts achieve relational justice, compose themselves, function for their members, and find better connections with their environment.

This small volume seeks to map out the essential functioning of families as natural, self-constructing, relational systems at different stages of transition and development. It seeks to delineate social work intervention with families in capsule form. It seeks to introduce the reader to foundational concepts that will be useful as practice in the field continues to develop. It seeks to summarize a continuum of therapeutic and educational interventions that social workers may use to help family members, as well as the family system itself, develop and function better. For the moment, it is necessary to orient ourselves to a way of thinking about the natural basis for social work practice with families. In this chapter, we review key assumptions underlying this practice and a brief, conceptual history of a century of social work practice with families.

How Do Families Function in Society?

Family, a mediating system between persons and society, plays a crucial role in everyone's life. It is the fundamental crucible of human identity, attachment, and interaction—the basic membership system for human well-being. A long record of research on human development and well-being points out the necessity and the benefits of family membership and the effects on its members when family does not go well (Waite & Gallagher, 2001).

Ernest Burgess (1926; Burgess & Locke, 1953) recognized the family as a "unity of interacting personalities." Seen from the inside, the family is a self-generating, relational network held together by bonds of mutual understanding and social obligations. Being part of a family involves a balance between *agency*, the capacity of members to initiate action within and outside the family, and *communion*, the capacity within the family for membership and for intimate fellowship. *Agency* is always in delicate balance with *communion*. Indeed, agency is not possible without communion, and vice-versa. With communion comes *membership*, bringing obligations, relationships, and established commitments. Adolescents often think of family simply as a static background for what they do as individuals, for their agency. Life circumstances will bring them to recognize their dependence on a reliable family system. Other family members, such as a parental child, can get lost in obligations. Paradoxically, when the family is understood as simply a background for what the individual does or as a set of obligations, it is no longer a family. It loses its uniqueness, its power, and even its value for its members and for society. There must be a balance between agency and communion if the family and its individual members are to function well.

Family is a complex network of related (and changing) persons, linked by generations and held together by bonds of empathy and obligations. In many cultures, this nuclear family can extend to a large kinship unit. In some cases, an unrelated person—for example, the "auntie" in African-American culture—may assume a very effective and important family status. Many variations of family are linked to culture and other factors, but if family is to work, it must be seen as a set of commitments beyond individual self-interest. As members grow older and generations mature, families go through life cycle phases. Family structures shift. Members are often left to catch up with these shifts. Social workers work with these personal changes and structural shifts: with the heat, light, and confusion they generate, with the needs of family members, and with the family's environment.

Families are vulnerable to the dysfunctions of their surrounding environmental systems. The price of poverty is paid for by families. When employment is not available or takes over family functions, it affects the family. When health systems disregard families, when schools and neighborhoods become unsafe places—families are affected. At first families may attempt to cope with an impingement by ignoring it. Yet their needs for these environmental resources can be profound. Their survival as a functioning family is often at stake. Social workers have long known that arranging a shift in the impinging environment, while simultaneously working with family members, often makes a great difference in the family's ability to cope.

The family, seen from the outside, is the elementary cell of social life; it is the basic social institution that mediates between persons and their environments. It is here that mutuality is first experienced and civility first taught (Etzioni, 1983). In every society, the family, lived in various cultural contexts, becomes the basic system of personal belonging, of development and identity, of mutual support and resource distribution. It works for society as the source of its continuation and its civility. It is the basic informal social welfare system.

Other social institutional systems, external to the family—health, education, justice, work—do their work best when they help the family function better without taking the family's place. These social institutional anchors and societal guidance systems are meant to contribute to the family's ability to act effectively. They also can limit its actions and possibilities. In modern society, families cannot really act effectively without simultaneous interaction with societal institutions of health care, education, work, welfare, law, justice (especially laws regulating family), and religion. Family often mediates its members' access to and use of these institutions, and these institutions often mediate family structure. Nor can the institutions be successful without collaboration with families. Without these crucial institutional links, families would quickly experience stress and face breakdown. Often families bear the brunt of what is essentially institutional failure (Ryan, 1971). It is no accident that in working with families, social workers also work with (and often for) each of these social institutions.

The Diversity of Families: Some Functional Commonalities

At present it is impossible to point to a "typical" family arrangement. Philip Cohen (2014a; 2014b) outlines the diversity of family forms found in the contemporary United States. Among 100 representative children, 34 live with dual-earner married parents, 22 live in a married, male breadwinner family, 23 with a single mother (only half of whom have ever been married), 7 with a parent who cohabits with an unmarried partner, 3 with a single father, 3 with grandparents instead of parents, and 8 in other categories (Cohen, 2014b, p. 1). None of these diverse arrangements changes the essential tasks of families or the scope of social work with families. Such diverse families still face an array of tasks:

1. Developing and ensuring solidarity among members
2. Providing for the human development and differentiation of members
3. Coping and helping members cope with the external world
4. Coping with the special needs of members
5. Defining themselves, their adequacy, and their strengths in an often confused environment that may devalue them
6. Coping with their own unique developmental and structural needs, so to perform the above tasks

It is through these tasks, carried out at different life cycle stages, that the family constructs itself. They are developed in different ways and through different examples throughout the book. They are also the point of entry for the social worker. In many cases, with certain family arrangements, the tasks may become more difficult. There may be confusion among family members about these tasks. Some of the social/institutional environment may be distinctly unhelpful to them. There are always gaps between family members and their social institutional environment. If the family is to deal resiliently with these gaps, often it needs time for a healing process to take place. And it often needs healing persons to help this process.

What Is the Scope of Social Work with Families?

Social work has been rooted in work with couples and families for more than a century. Social workers work on both the inside and the outside of families. Their work encompasses couple therapy and family therapy, family life education (FLE), and environmental intervention. They work with family members who struggle with the implications of their membership and attachments and who are coping with particular developmental tasks, needs, or stresses, as well as with the needs, stresses, or tasks of the family itself. Family relational patterns are experienced, developed, melded, and changed again and again in new relationships and new structures and stages of family life, but there is a certain consistency in these changes. The patterns are especially relevant when, acting with others, people form new families, combining the well-trodden pathways, the places and persons known, with new possibilities. The conversational dance of development, the shifts in current relationships in each person's life, can revise patterns and gradually shift even the personal meanings of memories (Lewis & Gossett, 1999).

Families and Social Institutions   Social workers work on the outside of families with societal institutions that include schools, health care systems, justice systems, welfare systems, and work systems that often regulate and set the parameters of what families are able to do. Working between institutions and family members in relation to each other, the combination of family and institutional intervention constitutes an intervention approach with range and power to affect people's lives and development.

WHAT IDEAS HAVE SHAPED SOCIAL WORK WITH THE FAMILY OVER ITS HISTORY?

Although concepts of family practice developed in response to historical circumstances, they provide a rich organizing framework for understanding what it is. We review these concepts as they have developed over the course of a century.

A Helping Relationship for Change   From the beginning, social workers served families. For early social workers in Charity Organization Societies (COS), such as Mary Richmond, social work was family service (Richmond, 1907, pp. 32–37; 1917). Her basic unit of assessment and intervention, the *case*, foreshadowed the basic person-in-environment framework. The person's perspective and situation were important: a helper must begin where the client is. The case inevitably contained the family. She made it clear that no help could be provided without respecting the family's ways of operating, its decision making, its hierarchy, and its cultural patterns: what would later be called *family structure*. Assistance given without respecting family structure would only undermine the family itself (Richmond, 1907, p. 36). With the focus on persons, mostly in families, interacting to secure needs, the *case*, and later the *situation*, would become the basic units of assessment and intervention. The COS motto—"not alms, but a friend"—denoted an early redirection of the helping process from provision of goods alone toward providing a relationship that would help persons take action on a problem or situation. The first COS agencies did provide material assistance—in the form of groceries, rent assistance, and later cash assistance. They reached out to families, often unable or afraid to come to the agency, through home visits, long a tradition in social work practice. However, the personal support and counseling provided—first by volunteers and later by professional social workers—was more important than the material assistance. Implicit in this was a shift in emphasis from charitable giving to a concern for persons' organizing their own worlds, using the assistance to cope with their own situations.

The shift from charitable giving to helping persons organize their own worlds involved a shift of focus to the helping process. The focus on persons interacting with each other and with institutions would allow social workers to adjust their responses to the needs and meanings inherent in a particular situation. Reflecting this perspective, the first professional journal in social work, *The Family*, was founded in 1919. At the same time, the American Association for Organizing Family Social Work (1919 to 1930) was founded; it would later become the Family Service Association of America (FSAA). FSAA brought together approximately 200 COSs (later to become family service agencies) in major cities and small towns. From its inception in 1911, its goals were twofold: "casework to help individuals and families attain self-sufficiency, and research and dissemination of knowledge to prevent the causes of poverty and other social ills" (Hansan, 2013). Family service agencies gradually took over the COS functions in the 1920s, bringing an increased emphasis on individual, marriage and family counseling, then in its infancy. Individual, marriage, and family counseling, historically a cornerstone of the social work profession, would be developed beginning in this period. When public welfare departments were established in every state during the Great Depression (1929 to 1940), the COSs could shift their focus from providing material relief to providing skilled family counseling in what were now family service agencies. Over the following few decades, skilled family counseling in these agencies was the exclusive province of professional social workers (Popple, 1995, p. 2286). This situation only began to shift in the broader field during the mid-1950s, when other professions, such as psychology and psychiatry, got more involved in family work, and in the 1960s, with the contributions of an interdisciplinary family therapy movement (which still predominantly included social workers).

Family Life Education Broadens the Focus   In addition to assisting individuals and families, social workers also were involved in the early development of Family Life Education (FLE). The origins of FLE can be traced to the 1880s in organizations specializing in parent education, such as the Child Study Association of America. Parents met informally to learn about their children, using books as guides. Later these sessions adopted lecture discussion formats. The FSAA has been involved in FLE since the 1930s (Riley, 1995, p. 960). Although the initial formats were mainly educational, by the 1960s and 1970s there was a shift toward the parents' developing more effective skills and attitudes. This culminated in the eventual growth of marriage and relationship education (MRE) (Fagan, Patterson, & Rector, 2002; Lebow, 2013) and other group-related methodologies, discussed later in this book.

The Art of Helping People Out of Trouble   By the 1920s, social work could be conceptualized as the art of helping people out of trouble (DeSchweinitz, 1924). The focus of this art rested on helping persons cope with their situations. Methods of helping—whether with individuals, groups, families, or the institutional environment—would develop over the next twenty years. These methods eventually became teachable, with a theoretical base and a literature. They were then much more than simply an "art." Methods of helping would become ways the social worker could assist coping. They would become aids for people to recompose their situations, revise their personal patterns and relationships, find resources, and get out of "trouble." The natural basis for social work with families was becoming more clear: It would focus on the interactions of people with each other and with institutions, these interactions aiming to meet complex personal and family needs.

How to Think of a Network in Interaction with Its Environment   It was clear that a term was needed to describe this dynamic geography that was unique to social work. Ada Sheffield (1937) broadened the initial focus on the individual and the family to include the relations of the family with an institutional environment—the entire "situation"—as a focus for intervention. The basic context of social work and the boundaries for assessment and intervention would be contained in the situation. The situation brings together personal, familial, and institutional environments in an interactive context. It is a particular picture of persons, families, and a network of community institutions and resources; it takes the form of a social system or group focused in action around a problem, a need, or a resource (Siporin, 1972a, p. 237; 1972b, pp. 91–109). Individuals, families, and their institutional connections remained the basic frame of reference for the case or now the "situation."

Fields of Social Work Practice with Families   Early in the history of social work, the COS model, with its emphasis on persons' acting in a broader context, was adopted by other developing areas of practice. Experiments with social work in schools, hospitals, courts, and child welfare agencies became the basis for fields of practice. Each field of practice was different and reflected its social institutional context. Much of this practice had to be learned by apprenticeship. Within these different contexts each field of practice would develop its appropriate practice on a common foundation, later identified as the casework method.

From the first decades of the twentieth century, school social workers in New York City had been working, between home and school, with immigrant families and their children. In Hartford, Connecticut, social workers took part in the first school guidance teams, working with families, pupils, and school (Lide, 1959; Costin, 1969). In Massachusetts General Hospital, physicians and social workers expanded medical intervention to the social and familial world of the patient (Nacman, 1977; Carlton, 1984). The field of child welfare work moved from its early roots in the orphanage to work with children in foster families and in their own families. During World War I, the Red Cross developed counseling for families of servicemen, in those days including virtually everyone (Watts, 1964). After the war, services for psychiatric patients and their families soon followed (Southard & Jarrett, 1922). In seeking to understand all this diversity and seeking to integrate multiple theories, a functional model of the helping process gradually emerged. Social work "functions," each different in what they addressed, developed through a picture of the interaction between social institutions, families, and individuals (Witmer, 1942).

This would differentiate social work practice as it took place in different fields of practice with individuals and families. Later work in "functional social work" would develop a useful, interactional framework for the helping process, whether in casework (Smalley, 1967) or group work (Schwartz, 1977). Many services in the private sector were sponsored by religious organizations and cultural subgroupings. Here the emergent personal focus was adapted not only to a function, but also to the particular needs of a community of membership, although services would usually be extended to others not of that community.

Casework: An Underlying Method   At the same time when services were developing in different fields of practice in social work, there was an effort to conceptualize a common teachable base for all social work fields of practice. Such a base came in the form of methods, principally casework—which at that time meant work with individuals and families. Basic issues in the maturation of social work practice and theory were laid out in the Milford Conference Report (American Association of Social Workers, 1931). It was necessary to establish a distinction between fields of practice and the generic base for practice in these fields. Casework, identified as "generic," would provide an underlying base for its concrete manifestation in different fields. The distinguishing concern of social casework would be the capacity of individuals to structure their social activities within a given environment (person-in-situation) (Brieland, 1995, p. 2250). The person-in-situation would include a family and community environment.

An Individual Focus for Casework: Some Problems   During the 1920s, a psychotherapeutic or "clinical" orientation emerged, and accordingly some practice began to focus more on the person. After World War II, in response to the combination of increased professionalization and the greatly revived mental health movement, the general focus of social workers in many fields came to rest on the psychotherapeutic uses of casework. Private family service agencies were well developed and provided a range of services to middle-class clients, as well as families in poverty. Social workers still focused on families, but the family often took a back seat to the person. Such practice could take on a medicalized cast with a focus on mental health and a lessened reference to the person's dynamic context (Hartman & Laird, 1983, pp. 3–22). This trend lasted through the late 1960s and continues to some extent today, although most social work now uses multiple methods of working—with individuals, couples, families, and groups within an interactional context. It deals with multiple systems; its goals are broader than a focus on mental health alone.

The Transaction between Persons and Environments   The 1960s and 1970s saw many developments in areas, such as family therapy, that needed integration into the knowledge base. Dissatisfaction with an overindividualized and medicalized practice led to a search for the roots of practice. There was need for integration between theories focused on individuals, theories used to understand the family as a unit, and theories related to an institutional and community environment, each perceived at the time within their separate orbits. Social work theory needed to clarify its focus and integrate knowledge from different areas into a picture, which reflected practice in its fullness. Although knowledge about families could be found in disciplines, such as sociology, psychology, and psychiatry, no single, core discipline could adequately explain practice. The response to this situation was that social work theory needed to be *built* on an architecture of social relations and a picture of persons coping within relational fields (Gordon, 1969; Bartlett, 1972). The best summary of this very general foundational work appeared in the 1979 report of the Joint NASW-CSWE Task Force on Specialization:

> The fundamental zone of social work is where people and their environment are in exchange with each other. Social work historically has focused on the transaction zone where the exchange between people and the environment which impinges on them results in changes in both. Social work intervention aims at the coping capabilities of people and the demands and resources of their environment so that the transactions between them are helpful to both. Social work's concern extends to both the dysfunctional and deficient conditions at the juncture between people and their environment and to the opportunities there for producing growth and improving the environment. It is the duality of focus on people and their environments that distinguishes social work from other professions (Joint NASW-CSWE Task Force on Specialization, 1979).

Systems Perspective A system is a holistic, organized unit of independent transacting and mutually influencing parts within an identifiable environment (Siporin, 1972a, p. 106). Systems theory, which was used by social work during the 1960s and later, would allow for a broadening of focus to include the family and institutional systems people interacted with. It would allow for the interaction of persons in family units, institutions, and whole communities to be better understood and mapped out (Hearn, 1969; Hartman & Laird, 1983). The systems perspective was gradually appropriated by social workers and the family therapy movement as a means of mapping out this interaction, even becoming a way of distinguishing a broader approach from one that predominantly focused on individuals.

The Family Therapy Movement Since the early 1960s, interdisciplinary groups of social workers, psychologists, and psychiatrists, whose fundamental frame of reference is the family, have been informally working to develop theory and practice, as well as to differentiate work with families from ways of helping individuals. In this book we draw heavily upon family therapy theories in the context of family structure and family development—how families compose themselves at different stages of development and the characteristic focus and tasks of social work practice with families. Because the family therapy model reflected what social workers had already been dealing with since the beginnings of their profession, social workers, such as Virginia Satir and others, have been a most important part of this movement.

After all, social work family intervention had a fifty-year history, far longer than other professions. Early family therapists, intervening with various parts if the family system, created different theoretical languages to describe their practice. For a time, family therapies represented a wide range of competing approaches to theory and practice, each connected with the aspect of family functioning they addressed. Table 1.1 examines these different aspects of family functioning and the common human needs families satisfy. Table 4.1 relates the different approaches to family therapy to these common needs and aspects of family functioning. Although social workers, among others, were pioneers in these different particular approaches, the social work perspective never lost its underlying approach to the family as a whole. In prac-

Table 1.1

Components of Family Functioning and Human Needs

Human Needs and Capacities	Components of Family Functioning					
	Personal Development and Intrapersonal Process	Family Communication and Meanings	Interpersonal and Spiritual Narratives and Stories	Family Developmental Processes	Family Structure	Family Environmental Systems
Safety	X	X	X	X	X	X
Belonging	X	X	X	X	X	X
Capacity for effective communication	X	X	X	X	X	X
Capacity to choose in an ethical, relational framework, to be concerned for self and others	X	X	X	X	X	X
Capacity to grow, to interact, and to take care of self and others— to love	X	X	X	X	X	X

tice, family therapy approaches often were less a matter of dogma than emphasis. Moving between one level of family functioning and another as the situation and the assessment dictated, family practitioners often quietly used techniques from competing approaches in their work long before theoretical frameworks would begin to integrate these approaches in a common picture of family functioning. Most therapists, describing themselves as "integrative," would have a dominant, organizing, and central "home theory" that guided their overall perspective and understanding of the change process. They would import ("assimilate"; Messer, 2001) selected techniques from other approaches into this home theory on a case-by-case basis (Gurman, 2011, p. 287).

Toward Synthesis: Practice Theory and Effectiveness Research

By the 1990s, both family therapy theory and practice were beginning to move toward synthesis (Bruenlin, Schwartz, & Mac Kune-Karrer, 1992; Lebow, 1997; Pinsof, 1995; Lebow, 2003; Bruenlin, Pinsof, Russell, & Lebow, 2013; Pinsof, Bruenlin, Russell, & Lebow, 2013). By 2001 "assimilative intervention" became the hallmark of a move toward a practice synthesis of different theoretical perspectives (Messer, 2001). In the meantime, effectiveness research was validating couples and family intervention. A number of approaches to couples intervention were validated by random clinical trials (RCT) (Gurman, 2011, p. 282). One example, emotionally focused couple therapy (Johnson, 2003; Johnson, 2004), assimilated a variety of techniques into a well-organized attachment theory and family systems base. Family intervention multisystemic therapy (Sheidow, Henggeler, & Schoenwald, 2003) and functional family therapy (Sexton & Alexander, 2003) assimilated community networking into an integrative, family systems base and achieved positive results on RCTs.

By 2008 both family practice and research had developed and come to the point where it was possible to identify a common thread of "family systemic therapy" from among a large number of studies appearing in the international literature (German, Spanish, English, Mandarin Chinese). These studies addressed various problems of children, adolescents, and adults in families. The studies were now sufficiently numerous and sophisticated—with large enough numbers of participants and adequate resources—to test the effectiveness of their interventions through RCTs. The international selection criteria for these approaches required that: (1) they perceive behavior and mental symptoms within the context of the social systems people live in; (2) they focus on interpersonal relations and interactions, social constructions of realities, and the recursive causality between symptoms and interactions; (3) they include family members and other important persons (e.g., teachers, friends, professional helpers) directly and indirectly through specific interventions, such as systemic questioning and developing intervention hypotheses that included the entire family unit; and (4) they appreciate and use the client's perspectives on problems, resources, and preferred solutions. Such identification and testing of family systemic therapy would be a significant watershed in the development of family practice.

From 2008 to 2011, a German study identified thirty-eight RCT studies of family intervention dealing with adult patients in the international literature (Sydow, Beher, Schweitzer, & Retzlaff, 2010), forty-seven RCT studies of child and adolescent externalizing behavior (ADHD, conduct disorders, substance abuse) (Sydow, Retzlaff, Beher, Haun, & Schweitzer, 2013), and thirty-eight RCT studies of child and adolescent internalizing and other behaviors (mood disorders, anxiety disorders, eating disorders, suicidality, etc.) (Retzlaff, Sydow, Beher, Haun, & Schweitzer, 2013). The researchers compared each group through meta-analysis, studying the effectiveness of the interventions with the different problem categories. In these studies, described in greater detail in chapter 12, for the broad majority of each group (34/38, 42/47, 33/38), systemic therapy was either significantly more efficacious than control groups without a systems-oriented intervention, or systemic therapy was more efficacious than other evidence-based interventions (Sydow, Beher, Schweitzer, & Retzlaff, 2010; Sydow, Retzlaff, Beher, Haun, & Schweitzer, 2013; Retzlaff, Sydow, Beher, Haun, & Schweitzer, 2013). Such research is evidence of common, interdisciplinary orientations to family intervention, emerging internationally, in sufficient number that they can be identifiable, comparable, and effective. Although social workers have a broader problem focus, the general assumptions behind "family systems" therapy are not different from those behind the practice of social work with families. The emergent framework is very familiar to social workers. What made these (still) loosely categorized approaches so effective? In the remainder of this book we will develop a framework for the practice of social work with families and provide a social work practice framework that would begin to answer the question.

A SOCIAL WORK FRAME OF REFERENCE FOR WORKING WITH FAMILIES

What Needs Do Families Uniquely Provide For?

What Do Persons in Families Seek?   The natural beginning point of any understanding of family functioning is human need. Persons take part in families to realize basic, uniquely personal needs that are so important for their own development that they cannot be ignored. They become a matter of (relational) justice for persons in a family. Among the basic needs and personal capacities that persons seek to realize in a family and that family uniquely can promote better than any alternative, are the following:

- *The need for safety.* Where there is safety and discretion, the persons and fragile identities of others in the family are protected, and belonging is possible.
- *The need for belonging.* Where there is belonging, the family can be a secure base for communication and action.
- *The capacity for communication.* Where there is communication, one can comfortably express one's own feelings and accept and respond to the feelings and thoughts of others in the family.

- *The capacity to choose in an ethical, relational framework.* In a relational framework of appropriate concern for the worth and dignity of self and others, one can have the capacity to choose. Where there is a degree of personal agency that respects one's own and others' dignity, there can be the capacity to grow as a person and to change.
- *The capacity to grow, to interact, to care, and to love.* Growth takes place in a context of interaction, communication, care for the needs of the self and others, and role differentiation. Where there is the capacity to grow as a person and to interact with others, there can also be the capacity to care appropriately for the needs of the self and others and, ultimately, to love.

What Is Relational Justice? Every one of these human needs—safety, belonging, communication, personal agency, and so on—can be sometimes profoundly violated within particular families. Furthermore, the needs of individual family members as they move through their personal life cycles may also be in conflict. That needs are violated argues for the interest of the community in protecting family members, as well as for a professional approach to working with them. When these needs are grossly violated, the surrounding community with its organized social welfare institutions steps in. This often creates greater difficulty as family members struggle to deal with possible colonization by outside institutional structures—perceived by families as representing a different culture or class—as well as influences from the market, money, images from the mass media, and the like.

Perceived injustice, reinforced by a community response, unbalances the family system. In case study 5.7, the J. family are overseas Chinese from Singapore, now living in San Francisco. On the inside of the family, how does each member of the family find new relational balances after the father beat the 13-year-old son, Kwak, with a broomstick when Kwak talked back to him? On the outside of the family, how does the family find its own balance with the California child welfare system and the court when the abuse was reported? Such internal and external problems and tasks are interrelated. The family needs to work to restore substantive justice for every member while restoring its internal and external balances. Often this cannot be done well without outside assistance that respects the family and its delicate functional balances, but is also connected with the larger systems.

How Can Families Meet Their Members' Needs?

Table 1.1 maps out relations between human needs, capacities, and family functioning. Families provide the context for personal development and the relationships of members with each other. They are vehicles for communication and meanings. They are the background for our life narratives. Their relational structure develops and changes as we develop and as the others develop. They provide the context and, in many cases, the reasons for our exchanges with the environment. From the family's perspective, each of these components of functioning addresses and constructs in different ways the goods that can emerge from family interaction. Social work inevitably deals with all of these components. In table 4.1, we see the particular connections and the contributions of differing approaches to family therapy practice and theory to each of these components of family functioning.

What Do Social Workers Do That Helps Families Achieve These Needs?

In outline form, social workers work on seven levels to assist families to compose themselves and to meet needs of family members:

1. Working with individual family members on personal and relational tasks
2. Working to change family communication and meanings
3. Working to reframe the family's interpersonal narratives and stories of their experience
4. Working to assist families with family life cycle developmental tasks in which they have become "stuck"
5. Working to change the family's relational structure, and from this to change members' experience of each other
6. Working to change the family's relationship with environmental systems
7. Working to assist environmental systems to help families (and their members) to function better

A Framework for Family Intervention

Table 1.2 shows a basic framework for the interaction between personal needs and family needs, the response of the social worker, the response of the family, and principles of practice. The interactions of family members create the context, the goals, and the boundaries of the helping process. Per the table, the social worker would respond to the family's needs by helping family members construct their relationships with each other, develop personal capacities for membership, and ultimately modify the family structure. The social worker responds to the family members with whom he or she has chosen to work, as well as simultaneously to the family as a whole. The social worker's choice of where in the family to work is based on an assessment of family functioning, structure, and relational tasks in a systems framework, as well as the possible parallel interventions within the environment and social institutional worlds. For example, work with the parents may be the most powerful way to affect children. Indeed, choosing to work with children without some work with the parents would undermine parents and thus the functionality of the family system.

Table 1.2 focuses on the internal dynamics of the family meeting needs and on the possible response of the social worker, as a relational coach. It makes a connection between generic principles of social work practice and family structural change. Following the flow of the table, members of families seek certain personal and social goods, which families can uniquely provide. These—safety; belonging; communication; the capacity to choose in an ethical, relational framework; the capacity to grow, to interact, and to care—are illustrated in the first column of table 1.2. Fam-

Table 1.2

Needs of Persons in Families, Response of the Social Worker, and
Ethical-Technical Practice Principles

First Direction	Second Direction	Third Direction	Fourth Direction
Persons interacting at individual and family life cycle stages establish family structure and satisfy human needs	*The response of the social worker*	*The awareness and response of persons in the family*	*Ethical-technical practice principle (to help the family unit to . . .)*
I Safety			*Develop confidentiality, discretion, and trust*
To maintain safety and discretion, protecting the dignity and fragile identities of others	The social worker responds to these needs, the family's personal and relational tasks, by helping family members, individually and with each other, to communicate, to respond to each other's needs, to accomplish developmental tasks, and to create a network of understandings (family structure).	The family members respond to the social worker's sensitivity, understanding, and response to them and to the identification of personal and relational tasks in the sessions. They begin to learn to respond appropriately to each other and develop a climate of understanding and support with each other in which these tasks can be accomplished.	
II Belonging			*Support the worth, dignity, and uniqueness of each person*
To be treated as a unique person of worth; to respond to others in this way; to withhold negative judgments of worth			
III Communication			*Develop purposeful, skillful, and constructive communication*
To respond accurately to the feelings and thoughts of others; to express one's own feelings and thoughts			
IV Capacity to choose, to be concerned for self and others			*Support self-determination, principled choices, and altruistic beliefs*
To grow into making choices and decisions in an ethical–relational framework; to respect others' similar freedom			
V Capacity to grow, to interact, and to take care of self and others			*Support differentiation of self and care for others in revised family structure*
To carry out developmental tasks with family support; to care appropriately for the needs of self and the others			

ily members need to work together for the family to achieve these basic human goods for their members. The work of constructing a family is inherently concerned with what persons need to grow and develop as human beings, that is, with relational justice. In this sense, the value issues are already inherent to the situation and to family intervention (Constable, 1983; 1989). The environment, reflected in family interaction, provides another set of related systems. For example, in case study 10.1, in the case of Alan, the major focus was Alan's process in school. However, the school social worker intervened with Alan, his teachers, and his parents, each in relation to the embedded meanings of Alan's suicidal ideation and functioning in the family and in the school. Without interdisciplinary work in every sector, the situation would not have been successful. And the school was the only place where Alan and his family were reachable at the point when he had expressed suicidal ideation.

How Do Resilient Families Cope?

Strengths-Based Family Intervention   We can come to a deeper understanding of how families may discover their strengths through an understanding of the resilient family. Often functioning under extreme conditions, the resilient family forges transformation and growth *from* adverse circumstances (Walsh, 1999; 2003; 2012

Resilient families are able to carry on through difficult and stressful situations. Cultural groups who have experienced extreme stress—such as slavery and subsequent discrimination, the Holocaust, deportation to Siberia, migration, or refugee flight—may carry with them the pain imposed by oppressive conditions, but also the qualities that have allowed them to survive in inhuman conditions. However, resilience is not a matter of one particular family structure, but rather of how family members together learn to process their internal and external environments. For most families the effects of oppressive conditions could act to suppress the very qualities that could lead to survival. The resilient family becomes stronger in the midst of difficulty. It develops its meanings, interacts with its circumstances, and adapts creatively to them, preserving its own values. Family members are still able to communicate their needs and solve problems. The family shows some ability to:

- Approach adversity as a challenge shared by the whole family
- Normalize and contextualize distress
- Use adversity to gain a sense of its own coherence
- Make sense of how things have happened through causal or explanatory attributions
- Have a hopeful and optimistic bias
- Master the art of the possible
- Draw upon spiritual resources
- Develop flexibility and adaptability
- Develop its internal connections
- Use social and economic resources appropriately
- Communicate clearly and openly with each other
- Solve problems collaboratively

The key processes in family resilience are developed in greater detail in table 1.3. The discussion of the resilient family provides an excellent example of how *agency*

Table 1.3
Key Processes in Family Resilience

Belief Systems
1. Make Meaning of Adversity
   - View resilience as relationally based versus being a "rugged individual"
   - Normalize and contextualize adversity and distress
   - Sense of coherence: crisis as meaningful, comprehensible, manageable challenge
   - Causal/explanatory attributions: How could this happen? What can be done?

2. Positive Outlook
   - Hope, optimistic bias; confidence in overcoming odds
   - Courage and en-*courage*-ment; affirm strengths and focus on potential
   - Active initiative and perseverance (can-do spirit)
   - Master the possible; accept what can't be changed

3. Transcendence and Spirituality
   - Larger values, purpose
   - Spirituality: faith, congregational support, healing rituals
   - Inspiration: envision new possibilities; creative expression; social action
   - Transformation: learning, change, and growth from adversity

Family Organizational Patterns
4. Flexibility
   - Open to change: rebound, reorganize, adapt to fit new challenges
   - Maintain stability during disruption: continuity, dependability, followthrough
   - Strong authoritative leadership: nurturance, protection, guidance
   - Varied family forms: cooperative parenting/caregiving teams
   - Couple/co-parent relationship: equal partners

5. Connectedness
   - Mutual support, collaboration, and commitment
   - Respect individual needs, differences, and boundaries
   - Seek reconnection, reconciliation of wounded relationships

6. Social and Economic Resources
   - Mobilize kin, social, and community networks; seek models and mentors
   - Build financial security; balance work/family strains

Communication/Problem Solving
7. Clarity
   - Clear, consistent messages (words and actions)
   - Clarify ambiguous information; truth-seeking/truth-speaking

8. Open Emotional Expression
   - Share range of feelings (joy and pain, hopes and fears)
   - Mutual empathy; tolerance for differences
   - Take responsibility for own feelings, behavior; avoid blaming
   - Pleasurable interactions; humor

9. Collaborative Problem Solving
   - Creative brainstorming; resourcefulness; seize opportunities
   - Shared decision making; conflict resolution: negotiation, fairness, reciprocity
   - Focus on goals; take concrete steps; build on success; learn from failure
   - Proactive stance: prevent problems; avert crises; prepare for future challenges

SOURCE: *Family Process* 42, no. 1. © 2003 FPI, Inc. (Walsh, 2003).

and family *communion* interact within a family. For family members to have agency, the family needs communion, and for the family to have communion, at least some of the members must have agency. One supports the other in a complex circular relation.

A Natural Basis for Social Work with Families

The family is a primary, social institution. Despite their diversity, they are natural, self-constructing, relational systems, which we encounter at different family life cycle stages of transition and development. When they work well, they sustainably meet the human needs of their members as no other arrangement can. A natural basis for social work with families builds on the assumption that family is the protagonist, seeking to perform life cycle tasks, and that social workers may help their members do this effectively. And so, social workers intervene *with* families to help family members do what they must do in any case. They intervene *between* families and social institutions, and *with institutions* so that those institutions can carry out their societal mandates as well

They use a wide range of methods in the process of helping individuals, families, and institutions to compose themselves, to achieve purposes, and to carry out relational tasks inherent to the human condition. These are not simply personal tasks. *Relational* tasks are the tasks of members of a family network in interaction. Social work practitioners have routinely found that they must draw from different bodies of available method theory depending on where in the system they may best intervene (Corcoran, 2000; Cocozzelli & Constable, 1985; Constable & Cocozzelli, 1989; Jayaratne, 1978). With an appropriate organizing framework, the social worker can use a variety of approaches to intervention in different situations and in different institutional and cultural contexts. Methods are assimilated into the helping process (Gurman, 2011, p. 287) to best serve the family's needs, assimilation which most family practitioners actually do (Nichols, 2013, pp. 297–306).

Relational justice means that in the family every person needs human dignity and the prerequisites to grow and flourish. When Mr. J. was abusive to his son, each member of the J. family had to do personal and relational work to cope with the challenges to their relationships brought about by the father's abuse and by the intervention of the court. The question of relational justice is embedded in every family question. What should I do in this situation? What should one family member expect from others—or from society? What should he or she contribute? Things often fail, and these failures become a reason for intervention (Tillich, 1962). On the inside of the family, the delicate networks of empathy and obligation can fail. When they fail, families may become less able to operate in the broader society and to use the resources of surrounding institutions. They may become less able to carry out their very personal function for each of their members. Persons who reflect such societal and familial confusion and conflict can experience difficulty developing their own potential as participants in family and in society. On the outside of the family, institutions and communities can fail. External systems, such as employment, justice, human welfare, and education, may fail to carry out their own assigned functions of healing, educating, ensuring justice, distributing work, and ensuring human welfare. In the diversity and complexity of society, where economic and political power privileges certain groups over others, conflicts and discrimination unfortunately take place.

Power, Dominance, and Autonomy: The Feminist Critique During the 1980s, a number of prominent women in the family therapy movement (who were social workers) challenged an implicit acceptance of gender dominance in theory development and in practice (McGoldrick, Anderson, & Walsh, 1989; Walters, Carter, Papp, & Silverstein, 1988; Weingarten, 1991). People need to find respect, space, and equality in their relations with each other. The concept of dominance needs to be distinguished from legitimate functional power, coming from one's role. And no one is fully autonomous. Although the socialization process demands different levels of *authority*, the language of dominance never works well in family relations. For example, for the socialization of young children to take place, parents need a certain amount of functional power, but power alone will not accomplish socialization. Relational justice demands that parents' legitimate control over certain contingencies be recognized both morally and socially. This is not dominance—the imposition of one's personality or one's preferences. It is not the personal need to *control* another person.

The societal shifts in gender awareness heightened the feminist critique of relational injustice. These shifts pushed theory to clarify the necessary spousal equality. It brought theory to make distinctions between personal dominance and the functional power that parents need if they are to be effective. The shifts pushed social workers who were working with families, spurring them to find ways of helping family members move to more balanced positions, gradually coming to a balance of needs, rights, and obligations. Depersonalized or skewed family relationships, ones that sacrifice one person for another, are dysfunctional. There are better solutions as families find balance and persons find *co-responsibility*. The co-responsible person is neither the total master nor the total victim of one's fate; he or she is neither fully responsible for, nor unconcerned about, the other. These themes are still being developed in the family field.

Diverse Family Situations

Families are diverse in their form and their interaction (McGoldrick & Carter, 1999). Culture, gender, generational divisions, and simple human differences recognize that, in family situations there is great diversity. There is not one picture of a "good family." Families may do the same relational work effectively in many different ways. The experienced practitioner learns to understand this diversity—what can work and what might not. Parts of the job of parenting, for example, are done in a family by birth parents, grandparents, siblings, aunts, adoptive parents, single foster parents, day care providers, "aunties," and others having a wide variety of beliefs about themselves and the family relations they are constructing together. Different families have different visions and different patterns of seeking the same values. There are inevitable collisions within families and between family members and the larger society, but such collisions can be either destructive or creative. Familiar with this general territory, the social worker offers the possibility of an informed helping process, one that can assist family members in coming to terms with and finding some resolution for some of the differences and dilemmas inherent in their situation or (often) imposed by outside forces. The social worker needs to understand the many ways in which families can resolve these dilemmas. Within the normal constraints and consequences of society, the issues are for the family to resolve. The alternate is no longer to function as a family.

The Transcultural Perspective   The same philosophy of working with difference applies to the many cultural variations of today's society. In today's global society, rapid cultural change is taking place both within families and in their relationships with their surroundings. A transcultural perspective is inherently a dynamic perspective that recognizes the reality that both families and society are in flux. It assumes that culture is dynamic and adaptive and that families often identify for themselves narrower beliefs than their actual capabilities. As described in greater detail in chapter 5, it assumes that all persons actively seek to construct secure relational bases; they hope to secure similar basic needs and relational goods. However, there are shifting concepts of what that base is, how it may be secured, and what is due in relational justice. Family members may have different understandings of relationships and may interact with each other in different ways based on these understandings. It is challenging for families to find their internal and external balances in this situation. The J. family, overseas Chinese from Singapore living in San Francisco, has a long cultural history of adaptation while retaining a strong relational core. Within the family there were different understandings about what their external environment called child abuse. And there were different understandings of the shame of the family and of their father and, called before the court to correct this problem.

In the context of such rapid changes and differences, the transcultural work of family members is already embedded in their relational tasks. There may be differences in how families conceive and carry out these tasks. There may be differences in how families transact with social institutions. But all families search for secure relational goods—for the ontological meanings of *being with* each other. It is not enough to concentrate on different perceptions or whatever *barriers* to their aspirations the J. family might encounter. When there are obstacles, a transcultural perspective looks for possibilities of redeveloping *connections* within families and between families and social institutions. The key to their transcultural understanding cannot be found in some ideal state. Rather, it is found in the helping process itself, in the search for the relational goods of being with each other. These are different rivers flowing into one sea.

What Is Family Education?

Family education broadens the helping focus from helping families one by one to helping groups of family members, learning to deal with common family situations or developmental concerns. Family education began over the last century as marriage preparation, frequently sponsored by churches. In the early part of the twentieth century, social workers in private, community family agencies in the United States were developing "family life education." Training for these programs was routinely offered by the Family Service Association of America. Much of the focus of family life education at that time was informational in contrast to direct work with families, done in the same agency one family at a time. By the late 1960s well-developed and popular programs were emerging in a variety of other fields serving families. There was the greatest development in marriage and relationship education (MRE) with couples contemplating marriage and couples in the early stages of their marriage. These programs were moving from information to an emphasis on skills, such as couple communication or relationships with one's children.

By 1985, the time of the first major evaluation of family education (Giblin, Sprenkle, & Sheehan, 1985), many programs existed that used a variety of formats to help couples and family members with different problems. For example, for families dealing with a member with special needs, family education groups afforded an opportunity (1) to recognize and normalize their situation, (2) to find family-friendly ways of collaborating with specialized help and remedial programs, which otherwise might put pressure on individual family members, (3) to deal with the internal family structural implications of having a member with special needs, and (4) to learn new ways of dealing with the member, such as managing strong expressed emotion with a schizophrenic member. Such programs left families in charge of their own situations. For the amount of professional time investment developing and fostering the group, the possibilities of good outcomes were high. Social workers, with their group work and family orientation as well as their professional history, are able to provide many of these services.

SUMMARY

Social workers have been working with families for more than a century. They have learned that to be effective, they need to focus on families as unique and self-constructed relational systems, as well as on what family members actually do when they construct (or reconstruct) relational realities. Because what they do involves persons' interacting both with each other and with institutional realities, social workers are prepared to act within this arena. The identity and position of social work permits it to draw readily from social psychology, family therapy, and other areas, such as pastoral counseling and nursing, without the contradictions that would come if social work were referenced primarily to one or two methods or if it addressed only one level of or one approach to human functioning. Intervention is based on a strengths-based picture of families' composing themselves to carry out what families themselves are uniquely able to do, for which no other institution can easily substitute. In the following chapters, we identify a life cycle history of family development, family structure at points of the life cycle, and family intervention—the content, process, and narratives of social work practice at different points in the life cycle. We draw freely from larger bodies of family intervention theory, integrating these theories into a picture of social work practice with couples and families. Our capsule treatment confines itself to an outline of content, process, and the integration of theory in practice in a dynamic, transcultural context. Theory is integrated through practice, using case situations. These are composites of the many family situations we have encountered in practice and in teaching. They are emblematic of the people and situations that social workers encounter every day.

REFERENCES

American Association of Social Workers. (1931). *Social casework: Generic and specific*. New York: Author.

Bartlett, H. (1972). *The common base of social work practice*. New York: National Association of Social Workers.

Brieland, D. (1995). Social work practice: History and evolution. In R. L. Edwards & J. G. Hopps (Eds.), *Encyclopedia of social work* (pp. 2247–2257). Washington, DC: National Association of Social Workers.

Breunlin, D. C., Pinsof, W., Russell, W., & Lebow, J. (2013). Integrative problem-centered metaframeworks therapy I: Core concepts and hypothesizing. *Family Process, 50*(3), 293–313.

Breunlin, D. C., Schwartz, R. C., & Mac Kune-Karrer, B. (1992). *Metaframeworks: Transcending the models of family therapy*. San Francisco: Jossey-Bass.

Burgess, E. W. (1926). The family as a unity of interacting personalities. *The Family, 7*, 3–9.

Burgess, E. W., & Locke, H. J. (1953). *The family: From institution to companionship*. New York: American Book.

Carlton, T. O. (1984). *Clinical social work in health settings: A guide to professional practice with exemplars*. New York: Springer.

Cocozzelli, C., & Constable, R. T. (1985). An empirical analysis of the relation between theory and practice in clinical social work. *Journal of Social Service Research, 9*(1), 47–63.

Cohen, P. (2014a). *The family: Diversity, inequality and social change*. New York: W. W. Norton.

Cohen, P. (2014b). *Family diversity is the new normal for America's children*. Council on Contemporary Families, September 4, 2014. Retrieved from https://contemporaryfamilies.org/the-new-normal/.

Constable, R. T. (1983). Values, religion and social work practice. *Social Thought, 15*(2), 29–40.

Constable, R. T. (1989). Relations and membership: Foundations for ethical thinking in social work. *Social Thought, 15*(3–4), 53–66.

Constable, R. T., & Cocozzelli, C. (1989). Common themes and polarities in social work practice theory development. *Social Thought, 15*(2), 14–24.

Corcoran, J. (2000). *Evidence-based social work practice with families.* New York: Springer.

Costin, L. B. (1969). A historical review of school social work. *Social Casework, 59,* 439–453.

DeSchweinitz, K. (1924). *The art of helping people out of trouble.* New York: Houghton.

Etzioni, A. (1983). The essential family. *JCPenney Forum.* May 1983, p. 20.

Fagan, P. F., Patterson, R. W., & Rector, R. E. (2002). *Marriage and welfare reform: The overwhelming evidence that marriage education works* (Backgrounder #1606). Washington, DC: The Heritage Foundation. Retrieved from http://www.heritage.org/research/reports/2002/10/marriage-and-welfare-reform.

Giblin, P., Sprenkle, D. H., & Sheehan, R. (1985). Enrichment outcome research: A meta-analysis of marital, premarital and family interventions. *Journal of Marital and Family Therapy, 11,* 257–271.

Gordon, W. E. (1969). Basic concepts for an integrative and generative conception of social work. In G. Hearn (Ed.), *The general systems approach: Contributions toward an holistic conception of social work.* New York: Council on Social Work Education.

Gurman, A. S. (2011). Couple therapy research and the practice of couple therapy: Can we talk? *Family Process, 50*(3), 280–292.

Hansan, J. E. (2013). Family Service Association of America: Part I. The Social Welfare History Project. Retrieved from www.socialwelfarehistory.com/organizations/family-service-association-of-america-part-I.

Hartman, A., & Laird, J. (1983). *Family-centered social work practice.* New York: Free Press.

Hearn, G. (1969). *The general systems approach: Contributions toward an holistic conception of social work.* New York: Council on Social Work Education.

Jayaratne, S. (1978). A study of clinical eclecticism. *Social Service Review, 52*(4), 621–631.

Johnson, S. (2004). *The practice of emotionally focused couple therapy.* New York: Brunner-Routledge.

Johnson, S. (2003). Emotionally focused couples therapy: Empiricism and art. In T. L. Sexton, G. R. Weeks, & M. S. Robbins (Eds.), *Handbook of family therapy* (pp. 263–280). New York: Brunner-Routledge.

Joint NASW-CSWE Task Force on the Development of Specialization in Social Work. (1979). *Specialization in the social work profession* (NASW Document No. 79-310-08). Washington, DC: National Association of Social Workers.

Lebow, J. (2013). Programs for strengthening families. *Family Process, 52*(3), 351–354.

Lebow, J. (1997). The integrative revolution in couple and family therapy. *Family Process*, 36(1).

Lebow, J. (2003). Integrative approaches to couple and family therapy. In T. L. Sexton, G. R. Weeks, & M. S. Robbins (Eds.), *Handbook of family therapy* (pp. 201–225). New York: Brunner-Routledge.

Lewis, J. M., & Gossett, J. T. (1999). *Disarming the past: How an intimate relationship can heal old wounds*. Phoenix, AZ: Zeig & Tucker.

Lide, P. (1959). A study of historical influences of major importance in determining the present function of the school social worker. In G. Lee (Ed.), *Helping the troubled school child*. New York: National Association of Social Workers.

McGoldrick, M., & Carter, E. (1999). Self in context: The individual life cycle in systemic perspective. In B. Carter & M. McGoldrick (Eds.), *The expanded family life cycle: Individual, family and social perspectives* (3rd ed., pp. 27–36). Boston: Allyn & Bacon.

McGoldrick, M., Anderson, C., & Walsh, F. (1989). *Women in families: A framework for family therapy*. New York: Norton.

Messer, S. B. (Ed.). (2001). Special issue on assimilative integration. *Journal of Psychotherapy Integration*, 11(1).

Nacman, M. (1977). Social work in health settings: A historical review. *Social Work in Health Care*, 2(4), 407–418.

Nichols, M. P. (2013). *Family therapy: Concepts and methods* (10th ed., pp. 297–305). Boston: Pearson.

Pinsof, W. M. (1995). *Integrative, problem-centered therapy*. New York: Basic Books.

Pinsof, W. M., Breunlin, D., Russell, W., & Lebow, J. (2013). Integrative problem-solving metaframeworks therapy II: Planning, conversing and reading feedback. *Family Process*, 50(3), 314–336.

Popple, P. R. (1995). Social work profession: History. In *Encyclopedia of social work* (pp. 2282–2292). Washington, DC: National Association of Social Workers.

Retzlaff, R., Sydow, K. v., Beher, S., Haun, M. W., & Schweitzer, J. (2013). The efficacy of systemic therapy for internalizing and other disorders of childhood and adolescence: A systematic review of 38 randomized trials. *Family Process*, 52(4), 619–652.

Richmond, M. (1917). *Social diagnosis*. New York: Sage.

Richmond, M. (1907). *The good neighbor*. Philadelphia: Lippincott.

Riley, D. R. (1995). Family life education. In *Encyclopedia of social work* (pp. 960–965). Washington, DC: National Association of Social Workers.

Ryan, W. (1971). *Blaming the victim*. New York: Pantheon Books.

Schwartz, W. (1977). The interactionist approach. In *Encyclopedia of social work* (pp. 1328–1338). New York: National Association of Social Workers.

Sexton, T. L., & Alexander, J. F. (2003). Functional family therapy: A mature clinical model for working with at-risk adolescents and their families. In T. L. Sexton, G. R. Weeks, & M. S. Robbins (Eds.), *Handbook of family therapy* (pp. 323–350). New York: Brunner-Routledge.

Sheffield, A. (1937). *Social insight in case situations.* New York: Appleton-Century Crofts.

Sheidow, A. J., Henggeler, S. W., & Schoenwald, S. K. (2003). Multisystemic therapy. In T. L. Sexton, G. R. Weeks, & M. S. Robbins (Eds.), *Handbook of family therapy* (pp. 303–322). New York: Brunner-Routledge.

Siporin, M. (1972a). *Introduction to social work practice.* New York: Macmillan.

Siporin, M. (1972b). Situational assessment and intervention. *Social casework, 53,* 91–109.

Smalley, R. (1967). *Theory for social work practice.* New York: Columbia.

Southard, E. E., & Jarrett, M. C. (1922). *The kingdom of evils: Psychiatric social work presented in 100 case histories.* New York: Macmillan.

Sydow, K. v., Beher, S., Schweitzer, J., & Retzlaff, R. (2010). The efficacy of systemic therapy with adult patients: A meta-content analysis in 38 randomized controlled trials. *Family Process, 49*(4), 457–485.

Sydow, K. v., Retzlaff, R., Beher, S., Haun, M. W., & Schweitzer, J. (2013). The efficacy of systemic therapy for child and adolescent externalizing disorders: A systematic review of 47 RCT. *Family Process, 52*(4), 576–618.

Tillich, P. (1962). The philosophy of social work. *Social Service Review, 36,* 513–516.

Waite, L., & Gallagher, M. (2001). *The case for marriage: Why married people are healthier, happier and better off financially.* New York: Doubleday.

Walters, M., Carter, E., Papp, P., & Silverstein, O. (1988). *The invisible web: Gender relations in family relationships.* New York: Guilford.

Walsh, F. (1999). *Strengthening family resilience.* New York: Guilford.

Walsh, F. (2003). Family resilience: A framework for clinical practice. *Family Process, 42*(1), 1–18.

Walsh, F. (2012). Family resilience: Strengths forged through adversity. In Walsh, F., *Normal family processes* (4th ed., pp. 399–427). New York: Guilford.

Watts, P. A. (1964). Casework above the poverty line: The influence of home service in World War I on social work. *Social Service Review, 27*(3), 303–315.

Weick, A., Rapp, C., Sullivan, W. P., & Kisthardt, W. (1989). A strengths perspective for social work practice. *Social Work, 34,* 350–354.

Weingarten, K. (1991). The discourses of intimacy: Adding to a social constructionist and feminist view. *Family Process, 30,* 285–306.

Witmer, H. L. (1942). *Social work: An analysis of a social institution.* New York: Farrar & Rinehart.

CHAPTER 2

The Relational Person: Differentiation, Attachment, Interdependence

KEY TOPICS

Relational Processes in Families
The Relational Person: The Demands and Dilemmas of Family Membership
Persons, Relationships, and Commitments
Agency, Communion and Autonomy
Obligations and Relational Justice
The Person-in-Relation
The "I" and the "Me"
Ego-Oriented Casework
Relational Tasks and Attachment Theory
Attachment and Membership
Commitment and Fidelity
Reworking Attachments
Relational Change and Development

RELATIONAL PROCESSES IN FAMILIES

Without a frame of reference for social work with families, different theoretical languages will be uncritically imported from other areas. A major problem for social work theory is how to conceptualize the relational work of the family and the persons in it, and then the work of the social worker helping persons to reconstruct family life. What does membership in families mean? What is the work of a family member? What are the personal relational tasks that make family sustainable? What family structure results from this interaction? What social work practice with family members results from this picture?

Such is the problem of creating harmony between human agency and communion in the human condition. What life-ways bring some to survive, to adapt, and to differentiate themselves, to find solutions to problems and needs, whereas others are wedded to the structure? It is not simply a matter of focus on one or another aspect of this picture. When we focus on the family patterns alone, we can blur individual differences of the members and vice versa. How do these differences themselves create the patterns? When we focus on individual differences alone, the patterns can be lost. How are these patterns created out of shared relationships and understandings? Obviously both are necessary.

We begin to answer these questions with the assumption that every person is inherently relational, *incomplete unless that person has connection and social membership—first of all in a family and then extended to a multiplicity of other relationships and memberships.*

THE RELATIONAL PERSON: THE DEMANDS AND DILEMMAS OF FAMILY MEMBERSHIP

The concept of the relational person has a long history. Toward the end of the nineteenth century, William James developed a concept of the "social self": "A person "has as many social selves as there are individuals who recognize him and carry an image of him in their mind" (James, 1981, pp. 281–282). Later, his students John Dewey and George Herbert Mead developed further the concept of the social nature of mind, the social self, and its relations to society. Mead's (1934) concept that *mind* had its birth in social relationships had considerable impact on Jessie Taft and on the functional school of social work. Indeed, Mead was Taft's doctoral mentor at the University of Chicago. Otto Rank's related ideas of the birth of the self through differentiation and reconnections with others would have a useful fit with Taft's ideas (Rank, 1947, pp. 195–220).[1] The functional school, and later mainstream social work theory, drew heavily from these concepts.

In a parallel process, Mary Richmond (1917; 1907) took up the theme of the centrality of social relations in the beginning of *Social Diagnosis*:

> One of the most striking facts with regard to the consciousness of any human being is that it is interwoven with the lives of others. It is in each man's social relations that his mental history is mainly written, and it is in his social relations likewise that the causes of the disorders that threaten his happiness and his effectiveness, and the means for securing his recovery are mainly sought. (1917, p. 4)

At about the same time, Harry Stack Sullivan, also influenced by Mead, was developing similar concepts in an interpersonal psychotherapy (Sullivan, 1938–1939). In the middle of the twentieth century, despite a renewed focus on treatment methods for individuals, there remained latent a focus on persons interacting with each other. Family therapy developed from this interactive emphasis often nourished by contact with social workers who had generally retained a family focus. Some theories we will discuss at a later point: object relations theory (Greenberg & Mitchell, 1983), attachment theory (Bowlby, 1969; Ainsworth,

---

[1]Otto Rank was an early psychoanalyst, a disciple of Freud, whose work strongly influenced the functional school of social work in the 1930s.

Bleher, Waters, & Wall, 1978; Ainsworth, 1973) self psychology (Kohut, 1977; Kernberg, 1976), membership (Falck, 1988), and family therapy theories (Nichols, 2013; Nichols & Schwartz, 2001; 2008) would, each in their own ways, develop approaches to what were essentially related.[2]

Similarly, developmental theory is shifting from a single focus on the developing individual to a progressive exploration of relational space and the ways that people are connected with each other as they develop. The recurrent findings that interdependence is inherent to the human condition dominate the discussion of personal development. Daniel Stern (1985) and others see maturation of development as greater differentiation throughout the life cycle within the context of interdependence (Fishbane, 2001; McGoldrick & Carter, 1999, pp. 27–44; McGoldrick & Shibusawa, 2012, pp. 375–398).

Persons, Relationships, and Commitments

Agency, Communion, and the Myth of Autonomy   The autonomous person, "self-made," self-determined, master of the environment, is very much a myth, a construct, while it also has been a dominant narrative of Western society. Narratives of autonomy influence the way North Americans think and set Western standards for mental health. They influence approaches to gender, marriage, child-rearing, and educational policy (Fishbane, 2011; 2001). Autonomous persons are often considered to be progressive and evolutionary, having arrived at "a state of maturity arrived at as the outcome of a developmental process" (Haworth, 1986, p. 8). The autonomous person would be minimally bound by obligations. These obligations would be only rooted in and limited by individual contract. Social relations would be entirely voluntary. They could be dissolved. Nature can be mastered. These beliefs, if carried to their implicit conclusions, would make it a challenge to live effectively in a family. Personal goals and a drive for achievement can overshadow the relational commitments necessary for family life.

Over a century of experience with autonomous pictures of the person, there has been a gradual shift in the West to relational ones, but the issue is by no means resolved. In Italy, relational sociology is developing as a critique of overindividualized images of the person. These images distort observable social realities. They undermine social institutions, including family, and make them ineffective (Donati, 1991; 2001, pp. 147–177; 2012). Autonomy, with its accompanying societal sentiments, is in crisis. Its assumptions clash with life as it has been observed, experienced, and studied. Autonomy overrides values such as intergenerational loyalty, obligation, or interdependence and sends them underground (Bellah, Madson, Sullivan, Swidler, & Tipton, 1986). Autonomy clashes with the growing awareness of ethnic subcultures (McGoldrick & Carter, 1999) and of women (Gilligan, 1982;

---

[2]There is a long history of theory dealing with this issue, recently summarized by Christian Beels (2002), a psychiatrist and family therapist.

McGoldrick, Anderson, & Walsh, 1989; Walters, Carter, Papp, & Silverstein, 1988; Weingarten, 1991). Communitarian sociologists and political scientists (see Etzioni, 1993) are beginning to explore other solutions to this problem in the development of countervailing concepts of civil society. In the United States in the final decades of the twentieth century, a movement for the invigoration of family values began to develop and gain considerable strength (Blankenhorn, Bayme, & Elshtain, 1990).

In family life, a rigid belief in one's autonomy can create an inability to agree on and to develop with others balanced roles or commitments. This is hopefully a temporary disorder experienced by adolescents, who are appropriately experimenting with greater autonomy. However, in some families, relentless patterns of autonomy can make relational civility impossible. As it is lived in civility, family membership involves a balance between the ability to initiate action, personal *agency* and the capacity for membership, *communion*. Agency always is in delicate balance with obligations, relationships, and established commitments. A picture of human agency, developing amid systemic/structural constraints, needs to be balanced by communion. The relational person can be concerned for the other without losing one's self; indeed, the person becomes more a person through these concerns and through giving to the other. The malaise of the autonomous life style of the twentieth century runs headlong into needs for connectedness and a belief in the importance of obligations of the twenty-first century. When these images collide, there is born a pressing need for *relationality*, never quite far from the surface of life as it has to be lived.

Can the Family Unit Become Personal? The basic concern behind both relational justice and functional family assessment is whether the family unit can become *personal*—whether the family unit can support the development and needs of persons. Persons are members of families. Family members want productive interpersonal relations and a sense of a genuine, intertwined interdependent narrative. They also become aware that some of their patterns of interaction are dysfunctional, unproductive—even hurtful. Overcoming those patterns becomes a task and a challenge for family members.

For the *relational* person, life is and should be experienced with others. As life is experienced, autonomy is useful, but not primary. Freedom could not exist for one without a corresponding responsibility for others. Responsibility becomes a person's ability to be responsible in relation to others and to take into account the relational consequences of his or her own actions (Fishbane, 2001, p. 276; Fishbane, 2011). Indeed, "agency" is lived when one is an agent of another or of society. Obligations and legacies become an inherent part of living and of relational justice. Building on a more complex sense of obligations and legacies, roots become important. And so with roots come established relationships and family legacies. Such are major concerns of contextual family therapy, which develops these concepts into a particular model for family practice, which emphasizes the invisible power of obligations and legacies (Boszormenyi-Nagy & Spark, 1973).

Obligations and Relational Justice   With life experience, we accept that unattended things can fail, whether inside or outside the family. The relational circle can be broken. People can be treated badly. Family members can fail to respond to the needs of others. Children can experience abuse and neglect. Injustice, whether relational or societal, can create further injustice in a never ending spiral. Social workers cannot take up this whole burden. Nor can they remove the responsibility of family members and society itself to be just and fair and to act for the common good of all, especially the most vulnerable. Social workers, however, have a special responsibility to be instruments of relational justice in the situations they encounter. In families, they challenge patterns of exploitation, dominance, and abuse. Issues of injustice are often carried from generation to generation. Debts and legacies, passed across generational lines, can either limit or expand possibilities for family members. Working between generational lines, social workers can help family members rebalance debts and legacies in a person's own self concepts and with others in the family. This *rebalancing in the interest of development* presupposes the complexity and dynamics of developing social relationships and cultural expectations. It puts relational justice into practice in a changing society (Boszormenyi-Nagy, Grunebaum, & Ulrich, 1991).

Readiness for the Relational   The autonomous person expects to clearly understand and communicate her own needs and desires. Without losing any clarity about self, in the larger context of relationships, clarity about the other is also needed. Agency and communion need to be in balance with the other. Marsha Mirkin describes "readiness for the relational":

> By readiness for the relational I mean a willingness to be moved by the other, to see and be seen, to stay connected even through conflict, to hear the other's narrative, even while articulating one's own, and to negotiate differences without resorting to "power over" tactics. Readiness for the relational also entails relational accountability to the other, and an openness to being affected by the other's response. (quoted in Fishbane, 2001, p. 276)

This balance of self and other becomes a learned interdependence in the context of family life. And this is the way people live in families. People at most life cycle stages form interdependent bonds with each other (Cohler & Geyer, 1982; Galatzer-Levy & Cohler, 1993; McGoldrick & Carter, 1999); the maps of our need for each other can be traced and observed in the consciousness and cognitive growth of persons (Kohlberg, 1969; Mahler, Pine, & Bergman, 1975; Piaget, 1954). Object relations theorists (Greenberg & Mitchell, 1983; Kernberg, 1976) and attachment theorists (Atkinson & Zucker, 1997; Bartholomew & Horowitz, 1991; Levy, 2000; Lewis & Gossett, 1999; Sperling & Berman, 1994, p. 189) emphasize the empirical and theoretical implications of interdependence.

Membership   In contrast to the notion of individuality, which emphasizes separation, the human condition is one of membership. Membership is a fact of every person's social living. It is an acknowledgement of the inherent interdependence of every person's life situation. For every person, membership spans many contexts: family of origin, immediate family, extended family, occupational groups, friendships, neighborhood ties, religion, culture, ethnicity, and so on (Carlton, 1984). Being a member is inconceivable without others. Indeed the identity of a member is bound up with that of others. The actions of a member are derived from and contribute to a social bond. An individual's differences lead to separation. A member's differences create tensions that lead to growth, group cohesion, and group conflict. An individual's freedom may be considered the absence of constraint. A member's freedom is not the absence of constraint, but rather a bond of simultaneous concern for self and others (Falck, 1976). Membership assumes that there are already reasons for commitment—that there is already a normative context for relationships. It is a type of socialized connectedness. Membership extends to a continuous interaction with others who become parts of the self "both seen and unseen"—that is, in current experience and in memory (Falck, 1988, p. 30). Social workers render professional aid to manage the complexities of membership (Falck, 1988, p. 56).

THE PERSON-IN-RELATION

The basis of family membership is the person-in-relation seeking to develop as a human being, seeking relational safety, belonging, communication, growth, friendship, and other human goods within the fold of the family. A person-in-relation is different from a statistical "individual." Although the concept of the individual signifies a separable unit, personhood includes the necessary relations with the outside world, that become parts of our selves.

Frederick Allen, a pioneer in psychiatry, reflecting Harry Stack Sullivan, discusses these relations that get to the core of a person's being. These are learned patterns of interaction with others, structures of which we have become part, and processes that place us on a line of development. These give us a past and a future. Persons learn and become unique through their stories: their experiences of present and past relationships with other persons, their relations to larger social units and to institutional structures and through persons who are significant others to them. They learn through the reflected expectations of societal contexts, both those that they have chosen and those that have been thrust upon them. Growing and becoming a person reflect an ever more complex, progressive relation of person with environment. From the sense of oneness with the environment experienced by the infant through a progressive differentiation of self, the relation between individual and environment continues. Growth can bring new levels of consciousness of the relation of self and other, of choice, and of capability for forming new social units in relations with others. Growth is a continuous process of the formation of new wholes from the elements of the preceding ones (Allen, 1942). Persons are capable of growth in a process of progressive differentiation of function that results in a more complex unity.

The self-process is ongoing, ever-changing, and dynamic, carried out in relation to and in interaction with others. The process of growth moves from the initial differentiation of the parts of one's body from one's surroundings to the discovery and development of inclinations, tendencies, and traits. Persons gradually acquire the ability to distinguish between those parts of their experience that are a part of their own selves and those parts that are not of their own selves. We each become a self through social interaction, through connections with others at greater levels of maturity, through the progressive awareness of difference, of the "not self," through the taking and making of roles, and through a developed understanding of the role of the other and the other's relations with us. These characteristics are formed in a process of finding similarity and differences from others.

The "I" and the "Me"

Each person is a blend of the "I" and the "me," the spontaneous and the patterned (Burr, Hill, Nye, & Reiss, 1979, pp. 47–48), the qualities that reflect human agency and the qualities that reflect communion and connectedness. The "I" is a creative, acting self, a subject, normally the initiating and the mediating part of the person.

The self-process is an internal, reflective conversation of consciousness through which the individual can delay responses, see himself or herself from the perspective of the other, review the past, and envision the future (Shibutani, 1961). The "I" can be unpredictable, spontaneous, and unique to a particular person. The "I" need not be reduced to a part of the self. It becomes the will, an essential life force, self-organizing, central to growth, and seeking to transform its world (Smalley, 1967, pp. 81ff).

When the "I" is engaged, it becomes central to the helping process. The "I" is present in the language and discourse of compassion. Indeed, the discovery that one can speak of suffering to another, that both can listen and acquire a compassionate language of their own, may be the chief tool of a healing process. It is the "I" who finds words, then a language, for discourse; it is the "I" who can listen and respond. While it may be colonized or paralyzed by unspeakable injustices or by suffering, the "I" can also discover itself and its newly found ability to respond. It discovers its difference from the injustice, from the event, or from the circumstance. The "I" need not be encapsulated by the suffering that takes place, such as when one discovers an incurable cancer. It allows us to find a way to recognize and still transcend the injustice and the suffering that comes with this circumstance (Reich, 1989).

Postmodern family therapists have developed a powerful narrative of the outsider witness (Weingarten, 2000) who helps the person retell his or her story in a way that "regrades" (rather than degrades) the person's life situation and narrative (White, 2007, p. 165). It allows the person to recover an appropriate position in his or her life story as an agent, rather than as a victim. From Kaethe Weingarten's perspective, when a person is aware and empowered in the context of a relationship, that person may seek the pathways of *reasonable hope*, at the same time being able to accommodate doubt, contradictions, and despair. People may feel despair, but "do" hope (Weingarten, 2010). They may take on the position of agent in their own narrative, in their own story (Kotze, Hulme, Geldenhuys, & Weingarten, 2013).

The constellation of patterns, learned through continuous social interaction, is the "me." These parts of the self are learned and repetitious, patterns that denote an actor's response to the expectations of significant others. These are the parts that others learn they can rely on. They are social parts in that they are drawn from the response to these perceived expectations. There may indeed be many different "me's," many patterns of feeling and behaving, drawn from different experiences and from memories. There is a "me" that becomes anxious and fearful in certain circumstances. There is a "me" that becomes sad. There is a "me" that is confident, and so forth. It is like an internal family, sometimes ordered, sometimes riotous, sometimes confused and conflicted. As with parents in families, in not all cases is the "I" fully in charge, able to help these different parts of the self or use fully their great potential contributions. In a parallel sense, Richard Schwartz (1995) points out that the aim of help is for the leadership part of the person (equivalent to the "I") to become fully in conversation with the many other parts, the internal family of the person—for the self to become a principle of harmony.[3]

Ego-Oriented Casework

Social work has a long tradition of working with persons in families. As ego-oriented casework (Hollis, 1972; Goldstein, 1995; Parad, 1958) developed during the mid-twentieth century, its historical heritage (discussed in chapter 1) gave it a natural focus on the person. However, rather than beginning with the person alone, its focus was on person-in-situation. Essentially, it would engage the person from the "outside in" (Simon, 1960, pp. 33–36), from reality tasks to the relation of these tasks to ego functioning. The social worker works with the client in a professional dialogue, using combinations of ego support, clarification and insight development. The goal would be to improve ego functioning through work on psychosocial tasks (Goldstein, 1995, p. 1950).

CASE STUDY 2.1: GLORIA

Gloria, a single Filipina pediatric nurse in her late thirties, struggled every day with her obsessions about her beloved boss, Dr. Smith, who was married with several children. She remained very productive at work. When she was not focused on her work, her feelings about him filled the empty spaces of her life. She was fearful that her way of dressing (the colors she chose to wear) and other actions, which others would consider insignificant, would hurt him. She would worry when she didn't say "good morning" to him halfway

---

[3]The concept of an "I," the leadership part of the person, the subject, the self, is a theme that has been explored throughout the history of philosophy and theology, but particularly in the twentieth century by Martin Buber (1958; 1965), among others (see the discussion in Shivanandan, 2001).

down the hall or when she spoke to another man in his presence. These obsessions often put her in embarrassing situations. She would want to ask him, "I didn't hurt you, did I?" or do other somewhat unusual things to reassure herself. Her obsessions were torturing her. Dr. Velu, her psychiatrist, considered her "quite fragile." The social worker, working with Velu, took a modified cognitive and problem-solving approach, helping Gloria to identify her strengths as well as those parts of herself, left over from childhood experiences, which were making her insecure and pushing her to obsessive behavior. Each week, in what was the starting point of the helping relationship, her major focus was on her daily activities and perceptions, and on what she could do about the situation in which she found herself. There was support for her strengths; her weaknesses were buttressed (Simon, 1960).

With the help of her social worker, Gloria corrected some of her perceptions in the context of her active coping. She began an exercise program and made an effort to broaden her friendships with other women. She began to become reflective, to see her own strengths and to see that she could gently take leadership of her self with her own wisdom and experience. She could reassure the parts of her that became anxious, even trying to lead those parts to a better understanding. She also began to try to see her behavior as her boss might perceive it. This helped her enormously, since she didn't want to displease him. Eventually she could learn to laugh at the absurdity of some of her beliefs. Although many of her difficulties continued, she was gradually learning to reassure herself, to maintain her unimpaired professional competence, and to avoid many of the problems into which she had fallen previously. She received an award for her work. While accepting her fears and obsessions as part of her, she gradually saw herself beginning to transcend the fears and obsessions, that previously had controlled her so completely.

Gloria's concerns will not change quickly. She needs to discover her capacity to sort all this out. She is alone and isolated. She will need to find other friendships and resources. In working with an individual client, such as Gloria, the social worker is helping her to learn, to grow, and to cope. Working with families is somewhat more complex. The social worker will shuttle from personal to relational tasks with different family members within individual sessions and within the overall process, always within the context of family as a network of relations and the relational tasks that flow from this reality. In the second part of the case of Armand and Rosalind (case study 4.3) the social worker had only Armand to work with directly. Nevertheless, keeping Rosalind in the picture, the worker coached Armand, now alone, to restore a relational balance. Rosalind responded to this.

The Empathic Relationship as a Holding System   *Empathy* arises between two persons. The act of empathy is a spiritual process that can transcend anger, misunderstanding, and confusion to bring peace. Thich Nhat Hanh of the Zen Buddhist tradition writes: "To develop understanding you have to practice looking at all human beings with the eyes of compassion. When you understand, you love. And when you love, you naturally act in a way that can relieve the suffering of people" (Hanh, 1987, pp. 14–15, in Anderson & Worthen, 1997). Compassion (or *misericordia* in the Western spiritual tradition) involves an active reaching out to the sadness or shame of the other to transform it. Compassion cannot come without reflective selves, however—often made possible through a deeper understanding of one's own experience of being the recipient of compassion from another. Gloria (case study 2.1) gradually discovered that she could begin to test, even transcend, the limits of her obsessions in the context of an empathic relationship—that she could see others not simply as an extension of herself and her fears and beliefs.

The Self Is Spiritual   In the "I" there can be a growing inner awareness of its own spirituality, of a certain ability not to be fully defined by—indeed, transcending—some of the limitations of concrete experience (space, time, and language) in its search for meaning and its leadership. Ed Canda (1986), a social worker, considers the central dynamic of spirituality to be the reality of every person's search for a sense of meaning and purpose through relationships between self, other people, the nonhuman world, and the ground of being. This theme is inherent in human nature: a search for connection with a higher power. For many, this takes the form of the search for a personal Creator-God. Augustine (1960) in the fourth century AD summarizes his discovery of who he is in this relationship: "You have made us for yourself alone, and our hearts cannot rest until they rest in you." Spirituality is a family resource, as well as an individual one. It is profoundly social, a manifestation of membership in a faith community, of prayer, of meditation, and of forgiveness (Walsh, 2012, pp. 347–374). The general contents of religion are the specific, concrete, and necessarily social expressions of spirituality, coalesced into particular forms: rituals, sacred scriptures, doctrines, rules of conduct, and other practices.

The Self Is Relational   Self is a relational, dialogical concept (Anderson, 2012, p. 11). The relational self becomes itself through communication "in the spaces between" (Buber, 1958; 1965; Josselson, 1992), human interaction and development. Thich Nhat Hanh (1991, p. 96, in Anderson & Worthen, 1997) explains, "To be is to inter-be. We cannot just be by ourselves alone. We have to inter-be with every other thing." Compassion provides the link between our selves and others.

The Internal Family System   From Richard Schwartz's perspective, reflecting Assagioli (1975) and Gazzaniga (1985), the mind is an internal family of parts and a self. The parts are like subpersonalities: sometimes they are in contention, sometimes in agreement, sometimes balanced with different parts, sometimes in extreme positions. Sometimes they are a squabbling family; sometimes a silently polarized one; sometimes confused and uncertain, sometimes riotous. Sometimes they are stuck in a very young phase, needing to grow up, to become stronger and more worldly wise. Schwartz writes about the leadership part, "the self," which can have the clarity of perspective to lead effectively. When the self is fully differentiated—for example, when persons are asked to climb a mountain in their minds, leaving their parts in the valley—they describe feeling "centered," a state of calm well-being and lightheartedness, confident, free, and open-hearted (Schwartz, 1995, p. 37).

RELATIONAL TASKS: CONCRETE LINKS TO A FAMILY NETWORK

Relational tasks develop the connection of the relational self with its necessary context. They are inherent in being a member of a family. They are in one sense personal tasks, but they are always done with and on behalf of others. Persons form social units (couples, families) through these relational tasks. Out of these tasks the family either is constructed or declines as a relational network. Accomplishment of these relational tasks depends as much on the other(s) as on the self. The uncertainty of the other's real involvement makes them unpredictable and difficult. Additionally, there are many obstacles to their accomplishment: fears, disappointments, legacies from the past, problems with the other, environmental deficits, and so on. On the other hand, even with the uncertainties—the obstacles to their accomplishment, whether other actors will be appropriately involved—there is a natural thrust toward doing relational tasks in one way or other. Thus, even if there are obstacles, there is a certain universal thrust toward getting tasks done within a culturally acceptable framework of meanings. The tasks and the obstacles become the focus of the helping relationship.

Generational Justice   A number of family therapists include multiple generations as the context for relational tasks. Ivan Boszormenyi-Nagy takes such a contextual approach to problems occurring in the present generation. We all reflect the contexts and images of the family's past; there is really no self-made person. There are issues of loyalty between generations. There is also a need for an ethical balance of give and take among persons in a family. This creates a pull between one's learned patterns, hidden "loyalties" and legacies from family of origin, and the give and take with one's partner, who also has hidden loyalties and bonds (Boszormenyi-Nagy & Spark, 1973). Disconnection from family of origin can result in loyalties' becoming invisible and bonds' going unacknowledged. It can result in self-defeating or destructive behavior in one's own life (Fishbane, 2001). Accordingly, the helping process cannot remain fixed in the present as if there were no history.[4] An example can be taken from the need of each person in a new couple unit to rework ties to his or her family of origin at the same time as the couple is forming relationships with each other. Family-of-origin work is work that can only be done with one's own family and one's self. The partner would do best to take only a supportive role in this. Reworking ties to their own families-of-origin, they can then begin to integrate some of their separate patterns with each other. We will see an example of this in case study 3.1 (Sarah and Phil).

---

[4]For more extensive discussion of this theoretical base, see Nichols (2013, pp. 158–160; Nichols and Schwartz, 2001, pp. 427–433).

Self-Differentiation and Connectedness—Murray Bowen   Murray Bowen (1978) developed concepts of self-differentiation and connectedness as keys to his theory of family intervention. Bowen, a psychiatrist, saw anxiety as the fusion of thinking and feeling, which he observed in disturbed states. From his perspective, the degree to which self-differentiation occurs in a person reflects the extent to which that person is able to distinguish between the intellectual process and the feeling process that he or she is experiencing without the paralysis brought by anxiety. Self-differentiation is demonstrated by the degree to which a person is able to avoid having his or her behavior automatically driven by feelings. This should lead not to a denial of feelings, but rather to a balance of thinking and feeling. On the one hand, the person's thinking is not limited by feelings. On the other, the person is able to express feelings spontaneously and appropriately. Such differentiation is more of a process than an attainable goal (Goldenberg & Goldenberg, 1996). Differentiation is tested in the presence of anxiety and strong feeling, particularly in family relationships. People who are differentiated can connect with others' experiences without losing themselves. For Bowen, family-of-origin work is crucial to self-differentiation and connectedness. Can a person creatively participate in family relationships without getting drawn automatically into the feelings of others and without being taken over by a shared anxiety? As persons make forays into the family of origin, can they remain nonreactive but reconnect and, when necessary, challenge old rules (Fishbane, 2001)? Goodrich (1991, p. 21), with a particular interest in women's development, clarifies that this differentiation is not disconnection. Rather it is an aspect of connectedness, a differentiation *with* rather than differentiation *from*.

Attachment and Membership   Attachment and membership are two concepts that, along with relational tasks, bridge the relation of persons with their environment. Attachment and membership are the product of relational tasks performed with others. Using attachment theory, psychiatrist Jerry Lewis understands relationships through qualities of connectedness and separateness. Connectedness involves the commitment of one person to another. There is priority over other relations and involvements; closeness, a sharing of values, interests, activities and friends; and psychological intimacy. Psychological intimacy is the mutual sharing of vulnerabilities. It is the ability of persons to talk directly and openly with each other about very personal experiences and feelings that rarely are discussed with anyone else. It involves, most of all, the ability to listen to each other, to feel understood and safe, and ultimately to trust another with vulnerable parts of one's self. Such connectedness is similar to our concept of communion. Separateness involves the capacity to experience one's self as a distinct person with a unique blend of both assets and liabilities, to manage one's life effectively independently of others, and to appreciate solitude as well as togetherness with others (Lewis & Gossett, 1999). This is similar to our concept of agency.[5]

---

[5]See more extensive discussion of Bowen's theory in Nichols (2013, pp. 90–93; Nichols and Schwartz, 2001, ch. 5); and Goldenberg and Goldenberg (1996, ch. 8).

Cultural Meanings of Attachment and Membership   The concepts of connectedness and separateness (or autonomy) are profoundly related to culture. Tamura and Lau (1992), two Asian psychiatrists, discuss the contrasting relational value systems of Japan and Britain. The most significant difference in value systems between the two cultures is the Japanese preference for connectedness and the Western preference for separateness. The Japanese person is seen as a part of the embedded interconnectedness of relationships, whereas British norms prioritize separateness, clear boundaries in relationships, individuality, and autonomy. This value orientation is manifested in the Japanese language, the hierarchical nature of the family structure, the family life cycle, and the implicit communication style. According to Tamura and Lau, the preferred direction of change for Japanese families in therapy is toward a process of integration—how a person can be effectively integrated into the given system—rather than the process of differentiation popular in the West. Different cultures may emphasize the communal or the individual (human agency and communion), human relational capacity and capacity to act together (see table 2.1). In the human condition, both are necessary and interde-

Table 2.1
Contrasting British and Japanese Families

	Britain	Japan
Value System	SEPARATENESS	CONNECTEDNESS
Worldview	Dualism (Cartesian split)	Holism (Buddhism)
Family Strucrure	Egalitarian Nuclear family	Hierarchical Extended family
Emphasized Relationship	Husband–Wife	Mother–Child
Family Life Cycle	Process of individuation Leaving home	Process of integration Arranged marriage Reunion with elderly parents
Communication	Verbal Explicit (maximize the difference)	Nonverbal Implicit (minimize the difference)
Direction of Change (solution)	DIFFERENTIATION Individuality Autonomy	INTEGRATION Support network Sensitivity
Role of Therapist	Third party "Neutral"	Connected Directive, authoritative
Mode of Psychotherapy	Verbal Talking through Therapeutic debate Externalize Unconscious → Conscious	Nonverbal Meditation Silence Internalize Conscious → Unconscious

SOURCE: Tamura and Lau (1992). © 1992 FPI, Inc.

pendent. Rather than being an absolute dichotomy, it is a matter of cultural meanings and emphasis.

ATTACHMENT THEORY

Just as *communion* is a precondition for human *agency*, attachment is an essential part of the human condition. Attachment builds on the assumption that attaching behaviors, bringing developing persons closer to their caregivers, are prerequisites to every person's security, safety, and further development (Ainsworth, Bleher, Waters, & Wall, 1978; Bowlby, 1969). When a child experiences sufficient reciprocal, affectionate reactions with a caregiver who is available and responsive to the child's appropriate needs, the bond that is formed between them is described as *secure attachment*. Secure attachment develops as the result of thousands of daily interactions in which the caregiver achieves affective attunement with the child, eventually becoming a secure base from which the child can tackle new tasks and new relationships with the consistent expectation of being successful and loved (Ladnier & Massanari, 2000; Hughes, 1997). Problems of attachment with parental figures may be generalized to a larger network of relationships. A child attaches not only to his or her primary caretaker(s), but also through the primary caretaker(s) to the total network of relationships of which the mother and child are a part (Donley, 1993). John Byng-Hall (1995), emphasizing the network concept, defines a secure family base as follows:

> A secure family base is a family that provides a reliable network of attachment relationships in which all family members of whatever age are able to feel sufficiently secure to explore. The term "network" implies a shared family responsibility that assures everyone that any member who is in need of help will be cared for. For small children, it means an expectation of reliable handover and hand-back within the family network, or with appropriate outside caregivers. Children need a sense that relationships between the adults are sufficiently collaborative to insure that care is available at all times. A secure family base involves a shared awareness that attachment relationships need to be protected and not undermined. The shared working model of the secure family base is of family members supporting each other to care for their members.

Patterns of secure attachment, carried into further development, result in two crucial sets of skills—self-regulation and relationship skills (Ladnier & Massanari, 2000, p. 36):

Self-Regulation Skills
- impulse control
- self-soothing
- initiative
- perseverance
- inhibition
- patience

Relationship Skills
- empathy
- trust
- affection
- reciprocity
- expression
- respect

Children who fail to receive consistent, predictable, reassuring responses from their primary caregivers are considered likely to learn insecure patterns of attachment. The child who does not learn to use his or her caregiver as a secure base for exploring the world could be at risk for problems in social relationships, emotional development, behavioral control, and cognitive capacity (Hughes, 1997).

Three subtypes of insecure attachment have been identified in work with infants: ambivalent, avoidant, and disorganized. *Ambivalent* attachment involves confusion over how to feel safe and secure (Lewis & Gossett, 1999). Infants whose attachment was considered ambivalent were, in general, more likely to cling to their mothers in an unfamiliar environment and less willing to explore on their own. When separated from her, they appeared anxious, agitated, and tearful. When the mother returned, they tended to seek contact with her but simultaneously rejected her attempts to soothe them. Infants considered *avoidant* generally gave the impression of being independent and self-sufficient. They tended to explore the unfamiliar environment with little concern for their mother's whereabouts, just like children who were considered to be securely attached. They differed, however, from the securely attached children in that they seemed unaffected by separation from the mother and either rejected or avoided her when she returned (Ladnier & Massanari, 2000). Infants with *disorganized* attachments lacked a consistent strategy for organizing their comfort-seeking behaviors in times of stressful separation or reunion with the mother. Their disorganized reactions would include such things as apprehension, helplessness, and depression. Some demonstrated desperate reactions such as prolonged motor freezing or dissociation alternating with agitation in unpredictable ways (Ladnier & Massanari, 2000).

Adult Attachment, Reciprocity, and Commitment

Adult attachment involves the development of working models—mental representations of the attachment relationships a person experiences throughout his or her life span. These working models organize interpersonal cognition, affect, and behavior; guide affect regulation; shape self-image; and are the definitional component of the person's attachment style (Clulow, 2001; Baldwin, Keelan, Fehr, Enns, & Koo-Rangarajoo, 1996, in Mikulincer & Florian, 1999). As a person grows and develops more complex attachment with significant others, the social relational dimensions of reciprocity and commitment become more important. Reciprocity implies a more complex exchange. The development of commitment to the other extends reciprocity to a type of guarantee of the relationship continuing in good times and in bad. The relationship, strengthened by trust and mutual commitment, becomes a secure base for development (Mikulincer, Florian, Cowan, & Cowan, 2002).

The adult with a secure style of adult attachment demonstrates confidence in the availability of attachment figures in times of need, and comfort with closeness and interdependence. The avoidant style involves insecurity at others' responses and a desire for emotional distance. The anxious ambivalent style shows similar insecurity but also has a strong desire for intimacy and a high fear of rejection (Hazan &

Shaver, 1987). Based on adult attachment theory, emotionally focused couple therapy (Johnson, 2004; Greenman & Johnson, 2013, pp. 46–61) has good empirical support as an intervention for distressed couples. In a first phase of therapy, the couple works at deescalating their negative and problem-generating cycles. In a second phase, they work to achieve a secure attachment bond with each other.

Commitment   For many persons, attachment does not automatically mean commitment. Commitment is a learned and socially constructed sentiment. It is not necessarily mutual, but there are expectations that it be mutual. Recognition of lack of mutuality can lead to a rapid deterioration of the relationship. Love unrequited is the stuff of ballads and stories, but it is also a sad reality of everyday life. On the other hand, difference is inherent in every relationship. Such difference is not necessarily problematic unless one demands sameness from the other. As we will discuss in the following chapters, a productive relationship mutually and continually acknowledges the difference that is a natural and real part of the relationship. It works with this difference so that the relationship is truly changed for both members. A person with mature commitment loves the other for what the other *is*, not for what the person may want the other to be. This deepening of the attachment relationship is a natural process that, when it takes place, can stabilize the relationship into faithful, unqualified, mutual attachment sentiments: love and fidelity. To be able to love the other as other, not simply as a reflection of the self, is an important step in interpersonal maturity (Shivanandan, 2001).

Fidelity   Opinion surveys of married and single respondents place "trustworthy/faithful" as by far the most important trait of a marriage partner over other traits: intelligent, romantic, thoughtful, handsome, pretty, wealthy, and so on. This is not a surprising finding in light of the inherent personal vulnerability in such a relationship. Can each be faithful despite the inevitable changes in the other that life brings? Because change and growth is essential to being a person, mutual fidelity in a personal context would become a mutual openness of two selves to the changing and unfolding reality of the other, a reality that never can be known in advance (Grisez, n.d.). Constructing this type of relational openness, authentic delight in what is new with the other, is a lifetime project that changes with the developmental tasks that emerge. In chapter 6 we will discuss the contents of a covenant which some couples may expressly choose to be the basis of marital commitment. In any case, fidelity is not simply a quality of a person, but rather something constructed and differentiated in a concrete relationship. Outside a marriage bond, the fidelity to a parent, a friend, or a sibling may also be quite strong. The constructed bond of fidelity continues the protection of attachment through adulthood. It is inevitable that persons and circumstances will change. Accordingly, some fidelity to the person is essential to the architecture of effective, lasting relationships. Nevertheless, the human condition is filled with losses, betrayals, inadequate resources, unequal power, and poverty. The memory of losses and betrayals can have a lasting influence on one's perceptions and patterns. A person could be afraid to make a commitment.

Or he may assume that no commitment should be taken seriously. These issues are very much a part of work with couples throughout their relationship processes. They are inherent to almost any couples' case study in this book. The strengths-based social worker seeks to support a prudent and resilient human response to difficult and inherently insecure conditions.

Reworking Attachments

The process of reworking attachment and commitment, connectedness and separateness, is crucial to an understanding of what relational tasks are about. As we will see in our discussion of the shifts in relations that come with developmental stages, the shifts in relationship, going from one stage to another, are shifts in attachment. These shifts—anticipated, perhaps dreaded, by ego and perhaps avoided by alter—create the friction, the light, and the heat of a developmental stage.

CASE STUDY 2.2:
MARISA ANTONELLI

Marisa Antonelli, 17 years old, rocketed herself into pseudo-independence by enmeshing herself into relationships and risky practices with friends. Her parents see that the enmeshed closeness and intimacy they have always had with their only child will change. They feel as if they have lost her. They react with the watchful, protective behavior that seemed to work when she was younger. Now their watchfulness becomes extreme. They police her behavior, record her phone messages, and check her purse when she is out. The daughter's response is to continue her risky behavior, now at a further extreme. The resulting cat-and-mouse game takes over the normal processes that work out family relationships when a member is developing. It prevents family members from dealing with the underlying issues of her steps toward a revised bond with her parents and toward adult relationships and responsibility. The game puts aside their historic commitment to each other. For the relationship to continue in any real sense, commitment will need redefinition.

Attachment theory connects with family development in the process of formation of bonds, discussed in the next two chapters. The issues, which have become part of an earlier bonding process, can be re-experienced with formation of a new bond. On the other hand, the new bonding process may allow reworking of some of the attachment issues.

RELATIONAL CHANGE AND DEVELOPMENT

A picture emerges of a systemic dance of change taking place at each different family life cycle stage. Family structures develop and change as the persons within them develop and change. Structural changes and personal development of family members are keyed to each other. Structural changes and personal changes create tasks for family members at each stage. These tasks are both relational and personal. The social worker intervenes within the family structure and with family members around these tasks. Working between individual members and the particular family unit in formation at any stage of family development, the social worker is a mentor for the accomplishment of these tasks when their accomplishment is at risk.

In the next chapter, we will focus on the process of family development as it occurs over the family life cycle and creates family structure through language and communication. The family life cycle takes place in time; and so there are sequences of change. It takes place in space as family members become part of a relational structure.

REFERENCES

Ainsworth, M. D. S. (1973). The development of infant-mother attachment. In B. M. Caldwell, & H. N. Ricciutti (Eds.), *Review of child development research*, vol. 3 (pp. 1–94). Chicago, IL: University of Chicago Press.

Ainsworth, M. D. S., Bleher, M. C., Waters, E., & Wall, S. (1978). *Patterns of attachment: A psychological study of the strange situation*. Hillsdale, NJ: Lawrence Erlbaum Associates.

Allen, F. (1942). *Psychotherapy with children*. New York, NY: Norton.

Anderson, D. A., & Worthen, D. (1997). Exploring a fourth dimension: Spirituality as a resource for the couple therapist. *Journal of Marital and Family Therapy*, 23(11), 3–12.

Anderson, H. (2012). Collaborative relationships and dialogic conversations: Ideas for a relationally responsive practice. *Family Process*, 51(1), 8–24.

Assagioli, R. (1975). *Psychosynthesis: A manual of principles and techniques*. London, UK: Turnstone Press.

Atkinson, L., & Zucker, K. (1997). *Attachment and psychopathology*. New York, NY: Guilford.

Augustine. (1960). *The confessions of St. Augustine*. Garden City, NY: Image Books.

Baldwin, M. W., Keelan, J. P. R., Fehr, B., Enns, V., & Koo-Rangarajoo, E. (1996). Social cognitive conceptualization of attachment working models: Availability and accessibility of effects. *Journal of Personality and Social Psychology, 71*, 94–109.

Bartholomew, K., & Horowitz, L. (1991). Attachment styles among young adults. *Journal of Personality and Social Psychology, 61*, 226–244.

Beels, C. (2002). Notes for a cultural history of family therapy. *Family Process, 41*(1), 67–82.

Bellah, R. N., Madson, R., Sullivan, W. M., Swidler, A., & Tipton, S. M. (1986). *Habits of the Heart*. Berkeley, CA: University of California Press.

Blankenhorn, D., Bayme, S., & Elshtain, J. B. (1990). *Rebuilding the nest: A new commitment to the American family*. Milwaukee, WI: Family Service America.

Boszormenyi-Nagy, I., & Spark, G. (1973). *Invisible loyalties: Reciprocity in inter-generational family therapy*. New York, NY: Harper & Row.

Boszormenyi-Nagy, I., Grunebaum, A., & Ulrich, D. (1991). Contextual therapy. In A. S. Gurman & D. P. Kniskern (Eds.), *Handbook of family therapy II* (pp. 200–238). New York, NY: Brunner-Mazel.

Bowen, M. (1978). *Family therapy in clinical practice*. New York, NY: Jason Aronson.

Bowlby, J. (1969). *Attachment and loss*, vol. 1: *Attachment*. New York, NY: Basic Books.

Buber, M. (1958). *I and thou*. New York, NY: Scribners.

Buber, M. (1965). *The knowledge of man*. New York, NY: Harper-Collins.

Burr, W., Hill, R., Nye, F. I., & Reiss, I. L. (1979). *Contemporary theories about the family*. New York, NY: Free Press.

Byng-Hall, J. (1995). Creating a secure family base. *Family Process, 34*(1), 45.

Canda, E. (1986). *A conceptualization of spirituality for social work: Its issues and implications*. Unpublished doctoral dissertation, Ohio State University, Columbus, OH.

Carlton, T. O. (1984). *Clinical social work in health settings: A guide to professional practice with exemplars*. New York, NY: Springer.

Clulow, C. (Ed.). (2001). *Adult attachment and couple psychotherapy*. London, UK: Brunner-Routledge.

Cohler, B., & Geyer, S. (1982). Psychological autonomy and interdependence within the family. In F. Walsh (Ed.), *Normal family processes*. New York, NY: Guilford.

Donati, P. (1991). *Teoria relazionale della societa* [A relational theory of society]. Milano, Italy: FrancoAngeli.

Donati, P. (2012). *Family policy: A relational approach*. Milano, Italy: FrancoAngeli.

Donati, P. (2001). Freedom vs. control in relational society. In L. Tomasi (Ed.), *New horizons in sociological theory and research*. Ashgate, UK: Aldershot.

Donley, M. (1993). Attachment and the emotional unit. *Family Process, 32*(1), 3–30.

Etzioni, A. (1993). *The spirit of community: Rights, responsibilities and the communitarian agenda*. New York, NY: Crown.

Falck, H. S. (1988). *Social work: The membership perspective*. New York, NY: Springer.

Falck, H. S. (1976). Individualism and communalism: Two or one? *Social Thought, 2*(3), 27–44.

Fishbane, M. D. (2001). Relational narratives of the self. *Family Process, 40*(3), 273–293.

Fishbane, M. D. (2011). Facilitating relational empowerment in couples' therapy. *Family Process, 50*(3), 337–352.

Galatzer-Levy, R. M., & Cohler, B. (1993). *The essential other: A developmental psychology of the self*. New York, NY: Basic Books.

Gazzaniga, M. (1985). *The social brain*. New York, NY: Basic Books.

Gilligan, C. (1982). *In a different voice: Psychological theory and women's development*. Cambridge, MA: Harvard University Press.

Goldenberg, I., & Goldenberg, H. (1996). *Family therapy: An overview*. Pacific Grove, CA: Brooks-Cole.

Goldstein, E. (1995). Psychosocial approach. In Hopps, J. G. (Ed.), *Encyclopedia of social work* (19th ed., 1948–1954). Washington, DC: National Association of Social Workers.

Goodrich, T. J. (1991). Women, power and family therapy: What's wrong with this picture? In Goodrich, T. J. (Ed.), *Women and power: Perspectives for family therapy*. New York, NY: Norton.

Greenberg, J. R., & Mitchell, S. A. (1983). *Object relations in psychoanalytic theory*. Cambridge, MA: Harvard University Press.

Greenman, P. S., & Johnson, S. (2013). Process research on emotionally focused therapy (EFT) for couples: Linking theory to practice. *Family Process, 52*(1), 46–61.

Grisez, G. (n.d.). *Fidelity today*. Privately printed document.

Hanh, T. N. (1987). *Being peace*. Berkeley, CA: Parallax.

Hanh, T. N. (1991). *Peace is every step: The path of mindfulness in everyday life*. New York, NY: Bantam.

Haworth, L. (1986). *Autonomy*. New Haven, CT: Yale University Press.

Hazan, C., & Shaver, P. (1987). Romantic love conceptualized as an attribution process. *Journal of Personality and Social Psychology, 52*, 511–524.

Hollis, F. (1972). *Casework: A psychosocial therapy*. New York, NY: Random House.

Hughes, D. (1997). *Facilitating developmental attachment: The road to emotional recovery and behavioral change in foster and adopted children*. Northvale, NJ: Jason Aronson.

James, W. (1981). *Principles of psychology*, vol. 1. Cambridge, MA: Harvard University Press.

Johnson, S. (2004). *The practice of emotionally focused couple therapy* (2nd ed.). New York, NY: Brunner-Routledge.

Josselson, R. (1992). *The space between us: Exploring the dimensions of human relationships*. San Francisco, CA: Jossey Bass.

Kernberg, O. F. (1976). *Object relations theory and clinical psychoanalysis*. New York, NY: Jason Aronson.

Kohlberg, L. (1969). *Stages in the development of moral thought and action*. New York, NY: Holt Rinehart and Winston.

Kohut, H. (1977). *The restoration of the self*. New York, NY: International Universities Press.

Kotze, E., Hulme, T., Geldenhuys, T., & Weingarten, K. (2013). In the wake of violence: Enacting and witnessing hope among people. *Family Process, 52*(3), 355–367.

Ladnier, R. D., & Massanari, A. E. (2000). Treating ADHD as attachment deficit hyperactivity disorder. In T. M. Levy (Ed.), *Handbook of attachment interventions*. San Diego, CA: Academic Press.

Levy, T. M. (2000). *Handbook of attachment interventions*. New York, NY: Academic Press.

Lewis, J. M., & Gossett, J. T. (1999). *Disarming the past: How an intimate relationship can heal old wounds.* Phoenix, AZ: Zeig & Tucker.

Mahler, M., Pine, F., & Bergman, A. (1975). *The psychological birth of the human infant.* New York, NY: Basic Books.

McGoldrick, M., & Carter, E. (1999). Self in context: The individual life cycle in systemic perspective. In B. Carter & M. McGoldrick (Eds.), *The expanded family life cycle: Individual, family and social perspectives* (3rd ed., pp. 27–36). Boston, MA: Allyn & Bacon.

McGoldrick, M., & Shibusawa, T. (2012). The family life cycle. In F. Walsh (Ed.), *Normal family processes* (4th ed., pp. 375–398). New York, NY: Guilford.

McGoldrick, M., Anderson, C., & Walsh, F. (1989). *Women in families: A framework for family therapy.* New York, NY: Norton.

Mead, G. H. (1934). *Mind, self and society.* Chicago, IL: University of Chicago Press.

Mikulincer, M., & Florian, V. (1999). The association between parental reports of attachment style and family dynamics and offspring's reports of adult attachment style. *Family Process, 38*(2), 243–257.

Mikulincer, M., Florian, V., Cowan, P. A., & Cowan, C. P. (2002). Attachment security in couple relationships: A systemic model and its implications for family dynamics. *Family Process, 41*(3), 405–434.

Nichols, M. P. (2013). *Family therapy: Concepts and methods* (10th ed.). Boston, MA: Pearson.

Nichols, M. P., & Schwartz, R. C. (2001; 2008). *Family therapy: Concepts and methods.* Boston, MA: Allyn & Bacon.

Parad, H. (1958). *Ego psychology and dynamic casework.* New York, NY: Family Service Association of America.

Piaget, J. (1954). *The construction of reality in the child.* New York, NY: Basic Books.

Rank, O. (1947). *Will therapy and truth and reality.* New York, NY: Knopf.

Reich, W. (1989). Speaking of suffering: A moral account of compassion. *Soundings: An Interdisciplinary Journal, 72*(1), 83–108.

Richmond, M. (1907). *The good neighbor.* Philadelphia, PA: Lippincott.

Richmond, M. (1917). *Social diagnosis.* New York, NY: Sage.

Schwartz, R. (1995). *Internal family systems therapy.* New York, NY: Guilford.

Shibutani, T. (1961). *Society and personality.* Englewood Cliffs, NJ: Prentice-Hall.

Shivanandan, M. (2001). Subjectivity and the order of love. *Fides quaerens intellectum, 1*(2), 251–274.

Simon, B. (1960). *Relationship between theory and practice in social work.* New York, NY: National Association of Social Workers.

Smalley, R. (1967). *Theory for social work practice.* New York, NY: Columbia.

Sperling, M. B., & Berman, W. H. (1994). *Attachment in adults.* New York, NY: Guilford.

Stern, D. N. (1985). *The interpersonal world of the infant: A view from psychoanalysis and developmental psychology.* New York, NY: Basic Books.

Sullivan, H. S. (1938–1939). A note on formulating the relationship of the individual and the group. *American Journal of Sociology, 4*, 932–937.

Tamura, T., & Lau, A. (1992). Connectedness vs. separateness: Applicability of family therapy to Japanese families. *Family Process, 31*, 319–340.

Walsh, F. (2012). The spiritual dimension of family life. In F. Walsh, *Normal family processes* (4th ed., 347-374). New York, NY: Guilford.

Walters, M., Carter, E., Papp, P., & Silverstein, O. (1988). *The invisible web: Gender relations in family relationships.* New York, NY: Guilford.

Weingarten, K. (1991). The discourses of intimacy: Adding to a social constructionist and feminist view. *Family Process, 30*, 285–306.

Weingarten, K. (2000). Witnessing, wonder and hope. *Family Process, 39*, 389–402.

Weingarten, K. (2010). Reasonable hope: construct, clinical applications and supports. *Family Process, 49*(1), 5–25.

White, M. (2007). *Maps of narrative practice.* New York, NY: Norton.

CHAPTER 3

The Family Life Cycle, Relational Tasks, Language, and Communication

KEY TOPICS

Relational Tasks at Family Life Cycle Stages
Stages of the Family Life Cycle
Relational Architecture: Transitions to Personal Communication
A Well-Differentiated Family
Personal Components of Process and Structure
Differentiation from and Reengagement with the Family of Origin
Getting Married
The Systems Perspective Applied to Persons in Families
Language and Communication: The Newly Married Couple
Stress and Relational Tasks
Assessment

At every particular stage of the family life cycle, there is an emotional process of transition. There are transactional patterns typical to the stage. Implied in this transition are relational tasks for family members. These patterns and tasks are governed by the generational needs and issues characteristic of the stage (McGoldrick & Shibusawa, 2012, pp. 375–399; McGoldrick, Carter, & Garcia-Preto, 2010). Table 3.1 outlines some of these patterns at each stage. There is a thrust toward fulfillment of these tasks and emergent needs in one way or another. There is also a contrary thrust toward maintenance of aspects of an older relational system. One's previous life history and the relational environment will influence whether and how those needs are fulfilled and the tasks accomplished.

RELATIONAL TASKS AT FAMILY LIFE CYCLE STAGES: THE FOUNDATION FOR FAMILY INTERVENTION

Relational Tasks   Relational tasks have to do with interactive relationships with others that establish interpersonal patterns. They are carried out by family members in order to cope with what becomes necessary for the development of a workable family structure at a particular stage of development and in relation to a particular set of circumstances.

Each stage of family development has its own personal and relational tasks for family members. The more difficult, complex, and uncertain tasks are those of second-order change, shown in table 3.1. They involve the reworking of connectedness and separateness in current relationships with others. Because we also are creatures of our past relationships, as we rework connectedness and separateness in present

Table 3.1
Family Life Cycle Stages, Relational Transitions, and Relational Tasks

Life Cycle Stage	Shifting Memberships and Emotional Transitions	Relational Tasks
Young adulthood	Independence/dependence Responsibility for self/others	a. Relational differentiation with family of origin b. Development of relationships with peers c. Development of some financial independence through work and education
Emergent couplehood	Couple system becomes primary; other systems shift	a. Sharing goods and life goals; sharing closeness and intimacy; development of commitment b. Qualitative changes with (the now broadened) extended family and with friends to accommodate new couple
Families with young children	Couple becomes secure base for children; other relationships realign	a. Creating relational space for children b. Shifting/sharing child-caring and financial tasks c. Realignment with extended family/grandparents; development of outside relationships around child care, schooling, and activities
Families with adolescents	Responding appropriately to the adolescent's often risky maturational struggles and exploration; responding to shifts in the older generation	a. Shifting the couple relationship to accommodate the adolescent's differentiation/ exploration and need for a qualitatively different relationship with family b. Responding to midlife marital, personal, and career issues c. Responding to changes in the older generation
Families with young adults	Supporting differentiation in relations with children; retaining connectedness; couple finding/deepening new personal connections and involvement	a. Development of appropriate relationships with adult children b. Rediscovering/deepening and broadening the couple relationship c. Shifting relationships to work; preparing for retirement d. Dealing with emergent needs and relational shifts in the older generation
Families in later life	Shifting centrality to the middle generation; connections with grand-children; maintaining couple and personal identity	a. Compensating for each other's physical changes b. Developing/differentiating couple functioning c. Using time/space of retirement to balance productivity and relationships d. Accommodating relational shifts and reversals with the middle generation; developing relationships with grandchildren who are now exploring independence e. Sharing experience and wisdom with others without the need for agreement or control f. Dealing with losses; preparing for one's own passing

important relationships, we are also reworking attachment—thus the connection between attachment and relational tasks. For each family, the relational architecture of every stage may be different in response to the needs and narratives of family members and the external environment.

Personal Tasks Personal tasks have to do with what each person does within himself or herself to "get ready" for the task ahead or to respond to the implicit expectations of the family life cycle stage. Personal tasks come from an internal conversation in relation to our perception of the outside relational world of persons, of units of belonging, of institutions, of expectations, and of potential resources. Our memories of significant relationships, our anticipation of the future, and our present interaction with the other(s) is linked with an internal conversation with the "I" and the "me," the self and its parts. Through this conversation of the "I" with the "me," the person can delay responses, attempt to see himself or herself from the perspective of the other, review the past, and envision the future. Because of these capacities, the creative acting self or "I" can make choices between alternatives. "I" would be expected to direct thinking and behavior (Shibutani, 1961; Schwartz, 1995). Our human condition, however, is different from this ideal image. Persons are often similar to discordant families. Parts of us may believe we can or should do something; other parts may take a different tack (Schwartz, 1995). The leadership part, the "I," can mediate between these parts and join with others on the outside for support. The person may in fact not believe that he or she is able to do all this. A person who is overwhelmed by sadness, fear, anger, or obsessions, such as Gloria (see case study 2.1), clearly does not believe it is possible. As Gloria's reflective understanding of herself strengthened, she gradually began to be able to deal with her obsessions and the world outside.

Each person who develops a relationship with another that may eventuate in the development of a new relational structure, such as a new family or a new structure in an already-existing family, is also beginning a series of relational tasks with another. Since understandings and patterns need to be established jointly, the process depends on that other person as much as on the self. As such, the relational tasks of the couple, and later the couple plus children, can be accomplished only interpersonally. These tasks take time and it is not fully certain how they will be accomplished.

CASE STUDY 3.1:
SARAH AND PHIL

Sarah and Phil have been married for fifteen years. Sarah's recent severe back ailment demanded that she and Phil rearrange household tasks and the jobs of ferrying two adolescents and two preteens from one activity to another. In addition, Sarah is showing early signs of the recurring depression with which she has struggled since adolescence. It was only with the onset of Sarah's back trouble that both realized that they had taken much for granted from previous experience. They had assumed that the house should always be kept as immaculately as Phil, who grew up as an only child surrounded by helpful aunts and uncles, had experienced. They had assumed that their children had a natural right to be taxied any place where they had an activity, regardless of the difficulty involved. Their children had assumed the same. If they were going to develop their own patterns and adapt expectations to the realities of their resources of energy and time, they needed to communicate with other members of the family and work out the resulting issues with each other. They needed to ask their children to help and, with the children's participation, to work out priorities for transportation as part of an exchange. They had no language of meanings or communication patterns to accomplish this. And so they felt, with Sarah falling into a helpless depression and Phil alternating between increasing demands on Sarah and confusion, that their relationship was rapidly spiraling out of control. It took a good deal of work for family members to find words and a language to use with each other for these unfamiliar transactions. In the process of developing a common pattern, there was a concrete shift in power from "the way Phil's family did it" to "the way we want to do it, given our needs and circumstances." They needed to develop their own pattern over time rather than adopting Phil's family patterns without further discussion. At the same time they had to work out a relationship that now felt strange and different to them.

Family Resilience

It took fifteen years and a back ailment for Sarah and Phil to discover the imbalances in their relationship and to begin to work things out with each other. They had to find their own way to develop cohesion, flexibility, communication, and problem solving skills. Celia Falicov (1995) suggests that resilience is a matter of internal fit of members with each other, rather than a model for all families. Froma Walsh (2012), reviewing this research, suggests that there are many pathways to relational resilience and these vary to fit diverse family forms, psychosocial challenges, resources, and constraints. Shared beliefs and narratives that foster a sense of coherence, collaboration, competence, and confidence are vital in coping and mastery. There is a balance between stress and protection at each family developmental stage, shifting between stressful events that heighten vulnerability and protective processes that enhance resilience, as well as a balance in the relative influence of family, peers, and other social forces (Walsh, 2003, p. 4). Table 1.3 illustrates the personal and family resources that resilient families call upon at every life cycle stage to cope with stressful events. Harry Aponte (1994) points out that in poor communities, where often families lack institutional or societal support and deal with racism, poverty, and dangerous and dehumanizing conditions, resilience is a matter of spirit. It is a question of building a sense of dignity, purpose, and future in families that could have surrendered hope, meaning, and self-worth to despair. Optimism and hope become core elements in resilience. Families also, however, require a responsive society and community to improve their conditions and prospects.

STAGES OF FAMILY DEVELOPMENT

An overall picture of the stages of family development emerges from a consideration of adult developmental tasks taken in a relational sense. The demands of developmental change unfold in different stages. At each stage the family unit needs to develop a secure base for what is emerging. Each stage denotes a shift to the construction of a new relational structure—thus there is always difficulty translating an earlier stage to a later one. Family members don't have a clear picture of what new structure is emerging. All of the patterns used to manage the earlier stage, even if successful, will seem obsolete in relation to the new stage. The new stage will at least demand some accomplishment of the earlier one, however. In any case, the tasks of the earlier stage are experienced again in relation to the newer stage.

Not every person or family unit goes through all these—not in the same way and not with the same cultural meanings. Not everyone differentiates and reengages with family of origin in the same way. Not everyone gets married, and there are very different meanings for marriage experienced by family members. Not everyone raises adolescents or takes care of the elderly in the same way. What is common to all persons are the issues of attachment, differentiation, and creation of a secure base for development. Chapter 9 describes the helping process with a few of the many variations on this theme—families going through divorce, single parents, and blended families, each reconstructing relationships in their own way and in relation to concrete circumstances. Each stage of family development involves development of new relational architecture. A new relational unit must emerge, but it can emerge only through the communication and interaction of the people involved in the new relational unit. At each stage, the attachment patterns, deep in each person's beginnings and later growth, are revisited, then related to the other person's changing physical and relational attachment patterns. In some ways, this co-construction of attachment patterns into a new unit can provide a wonderful opportunity to revise these patterns. To do this, the relationship developed needs to be able to transcend these patterns in a real way. As in the challenge Sarah and Phil faced in adapting to their own realities, these can be difficult moments. Perhaps this is one reason traditional religions do not consider marriage to be an arrangement subject to continuous negotiation. Many religions enshrine commitment and fidelity in covenant, in a sacrament. The covenant, an entirely different arrangement from a purely negotiable agreement, transcends certain individual considerations.[1] Paradoxically, it may be easier to work out particular differences and functional patterns within the security of a relationship that is already partially defined and meant to be committed, respectful, and personal—a secure base.

Relational Architecture: Transitions to Personal Communication

Many families are not so much based on friendship, communication, or role flexibility as on tradition. As cultures shift at a glacial pace from fixed-role expectations

---

[1]See chapter 6 for one illustration of sample language of a covenant.

to negotiated understandings and companionship, a combination of patterns often develops. Some understandings remain externally fixed by culture; some are worked out within the family. Sarah and Phil, a reasonably flexible, independent, and well-educated, middle-class couple, found that there were many arrangements in their marriage that they hadn't discussed with each other or with their children. Although they had been married for fifteen years, they hadn't developed the language or the communication patterns to discuss these arrangements. It simply hadn't occurred to them that they could or should discuss them. Elizabeth Bott (1971), in her study of east London working-class families, found the husband-wife relationship to be not particularly close or important. Husbands had their own friends and family of origin. Wives had theirs. The relationship, guided by some traditional beliefs, was almost taken for granted. It was not as *personal* as might be expected by the modern, individualistic, middle-class mentality. Such an arrangement continues in a variety of cultures, particularly among working-class families. The arrangement can be stable as long as the surrounding kinship and friendship support systems are available to uphold the relational arrangement and the spousal system is not challenged. When it is challenged, the structure needs to shift to accommodate the challenge (Minuchin, 1974). If the unit is to survive the challenge, a more balanced structure, based on friendship and communication, needs to be developed. But the transition has its perils. The following case study illustrates the development of a more balanced structure. Miguel and Juana, born in Mexico and living in a modern North American metropolis, are gradually moving from traditional understandings of family to a more relational one.

CASE STUDY 3.2: MIGUEL AND JUANA

Miguel and Juana have been married twelve years. Miguel, a construction worker, works hard in his father's business. When he is with his friends, he drinks fairly heavily. His mother runs much of his life and advises him on how to deal with Juana. He is often out with his friends. He gives his paycheck to Juana and leaves the child rearing to her. Juana is in control at home. Miguel frequently lies to Juana. When it becomes obvious, he simply smiles and admits he lied. What else could any man do? He takes it for granted that Juana will forgive him, and she usually does. He assumes that giving her the check and his support when she requests it should be enough. Juana, a skilled technician whose parents are still in Mexico, feels isolated. She is alienated from her mother-in-law, whom she sees as hostile to her. She feels Miguel allows his mother to direct their marriage. She is concerned with Miguel's drinking, which is getting out of control. Most recently their son, Jorge, 11 years old, has been challenging her with impunity. From her perspective, Jorge challenges her and disregards her in the same way that Miguel challenges and disregards her. Miguel seems to be supporting Jorge. Their insurance program had limited them to seven sessions of marital counseling at the company's expense. After that, they would have to pay the costs of marital counseling. From Miguel's initial perspective, married relationships were parallel relationships. He would have his role and Juana hers. Juana disagrees, partly because the relationship is unbalanced, with her bearing the brunt of their problems. Also, her long-lasting family support system is still in Mexico. She needed more closeness, more balance, and more trust with her husband.

Juana and Miguel did work together to develop communication both could trust, to help Miguel start to do something about his drinking, to sort out issues around Miguel's mother, and to develop a common strategy around Jorge. In the beginning, Miguel didn't take Juana's determination to see change seriously. When she held her ground, he responded. They worked fairly quickly over several months and seven sessions, and did make some progress on all of these issues. Miguel took more responsibility for Jorge, but only after discussing it with Juana. He now has a program to deal with his drinking, as well as a spon-sor. Juana began to trust Miguel more as it became more important to Miguel to be trustworthy. Miguel set some boundaries on his mother's involvement in their marriage, and Juana worked on developing a better relationship with her mother-in-law. As long as they could see the relational issues as tasks, they were willing to do them and enjoyed the process. They were pleased by the changes they experienced in their family. The development of a common pattern meant that Miguel had to be involved. He couldn't privilege himself in the relationship. Their relationship was slowly growing and a new balance was emerging between them. The closeness and balance of their relationship, however, was never their major concern. For the most part, they preferred to see their work as tasks that they had completed successfully within the seven sessions allotted by the insurance company. They did recognize that they had made changes for the better.

A Well-Differentiated Family

James Framo has developed Bowen's concept of self-differentiation and connectedness into principles of healthy family functioning. However, few families could meet these criteria. Indeed, most marriages are like Sarah and Phil's: somewhere in process, moving toward achieving these standards in the continuing drama of family life. Framo distills from his experience as a therapist what family development can aim for. The value of his criteria is that they are useful to understand what goals can be set. Families who arrive at these goals in their daily living would easily be at the upper quartile of self-differentiation/connectedness:

1. Parents are each well differentiated, having developed a sense of self before separating from family of origin.
2. Generational boundaries within the family are clearly separated, with the children free of the role of saving the parent or the parents' marriage.
3. Perceptions and expectations by parents of each other and of their children are sufficiently clear.
4. Loyalty to the family of procreation is greater than to the family of origin.

5. The spouses put themselves and each other before anyone else, including the children. The marriage, however, is not a symbiotic one that excludes the children; the children do not feel that to be close to one parent they are alienating the other.
6. Identity development and autonomy for all family members is encouraged; successful development in the children will mean that they will leave home at some point to start families of their own.
7. Nonpossessive warmth and affection is expressed between parents, between parents and children, and among the siblings.
8. The capacity to have open, honest, and clear communication and to deal with issues with each other is evident.
9. There is a realistic, adult-to-adult caring relationship between each parent and his or her parents and siblings.
10. There is an open family in the sense of involvement with others outside the family, including extended family and friends. Outsiders are allowed inside the family.[2]

Framo developed a similar picture of a healthy marital relationship, only achieved through the normal developmental challenges over a number of years. After fifteen years, Sarah and Phil are working on all these things.

1. The partners are more personally differentiated, and dependency on each other is voluntary.
2. They have come to terms with the roots of their irrational expectations of marriage and of the spouse derived from the family of origin.
3. They have developed a more empathic understanding of their mate.
4. They can meet each other's realistic needs in the face of their differentness.
5. They can communicate more clearly and openly.
6. They like each other more and enjoy sex with each other.
7. They have learned to deal with the issues between them.
8. They can enjoy life more and get pleasure from their work and their children.
9. They have developed flexibility in dealing with situational stresses and crises.
10. They have adjusted to the disenchantment of romantic love and have more realistic appraisals of the vicissitudes of mature de-idealized love. (Framo, 1981, pp. 139–149)

Personal Components of Process and Structure

Miguel and Juana saw their work as solving problems and carrying out tasks. It was only at the end that they began to see some of the relational changes that had taken place in this process. Sarah and Phil did not consciously set out to change their

[2]Adapted from Framo, 1981, pp. 139–140, © 2015. Reproduced by permission of Routledge, Inc., part of the Taylor and Francis Group

relationship as they wanted it to be: the changes became necessary when Sarah's back went out. There is opportunity at each stage of family development for the emergent family to define together the personal components of structure. What gets to be defined in one way or other would be autonomy and independence, vulnerability and obligation, and gender relations. The underlying issues are attachment and bonding, connectedness and separateness. As these get redefined and bonds need to be elaborated or to shift, the process generates light and heat. This always takes place in the context of broader societal meanings and the social institutions that reinforce them. What gets defined then is not simply structure, but also the values and expectations that will govern relationships. After they are defined, can they be taken for granted? Social institutions, such as religion, law and justice, education, and health care systems, will reinforce the emergent structure, or possibly create challenges. Each stage carries with it a certain risk that it will be accomplished badly, or not accomplished at all, or that family members will need assistance in its accomplishment. These risks increase when previous stages have not been accomplished well, when a family structure is rigid and unwilling to accommodate change, or when previous generations have had difficulty with a particular stage.

In addition, circumstances such as losses through death or divorce, a stepfamily, premature parenthood, an affair, mental illness, addictions, the birth of a child with a disability—all these create risks and potential crises. There is often a need for social work intervention with the family on the relational structure. The goal is that the stuck relational tasks be accomplished in a way that accommodates every member's developmental needs and that facilitates family functioning.

We now briefly examine the two earliest stages of family formation, the young person's differentiation and reengagement with the family of origin, and the related processes of two people planning for marriage and getting married. As we move through the book, we will use as examples case studies of different families transacting at different life stages, and of social workers assisting them in the personal and relational work related to these stages.

DIFFERENTIATION FROM AND REENGAGEMENT WITH THE FAMILY OF ORIGIN

The first stage of family development we consider is differentiation from and reengagement with the family of origin on the part of young people in their twenties. The personal task is one of *getting ready* to revise the previous parent-child relationship in the direction of independence and greater self-responsibility. In some ways, this task of getting ready is the obsession of adolescence, rarely fully realized because the adolescent is usually not in any position to take effective care of himself or herself. Indeed, there is often a prolongation of adolescence in various ways until the young person is ready to complete an education and establish himself or herself occupationally, financially, and, in some countries, through separate living arrangements. Interpersonal tasks at this stage include the following:

- Differentiating oneself in relation to family of origin
- Completing an education
- Establishing oneself occupationally
- Establishing oneself financially
- Developing close peer relationships
- Reengaging with family of origin with a different level of dependence/independence

In some societies, for many persons an often symbolic part of this personal and relational process is the concrete moving out of the home. In any case, for many young people, who may lack alternative housing arrangements, this stage can also be accomplished at home, with the family respecting the new boundary that develops and relying on the young person in a different way. If the process is not accomplished, the move into the next stage is much more difficult, because the previous relational tasks are now involved and implicit in another more complex set of personal and relational tasks.

Family-of-Origin Work

Family of origin work can be done at every stage of development, but it is at periods of sharp developmental transition that the work takes on paramount importance. This is particularly true at the stage of early adulthood and formation of a new family, or at a stage of loss of a family member. During "normal" times, James Framo routinely prescribes this work for couples experiencing marital problems. According to Framo (1981), when there is a focus on past and present issues in the family of origin, often the marital problems recede in importance. These are replaced by the dawning realization that maybe something can be done about that longstanding guilt over closeness or alienation from a mother, father, or sibling. Working out a better relationship with the family of origin frequently becomes a goal in its own right.

Getting Married

The next possible stage for some would be that of planning for marriage and getting married. After the previous stage of differentiation from and reengagement with family of origin, there may be a number of years before the person may decide that he or she is ready to form a more permanent couple bond with another, which would lead to a family. This is a shift from a single state with friends and family to a level of mutuality with another. The relational tasks are as follows:

- Disengaging (or altering the form of engagement of) oneself from especially close relationships that compete or interfere with commitment to the new marital relationships

- Accommodating patterns of gratifications of premarital life to patterns of the newly formed couple (marital) relationship
- Establishing a couple identity
- Establishing a mutually workable and satisfactory system of communication between the pair
- Developing mutually workable and satisfactory patterns of decision-making
- Establishing a mutually workable and satisfactory pattern with regard to relatives
- Establishing a mutually workable and satisfactory pattern with regard to friends
- Developing a mutually workable and satisfactory pattern with regard to employment
- Developing a mutually satisfactory set of expectations of marriage and children
- Developing mutually satisfactory pattern and sets of expectations regarding religious practice, ethical values of each, and education of children
- Planning specifically for the wedding, honeymoon, and the early months of marriage that lie ahead (Rapoport, 1963)

These tasks continue into later stages. For Miguel and Juana at a later stage, these tasks were implicit in Juana's desire to establish their own couple unit with its own patterns separate from Miguel's mother's expectations, as well as in Miguel's mild resistance to this.

This is complicated and difficult work. Expectations of each member are often different. Real communication about differences may not take place. When one realizes these differences, there is often a jarring personal crisis. The change process often goes slowly. The "I," who may want this relationship, converses with the "me" of one's set patterns. Different parts of the self may take different positions. For this new relationship with a new person, previous patterns will not suffice, even— especially—if one has had a close previous relationship with another. Each person is different. No one person can substitute for another. The process proceeds unevenly as both future partners struggle to communicate their expectations and needs and adapt to the other's. At the same time, there is a process of disengagement and reengagement with other meaningful relationships in one's life situation. These patterns remain at least partially unresolved and carried into marriage. It can easily take half a decade to "get married." Miguel and Juana had been married for twelve years, Sarah and Phil for fifteen. Some couples may never alter their previous personal patterns and accommodate each other's sufficiently to really be married.

DOES LOVE CONQUER ALL?

In Western European cultures and increasingly throughout a modernizing world, the process of developing a relationship leading to marriage is made much more complex by distorted societal beliefs about romantic love and marriage. Couples' counselors often see people who fall in love believing that love alone will keep them together and that nothing else matters. In contrast to the romantic search for one's self, one's desires, and one's preoccupations with the other, love and fidelity imply a realistic discovery of the other *as other*. This discovery is a process that will gradually unfold over a lifetime of mutual commitment. Couples quickly discover that their real experiences of working out their relationships do not match their beliefs. They may feel disappointed and think that there is something "wrong with us." Romantic beliefs say they should be soul mates. If this is not quickly accomplished, it becomes a sign that they are not really in love, and so on. Let us examine some clusters of popular marriage myths:

- I am in love, and that is enough. Don't bother me with the details. It is not important to learn to communicate, solve problems, and understand differences. If you are really in love, it is enough.
- If we have conflict—if you or I get angry—we must not be in love. If you don't know what I am thinking, you must not understand me or really love me.
- If marriage is to succeed, it must meet all my needs. There is a "right person" someplace out there who will do that.

These deny the daily hard work of developing and maintaining a good relationship in favor of a type of culturally acceptable narcissism attached to love beliefs. As couples test these myths and their expectations against the realities of their relationship, they often need professional help sorting them out and discerning their real relationship with each other as concrete persons. They often have very little frame of reference for this discovery—thus the need for a guided professional experience.

The following case study illustrates the process of sorting out the myth from the reality.

CASE STUDY 3.3:
BRIAN AND LISA

Brian and Lisa are an engaged couple in their late twenties. Brian is an only child. He has close relations with his parents, an older couple who dote on him. He is just beginning to establish himself in advertising, a high-pressure competitive occupation. His patterns are of hard work and all-night partying. He has many close male friends and enjoys them tremendously. He binge drinks with his friends with weeks of abstinence in between. Before he met Lisa, he had a close relationship with Bonnie, which never gelled. Brian returns to this relationship when he is feeling sad. Lisa is the oldest of six children, accustomed to taking responsibility, and accustomed to being in control. She is a lawyer, just beginning in her profession but quite unhappy with her current job in the district attorney's office. When Brian and Lisa announced their engagement, no one took Brian seriously. Lisa had her nagging doubts about his seriousness. She dealt with this by managing all the small details of planning for the wedding, and Brian was happy to let her do it her way. Brian and Lisa wanted marriage. Each felt the other met their abstract requirements for a spouse, but they kept getting surprised by characteristics of the other they hadn't anticipated. It was a learning process, but they wondered about it as they got closer to marriage. Brian liked Lisa's clear ideas of what she wanted and her sense of control. This was very different from his other flames. Parts of Brian felt ready to marry. However, he also found himself reacting to her set ideas and going back to one of his old friends for relief. His drinking contin-

ued off and on. He might take a weekend with his friends or talk things over with Bonnie. For her part, every time Lisa felt everything was settled, Brian would unsettle things by doing something she didn't anticipate. Lisa remembered her father, who was a lot of fun and never predictable, but who also had had a drinking problem. She was terrified, fearing that these patterns that she knew so well would repeat themselves. She and Brian broke off their engagement several times before coming to counseling. During sessions, Brian agreed to stop drinking altogether, and he did. He was tired of his lifestyle, and he didn't want to lose Lisa.

The social worker helped both Brian and Lisa to communicate better and to develop their plans together. They had to make an assessment, on the basis of their real communication, of whether they wanted to continue the relationship toward greater commitment. Brian had to let go of Bonnie if Lisa was to feel a sense of trust in his commitment and the relationship. Lisa had to back down from making decisions, even petty ones, for Brian. Brian needed to become more active in the relationship. Both needed to change and support the other's changes. They found some mutual friends both could enjoy without the pressure on Brian to drink. As they began to communicate around plans for the wedding, some of the different patterns that had ruled their families of origin came out. Both needed to form a third pattern together and, in the process of doing that, revise some of their previous patterns and relationships. Both had to work out their own friendship with each other and at the same time new relationships with parents, and in Lisa's case, with her siblings as well.

Brian and Lisa are essentially establishing a new set of patterns to govern their future relationship in common. It is a type of dance with each other in which simultaneously they establish their own pattern and work out different patterns with their respective families of origin and with friends. These are very important for many reasons, not least because Brian and Lisa need the concrete support of family and friends to establish this new relationship. Things also could go badly on the inside of the relationship. Brian and Lisa could develop extremely distorted communication patterns. Brian might be unable to refrain from binge drinking. Lisa could go into a serious depression. They might not be able, or it might not be advisable, to move to the next stage of their relationship: a deeper, exclusive, and more permanent commitment. On the other hand, external factors, such as war, unemployment, death of a parent, or pregnancy could change the process also, delaying it or speeding it up. These could place so much pressure on the couple that they would be unable to continue their plans.

There are several ways to examine Brian and Lisa's worlds. First, their interaction is not linear or mechanical. Rather it is recursive and reflexive. It needs to be seen from the systems perspective. Second, the normal relational work they do, accommodating two worlds in one, will have to go slowly. There will be plenty of fits and starts, even for this relatively well-adjusted couple. This is because the work has to proceed on two levels—personally and systemically. The process continues on its own, whether or not the social worker is working with the family. In the authors' experience, often a couple or family will break off contact after one or two sessions, only to reappear months or years later, having continued in the interim to work (sometimes quite successfully) on the tasks and concerns identified in the first contact.

THE SYSTEMS PERSPECTIVE APPLIED TO PERSONS IN FAMILIES

The systems perspective for understanding process and structure has proven itself to be a rich and powerful tool for that purpose and thus for understanding family interaction. The use of the systems perspective, particularly in the family area, has led to the evolution and use of common definitions of terms that have implications for understanding family interaction (Walsh, 1982; 1993). Fundamental principles of systems functioning are as follows:

1. *Circular Process.* This term defines the underlying recursive organization of all family systems. In any system, change in any one member affects other members and the group as a whole; this, in turn, affects the first individual in a circular chain of influence. Every action in this sequence is also a reaction. Causality is fundamentally circular rather than linear (Everett, Russell, & Keller, 1992).

2. *Communication.* Communication refers to behavior, both verbal and nonverbal, by which people share meaning with each other (Bateson, 1936). Every communication has two functions: a "content" (report) aspect, conveying factual information, opinions, or feelings, and a "relationship" command aspect, which, in conveying how the information is to be taken, defines the nature of the relationship (Watzlawick, Beavin, & Jackson, 1967).

3. *Homeostasis.* Systems maintain dynamic balances among themselves. All systems members contribute to the balance through mutually reinforcing feedback. When there is too much deviation from the system's norm, the negative feedback process regulates tension and attempts to restore a family equilibrium (Walsh, 1982). An example: if the environment is changed (e.g., via an effective therapist) the family's stable (homeostatic) functioning will be necessarily disrupted (Dell, 1982; Everett, Russell, & Keller, 1992).

4. *Family Rules.* Family rules are shared norms and values and mutual agreements that define relationships (Everett, Russell, & Keller, 1992). Rules are necessarily limited so that the family system is patterned and predictable to

its members. These rules, both implicit and explicit, organize system inter-action and function to maintain stability. They provide expectations about roles, actions, and consequences that guide the life of a system and its inter-action (Walsh, 1982).

5. *Equifinality*. Living systems differ from mechanical systems and are gov-erned by a certain "biology of purpose" (Sinnott, 1961). No matter how the seed is planted, one part of the plant grows toward the sun; the other sends roots to the soil. Similar outcomes may result from different initial conditions (Everett, Russell, & Keller, 1992; Von Bertalanffy, 1968). Two-well func-tioning family systems may have come from different initial conditions, or the same origin may lead to different outcomes. One family system may dis-integrate, the other come together in response to a similar stressor. The sys-tem's ongoing interactional patterns and responses to stress make the differ-ence (Walsh, 1982).

6. *Nonsummativity*. The system as a whole is greater than the sum of its parts. It cannot be described simply by summing up characteristics of individual members. The system's organization and interaction involves interlocking patterns of behavior of its members, and the patterns connect the members with each other (Walsh, 1982).

All these concepts of social interaction—circular process, nonsummativity, equifinality, and so on—apply to Brian and Lisa's relationship. The tasks with which Brian and Lisa are dealing will become very familiar, repeating themselves in dif-ferent ways at every stage of family development. In addition to the normal stresses and uncertainties of developmental shifts, there were other stresses in Brian's and Lisa's relationship. These add some personal tasks for each, making the relational shifts riskier and more difficult. Brian had an alcohol problem which he had to deal with. Lisa's own history would make this a particularly difficult area for her. She had a need for a very ordered world that she controlled. But she also had to allow Brian some control. Brian would have to take responsibility for his binge-drinking prob-lem. It would be almost impossible for them to form a real relationship if Brian remains "engaged" to alcohol. Lisa could complicate the situation by her own anx-iety and need to control the problem, rather than insisting that this was Brian's domain, and she expects change if they are to build their dreams together. She needs to deal with her own anxiety and need for control of things. Together they also need to sort out some of these issues before they move on. They also need to make their relationship secure, developing trust and fidelity. Depending on how the work proceeds, together they may make a mature decision not to marry or to marry.

LANGUAGE AND COMMUNICATION: THE NEWLY MARRIED COUPLE

The issues that Brian and Lisa had to face before marriage become even more important in the first years following marriage. Now they must develop a real and workable relationship and an understanding of each other, including ways of resolving normal differences. They must develop the common patterns that balance their relationship. They must truly make a permanent commitment to each other as "other"—that is, as not self, not a reflection of one's desires and experiences, not as "heavenly twins," but as real human beings. There is an other who is different, has needs and can contribute something to the relationship. In the beginning, the young couple, full of romantic feelings, marry their desires and illusions, and in this respect marry themselves. Depending on their experience and maturity, they may often be disappointed when their partner is not their expected image. Only later may they discover and hopefully begin to appreciate the "otherness" of their partner. They can then make the discovery and a commitment to the other as "other," and then to the "we" that eventually emerges (Hargrave, 2000). The process takes time. Language and communication are the key vehicles for developing the common patterns necessary for sharing a common life and a "we" relationship. This is true at every stage, but it is particularly important at the beginning. To carry out relational tasks, the couple needs to develop a relational language of meanings and to communicate with each other. For reasons having to do with socialization, family experience, and cultural meanings, this is difficult for men and women in a society dominated by competition, work, and a globalized economy but in which, paradoxically, the expectations for relational closeness have never been higher. These tasks are particularly difficult for men, whose goals and life patterns may be often geared to achievement, competition, and the work world and to denial of feelings. Each person's experience, language, meanings, and communication skills are profoundly shaped by his or her experience in the family of origin. Without language and communication, it may feel as if one has married a stranger. Intimacy may feel like exploitation. For the beginning social worker working with the newly married couple, development of language, meanings and communication skills becomes the pathway eventually to assist couples at any family life cycle stage to construct and reconstruct a relationship. Social worker Virginia Satir (1988), in her powerful discussions insisted that language and communication are the chief tools of relational change. When the couple learns to use these tools well, the effect is profound. Good communication acts as a catalyst for rapid change. On the other hand, the expectation of honest communication in a helping relationship, when unfulfilled, can also lead to a degeneration of the relationship. When one or the other partner is dishonest, the expectation of honest communication and its disappointment can shut down the relationship and can be a catalyst for rapid emotional divorce.

Communication is at best difficult. It is a learned skill, socially constructed as part of a relationship. Rather than really communicate, people often just make statements in the presence of the other as in a crisscross of monologues. Sometimes it takes a crisis to begin to have genuine communication. When communication takes place at all between two people, it always consists of two processes: an expression of thought and feeling by an initiator and a reflective response to the expression by a receiver. Then the process reverses, with an expression by the receiver and a reflective response by the initiator, until the issue reaches some resolution. In everyday discussion, the process often gets sidetracked for several reasons. First, the expresser may not have the language to be able to say what he or she is thinking or feeling. Second, the expresser may not fully intend to communicate. The expression becomes a smokescreen or is a self-justifying expression for him or herself rather than an authentic attempt at communication with the other. Receiving communication is even more difficult than expressing, because it involves careful listening to the other and an ability to respond without one's own feelings and preconceptions getting in the way. It involves an empathic ability to take the position of the other, to take some of the other's language, and then to respond to the other in that language. Most conversations go much too quickly for anything to get accomplished. The expression or the language may come too fast for the receiver to absorb. The receiver may be preparing a response to what he or she thinks the initiator is saying, rather than listening. There may be too much emotion, too great a merger of thoughts and feelings—even too much noise from the outside—for any genuine communication. "Noise from the outside" can take many forms—actual noise (such as traffic), but also interruptions (children, telephone) and even general societal pressure ("I know my father wants me to do well at this; I'd better. . .").

There has been a considerable amount of work in the areas of language, expression, response, and the use of real communication to develop a relationship. In the area of language, persons who have experienced posttraumatic stress or sexual abuse, who are dealing with serious illness, such as end-stage cancer, or who come from families where language was hardly used except for control, often have great difficulty finding language to express feelings and thoughts. This blockage can block the relationship in the area affected. Kaethe Weingarten (2000), Peggy Penn (2001), and others from the Ackerman Institute for the Family have done a good deal of work in this area.

It is becoming recognized that people struggling with extreme suffering, such as end-stage cancer, need to find different voices and languages to reflect their feelings and thoughts accurately. In the beginning, they may have no language to speak about personal suffering. What makes the suffering even more painful is that the perceived injustice of it takes over all other considerations. It is just as difficult for the helper to respond to a person speaking about suffering. At best, the initial response may simply be silence rather than empty words. The helper also must find a voice and a language to help the suffering person to express and reflect. There is a growth process on the part of the helper that parallels that of the suffering person (Reich, 1989). This is a process that every social worker needs to experience if he or she is to be effective with situations where language cannot be found to express thoughts. Empathy, put to words, demands reflective, meditative habits, but the rewards of this process go far beyond words.

Developing Language and Communication

Bernard Guerney (1977; 1982) over almost fifty years has developed a process he calls relationship enhancement. This is a controlled process of expressing and empathic responding that can be taught to individual couples or groups. As it has developed, it is a powerful tool for deepening and teaching empathic accuracy (Snyder, 1995). An initiator starts the conversation by some positive reflection on what they will be discussing. He or she then moves to "I" messages (Gordon, 1970) that describe in a non-accusatory way the effect of something to do with the other person on him or her. The "you" message, which focuses on an accusation of the other (you do . . .), rarely works. The receiver and responder needs to suspend his or her own reactions to what is being said and focus intensely on understanding the thoughts, wishes, desires, intentions, motives and inner emotional experience (be it fear, sadness, joy, anger, irritation, or any other emotion) of the speaker. The responder in some ways "becomes" the other and conveys this deep understanding to the speaker. He or she reserves one's personal responses, thoughts, and feelings until it is his or her turn to become the speaker and receive the gift of this same deep empathy from the other. When this communication emerges, the effect is relaxation on the part of both and often a reframing of the whole context for discussion. Sometimes, when one or the other has difficulty expressing or responding, the social worker—with permission—takes the role of the speaker or responder, "becomes" the person, expresses or responds for that person, and checks to see whether the person agrees or disagrees with the expression. If the "becoming" is accurate, the person agrees with the social worker's expression and moves with it. The response to this expression by the other moves the process along and avoids possible impasses. The following case study illustrates this process.

CASE STUDY 3.4:
JIM AND CHERYL

Jim and Cheryl, both 21 years old, had been married for five months. Already they were having severe arguments with verbal abuse and eventual physical abuse. Jim has a physically and verbally abusive mother and was protected from her only by his relationship with his father. Cheryl, together with her older sisters, constantly experienced physical and verbal abuse from both father and mother until she left home to marry. In their conversation, Jim tended to ignore Cheryl. Cheryl had great difficulty finding language to express herself and tended to get into circular discussions with herself in which she saw herself inevitably at fault, expecting herself

to be "wrong" but also being angry about it. In her speech and in her gestures she seemed to be saying, "I'm not good enough." Jim had difficulty penetrating this conviction. Her posture was hunched forward, almost to deflect a blow. Jim looked sideways at her, never directly. Neither could connect with the other, and this was frustrating to both. The social worker began the session by asking them to talk to each other about what they felt needed changing in their relationship and what they felt they could change. The person who would initiate, the "speaker," has a floor tile, "the floor," while the other reflected the speaker. Jim initiated the conversation. The social worker needed to help him to attend to Cheryl, use "I" messages, and start softly and positively.

He shifted to look intently toward Cheryl and talked with her seriously without criticizing her. He needed to help her to find a language to respond to him. She was taking whatever he said as criticism. With the social worker's help, he challenged what she was hearing—that somehow she was not good enough. When Cheryl finally responded accurately (with the worker's help) to Jim, she took "the floor." Jim gradually was able to learn to reflect her expressions. Midway in a two-hour session, Cheryl visibly relaxed. Her posture changed to attend to Jim. She took his hand, and in the discussion she said that after twenty-one years, she suddenly realized that things could be different and that she could do something about her relationship. It wasn't hopeless. In fact, it looked doable. Their relationship now felt like it could be a "craft project" to her. What she meant was that she was less overwhelmed, less paralyzed, and saw step-by-step how they could work on things, and improve them. She had never understood this before, and she was delighted. The couple would continue on this basis over a number of sessions, building their relationship and doing family-of-origin work. It was a very difficult process. Cheryl eventually began therapy for herself. Very close to divorce in the beginning, Jim and Cheryl stabilized their marriage and recommended marriage counseling to those of their friends who were having difficulty.

Additional Circumstances: Stress and Relational Tasks

Situational Stress   The stress and complexity of family development is often compounded by situational stress. Situational stress can delay or prevent the accomplishment of family developmental tasks. With Brian and Lisa, it was some of their older family issues and his binge drinking. In other cases, there are losses carried into the present tasks: hospitalizations and illness, migration issues of abuse, divorce, suicide, imprisonment, and poverty, all of which put a good deal of pressure on these relational tasks.

Loss of a family member is one example of such stress. Loss includes death— particularly suicide or homicide—but also loss through divorce, illness, hospitalization, or separation through war, prison, even extended travel for employment. Family members will struggle to replace the lost functioning and the lost relationship. In some ways, an ambiguous loss, where the person is at times available or could return—a spouse whose sailboat simply didn't return to port—may even be more difficult than the finality of death.

Part of this is the problem of change, which itself may feel like a loss. The unanticipated addition of a family member, whether coming home from prison or from war, the blending of stepfamilies, or even a child's coming at a difficult time also can create stress and relational tasks for family members. Family members may need to cope with external stresses, such as school problems, lack of health care, probation, parole or court supervision, or community conditions. Internal pressures on family members can arise from a mental or physical illness of a member, alcoholism, or internal conflicts between spouses or between parents and children (see Janzen & Harris, 1997). When these stresses and pressures occur, the social worker often works not only with the family but also with a school, a hospital, a court, or a child welfare agency to help the family manage these additional stresses and reorganize themselves when necessary. This work is described in greater detail in chapters 10 and 11.

Some deeper stresses are particularly devastating to the ability to communicate in a real sense with the other, to relate with intimacy and trust, or to take reciprocal roles with one another. An affair is destructive to trust and intimacy. In this case, the social worker needs to help the couple through the personal and relational tasks of repairing the damage and restoring trust, intimacy, and a balanced, collaborative relationship. In cases of alcoholism and other addictions, the partner is in some ways "married" to the addiction, so the partner must divorce the addiction and remarry the spouse with all of its implications of restoring trust, intimacy, and a balanced collaborative relationship. Similarly, a spouse who re-emerges from depression or mental illness needs to help develop a restored relationship from the time he or she was "away." The birth of a child who has a disability places the couple in a new and unanticipated situation, that will last their whole lives. They have to shift their relationship, balance their caregiving roles and their relations with other children and their families of origin, and mourn the loss of the "perfect" child they had expected. All of these, and other similar circumstances, generate new tasks that must be attended to if the couple is to survive. They place particular pressure on the couple's bond, and then on others in the family. A good example of this is found in chapter 7, in the story of the social worker working with Rita and Joav Green as they deal with the birth of a child with Down syndrome.

There are other stresses that are felt not only by the couple, but also, almost at the same level and intensity, by everyone in the family. Death—particularly the unanticipated, early death of a family member—is an example of this. Every family member mourns the lost and irreplaceable attachments to the person who died, the relationship with that person, and the individual meanings of that person's life. Every family member has to consider the personal and relational meanings of the death. The personal work of mourning is accompanied by a shifting dance in relationships of every member of the family. A suicide is particularly difficult to accommodate in one's personal world and in the relational world of a family. Divorce also brings about personal tasks of mourning and continuing relational shifts of every family member. The formation of a stepfamily is another example of relational shifts that are superimposed on the loss of a member. Often the stepfamily gets stuck between incomplete mourning for the lost member, the tasks connected with accommodation of the new member, and the development of new relationships. Risk comes when the tasks are not done well or geared toward any resolution of the problems. In this case, the entire family carries the constant weight of unresolved issues into its daily living and work situations. The weight is an unseen presence that cuts off members from the possible support of each other. Relationships can become ritualized, the family a hollow shell.

Poverty and Discrimination   Another profound influence on family life is poverty and discrimination. Harry Aponte, a Puerto Rican social worker who has done a great deal of work with poor families experiencing discrimination, writes about underorganized families. Although not all underorganized families are poor, the circumstances of poverty and discrimination can affect a family's organization and structure. An underorganized family has a limited number of relational structures to solve problems. Its members may be rigid in how they employ the structures they have and may be inconsistent in their use of these structures (Aponte & Van Deusen, 1981; Aponte, 1986; Aponte, 1994). The underorganized family needs to develop greater complexity of structures and thus needs to develop structures that it never previously had. The family cannot survive without a supportive external environment. Its members need resources to feel safe, to know that the children are taught well, to be healthy, to have a good place to live, to have good and rewarding jobs, to be able to launch the children into a good environment, and so forth. When the family lacks any control over the effects of the outside world, it may not develop the internal structure to deal differentially with the environment—to have different ways of working with different parts of the environment and with its own internal processes. The family experiencing poverty or discrimination may feel no ownership or association, may lack resources and be unable to draw upon or trust its surrounding institutional environment. No one from the police, the justice system, the schools, the health system, or from the employment system may have workable relationships with the family. Lacking a way to interact positively with people from these external systems, the family can lose some of its effective internal functioning as well (Aponte, 1986).

ASSESSMENT

Assessment involves an understanding of what is affecting the family and what needs to be done. Understanding the family dynamics of relational tasks and the additional stresses placed on the family members by external events and family history is essential. Relational tasks are geared to personal and relational action on the part of all members of the relational set. The social worker needs to decide who to include in a collaborative intervention process. When Brian and Lisa understand what they need to do individually and collectively, they can do something about it. When Brian stopped drinking altogether, and when he let go of some of the relationships and patterns characteristic of his bachelorhood, Lisa began to feel more secure. Both began to learn a different way of communicating in a real way with each other. Their commitment to each other did transcend some of the other issues. It was an opportunity for both to change. The actions they performed with each other and their personal work changed their individual patterns and reassured both that they could succeed in their relationship, although the fault lines would remain and would probably come up again at different times. The paradox is that both Brian and Lisa would do things for each other and for the emergent relationship that they would have never done for themselves. Brian might now let go of personal feelings of emptiness that led to binge drinking. Lisa might now let go of the anxieties that led to a need to control. It is important for the social worker to assess both the persons (for personal tasks) and the emergent relationship (for relational tasks). To intervene in one is to intervene in the other.

Normalization of One's Responses to the Situation   Another very powerful tool that goes with the family developmental perspective is the idea that the problem can be *normalized*. Even in extreme conditions, such as war or migration, a normalized problem is something that can be expected in the circumstances. There is nonblaming language for normalized problems, one that can more easily be converted into personal and relational tasks. A normalizing, demystifying framework carries with it the expectations that people will cope and eventually have some control over the problem (or live with the problem if that is appropriate) through their own shared and individual resources. Fear and uncertainty of something out of control often paralyzes coping. Brian's reaction to this discussion was simple: "I guess I just have to stop binge drinking—or any drinking, for that matter." And he did, because Lisa was important to him. Lisa let go of her anxious need to control. At the same time, she had to expect something of Brian. Both learned to communicate with each other, developing a better, more human understanding of each other, reassuring each other, and helping each other to soothe their own anxieties. Brian and Lisa could each let go, because the other was there for them. Their marriage would become more important to each than an established pattern. Perhaps love would make this possible.

SUMMARY

This chapter has explored systematic life cycle change processes in families and their vehicle in communication. Relational tasks are energized by human needs that family life can satisfy. Social workers work with family members who carry out these tasks together and, together with relevant social institutions, re-create workable relational structures. There is no quick or easy way to carry out a relational task. Indeed, it cannot be done except with another person—and therein lies the complexity. There are always older tasks buried in the newer ones. What is remarkable is that they get done at all. To the extent that they do get done, it is helpful to identify patterns, predict next steps to be done, and help family members take these steps with each other. Relational time and space are the dimensions of family process. In the next chapter, we move to a deeper understanding of social interaction that develops a relational architecture within families.

REFERENCES

Aponte, H. J. (1986). "If I don't get simple, I cry." *Family process*, 25(4), 531–548.
Aponte, H. (1994). *Bread and spirit: Therapy with the new poor*. New York, NY: Norton.

Aponte, H. J., & Van Deusen, J. M. (1981). Structural family therapy. In A. S. Gurman & D. P. Kniskern (Eds.), *Handbook of family therapy* (310–360). New York, NY: Brunner-Mazel.

Bateson, G. (1936). *Navan*. Cambridge, UK: Cambridge University Press.

Bott, E. (1971). *Family and social network: Norms and external social relationships in ordinary urban families*. London, UK: Tavistock.

Carter, E. A., & McGoldrick, M. (1999). *The expanded family life cycle: Individual, family and social perspectives* (3rd ed.). New York, NY: Allyn & Bacon.

Dell, P. (1982). Beyond homeostasis: Toward a concept of coherence. *Family Process, 21*(1), 21–41.

Everett, C. A., Russell, C. S., & Keller, J. (1992). *Family therapy glossary*. Washington, DC: American Association for Marriage and Family Therapy.

Falicov, C. (1995). Training to think culturally: A multidimensional comparative framework. *Family Process, 34*, 373–388.

Framo, J. L. (1981). The integration of marital therapy with sessions with family of origin. In A. E. Gurman & D. P. Knishkern (Eds.), *Handbook of family therapy*. New York, NY: Brunner-Mazel.

Gordon, T. (1970). *Parent effectiveness training*. New York, NY: P. H. Wyden.

Guerney, B. G., Jr. (1977). *Relationship enhancement: Skill training program for therapy, problem prevention and enrichment*. San Francisco, CA: Jossey-Bass.

Guerney, B. G., Jr. (1982). Relationship enhancement. In E. K. Marshall & P. D. Kurtz (Eds.), *Interpersonal helping skills* (pp. 482–518). San Francisco, CA: Jossey-Bass.

Hargrave, T. (2000). *The essential humility of marriage: Honoring the third identity in couple therapy*. Phoenix, AZ: Zeig, Tucker & Theisen.

Janzen, C., & Harris, O. (1997). *Family treatment in social work practice* (3rd ed.). Itasca, IL: Peacock.

McGoldrick, M., Carter, B., & Garcia-Preto, N. (2010). *The expanded life cycle: Individual, family and social components* (4th ed.). Boston, MA: Pearson.

McGoldrick, M., & Shibusawa, T. (2012). The family life cycle. In F. Walsh (Ed.), *Normal family processes* (4th ed., pp. 375–398). New York, NY: Guilford.

Minuchin, S. (1974). *Families and family therapy*. Cambridge, MA: Harvard University Press.

Penn, P. (2001). Chronic illness, trauma, language and writing: Breaking the silence. *Family Process, 40*(1), 33–51.

Rapoport, R. (1963). Normal crises, family structure and mental health. *Family Process, 2*(1), 76.

Reich, W. (1989). Speaking of suffering: A moral account of compassion. *Soundings: An Interdisciplinary Journal, 72*(1), 83–108.

Satir, V. (1988). *The new peoplemaking*. Palo Alto, CA: Science and Behavior Books.

Schwartz, R. (1995). *Internal family systems therapy*. New York, NY: Guilford.

Shibutani, T. (1961). *Society and personality*. Englewood Cliffs, NJ: Prentice-Hall.

Sinnott, E. (1961). *Cell and psyche: The biology of purpose*. New York, NY: Harper.

Snyder, M. (1995). "Becoming": A method for expanding systemic thinking and deepening empathic accuracy. *Family Process, 35*(2), 241–253.

Von Bertalanffy, L. (1968). *General systems theory*. New York, NY: Braziller.

Walsh, F. (1982). Conceptualizations of normal family functioning. In F. Walsh (Ed.), *Normal family processes* (pp. 3–44). New York, NY: Guilford.

Walsh, F. (1993). *Normal family processes* (2nd ed.). New York, NY: Guilford.

Walsh, F. (2003). Family resilience: A framework for current practice. *Family Process, 42*(1), 4.

Walsh, F. (2012). Family resilience: Strengths forged through adversity. In F. Walsh (Ed.), *Normal family processes* (4th ed.). New York, NY: Guilford.

Watzlawick, P., Beavin, J., & Jackson, D. (1967). *The pragmatics of human communication*. New York, NY: Norton.

Weingarten, K. (2000). Witnessing, wonder and hope. *Family Process, 39*(4), 389–402.

CHAPTER 4

Family Interaction and Structure

KEY TOPICS

Describing Family Interaction
Behavioral Research on Couples' Relationships
Communication Processes and Social Interaction
Bonding Processes and Vulnerability
The Process of Role Development
Socialization: The Acquisition of a Framework of Meanings
The Structural Perspective in Family Therapy
Relational Change through Interaction and Communication
Components of Family Functioning and Approaches to Family Therapy

This chapter explores the family relational structures people create and live in. As families go through life cycle changes, their beliefs, perceptions, and communication process create a relational architecture (family structure). This structure continues on through self-reinforcing patterns. Themes developed in this chapter are drawn from symbolic-interactionist social psychology, structural family therapy, and behavioral research on family communication and bonding.

THE BIRTH OF FAMILY STRUCTURES: PERCEPTIONS AND INTERACTION

Both social work and the family therapy movement assume that there is integrity and validity to how people see themselves and how they see others. For people working with families, the family needs to be understood from the inside as it is lived, in its complexity, as it maintains its precarious stability through internal and external change and as it changes to meet change. Many theories of the family have tended to see it as a social institution, whose changes can be more easily measured from the outside. Others see the family from the vantage point of an intervention method. Fortunately, there is a long tradition of theory, now confirmed by observational research, that deals with family as its members (and the family helper) experience it. The perceptions of family members (and helpers), mostly taken for granted, play an indispensable part in family interaction sequences, in relationship patterns, in its stability and change, and in the helping process. The milieu and each person's perceptions of it constitute an inseparable psychosocial phenomenon (Hoffman, 1981). Salvador Minuchin's comment (Minuchin & Fishman, 1981)—"Patients come to therapy because reality, as they have construed it, is unworkable"—pointed out what became a new paradigm in the understanding of family intervention. The paradigm recognizes the validity and power of human subjective experience. It recognizes the relation of subjective perceptions to an outside world and the tension often inherent in this relation. It is indispensable to the understanding of cultural perceptions and change in the dynamic sense necessary today. Its starting point is on the inside of the family as it is experienced by its members. In this chapter and the following ones, we will examine this body of theory in research observation and in practice experience.

Describing Family Interaction

Because it is mostly taken for granted, the delicate and elaborate relational (and intentional) architecture of family interaction cannot easily be described and analyzed. This task demands a systematic way of understanding and dealing with the validity of human subjective experience without reducing it to something else. Social psychology and relational sociology (Blumer, 1969; Burr, Hill, Nye, & Reiss, 1979; Cooley, 1922; Donati, 1989; 1991; Mead, 1934; Shibutani, 1961; Turner, 1970; Waller & Hill, 1951) have made some progress in developing an understanding of mutual communication, intentionality, and mutual action in families.

The Postmoderns   The postmodern work of Michael White (2007; Beels, 2009) and Kaethe Weingarten (2000; 2010) similarly opens the way for nonreductive, postpositivist understandings of the complexity of social relationships, human obligations and solidarity. They cultivate a refreshing openness to the lived worlds of each family, and indeed of each person, with a more immediate description of one's experience and ways. Each family is like a world unto itself. To understand and join the family the social worker must learn a special type of humility and curiosity. I must "enter" the family and experience it to understand it. When I, as a social worker become part of that family world, I am entering an alternate universe. Moreover, I can only enter the family as "I." To enter this world, we move from our abstract, relational language to a more personal language of "thicker" description (Ryle, 1971). At the same time, I remain a part of a broader world. I have the world of my understandings and commitments as a professional. And I have a parallel world of the understandings and commitments which come with this temporary quasi-family membership. And so I have learned to move back and forth between two worlds. I become a bit like a distant relative or visiting friend. I am curious and I want to understand this different world. I am unfamiliar with how things work, and I want to have the humility to let members teach me (Hunter, 2012).

However, I can only be accidentally a part of things. I am interested in what this family is doing, and I am concerned about them. Becoming a part of the family for a while, I have the advantage of unfamiliarity with its ways. Nothing is taken for granted. Although I may know a good deal in general about families, I don't really know *this* family, and so I must suspend for a while most of what I know about families to have a thicker understanding of the meanings implicit in what this family is doing together. I am not going to be encumbered by the thin understanding provided by premature judgments or by caricatures of, or even research about what is "typical" for a family in this cultural milieu. I am no longer satisfied with generalizations about families, and so, like an anthropologist joining a tribe, I aim for the *local knowledge* (Geertz, 2000) that comes only from quasi-family membership.

I am concerned that part of the problem is the "stories" about themselves that members of the family subscribe to. These stories often limit what they are able to do. For the moment I understand that entering the family's universe in this way, I can look for alternative stories (and alternative possibilities) from the thin generalizations of these stories, which both colonize them (Rober & Seltzer, 2010) and limit what members think they can do. In this vein I need to start from the position of "not knowing." What is different about this family from every other family? How do they manage with each other? There is a danger in taking a position that brings me to think that ultimately I am able to predict or control their processes. Whenever I work with families, I expect to be surprised by them, and this usually happens. If things are going well, I will be surprised and gratified many times as they discover and demonstrate parts of themselves and abilities I never knew they had. Nor did they know this. As a matter of fact I know that things are not going well when something prevents me from entering this alternate universe, when something prevents me from being surprised by them and when my own presumptions about them take over.

The Symbolic Interactionists The symbolic interactionist school (Blumer, 1969; Burr, Hill, Nye, & Reiss, 1979; Shibutani, 1961; Stryker, 1980), more systemic than the postmoderns, carries a long tradition of many theorists in social psychology (Cooley, 1922; Mead, 1934; Turner, 1968; 1970; 1974; 1979; n.d.; Waller & Hill, 1951) who have struggled with the problem of describing social interaction and its sources. All assume in one way or another that social relationships are created out of human experience and interaction. There are relations between the way people perceive reality, the way people act, their patterns of action, and the structures of relationships that they create. These structures in turn stabilize personal patterns and perceptions in a dense, complex, recursive and reflexive relationship.[1] There are three central assumptions of the school:

1. People act on the basis of the meanings they ascribe to things in their environments.
2. Meanings emerge through social interaction with others and the society.

---

[1]For a full description and development of this theoretical base, see Stryker (1980) and Blumer (1969, p. 163); also Burr, Hill, Nye, and Reiss (1979); Shibutani (1961); Doherty and Craft (2011, pp. 63–76). Thus Waller and Hill (1951) described "interlocking habit systems" developing between marriage partners. Ralph Turner (1968; 1970; 1974; 1979) has a theoretically integrated and developed description of role-taking and role-making as *process*, taking place on the basis of self-other interaction within a framework of social understandings. Every role is a performance, reciprocally related to other roles in a situation. Within this understanding of social process and the interaction of ego and alter, the role-taking (and making) process is *tentative*, *adaptive*, and *integrative* (Turner, n.d., p. 63).

3. Meanings are managed through an interpretive process used by the person dealing with the environment.

In this emergent picture, social relationships are created out of human experience and interaction. Let us draw these assumptions further into an understanding of social intervention:

- There are relations between the way people perceive reality, the way people act, their patterns of action, and the structures of relationships that they create.
- These structures in turn stabilize personal patterns and perceptions in dense, complex, reflexive relationships.
- The relation between people's patterns of behavior and their constructions of their worlds does not necessarily make behavior predictable in any linear or mechanical way. On the contrary, when we allow for people's differing perceptions, behavior becomes somewhat indeterminate.
- An intentional social world is an indeterminate social world. It is open to reconstruction through mutual communication, mutual commitments, and mutual action.
- In the world of practice, therapists intervene in people's interchanges and interactions: in the patterns and sequences, in communication, in the way relations with others are construed, and in what people are accustomed to doing.
- Through these guided interventions in human interaction, the phenomenal world is altered.
- The social worker assists family members to communicate appropriately and creatively and to make effective mutual commitments, thus assisting them to preserve relationships and to restructure their patterns of communication and interaction.

This body of knowledge about family relationships and interaction becomes the basis for a dual vision of family intervention, from the outside as a social institution and from the inside, through the interaction of its subjects (Turner, 1970, pp. 4–14). It is the interaction that creates the institution and can most account for both its stability and change. This interactional perspective on family is precisely what is needed by family helpers to understand their helping process (Constable, 1984).

The relation between people's patterns of behavior and their constructions of their worlds does not necessarily make behavior predictable in any linear or mechanical way. On the contrary, when we allow for differing perceptions, behavior becomes somewhat indeterminate and difficult to predict. An indeterminate social world is open to reconstruction through mutual communication and mutual action. In the world of practice, therapists intervene in people's interchanges and interactions—in the patterns and sequences, in communication, in the way relations with others are construed, and in what people are accustomed to doing. At one point, a marriage counselor might choose to interrupt a couple's conversation and refocus on their communication if they "stonewall" an issue in their session. Or she might elect to wait. In any case *through guided interventions in human interaction, the phenomenal world can be altered.* Assisting family members to communicate appropriately and creatively is the key to helping them preserve relationships and restructure their worlds, restructuring how they respond to each other and what they do with each other.

GENERAL CONCEPTS ABOUT SOCIAL INTERACTION

Social Process

People's self-consciousness, responsiveness, actions, and interactions proceed from their evaluations of themselves, their surroundings, and the significant others in their environment. These evaluations are perceived and communicated in different ways. They are the source of social agreements. William I. Thomas's (Thomas & Thomas) 1928 dictum "What men perceive as real are real in their consequences" brings together the interdependent realities of social structure and personality in social interaction. Social interaction, communication, and the development of social agreements are processes. Processes are interruptible and partially undetermined sequences, moving in their own direction, within which crucial events and turning points can occur (Turner, 1970, p. 12). Each event is less important for its immediate effects than for its contribution to cumulative developments (Turner, 1970, p. 8). An episode of interaction leaves a residue in the attitudes and memories of the participants. It makes a difference. With the passage of time, these episodes may determine cumulatively whether, for example, a couple stays together or breaks up (Turner, 1970, p. 20).

The Active, Constructive Self

Concepts of the active, constructive self, of social interaction, process, growth, the relative indeterminacy of the social world, and of the social nature of mind have long been recognized in social work, at least implicitly. Practitioners must be aware of the indeterminate realities they deal with. Many leading social workers were familiar with the more complex conceptions of social reality of the early social psychologists. However, in a century, which privileged what was quantitatively measurable, there was a struggle between mechanistic conceptions of social reality that could be more easily reduced and measured and more complex, qualitative conceptions of it. The former appeared to carry greater scientific weight. The more limited (positivist) measurements of relational and spiritual realities had generated a postmodern reaction, particularly when one needed to develop an understanding of persons acting together in a social world. Paradoxically, recent behavioral research, cited later in this chapter, points out that family interaction can be both observed and measured and that theories of interaction can be tested.

The data of experience (and of practice) points out that persons are active, coping, adaptive, and to some extent self-directed. The conception of the active person, currently becoming accepted in the field of developmental psychology (Angyal, 1940; Brazelton & Cramer, 1990; Coelho, Hamburg, & Adams, 1974; Hartmann, 1958; Rank, 1964; Stern, 1985; White, 1959) has a long history. A leading social work theorist, Jessie Taft (1926), discussing the active, constructive self and the social nature of mind, quoted her mentor, George Herbert Mead: "The conscious self arises out of its own social responses and . . . continues to exist as social process, an index of its changing relationships" (p. 10). The quote demonstrates use of Mead's social psychological theory to illustrate and explain the recursive processes that practitioners were experiencing. Taft rejected determinism and the simpler idea that persons would be "molded" by their environment in favor of the idea that they are active in their responses to it. They do not simply take roles, but "make" them within and sometimes beyond the limits of current social expectations.

Reflecting Taft's conceptions of social work, Ruth Smalley saw the human being as potentially able to be a person within a concrete environment of constraints and possibilities and an actor. According to Smalley, the person has a biological capacity and will to live, to grow, and to solve problems. There is a psychological urge to be a whole person, to be consistent with one's self. There is also a capacity to take from the outside and use what he or she takes for the experience of the creation of personhood (Smalley, n.d.). In this sense, engaging persons to discover and use their capacities for action—both personal and social—for agency and communion within implicit limits and circumstances becomes a goal of social work, sustained by practice experience.

BEHAVIORAL RESEARCH ON COUPLES' RELATIONSHIPS

Over the past thirty years there has developed a body of observational research on how couples actually behave with each other. Previous assumptions about couple interaction were constructed out of therapeutic experience with families, but they had little basis in observed interaction of families. Nor was there a focus on the complexity of multiple interrelationships rather than simply individuals in relationships (Gottman & Notarius, 2002). For three decades, John M. Gottman and others observed married couples' interaction as couples. On that basis, they began to form different hypotheses about couples' relationships. Because they focused primarily on interaction, their findings had interesting parallels with explanations of interaction provided by symbolic interactionist social psychology. In this chapter, we will connect Gottman's findings with symbolic interactionist theory and attachment theory. These theory bases give strength and explanatory power both to the research findings and to social work practice theory.

Gottman (1999) found that a certain level of conflict and difference is quite normal and even healthy in a relationship. The majority (69 percent) of couples experience and deal over many years with issues of difference with no resolution. Whatever the problem immediately experienced, it will also include (1) basic differences in the partners' personalities and (2) basic differences in needs that are central to their concepts of who they are as people. These differences are "perpetual problems" but would not indicate that the couple was unhappy. Gottman's research points out that happily married couples and unhappily married couples had about the same number of differences. What distinguished them was their ability to repair these differences satisfactorily. Romance, however, does have its place in this. Happily married couples had positive feelings about each other, and these overrode incidents of negative interaction. Moreover, even where there were few incidents of negative interaction, the absence of positive feelings about the other person predicted divorce within a North American context (Gottman & Levenson, 2000). Gottman concluded from his research that for marital quality and stability, the positive listening and expressing behaviors had to outweigh the negative by five to one. When negative behaviors and memories prevail, new communications and behaviors tend to be interpreted negatively. A cascade of increasing distance and isolation is established, and the marriage will move to a split (Gottman, 1999). Gottman's research shifts the focus from treating differences as a problem to the question of how couples process their differences.

COMMUNICATION PROCESSES AND SOCIAL INTERACTION

Gottman's research into couple interaction opens the way for the development of a deeper understanding of communication processes and social interaction in the family. As a first step, let us examine family interaction in the following episode of communication (c.f. Turner, 1970). It involves a married couple in their forties, Mark and Leslie; their daughter, Amber; and her college friend, Julie. They are having dinner together, and this is Julie's first meal with the family. On the previous day, Andrea, a friend of Leslie and Mark, had suffered a heart attack and was taken to the hospital. Mark had heard about the situation before dinner, but Leslie is hearing about it for the first time:

CASE STUDY 4.1:
MARK AND LESLIE

Mark: John called me today.

Leslie: I made the pasta sauce vegetarian this time. Is it okay?

Mark: [taking a breath] It's great—but wait, Leslie. John told me Andrea had a heart attack. She regained consciousness in the hospital, but she is paralyzed.

Leslie: What? Is she really paralyzed? How far paralyzed?

Mark: Well, she can't talk, but—

Leslie: Then she's really in a bad way. Will she recover? How much does it cost for her care with a specialist and all?

Mark: Well, it's—

Leslie: Will she be in the hospital long? I hope she gets better. Will she get any better, or is there a chance she'll die? Does the doctor know how much longer she'll be paralyzed? How does she eat?

Mark: She can't swallow, so they are feeding her intravenously, but—

Leslie: How much longer will she be in this condition? Did the doctor say? Why can't she swallow?

Mark: [getting angry] For heaven's sake, Leslie, please stop rattling away! How can I answer so many questions? You don't even let me talk.

Amber: [laughing] You're both getting crazy. How can Dad get a word in edgewise, Mom, if you just keep asking questions?

Julie: [laughing] Please. Tell us what happened. I'm dying of curiosity now.

Mark remains silent and just frowns for a few seconds, looking as if he is swallowing something painful. Suddenly he relaxes and smiles. The two girls burst out laughing, especially because of the way Mark looked when he was about to lose his temper. Leslie, who looked quite tense when Mark said she "rattled away," stopped, looked at the girls and Mark, put on a half smile, and then, shaking her head, started laughing herself.

Leslie: Julie, I do this all the time when I get worried about something. Mark is used to it. I'm sorry, Mark—I do talk fast, but I didn't think I was rattling.

Mark: [smiling] It's okay, and I'm sorry it got under my skin this time, and in front of the girls, too. Sometimes you just won't stop talking, asking questions. I can't get a word in edgewise when you do that. You don't let me talk.

Leslie: [leaning over and giving Mark a little hug] Yes. I know it gets to you when I do that. But I was terribly worried about Andrea. I just wanted to know as quickly as possible about everything. I'm sorry.

The conversation about Andrea continues comfortably.

The above episode is one of a long series of events in the progressive story of Mark and Leslie's marriage. Although there are tension points, Mark and Leslie have a workable marriage and are accustomed to dealing with these points. Mark begins with a "gesture," his statement about John's phone call. Leslie didn't want to discuss something that excluded the girls. Her first response was to ignore Mark's opening gesture and shift the discussion to the vegetarian pasta sauce. She had worked on the sauce and was very pleased with the result. Julie, their guest, is vegetarian. She was concerned that Mark seemed to be ignoring Julie and Amber. She felt this topic of conversation would recognize the girls as well as her work. She was also slightly irritated that Mark hadn't noticed the sauce and that he had started in this way with their guests present. Mark persists, making only a brief repair effort, because he knows that this information is important. Leslie reacts with concern when she realizes the importance of the news. She interrupts Mark and cuts him off several times. Mark's response is frustration. He is on the verge of anger. The daughter, Amber, softens the interaction, and the friend joins in the softening. Mark struggles with his anger and Leslie struggles at her hurt and embarrassment at Mark's talk of her "rattling away." Both know this is a hot-button term for her. The girls soften Mark and Leslie's interpretations of the other's gestures and responses.

Both Mark and Leslie have had many more positive than negative interactions in the past. As a consequence of this, neither one is overly watchful for responses of the other that they might take personally (Gottman, 1999). Also the presence of the girls prevents the episode from deteriorating. Otherwise Mark and Leslie might have gone further into reflections on past interactions and intensified criticism or defensiveness on either one's part (Gottman, 1999). The repair efforts are accepted for the moment. The episode is reinterpreted, and family and guest proceed with dinner conversation.

Later, in private, Mark and Leslie will still probably need to repair any leftover issues from the incident so that it doesn't carry over into future communication patterns and ultimately into the relationship. Leslie remembers Mark's remark about her "rattling away." She will think about it and remind him of his remark at an appropriate time. Mark remembers that Leslie cuts him off in different ways when he is trying to say something and doesn't always listen well—but then neither does he. Both also remember that that they mostly have a good relationship. Their meanings are eventually understood by the other. Their conversation "makes sense," and these little difficulties won't interrupt their mostly positive feelings. They can joke about them, but there are deeper meanings as well.

Mark and Leslie's episode is extremely important theoretically for several reasons. First of all, it is through interaction such as this that families construct or dismantle their relationships. We see the couple struggling with present communication and with memories of how they have communicated. There are differences, but research points out that this is less important than their ability to repair differences (Driver, Tabares, Shapiro, & Gottman, 2012, pp. 57–77; Gottman, 1999). Simply put, Mark and Leslie communicate with each other as real people, giving and receiving confirmation most of the time. The key is communication. Communication makes it possible to alter their picture of themselves and their roles in relation to each other. If they elect not to communicate about themselves or their conceptions of their roles, they are then conversing mostly with themselves or with their picture of the other person. Both the need for a better relationship and today's demand for communication about everything will push them to communicate and alter their pictures of themselves and their roles.

In Mark and Leslie's episode, Mark retreats from his picture of Leslie "rattling away"; Leslie modifies her original redirection of Mark's gesture. It is very important that they be able to modify their understandings and interaction. Not all couples are able to do this readily—or even at all. Mark and Leslie do listen to each other. Communication builds in a constructive process. It is real, rather than being circular. It would be circular if Mark would talk to his picture of Leslie (based on past experiences) but ignore the real Leslie. Leslie might talk to her picture of Mark in the same way. In reality, Mark and Leslie have had many more positive than negative episodes, and they can joke about the negative ones. This is the music of their couple communication.

However, this assumes that Mark and Leslie want to be close, to communicate and to repair their relationship. The couple could also have a parallel relationship, much as Elizabeth Bott (1971) found in East London marriages. Couples would communicate mainly about practical necessities. Their role conceptions were learned and *preset* through cultural influences, family-of-origin experience and other experiences, but not necessarily by their own couple interaction. Men were closer to other men than to their wives. Women were closer to women. This arrangement is not particularly unique and could be stable in a more traditional society. It would not work well, however, in conditions of societal change, when role conceptions are in conflict or the circumstances of their relationship demand communication. The social worker has the choice of supporting a parallel arrangement, when it is workable, or of helping the couple modify their relationship through developing some communication skills.

John Gottman's "Four Horsemen"

What might have made Mark and Leslie's relationship unworkable? If the episode between Mark and Leslie were left unrepaired, it could have deteriorated into cascading dysfunctional patterns. The research of John Gottman (1999, pp. 41–47) points out that four negative patterns of communication—*criticism, defensiveness, contempt,* and *stonewalling* ("the four horsemen")—if prolonged, almost unfailingly predict marital split. On the other hand, without the above four indicators of negativity, emotional disengagement also predicted a split (Driver, Tabares, Shapiro, & Gottmann, 2012, pp. 57–77; Gottmann, Driver, & Tabares, 2002). Mark might not bother to tell Leslie about Andrea or might completely stand apart from Leslie's reactions. Leslie might take the news without any relational comment or feeling at all.

Criticism   Criticism is any statement that implies that there is something globally wrong with the other, something that is probably a lasting aspect of the partner's character. "You always . . . rattle away, cut me off," and so on, are criticisms rather than constructive complaints. An "I" message is better. It can repair criticism, because it is not an attack on the other person, "Please wait, Leslie. When I was trying to say something about John, it confused me for a moment. It felt like you were going off with your own concerns before I could get back to what I was trying to say." Actually most couples would not be so diplomatic in real life. But then there may be less to repair, or the repair may not be made, eventually leading to bad memories. The antidote to criticism is making any statement of the problem that does not criticize (Gottman, Driver, & Tabares, 2002, p. 393), such as an "I" statement.

Defensiveness   Defensiveness is an attempt to defend oneself from a perceived attack. In marital interaction, it takes the form of the innocent victim posture. The message is, "What are you picking on me for? I didn't do anything wrong."

Mark: You interrupted me, Leslie. I was trying to tell you something.
Leslie: Why not? You always do that to me.

The antidote to defensiveness is accepting responsibility for even a part of the problem (Gottman, Driver, & Tabares, 2002, p. 393). The couple then can go back to the original communication and repair it.

Contempt   Gottman considers the third horseman, contempt, the "sulphuric acid" of a marriage. *Contempt* is any statement or nonverbal behavior that puts oneself on a higher plane than one's partner. It often sounds like mockery with a contemptuous facial expression. It stops positive communication completely because it is directly aimed at the other. According to Gottman's research, the amount of contempt in stable, happy marriages is essentially zero (Gottman, 1999, p. 47).

> Leslie: I made the sauce vegetarian today. Is it okay?
> Mark: There she goes again. Mrs. Rattle-Away. Amber, notice she never follows what I'm saying and I can't get a word in edgewise.
> Leslie: [smiling tensely and bitterly] Okay, Mr. Know-It-All. If you were really so smart, you might have noticed Amber's guest sitting over there.

The antidote to contempt is creating a culture of appreciation in the marriage (Gottman, Driver, & Tabares, 2002, p. 393). It is difficult to repair contempt except through a long period of positive work on the part of both partners on a greatly revised relationship. In this case, the matter gets complicated if Mark quickly moves to a possible alliance with Amber, who gets triangulated into the conflict with Mark and Leslie competing for the alliance with her. When couples come to this point, it is difficult to move back, and the move backward is a dance of three: Mark, Leslie, and Amber. As we will see at a later point, such alliances can both strengthen the dysfunctional couple patterns and at the same time foster serious problems in children.

Stonewalling   The fourth horseman, stonewalling, occurs when the listener withdraws from the interaction, shuts down, and is chronically unwilling to return to interact with the partner.

> Mark: [Getting angry] For heaven's sake, Leslie, please stop rattling away. How can I answer so many questions? You don't even let me talk.
> Leslie: [smiling coolly] Mrs. Rattle-Away will just shut up and find out for herself what happened, thank you. [pause] Amber, how was your English class today? Did you and Julie go together?
> Mark: Do whatever you want. I'm done.

It takes a great deal of repeated relational work and a real revision of the relationship to rectify stonewalling (Gottman, 1999). In the above vignette Leslie would stonewall if she would shut down the conversation with Mark, switching the subject and the focus to the girls. In doing this, she would reinforce an implicit alliance with the girls and further isolate Mark. His complaint, although angry and badly phrased, just wasn't important enough to deal with at all. Mark might reply by his own stonewalling. (Do whatever you want. I'm done.) Both are competing to shut things down now. Generally stonewalling is such an embedded pattern that the stonewaller is hardly aware of what he or she is doing. Mark and Leslie may think they are establishing peace, or at least an armistice. The antidote for stonewalling is finding productive ways of dealing with the topic, rather than abandoning it. This is easier said than done. Attempting to deal with the topic will increase tension and the possibility of the other shutting down. Each needs to self-soothe his or her own anger and take productive breaks, but ultimately both stay connected with the aim of resolving the issue. Because one or the other can shut down so easily, this can only take place over a long period and after many failed attempts (Gottman, Driver, & Tabares, 2002, p. 394).

There are some gender correlates in negative couple communication in North American samples. Research suggests that women tend to use criticism in a conflict; men tend to use defensiveness and stonewalling. In this connection, Gottman found that, in happy marriages, men do listen to women. Everything is fueled by the positive feelings about the other that we identify as love. Repairs are more important than the original problem and couples can learn to change negative communication patterns. Among newlyweds, even with high negativity, if they were able to learn to make effective repairs, 85 percent experienced happy, stable marriages six years later (Gottman, Driver, & Tabares, 2002).

In the last two examples of problematic exchange, the dysfunctional communication between Mark and Leslie is reinforced by attempts to realign with Amber against the other parent. In many ways, regardless of the age of the child (ten), an alignment of a child against a parent, what Jay Haley calls a "cross-generational coalition (Haley & Hoffman, 1968; Haley, 1980), seems closely related to problems with children, and of course it also undermines the marriage. Reinstating the coalition between the parents so that they form a united front (even if disagreements about the children continue in private) makes socialization of the children possible.

Communication: Repair Patterns and Change

In the original case study (case study 4.1), Mark and Leslie actually have relatively healthy communication and likely could successfully repair and reconstruct their relationship. However, the girls neutralized the issue, possibly because of their friend's presence, and this prevented Mark and Leslie from an immediate repair—Mark and Leslie may have to repair some of it later. In marital counseling, rather than neutralizing and covering over the issue, the social worker would generally interrupt the conversation and help them work out the issue, using their own natural communication with each other and some of the techniques discussed in these chapters. The focus would be on repairing and stabilizing communication patterns. Through this repair of communication, the couple's processes of decision making and bonding could also be strengthened in a longer and more determinate process. Ultimately they would learn to communicate differently.

This type of relational reconstruction demands real interaction both in session and out of session with a professional as a coach for the work to be done. Thus one key to the art of intervention is an understanding of interactive processes, of what needs to be done to repair and reconstruct relationships. Another key is an understanding of how and where to intervene in these processes while they are taking place before the social worker's eyes. One has a grasp of the process and of what needs to be done for a couple or family to reconstruct itself. The couple is in charge of their reconstruction. Then the professional social worker, as a coach, can choose from among a wide variety of methods that can be used to help the couple reconstruct their relationship, just as an artist can choose to work in a particular medium out of many possibilities. The professional could work with Mark and Leslie as a couple on couple issues, or with the whole family on issues involving the whole family.

For the most part Mark and Leslie do communicate fairly smoothly. With other couples, memories of previous interactions, perhaps not even with the same person, may be enough to stall the present interaction. Sometimes there is very little real communication—that is, of real people with each other. Ego communicates with memories or impressions of alter. Thus ego converses with self and not at all with alter. Alter does the same. And both are frustrated. Both react to their impressions of each other without really hearing what the other has said. Neither feels understood. However, as with Bott's East London couples in the 1960s, they may not feel a need to be understood by the other unless their relationship encounters change and demands some adaptability. In any case, neither may feel the friendship that goes with a more personal relationship. When they communicate, they may, for the most part, be communicating with themselves. Their communication only reinforces their present beliefs about the situation. This may need to change in a crisis. To change this condition requires persons to find some real communication with each other and, through that, manage the work they must do together in reconstructing their relationship. The social worker might assist this difficult process of changing one's patterns with the other.

SOCIAL INTERACTION

Social interaction is communication and action—with and in reference to other persons with whom we have a present or past relationship. Out of social interaction, persons communicate, develop bonds and connections with one another, experience conflict, learn and develop roles, develop expectations for the roles of others, make decisions, and carry out tasks. Not all couples have sufficiently rich verbal interaction to transact all of the above. They can communicate verbally mainly on practical details. They may get along well or poorly, depending on the fit of their interactional patterns. If the couple relationship is less important for both of them than their relationship with their parents, siblings, children, or their friends, conflict with the partner may not be considered a major problem.

For social workers, who have to decide whether or not to support a workable but undeveloped relationship, it is essential to know that social interaction can be maintained or modified through communication. To the extent patterns of social interaction can be modified, a relationship also can be modified. Processes of social interaction need to be understood by the social worker as interruptible sequences rather than inevitable events. The sum of these transactional processes—a network of social agreements—is experienced by each person through membership in groups, in families, at work, at play, and so forth. This is the work of social interaction. Social workers can intervene to reshape some of it in some cases.

BONDING PROCESSES AND VULNERABILITY

Bonds are powerful. Both membership and attachment are expressions of the interactive process of bonding. The stages of a bonding process correspond to the different stages of family formation. As illustrated in our earlier episode involving Mark and Leslie (case study 4.1), the bonding process is a reflection of the interaction of both the past and the present. As it is shaped by interaction, it can be subject to change. As Mark and Leslie inevitably change and as their circumstances change, so also must they continually work to stabilize their bond. As we saw from our examples of alternative conversations for Mark and Leslie, a bond could degenerate from clumsy handling, but the clumsiness of the past often can be rectified somewhat. A couple's bond inevitably reflects their past interactions and even their memories of bonding in their families of origin. Indeed, as internal and external changes occur, as the couple faces new circumstances, they must reconstruct this past in relation to their present. They are continually and actively in a bonding process. They cannot stop. If they did, certain bonds would deteriorate. On the other hand, Mark and Leslie already have a whole complex of bonds to each other. The vulnerability and deterioration of one set of bonds does not necessarily prevent other bonds from working. To clarify this point, let us examine the different types of bonds that exist in Mark and Leslie's case.

Our focus on the more personal bonds of friendship has been mainly on *identity* bonds. Identity bonds are bonds that can be made only with a particular and unsubstitutable person. These bonds often demand that a whole complex of sentiments of friendship and/or love be attached to them if they are to be seen as authentic. Not all bonds are so fully personal. Other quite powerful bonds are attached to a position or a task. These *status* bonds and *task* bonds may lead to identity bonds. We will discuss status and task bonds before discussing identity bonds in greater detail.

Status Bonds Status bonds are inherent to social membership and the social institution of marriage. Despite their name, these bonds are dynamic, not static. They are maintained by social interaction. Some status bonds come from the status of being married, of being a wife, a husband, a mother, a father, or a member of a family. The child, born into a family, is born into a status. Only later may more person-oriented bonds develop out of interaction. Nevertheless, the status bond of child to parent and parent to child is quite powerful, even when the relationship is not yet personal. Bott's (1971) East London families had powerful status bonds. In Western society there is the expectation that the family bond, and in particular the married bond, should be based on love. A marriage for status or position, or a loveless marriage, is considered tragic. Marriage is looked on as a desirable status, implying within many groups a certain level of maturity, of prestige, and of accomplishment. There are societal benefits and even financial benefits to the married state. The attraction of this bond may be such that rather than marrying another person, a person may simply marry marriage. In traditional societies, (such as those where marriages were arranged), this did take place to some extent, and it was hoped that other bonds related to the other person would later develop. In this sense, the status bond may be a pathway to the later development of more person-oriented bonds. The power of this bond may be seen in that, for example, even in Western society, there are considerable incentives to remain in a married state, even when for a time love is tragically absent. In the case of adoption, the original status bond of parent to child is dissolved, but another parental status bond is formed to replace it, eventually to develop into a personal bond.

Task Bonds   Collaboration in common or shared tasks is a bond. Although this bond as such dissolves when the task is completed, there are some tasks which will never be complete. The task bond is a well-used pathway to deeper bonding processes. Tasks infuse every other aspect of our lives. Being a part of a team or a school class, going through a stressful test together, taking wilderness training, going to summer camp—all these experiences may lead to deeper and more lasting friendships. Interlocking task roles in families develop interdependence between persons.

Individual developmental tasks and milestones, such as graduation from school, have a particular significance as task bonds and can be reasons for celebration in the family unit. Incomplete action is another type of task bond. Shared tasks and future aspirations, an expected graduation, even the bond of having a mortgage to pay off, bring family members together through the powerful bonds of incomplete action in a never ending search for the achievement of one and then another goal (Turner, 1970). A sports team (its participants and its spectators) are powerfully bonded by status, by their tasks together, and by the never-ending goals of beating a rival, accomplishing a title, or setting a record. Some communities are bonded by their football teams.

Response Bonds   The way alter (the other) habitually responds to ego (the self) as a person and ego to alter generates another kind of bond, the response bond. The response bond, the way ego and alter were with each other, is a very important component of the lasting memory of a relationship. The response evokes in ego both a kind of favorable self-image and an identification of "we." In this case, the interaction is continued into a relationship with expectations of continuing positive responses and treatment. The interaction of Mark and Leslie (case study 4.1) can be seen as a continual test of responsiveness and repair so that the meanings of the relationship, the self-conceptions, of one and the other and the relationship itself, the "we," are reinforced and maintained. When a relationship is disrupted through death, all of the bonds seem to be lost, but the lost "we," the lost response bonds, may be the most deeply felt. This is particularly true when relating to others who have known the "we." Feeling the loss of the other, they struggle to relate differently to the person remaining, and the person remaining would struggle to relate without the partner.

Identity Bonds   In Western society, with the expectation that the family bond should be based on the complex sentiment of love, the identity bond is extremely important. Identity bonds are bonds to a particular (and irreplaceable) human being based on an understanding of the other's experience as if that experience were one's own (Turner, 1970, p. 66). The complexity of Mark and Leslie's communication had everything to do with maintaining an understanding and acceptance of the other and the other's experience. Mark's hurt by being cut off by Leslie, or her not listening to him, was matched by Leslie's hurt when Mark said she was "rattling away." Both gestures were taken "personally" and thus went beyond the overt meaning of Andrea's hospitalization. Both tried to repair the slight and thus maintain an identity bond—that is, to be treated lovingly. If there was no attention to repairing the slight, the relation would become conflictual for each—that is, for their vulnerable identities. Ultimately it could deteriorate systematically into a relationship governed by criticism, defensiveness, contempt, and stonewalling, the "four horsemen" of Gottman. In this sense, identity bonds are quite vulnerable and demand constant relational work. Happily married couples learn to say "I love you" in their own many different ways every day and to say "I'm sorry" as soon as it is necessary.

Identity bonds rest on empathic foundations, an understanding of the other's experience as if it were one's own. These bonds are vulnerable, and because of this, the persons are vulnerable as well. People change in their experience of themselves and in their experience of the other. Gender barriers and the strains between generations inherent in socialization (when one generation is expected to take some responsibility for the other's behavior) create barriers. These barriers can weaken identity bonds. During periods of transition and strain, the status and task bonds become a type of safety net that can stabilize the relationship until the bond is repaired or new identity bonds are formed.

Empathic understanding denotes the ability to imagine what another person is feeling and to feel with him or her without becoming caught in that feeling and losing perspective. It is the foundation for a powerful bond that can reinforce a certain mutual understanding of one's worth as a person and that thus has the ability to provoke change. It also can stabilize a relationship. Empathic understanding of the other becomes an important tool in the repair of relationships. Social workers are continually working within the realm of empathic understanding, both in their own practice skills and in helping family members develop workable bonds with each other.

Breakdown of Identity Bonds

Identity bonds, denoting both connectedness and separateness, can easily turn themselves into the extremes of sympathy on the one hand or disengagement on the other. Sympathy involves feeling like someone without the presence of difference. One shares the same feelings, is identified with the same interests, becomes aligned with the person, and loves and hates the same things. Enmeshed families are excessively involved with each other. The family members are so tightly interlocked in its relationships with each other that boundaries, particularly generational boundaries, do not seem to be functioning. Alliances may exist across generational lines (e.g., cross-generational coalitions) rather than within generational lines. Any conflict or even difference is threatening to the family and is stifled. The extreme versions of this structure can stifle any growth and differentiation of its members.

At the other extreme, the disengaged family, in contrast, appears to be a family of unrelated, atomistic individuals with very little sensitivity to each others' messages or needs. The disengaged family provides few points of reference and very little support for members' efforts to cope (Minuchin, 1974). Disengagement denotes the feeling of alienation brought on by a failed identity bond. It involves a much stronger feeling than one might have for a stranger. In this sense, it is also a bond just as persons who go to great lengths to avoid each other are bonded. Empathic identity bonds, in contrast, are differentiated and allow for healthy connections and separation. They allow the other to be understood from the position of difference and thus allow flexible role development to proceed within the dyadic units of the family.

The concept of bonds, created through present interaction, is enriched by an understanding of invisible loyalties created out of past bonds, debts, and legacies, handed down over generations (Boszormenyi-Nagy, Grunebaum, & Ulrich, 1991). Thus, for the persons in a couple to develop an unimpeded relationship with each other, each may need to deal with the relational legacies from previous generations that affect current relationships. Current relationships are perceived as analogous to a past relationship and responded to accordingly. Personal work on the past relationships can be done in the context of the present relationship and vice versa.

Cross-Generational Coalitions   Since there are a large number of dyadic units in the family, it is probable that identity bonds of different quality will develop. Potentially this could lead to triangulated relations of persons on the inside or on the outside of different relationships. The common element in triangulation is an imbalance in a relationship of three persons, a triad. Two parties may remain close by distancing the third party or by making the third party an object of common concern. Two partners may remain distant while the third becomes a mediator or forms a coalition with one. Between parents and children, one problem is that a close bond between parent and child, with the other parent on the outside, will undercut the normal hierarchy of generations within the family. It can also affect the marital bond and the child's potential for a constructive relationship with the person on the outside. The child is "pulled in" on the side of one parent. Similarly the child who is a "mediator" stands between both parents, closer to each parent than the parents are to each other (Bell, Bell, & Nakata, 2001, p. 176; Vogel & Bell, 1960).

In another configuration, the marital couple's mutual focus on a symptomatic child may conceal strain within the marital relationship and postpone dealing with marital issues. Some research suggests that such triangulation can be unhealthy for the child because it interferes with accurate perception and response to the child's needs by the parents (Bell, Bell, & Nakata, 2001, p. 177). On the other hand, a certain level of triangulation is natural to all families with children. Indeed, it is inherent in a gender-identification process. The social worker may need to assist the parent on the outside of a close father-son or mother-daughter relationship, for example, to hold his or her own without getting drawn into needlessly challenging a developmentally healthy relationship.

THE PROCESS OF ROLE DEVELOPMENT

Roles are sets of expected behaviors arrived at and learned through social interaction. Role is often confused with the more static concept of status (Linton, 1936), but as we are using the term, it is a much more dynamic, relational concept, a product of interaction. To the extent that roles are actively taken by persons, these roles are capable of enormous variability within limits. With the present interlocking complexity of family tasks, roles are not so much prescribed by tradition as *taken* in relation to another person. That is, in order to take my role, I (ego) must understand it in relation to the other's (alter's) and the other's in relation to me. This demands not only that I learn and take my own role, but that I am also able to "take the role of the other" in relation to my role—to understand the reciprocal role of others in relation to my role. In Sarah and Phil's situation in case study 3.1, Sarah's back condition demanded that they shift and revise fixed concepts of role to something more adapted to each other's needs and their situation. To do this, they needed to develop communication with each other and with their children. They had to shift from an implicit understanding of roles to one that was more explicit and based on communication. For the interaction process out of which roles are developed, George Herbert Mead gives the example of ego and alter throwing and catching a ball. To throw a ball is to anticipate the motions of the person catching. To catch is to anticipate the motions of the person throwing (Mead, 1934). Phil has to understand and communicate with Sarah, and Sarah with Phil, if they are to resolve their role discussion brought on by Sarah's back. In these circumstances, the necessary family developmental shifts are made possible through appropriate communication.

An awareness of the roles of others may lead to an awareness of a conflict between one's habitual role expectations and the needs of others, as with Phil's expectations and Sarah's need. Family members often attempt to modify their own roles or innovate to meet the needs of another more accurately. A father may find that his expectations of his own role do not relate to his son's needs, and thus the father may have to modify his role. This modification could create considerable difficulty, and so the father may have to help the son modify his role expectations of him or work out a third solution that is satisfactory to both.

On the assumption that implicit understandings of roles can be modified, role learning and role making proceed reciprocally, involving ego and alter. Out of the principle of reciprocity—that my obligation is contingent on the other person's carrying out his or her own role—grow systems of mutual obligation and rules.

These rules rest on reciprocal relations of ego with alter. A violation of these understandings would release ego from obligations commensurate with the violation. In any case, this mutual agreement on role modification does not take place in a vacuum, since any change will affect and be affected by all relations, such as the father's relation to the mother and the son's relation to his siblings. For interaction to take place smoothly in a family group, clustering and segmentation of the many possible roles a person may carry generally occur. Each family member establishes a cluster of activities as his or her own. These activities often have some relation to each other, such as bookkeeping, tax payment, and bill payment. Each family member is generally expected to stay in his or her cluster and not dabble in the activities appropriate to another role (Turner, 1970). Family members often do take the others roles, when needed, but this should be accompanied by a negotiation process with the person who normally has the role.

Role boundaries are developed over time with frequent interaction. These boundaries can become seriously distorted, with one person approaching a role in a rigid, nonadaptive way, the other becoming overadaptive, and both supporting a less workable system of roles. Or a person can become so absorbed by implicit role expectations that there is no uniqueness or "I" separate from the "me" of network expectations. When this takes place, where relationships are potentially conflictual or risky for some members, the family could cease to be personal—that is, a place where persons can flourish as persons. When one person cannot develop, all the others in the unit are affected in different ways.

Once a system of roles has developed, family processes tend to preserve the balance that this establishes and to exclude the possibility of members playing different roles. If I cultivate the role of mediator in family conflict, others are likely to become even less restrained, instigating conflict, depending on me to mediate and restore an accustomed balance. Family interaction and the role system had become balanced and stabilized through my mediation.

In the episode of Mark and Leslie (case study 4.1), Amber, the daughter, very quickly moved in to mediate between her parents, although one could also detect some alliance with her father. Her speed and comfort in assuming the role indicate that she had played it previously. However, it is also possible that, as long as Amber is balancing the system in this way, her mediation actually shuts down the discussion and prevents Mark and Leslie from working out the conflict. This may be appropriate with her friend present. If this mediating role is a sustained quality of their interaction regardless of circumstances, her mediating role may be stabilizing and maintaining the immediate status quo at the expense of long-term stability. Her influence and standing in the family might depend heavily on her skills as a mediator, and her position might diminish when others do not play antagonist roles. A change in her role would cause normal family operations to slow down, and others could hold her responsible for any consequent breakdown of task accomplishment. If Amber had made herself so essential to her mother and father that without her they would be deadlocked, she also would be locked into a triangle, which then could become an essential part of their relationship. It could be difficult for her to leave that tight triangle to form a relationship with another. She could lose herself in the role. In a rigid relational system, forming a relationship with another would be very difficult without radically leaving the system. If Amber were to attempt to change, the family would need to endure confusion and misunderstandings until a new agreement on roles was developed and put into action.

FAMILY STRUCTURE AND COMMUNICATION

The pattern of roles adopted by the family has a certain permanence and develops through memory and communication into family structure. *Family structure* is a network of agreements that, once made, become essential for family operations. We can map out these different intensities of communication to form a sociogram of family structure. When we do this, we may locate the interlocking and conflictual three-person and two-person subgroups within the family. With specialization of role, there is often a certain stability of power over particular areas of decision making in this structure. As long as a subgroup can maintain its own internal agreement, it can develop alliances and coalitions and acquire power over decision-making processes in areas considered important.

Because these agreements involve the relatively fixed and expected behaviors of many actors, they are difficult to change. One person's attempts to change his or her role in this structure will inevitably be met with resistance. Others in the family subtly — or not so subtly — attempt to move the person back to his or her accustomed role. Even if the role is detrimental to the individual, family members may attempt to maintain the accustomed role, since their own definitions of family well-being and wholeness depend on the maintenance of family structure.

We often characterize a person in a family as dominant when we believe that person has a heavy influence on certain decision-making processes taking place in the family. The ability to influence decision making is closely tied to communication. Often the dominant person may be dominant only on some issues. This "dominance" may even be maintained by others who actually may have greater power over decision making but wish to preserve a belief in the superior power of one member. In most families, power grows in a more functional way, not as much from inherent authority as from the ability to communicate and develop alliances across the subgroups in the family. The greater the relative ability to communicate across family subgroups, the greater the ability to influence decision making, since a central "switchboard" can amplify or censor a message to manipulate others to go along. Miguel and Juana (case study 3.2) and to some extent Sarah and Phil (case study 3.1) in the previous chapter had to rebalance power and dominance as they rebalanced their patterns. They were becoming sensitive to the personal dimensions of their own relationship rather than mainly externally referenced roles.

Cultural values and the inherently conservative nature of family structure can provide a common set of reference points and a point of stability amid changing self-conceptions and behavior of members. Because structure reflects agreements made and power balances of the past, there is usually a lag between family structure and the changing identities of family members. Family structure, maintained through communication, is often a source of conflict between persons who want to change their interpretations of their roles and others in the family who are bent on maintaining an unchanged structure. The struggles between generations, each coping with changing self-definitions and the demands of their life stages, ultimately do create changes in family structure. The struggle may be more likely if there are forces outside the family supporting a different self-conception.

SOCIALIZATION: THE ACQUISITION OF A FRAMEWORK OF MEANINGS

Socialization is the medium through which family members learn to cope with each other and with society. From multiple and continuing interaction with significant others, persons organize a framework for the interpretation of reality, values, acceptable motives, and sentiments, as well as for the interpretation of the meanings inherent in the actions people take toward them. This framework of meanings is acquired through the process of seeing things, people's actions and roles, from the standpoints of the various actors in the person's experience. The ability to understand the role of the other is suggested by some developmental psychologists to be an important index of maturity (Kohlberg, 1969; Selman, 1976), particularly for developing persons, who are often family members. The framework contains conceptions of the self, of others, and of roles that become generalized into persistent coping patterns. If socialization is to be effective, it pervades all parent-child transactions and thus affects other aspects of family interaction, such as role differentiation and decision making. It also adds some specific sources of family tension and gratification.

Socialization is built upon the unequal authority of parents and children (Turner, 1970). A coalition of a parent with a child across generation lines would effectively undermine the other parent's socializing efforts and the hierarchy of the family. Family therapists note an association of the breakdown of appropriate boundaries around the parental dyad, lack of agreement of the dyad on socialization, or subtle alliances of one parent with a child with severe family conflict and breakdown of socialization. The parent, however, does not control all socialization influences on the child, and this is the irony of the parent's position in modern society. The parent is an agent of societal expectations and is made responsible by relatives, court systems, and children themselves for the results of socialization. The caricature of the uncle or grandparent who can indulge and enjoy the child without the responsibility for socialization is a source of continual triangulation within the family. It points out the pressures on the parents as agents of societal expectations that may actually be conflicted, contradictory, or impossible to achieve at one point or another in a child's development.

THE STRUCTURAL PERSPECTIVE IN FAMILY THERAPY

Family structure is a network of implicit and explicit agreements that, once made, become mutual patterns and eventually become essential for family operations. The concept of family structure was very quickly taken over in the 1960s and 1970s by the school of structural family therapy as a way of illustrating and clarifying the implicit understandings, bonds, and relationships that govern the way people behave in families (Minuchin, 1974; Minuchin & Fishman, 1981).[2] Some of the structural family therapy theory base is described here, particularly as developed systematically by Aponte and Van Deusen (1981). It is quite compatible with our discussion of symbolic-interactionist theory and expands it into the realm of practice.

Structures are the implicit understandings that regulate how family members relate to each other, what roles they should take, and so on. These structures are used to deal with the complex and changing internal and external worlds that families experience. Families need to manage their own relationships, the changes in individual members wrought by development, and at the same time cope actively with a changing and demanding environment. As a consequence of these changing internal and external tasks, families have to carry out a variety of functions. In the case of temporary absence or incapacity, members often have to take each other's roles. Thus every family needs to have a repertoire of structures to meet and integrate these complex internal and environmental changes. Some structures are dominant—that is, most family operations are based on a particular relational structure. Other structures are less frequently called upon, and thus are subordinate. The ability of a family to function well depends on the degree to which the family structures are well-defined, elaborated, flexible, and cohesive. A family with a limited number of structures to solve problems, whose members are rigid in the way they employ the structures they have, and who are inconsistent in the use of these structures is, by definition, underorganized (Aponte, 1986). This is a very important set of distinctions. Some families, such as Sarah and Phil (case study 3.1), dealing with somewhat dysfunctional dominant structures, may either modify those structures or call upon less used but available subordinate structures to deal with a problem. Some families on the other hand need to develop greater complexity of structures. These families are underorganized, and thus they may need to develop structures that they never previously had.

---

[2]For more extensive discussion of this approach to family therapy, see Nichols (2013, pp. 126–140), Goldenberg and Goldenberg (1996, ch. 9), Nichols and Schwartz (2001, ch. 8), and Aponte and Van Deusen (1981).

Every operation, indeed every transaction of the family, defines structure. Structure involves boundaries, alignment, and power.

Boundaries

Boundaries are the rules defining who participates: who is in and who is out of a family operation. To work in any operation, family boundaries need to be differentiated, relatively flexible, and permeable. The extremes of boundary making are as follow:

1. Enmeshment (where the boundaries are too low for an operation to work)
2. Disengagement (where the boundaries are too high for an operation to work)

There also is a violation of function boundaries where there is inappropriate intrusion of family members in functions that are the domain of other members (Aponte & Van Deusen, 1981).

Alignment

Alignment is the joining with or opposition of one member of the system to another in carrying out an operation. For example, the father may either agree or disagree with the mother about where to vacation. If he disagrees, he may join with the son in this disagreement. A *coalition* is a joining of two persons in opposition to a third person, as in the above example (Aponte & Van Deusen, 1981). An *alliance* is a joining of two members on the basis of common interests—father and son both enjoy fishing, for example, and form an alliance of fishermen in the family. An alliance is not necessarily energized by opposition to a third member. Dysfunctional alignments can take place through (1) a stable coalition, which is the joining together of two family members against another so that the pattern becomes a dominant, inflexible characteristic of their relationships, (2) a detouring coalition that occurs when stress between two family members is diffused by designating another party as the source of the problem and assuming an attacking or solicitous attitude toward that person, and (3) triangulation, which occurs when each of two opposing parties seeks to join with the same person against the other, with the third party finding it necessary to cooperate—now with one, now with the other of these opposing structures (Aponte & Van Deusen, 1981).

Power

Power, always relative to the family operation, is the influence of a family member on the outcome of an activity. Power is different from authority, since a person in authority may be utterly unable to influence a particular outcome. A baby will have great power over the sleeping and eating routines of family members, although that same baby is low in authority. Children in the family often have considerable power over certain operations. The power of a parent may be seen by who will prevail in a disagreement, and whether both parents can impose an agreed-upon rule on a child. Breakdowns of power in the system can come from disagreements and confusion, reflecting problems of boundaries and alignment. For socialization to work, there must be a certain hierarchy of parental power in relation to the children. Thus a weak executive undermines functional power in the family.

We can take Mark and Leslie, and Amber and Julie (case study 4.1), as simple examples of integration of systems concepts outlined in the previous chapter and also of concepts of interaction and structure outlined in this chapter. The interaction described in the case is a product of all of the persons, not of one involved alone. The causality of interaction and the results of interaction are circular rather than linear. Furthermore, the total communication episode cannot be understood by a focus on the individuals involved. Together they create something unique (nonsummativity). It is the pattern between Mark and Leslie that is constant, that can characterize them. They are different from each other and come from different backgrounds, but they have learned to heal and repair differences through interaction. On the other hand, if they ceased this pattern of repair, it could quickly break down into one or more of the four horsemen (equifinality). Everything that occurs takes place through and is referenced to communication and memory of past communication. There are rules governing their interaction—that is, there are implicit understandings—that continue. It is like a predictable dance. Mark and Leslie move to a certain point in their conversation of difference, and then they repair. Amber moves in when she senses tension. In this way, the family system maintains its balance, or steady state, (and is said to be in homeostasis).

System Rules

The family is too complex to do its work as if each instance is a totally new existential happening. There is a need for consistency and predictability in the relations and the sequences of relations in the family. People demand predictable relationships, even if they are adverse. The complex operations of the family in issues such as the socialization of children demand that the family develop patterns in its relationships. These patterns become established as system rules. Such relationship rules, both explicit and implicit, organize the interaction of the family and maintain a stable system by prescribing and limiting a member's behavior. The problem is that sometimes individual developmental needs place members where they see these patterns as no longer appropriate. As with Sarah and Phil (case study 3.1), Mark and Leslie (case study 4.1), Jim and Cheryl (case study 3.4), and Brian and Lisa (case study 3.3), this prompts the family, time and time again, to develop new ways of affiliating and preserving the essential bonds of membership in the middle of change. Often, in instances such as the loss of a member through death, a new form of family structure is needed to preserve family values and functions. Even the loss of children living at home, bringing couples to an empty-nest period, creates complex demands that the parents develop their relationships in a different way with each other and with their children not living at home.

Self-Reinforcing Patterns

When patterns and structure become dysfunctionally integrated with the daily inter-actions of a relationship, it may seem as if the relationship has turned into an unreal game. The pattern takes over any real communication or interaction. In chapter 2, Marisa Antonelli's relationship with her parents (case study 2.2), took on the quali-ties of a cat-and-mouse game, aimed at avoiding the real issues connected with Marisa's relational maturation. She and her parents were both caught up in this game. The game patterns are self-reinforcing because, from each party's perspective, one's own behavior appears to be a reasonable response to the other. Marisa's evasiveness brings on hypervigilance on the part of the parents, the parents' hyper-vigilance brings out more evasiveness, and so on. One's behavior brings out an intensification of the other's behavior until the interaction often goes out of control in a runaway episode. Each player draws oppositional energy from the energy of the other, and the pattern takes on a life of its own. Soon each needs the other to play the game. Unless the game can stop, boundaries get set, or the players simply with-draw from the field, something out of control, a "runaway" episode becomes inevitable. The runaway episode confirms each party's picture of the other and the reason for their extreme behavior. The solution would be to gradually make the game an "ungame." Restorative and stabilizing work can then take place during the temporary cessation of hostilities that the ungame stimulates. Parents and young adult can work out the terms of their relationship in a way that will gradually assist Marisa to take appropriate responsibility for herself and assist her parents to support her in this. The cat-and-mouse game is then no longer necessary, and the relation-ship can be stabilized into a more workable structure.

There are many possible forms of self-reinforcing patterns. Indeed, many of these patterns are quite normal in family interaction as long as they do not take over the family structure, polarize family members in extreme positions, prevent effective developmental and relational work from being done, and paralyze the normally benign operations of family relational structure (as in the Antonelli cat-and-mouse game). From the earliest development of family therapy, therapists from various schools—psychodynamic, Bowenian, structural, communication, and behavioral schools—each using somewhat different language, quickly identified a wide range of self-reinforcing patterns. These patterns, once identified, became the object of corrective work. In work with couples, some of the more important self-reinforcing patterns to emerge were the overfunctioning/underfunctioning (or overadequate/underadequate) pattern and the pursuer-distancer (or demand/withdraw) pattern (Christenson, 1990).

In the overfunctioning/underfunctioning pattern, the overfunctioning of one member in areas normally allocated to another brings out the underfunctioning of the other member in these areas, and vice versa. A simple example would be one person's speaking for another. Speaking for another can bring out silence on the part of the person being spoken for, or vigorous protest and conflict. When there is silence, it reinforces the need of that person to speak for the other, and so on. Both move to extreme positions. The speaker overshadows the other with his or her world but is less and less in contact with the real world of the other. The other is caught up in the speaker's world and loses an ability to speak for him or herself. The relationship becomes artificial and full of unspoken anger and disappointment, without any ability to correct itself through communication. Patterns similar to this can extend to every area of family structure, particularly where one member is already vulnerable and another is ready to act for the vulnerable person and in some ways to take over his or her reality. The overfunctioning person becomes dysfunctional; the underfunctioning person loses capacities he or she might otherwise possess or develop, particularly his or her voice in the relationship.

RELATIONAL CHANGE THROUGH INTERACTION AND COMMUNICATION

The Pursuer-Distancer Pattern   The pursuer-distancer or demand-withdraw patterns are so often encountered among couples seeking assistance that many approaches to couple therapy, such as emotionally focused therapy (Johnson, 2004), collaborative couple therapy (Wile, 2013), and behavioral family therapy (Christenson, 1987; 1990) give it primary importance. Both patterns are self-reinforcing and can be found in most problematic communication. When these patterns take place, one person will bring up an issue and the other person will minimize the issue or cut off discussion, or one person will initiate an activity and the other will disqualify or undermine it. The disqualifying response will energize the other to a position of further demand. The demand is disqualified, and both are now in extreme positions. The danger at this point is that pursue/distance very quickly becomes attack/withdraw or blame/withdraw. The following case study shows Maria and Tom shifting from pursue/distance to attack/withdraw (adapted from Wile, 2013, pp. 21; used with permission).

CASE STUDY 4.2: MARIA AND TOM

Maria (inviting): Hey, there. What do you say we go for a walk?

Tom (vaguely): Maybe later . . .

Maria (encouraging): Come on. Let's go now, while it's still sunny.

Tom: Not now. I'm enjoying this book.

Maria (pressing): You can read it when we get home. Come on. You'll feel different once we're out there.

Tom (not looking up): I really don't feel like it.

Maria: Well okay, we don't have to walk. Why don't we just hang out and talk for a while?

Tom: Really—I'm not in the mood.

Maria (shifting to attack): You're *never* in the mood.

Tom (shrugs) (Wile, 2013, pp. 20–21)

Maria stepped over a line when she suggested that Tom is never in the mood. Things could rapidly deteriorate. To make a repair, Maria could *soften* her gesture. For example:

> Maria: I guess I'm pushing you. We don't need to do this right now, and I'm sure that is an interesting book. We've been so busy lately. I just needed some time with you sometime today. What do you think?

Or Tom could soften his withdrawal:

> Tom: I'm sorry. You have been trying to get my attention. I wasn't paying attention, and you are getting frustrated with me. How about we talk after I finish this chapter and set something up. But I just don't feel like walking. Maybe something else.

In the context of their previous communication, softening could be quite difficult for either of them. They may be trapped in the pattern, so it could continue:

> Maria (blurting out a hidden fear): Admit it. You just don't want to do things with *me* anymore; *that's* it, isn't it?
> Tom (looks up for a second): That's not true.
> Maria (supplying evidence to support her case): Well, it is true. And that's how your *father* treats your mother. You're getting more like him every day.
> Tom (looks down at his book again)
> Maria: Aren't you going to *say* anything?
> Tom: I don't know what I *can* say.
> Maria (sarcastically): You could say, "Sure, let's go for a walk. What a great idea! Thanks for suggesting it. You always make things such fun."
> Tom (counterattacking): Do you always have to be so *sarcastic*?
> Maria. Do you always have to be so *withholding*? It's so passive-aggressive. (Wile, 2013, pp. 20–21; used with permission)

One very possible path is for the pattern to continue and repeat itself to the point of stonewalling. The game prevents constructive communication and relational work. As with the Antonellis (case study 2.2, case study 8.4), the general solution is to make the game an "ungame"—that is, not to play it and find a better, substitutable behavior. With Maria and Tom, there needs to be repeated softening and de-escalation. The initial response of the other to softening would be dramatic attempts to restore the game, and so the softening would need to be repeated. In any case, making the game an ungame will not fully resolve the problem. There needs to be a way gradually to begin to work out some of the underlying issues during the momentary period of confusion when, the other refusing to play, the game has lost its potency. We will see this in the following case study.

The following case study illustrates a process of repair that took some time after Rosalind found that Armand had an affair and lied to her about it.

CASE STUDY 4.3: ARMAND

Armand, an East Indian information technology specialist who shares his hobbies of tennis and cycling with his many male friends, has been married for five years to Rosalind, a medical professional from a large Greek family. They have a four-year-old girl, Anaya, whom Armand worships. In certain areas of their relationship, such as care of Anaya or recreation with each other, they get along quite well, despite the turbulence of other areas. During the early stages of the marriage, their personal relationship was rather undefined. It was as if they were trying to develop a common identity with little room for their own differences. When differences did arise, these immediately became a problem and severe conflict resulted. Fueled by Rosalind's intensity, Armand would take the "rational" side. When the conflict became chronic, Armand withdrew into an affair, which he denied. Suspicious at Armand's new coolness and sensing his ambivalence toward her, Rosalind pursued further. Sometimes they would argue all night. When Rosalind discovered clear evidence of the affair, she responded with extreme anger, severe depression, suicidal threats, and withdrawal from the relationship. Eventually she began an affair of her own. Armand now began to pursue and Rosalind to withdraw, but Rosalind withdrew only until Armand stopped pursuing. In the meantime both remained together in a precarious relationship. Approximately half of their day-to-day interactions were unhampered, but the other half reflected a demand/withdraw pattern that shuttled back and forth. A discussion of money, or anything involving emotional intensity, brought out the same dominant pattern. With their conflict so painful and unresolved, Rosalind asked Armand to leave, and Armand complied. When Armand suggested that they begin with a social worker, Rosalind's profound anger prevented her from taking part, but she did go to an individual therapist for her depression. She wasn't yet quite ready to start marital therapy and promised to come later (implicitly inviting Armand's pursuit of her on this issue). Armand cut off his affair and sought help from a social worker. After a short period, Rosalind invited Armand back home on condition that they maintain their separation at home. With assistance from the social worker, he came back home and went along with Rosalind's condition that they not resume their marital relationship. He slept on the couch but willingly went along with Rosalind's intermittent desires for intimacy. He did not respond in kind to her anger, which inevitably followed intimacy.

Gradually becoming conscious of the game, Armand was working with his social worker to end his part of it. He began to put names on the sequences of interaction—for example, that she would be angry and provocative after any intimacy, and that he shouldn't respond in kind. He had felt badly about the damage his affair had done, and he was self-consciously making up. The first step was to build enough boundaries for each within their own home so that the need for a separation, at least for a time, was less pressing. There needed to be some separation in their relationship so that both would be free. Armand was coached to construct healthy boundaries that respected Rosalind's choices, as well as to make their game an ungame. He would set goals for himself in his journal. He would be available to her when she was ready, but he wouldn't pursue her. He would want her to make up her own mind. When she needed him, he would be there for her, but wouldn't impose himself. He avoided angry confrontations—"I won't let her use my anger"—and learned to find calmer ways to resolve problems when he found them in himself. The social worker worked as a type of guru-coach, teaching him

about the game that had dominated their relationship and supporting his positive, constructive, and freeing interaction with Rosalind.

Rosalind's response was to test him, inviting him to the familiar pursuit but ready immediately to pounce on him or withdraw. When there was an opening in their relationship for real communication, he did try to use it as best he could. Only gradually were they able to give up the game and work together more constructively on their relationship. Both had been badly hurt, and both had to relearn trust in each other. At one point, a dramatic shift occurred, when Rosalind was able to tell Armand of her ambivalence and hurt. Armand listened, acknowledged her anger and hurt, and wordlessly took her hand. Rosalind responded, "I think I'll keep you." Despite this breakthrough, the work of reconstructing their relationship would take many years.

The case study points out both the persistence of a self-reinforcing pattern in the story of Armand and Rosalind and contextualizes its meaning. It also outlines a process of working with one person to manage relational issues. Although relationally focused, the methods used are somewhat similar to those used in working with Gloria in chapter 2 (case study 2.1), but now in a family systems framework. The family systems framework provides some theoretical predictability and allows the social worker to broaden the focus and act as a mentor to Armand. Where the focus was on Gloria, the focus now is on Armand's *interactions* with Rosalind and Rosalind's responses. Armand's improved communication helps Rosalind to respond differently. Gradually the two develop effective recursive patterns of communication and interaction. The process goes much more slowly than working with both members of a couple together. Eventually the angry confrontations dropped off and the couple was getting along better. But Rosalind was hurt and fearful. She was in no hurry to give up her anger and hurt too quickly, as she felt she would have to in couples' counseling. Armand respected this. The counseling format went at about the right speed for the situation. It was important to use the time to move from an ungame to a real healing relationship. When this took place, Rosalind did want to talk with Armand about her own ambivalence and hurt. When Armand listened and validated her feelings, she responded to him, and both were able to stabilize their relationship.

COMPONENTS OF FAMILY FUNCTIONING AND APPROACHES TO FAMILY THERAPY

In the relatively short time that family therapy has been developing, much of the initial focus has been on its leaders, each developing a particular approach to working with families. Throughout the 1970s and 1980s, these competing approaches multiplied. Each approach had something to say about how people function in families and how families themselves function. Each tried to balance human agency with communion. Possibly because of this, each had a certain level of effectiveness over interventions that focused on individuals. In the absence of an organizing framework, these approaches competed with each other. It was obvious that no approach was a panacea. Each could be more or less appropriate to a particular problem. Most practitioners were practicing from one perspective, but borrowing techniques from other perspectives. A unifying approach to family therapy theory and practice is now gradually emerging.

We can begin our discussion by making connections between levels of family functioning and the different approaches to family therapy. These connections are illustrated in table 4.1.

Each approach is a useful abstract, taken from a much richer picture of the whole—the social functioning of persons in families fully considered in all of its aspects and complexity. Each school contributes a great deal to the holistic perspective. However, in an actual practice situation neither social work nor family

Table 4.1
Components of Family Functioning and Approaches to Family Therapy

Personal Development and Interpersonal Process	Family Communication and Meanings	Interpersonal and Spiritual Narratives and Stories	Personal Developmental Processes	Family Structure	Family Environmental Systems	Integrative Approaches
Psychodynamic approaches	Bernard Guerney	Michael White	Bowen family systems	Structural family therapy	Ecological systems theory	John Gottman
Attachment theory	MRI Interactional family therapy	Froma Walsh				Doug Bruenlin
Object relations theory	Strategic family therapy	Contextual therapy				Richard Schwartz
Cognitive–Behavioral	Experiential family therapy					Betty Karrer
	Virginia Satir					William Pinsof

therapy could really be reduced to an abstract methodology or a partial picture of the family functioning. The holistic perspective, which relates to every aspect of human social functioning, has always been a characteristic of social work practice. Each school contributes a great deal to this holistic perspective. This book will relate the many schools of family therapy to the content and process of social work with families. It cannot, however, cover each school in a comprehensive way.[3]

Unifying Approaches to Family Therapy

The picture of competing approaches to family therapy has gradually changed over the period of the mid-1990s through the present. Studies of the effectiveness of differing approaches to family, together with the experience of practitioners dealing with families, created a shift in the field from particular approaches to intervention to broader organizing frameworks for family intervention and theory (Pinsof & Wynne, 1995). Family therapists themselves had moved from competing approaches to some integration of approaches. Practitioners had been drawing from different schools, rather than limiting themselves to a particular set of interventions. Theorists began to find it more useful and appropriate to integrate these different approaches into an overarching picture of practice (Breunlin, Schwartz, & Mac Kune-Karrer, 1992; Pinsof, 1995). Effectiveness research found that utilizing several of these differing approaches to practice with families were at least as effective, if not more, than individual approaches, and often worked more quickly (Pinsof & Wynne, 1995). However, each approach carried with it its own limitations of perspective on the family as a whole. Theorists, researchers, and practitioners began to assume that a broader focus integrating different approaches would be more effective. The key question then became: what then were the common properties and underlying dimensions of these more or less effective approaches? What made them effective at all? Recognizing this fieldwide trend as a second stage of theory and practice, Lebow (1997) suggested that integration presumed a more extensive melding of approaches into a metalevel theory.

As a first step in doing this, Breunlin, Schwartz, and Mac Kune-Karrer (1992) posited six levels of theory, or *metaframeworks*, that applied to family therapy. Rather than being opposed to each other, these were simply different levels of the complex realities that families experience and thus different components of valid understandings of intervention in families:

1. The mind and the self
2. Sequences of interactional patterns
3. Organization and structure of the relational contexts of our experience
4. Life cycle development

---

[3]The reader is referred to original work from different schools (listed in the reference list) or to texts that cover this vast area in a more comprehensive way, such as Nichols (2013).

5. Multicultural understandings of experience and interaction
6. Gender issues

William Pinsof (1995) approached the same theoretical issues, but from the understanding that the differing family problems demand different responses. From Pinsof's point of view, there are different spheres of problems or *systemic constraints* to functional relations and interaction. These systemic constraints maintain family problems. He posited six spheres of systemic constraints that could operate at the same time, but on different system levels, to maintain family problems:

1. Organizational constraints: how the (client) system organizes and conducts itself in relation to the problem
2. Biological constraints: how the system operates as a biological and physical system in relation to the presenting problem
3. Meanings and attributions: how the system thinks and feels in relation to itself and to the problem
4. Transgenerational constraints: issues and processes that derive from families of origin
5. Object relations constraints: the way in which the psychodynamic parts of members are organized in relation to the problem
6. Self-system constraints: the way in which the collective self system and individual self structures interact with the problem.

Over the past decades Pinsof, Breunlin, and others have combined these approaches into integrative problem-solving metaframeworks therapy (Breunlin, Schwartz, & Mac Kune-Karrer, 1992; Breunlin, Pinsof, Russell, & Lebow, 2013; Pinsof, Breunlin, Russell, & Lebow, 2013; Pinsof, 1995). In developing the relation between different theories and approaches to practice, they, together with other integrative approaches (Gottman, 1999; Johnson, 2004) contribute to some needed order within the many theories of family intervention.

Social work has had a long history of working with families using multiple methodologies. Its basic paradigm is the person-in-environment. Much of social work is done in social institutional practice contexts. There is an inherent orientation to justice. In this sense, its commitment to broader societal processes and to relational justice has always been clear. There are many places and ways to assist families and family members to restructure their internal and external relationships, but, like Armand and Rosalind, members cannot do it apart from the other. They must do it with each other. Personal and relational tasks create family patterns and structure. Such structure gets to be taken for granted by those who participate in it. It becomes the air they mutually breathe. Social workers can connect with families and with their members through these tasks, which are already present in the situation, when the situation is adequately understood. The three key issues considered throughout the remainder of the book are: what these personal and relational tasks are, what relational structures result from these tasks, and how social workers might respond to all of this. The social worker helped Armand and Rosalind to resolve their dysfunctional relational and communication patterns and to reconstruct a relationship (case study 4.3) that each could trust. However, to reduce Armand's and Rosalind's relational work to communication, to attachment, to narrative, or to structural change is not a fully accurate picture of what actually happened when they worked with each other to rebuild the trust that was lost.

SUMMARY

In chapters 3 and 4, we have studied the process of family development through relational tasks at the personal and at the family level and through family structure. These tasks, as they are attempted and carried out at both levels, create structure. Change often takes place slowly. It is dependent on many common factors. There is an investment in the current balance maintained among all the different elements that comprise the family. There are also pressures to change from inside and outside the family. When the time is ripe, change can occur very quickly. The social worker assesses the family in motion: the potential for change, the family process, the relational structure and the personal components. Based on this assessment and his or her working agreement with key members of the family, the social worker can be a catalyst for the development of family structure for the benefit of its members. These interventions take place through different family life cycle stages, with different levels of family complexity and with different social institutions—all explored in subsequent chapters.

REFERENCES

Angyal, A. (1940). *Foundations for a science of personality.* New York, NY: Commonwealth Fund.

Aponte, H. J. (1986). "If I don't get simple, I cry." *Family Process, 25*(4), 531–548.

Aponte, H. J., & Van Deusen, J. M. (1981). Structural family therapy. In A. S. Gurman & D. P. Kniskern (Eds.), *Handbook of family therapy* (pp. 310–360). New York: Brunner-Mazel.

Bell, L. G., Bell, D. C., & Nakata, Y. (2001). Triangulation and adolescent development in the U.S. and Japan. *Family Process, 40*(2), 173–186.

Beels, C. (2009). Some historical conditions of narrative work. *Family Process, 48*(3), 363–378.

Blumer, H. (1969). *Symbolic interactionism: Perspective and method.* Englewood Cliffs, NJ: Prentice Hall.

Boszormenyi-Nagy, I., Grunebaum, J., & Ulrich, D. (1991). Contextual therapy. In A. S. Gurman & D. P. Kniskern (Eds.), *Handbook of family therapy*, vol. 2 (pp. 200–238). New York, NY: Brunner-Mazel.

Bott, E. (1971). *Family and social network: Norms and external social relationships in ordinary urban families.* London, UK: Tavistock.

Brazelton, T. B., & Cramer, B. G. (1990). *Earliest relationship: Parents, infants and the dawn of early attachment.* Reading, MA: Addison-Wesley.

Breunlin, D. C., Pinsof, W., Russell, W., & Lebow, J. (2013). Integrative problem-centered metaframeworks therapy I: Core concepts and hypothesizing. *Family Process, 50*(3), 293–313.

Breunlin, D. C., Schwartz, R. C., & Mac Kune-Karrer, B. (1992). *Metaframeworks: Transcending the models of family therapy.* San Francisco, CA: Jossey-Bass.

Burr, W., Hill, R., Nye, F. I., & Reiss, I. L. (1979). *Contemporary theories about the family.* New York, NY: Free Press.

Christenson, A. (1987). Detection of conflict patterns in couples. In K. Hahlweg & M. J. Goldstein (Eds.), *Understanding major mental disorders: The contribution of family interaction research* (pp. 250–265). New York, NY: Family Process Press.

Christenson, A. (1990). Gender and social structure in the demand-withdraw pattern in marital interaction. *Journal of Personality and Social Psychology, 59,* 73–82.

Coelho, G. B., Hamburg, D., & Adams, J. (1974). *Coping and adaptation.* New York, NY: Basic Books.

Cooley, C. H. (1922). *Human nature and the social order.* New York, NY: Scribner.

Constable, R. T. (1984). Phenomenological foundations for the understanding of family interaction. *Social Service Review, 58*(1), 117–132.

Doherty, W. J., & Craft, S. M. (2011). Single mothers raising children with "male-positive" attitudes. *Family Process, 50*(1), 63–76.

Donati, P. (1989). *La Famiglia come relazione sociale* [The family as a social relation]. Milano, Italy: FrancoAngeli.

Donati, P. (1991). *Teoria relazionale della societa* [A relational theory of society]. Milano, Italy: FrancoAngeli.

Driver, J., Tabares, A., Shapiro, A. F., & Gottmann, J. M. (2012). Couple interaction in happy and unhappy marriages. In F. Walsh (Ed.), *Normal family processes* (pp. 57–77). New York, NY: Guilford.

Geertz, C. (2000). *Local knowledge: Further essays in interpretive anthropology.* New York, NY: Basic Books.

Goldenberg, I., & Goldenberg, H. (1996). *Family therapy: An overview.* Pacific Grove, CA: Brooks-Cole.

Gottman, J. M. (1999). *The marriage clinic.* New York, NY: Norton.

Gottman, J. M., & Notarius, C. I. (2002). Marital research in the 20th century and a research agenda for the 21st century. *Family Process, 41*(2), 159–198.

Gottman, J. M., Driver, J., & Tabares, A. (2002). Building the sound marital house: An empirically driven couple therapy. In A. S. Gurman & N. S. Jacobson (Eds.), *Handbook of Couple Therapy* (3rd ed.). New York, NY: Guilford.

Gottman, J. M., & Levenson, R. W. (2000). The timing of divorce: Predicting when a couple will divorce over a 14-year period. *Journal of Marriage and the Family, 62,* 737–745.

Haley, J. (1980). *Leaving home: The therapy of disturbed young people.* New York, NY: McGraw-Hill.

Haley, J., & Hoffman, L. (1968). *Techniques of family therapy.* New York, NY: Basic Books.

Hartmann, H. (1958). *Ego psychology and the problem of adaptation.* New York, NY: International Universities Press.

Hoffman, L. (1981). *Foundations of family therapy.* New York, NY: Basic Books.

Hunter, S. V. (2012). Walking in sacred spaces in the therapeutic bond: Therapist's experience of compassion satisfaction coupled with the potential for vicarious traumatization. *Family Process, 51*(2), 179–192.

Johnson, S. (2004). *The practice of emotionally-focused couples' therapy: Creating connection.* New York, NY: Brunner-Routledge.

Kohlberg, L. (1969). Stage and sequence: The cognitive-developmental approach to socialization. In D. Goslin (Ed.), *Handbook of socialization theory and research* (pp. 347–480). Chicago, IL: Rand McNally.

Lebow, J. (1997). The integrative revolution in couple and family therapy. *Family Process, 36*(1), 1–17.

Linton, R. (1936). *The study of man.* New York, NY: Appleton-Century-Crofts.

Mead, G. H. (1934). *Mind, self and society: From the standpoint of a social behaviorist.* Chicago, IL: University of Chicago Press.

Minuchin, S. (1974). *Families and family therapy.* Cambridge, MA: Harvard University Press.

Minuchin, S., & Fishman, C. (1981). *Family therapy techniques.* Cambridge, MA: Harvard University Press.

Nichols, M. B. (2013). *Family therapy: Concepts and methods* (10th ed.). Boston, MA: Pearson.

Nichols, M. B., & Schwartz, R. C. (2001). *Family therapy: Concepts and methods.* Boston, MA: Allyn & Bacon.

Pinsof, W. M. (1995). *Integrative, problem-centered therapy.* New York, NY: Basic Books.

Pinsof, W. M., & Wynne, L. C. (1995). The effectiveness and efficacy of marital and family therapy: Introduction to the special issue. *Journal of Marital and Family Therapy, 21*(4), special issue, 341–343.

Pinsof, W. M., Breunlin, D., Russell, W., & Lebow, J. (2013). Integrative problem-solving metaframeworks therapy II: Planning, conversing and reading feedback. *Family Process, 50*(3), 314–336.

Rank, O. (1964). *Will therapy and truth and reality.* New York, NY: Knopf.

Rober, P., & Seltzer, M. (2010). Avoiding colonizer positions in the therapy room: Some ideas about dealing with the dialectic of misery and resources in families. *Family Process, 49*(1), 123–137.

Ryle, G. (1971). The thinking of thoughts: What is le penseur doing? In *Collected Papers* (pp. 450–496). London, UK: Hutchinson.

Selman, R. L. (1976). Social-cognitive understanding: A guide to educational and clinical practice. In T. Likona (Ed.), *Moral development and behavior* (pp. 299–316). New York, NY: Holt, Rinehart & Winston.

Shibutani, T. (1961). *Society and personality*. Englewood Cliffs, NJ: Prentice-Hall.

Smalley, R. (n.d.). *Mobilization of resources in the individual*. Philadelphia, PA: University of Pennsylvania School of Social Work.

Stern, D. N. (1985). *The interpersonal world of the infant: A view from psychoanalysis and developmental psychology*. New York, NY: Basic Books.

Stryker, S. (1980). *Symbolic interactionism*. Menlo Park, CA: Benjamin Cummings.

Taft, J. (1926). The effect of an unsatisfactory mother-daughter relationship upon the development of a personality. *The Family, 7*, 10–17.

Thomas, W. I., & Thomas, D. S. (1928). *The child in America*. New York, NY: Knopf.

Turner, R. (1968). Role: Sociological aspects. In *International encyclopedia of the social sciences*, vol. 13 (552–557). New York, NY: Macmillan and the Free Press.

Turner, R. (1970). *Family interaction*. New York, NY: Wiley.

Turner, R. (1974). Rule learning as role learning. *International Journal of Critical Sociology, I*, 52–73.

Turner, R. (1979). Strategy for developing an integrated role theory. *Humboldt Journal of Social Relations, 7*(1), 123–139.

Turner, R. (n.d.). *Role taking as process*. Unpublished manuscript.

Vogel, E. F., & Bell, N. (1960). The emotionally disturbed child as the family scapegoat. In N. F. Bell & E. F. Vogel (Eds.), *A modern introduction to the family*. New York, NY: Free Press.

Waller, W., & Hill, R. (1951). *The family: A dynamic interpretation*. New York, NY: Dryden Press.

Weingarten, K. (2010). Reasonable hope: Construct, clinical applications and supports. *Family Process, 49*(1), 5–25.

Weingarten, K. (2000). Witnessing, wonder and hope. *Family Process, 39*(4), 389–402.

Wile, D. B. (2013). Opening the circle of pursuit and distance. *Family Process, 52*(1), 19–32.

White, R. D. (1959). Motivation reconsidered: The concept of competence. *Psychological Review, 66*, 297–333.

White, M. (2007). *Maps of narrative practice*. New York, NY: Norton.

CHAPTER 5

Assessment and Intervention with Families in a Multicultural World

KEY TOPICS

The Importance of Culture
Rivers Flowing into the Sea
Functional Family Assessment
Multicultural Perspectives
A Transcultural Perspective
Intergenerational Patterns
Transcultural Assessment
Transcultural Intervention
Working with Families with Children
The Use of Metaphors and Culturally Congruent Approaches
Home Visits
The Ending Phase
Same-Sex Relationships
Resource List for Work with GLBTQ Couples

In the previous chapters, we developed a comprehensive frame of reference for social work practice with families, built on transactions on the inside and the outside of families (chapter 1). We developed social work theoretical frameworks for understanding the relational person (chapter 2), family developmental processes (chapter 3), and family relational structures (chapter 4). The transcultural work of family members is already embedded in their relational tasks and in the relational structure these tasks create. This is the dynamic, complex and changing context, which culture provides to family intervention.

THE IMPORTANCE OF CULTURE

The transcultural perspective is inherently a dynamic perspective that assumes that all persons actively seek to construct secure relational bases in a world that is already experiencing rapid cultural change. They hope to secure similar basic needs and relational goods. However there are shifting concepts of what the base is, how it may be secured, and what is due in relational justice. Family members have different understandings of relationships. They interact with each other in different ways based on these understandings. Families are challenged to find their internal and external balances. The transcultural perspective recognizes the already-existing diversity of transactions within and across cultures and the reality that these cultures are themselves in dynamic motion. There are thus many paths to developing good family environments; there are many cultural meanings, even in what appears to be a single culture. Recognizing with family members the dynamic cultural meanings in these different paths, the social worker can assist family members to develop an environment that is workable for all the family's members.

The following cases point out some problems and solutions within this complex, multicultural society.

CASE STUDY 5.1:
HMONG CLAN FAMILY

A Hmong family, who had been relocated as refugees from the mountains of Laos to Columbus, Ohio, learned that their child's cancerous eye needed to be removed to prevent the cancer from spreading. Not understanding the decision or having been involved in it, the father took the child out of the hospital without notification and ran away. The state invoked the child protection law and searched for the family. This event became a top news item. Unfortunately, no helping professionals in the situation had a cross-cultural understanding of the meanings of the family's cultural beliefs and the fear and trauma behind its flight. The surgical removal of the eye, an appropriate course by Western medical treatment standards, would seem to the family like a death sentence for the child. Cross-cultural consultation, carefully combined with spiritual rituals of consolation, psychoeducational approaches to this family, and mediation by the clan group leaders, in addition to modern medical practices, could have prevented the many unfortunate outcomes of the situation.

CASE STUDY 5.2:
FAMILY HEALING SPACE

Samoans from a Pacific Islander community expressed their concerns for spiritual space when one of their family members became sick and was hospitalized in Hawaii. It is their cultural practice that healing take place through joining together with the sick person as a group of extended family and kin. However, the time, the space, and the limited number of visitors allowed in the hospital room prevented this communal practice of spiritual healing from taking place. Although it took some time to change, the hospital later not only modified its regulations for visitation, but also made space available for a group visitation and spiritual practice.

RIVERS FLOWING INTO THE SEA

Working with families in a complex, multicultural society is like working with many rivers with different sources. Assessment and intervention within a family's relational structures is intervention within a complex cultural framework. The cases already cited in previous chapters and in the introduction to this chapter involve persons from many different cultures. Yet with all this diversity, there are still common threads. People do things that any person, knowing one's self and one's own relational sources, could understand. In each case, family members struggle to define their family relationships. However, now the struggle takes place in the context of an increasingly media- and market-dominated North American society, which has itself an enormous and diverse cultural substructure. The example of the Hmong family suggests that a process could have taken place with the family and elders of the clan that would have respected their own cultural meanings. The Western medical community should have recognized the status of the elders and the family, the cultural functions of vision and medicine, and the broader cultural meanings of the situation. In the second case, a shift in hospital procedures did accommodate the needs of Samoan culture.

FUNCTIONAL FAMILY ASSESSMENT

Family assessment in a complex and multicultural world demands the development of a *functional family assessment* at the beginning of one's contact with the family. This is an initial assessment of how (and whether) the family unit is able to construct appropriate responses to the needs mentioned in chapter 1: safety, communication and belonging, appropriate choice, and the conditions conducive to growth within the context of the culturally referenced ways the family has of doing things. The family is asked to define its cultural reference points. Without these reference points, it is easy to get lost in a myriad of different interpretations and assumptions that are the social worker's, not the family's.

Functional family assessment comes from a consideration of how the family relational structure is working, how its members might construct relationships with each other, the cultural meanings of these relationships, and the relational work to be done. Relational structures, internal to the family, emerge at particular stages of family development. These relational structures can be tremendously varied, reflecting culture and other factors in the environment. Their functions, however—the prerequisites for the optimal development of persons—remain the same. For these relational structures to work inside the family, they need the support of a surrounding complex of family and societal arrangements, these also having their own systems of meaning. Social workers work between the internal relational structures and the external societal arrangements so that family members are able to construct these essential functions and relational qualities in their own way, but with reference to learned cultural patterns.

One of our principal assumptions has been that in a diverse, multicultural society, where economic and political power inevitably privileges certain groups over others, conflicts and discrimination unfortunately do take place. Because social workers are positioned at the juncture of major institutional sectors of society and with families, they have to deal with these power issues even more than members of other helping professions. Where there is pain and discrimination, social workers usually are the first to deal with the dilemmas they bring.

The transcultural work of the family members is already embedded in their relational work, that is, in their internal relational work and in their external work with social institutions. It waits only for recognition and appropriate support. The internal work has to do with family developmental tasks, which are transcultural tasks as well. The external work involves complex transactions with social institutions, which often do not by themselves understand the family. Such work usually involves a diverse, larger community with its political and economic structures. A transcultural perspective integrates into practice multicultural perspectives on the experiences and life ways of different cultural groups. Such practice with the emergent blend of family cultures in North America is already taking place. It is no longer seen simply as a matter of respecting cultural differences and the life-ways of different groups. A key to understanding the family from a strengths and resilience perspective is realizing how it deals with its own differences while retaining connectedness. The dialogue of family members at any stage is a dialogue of many types of differences and connections. Many of the effective ways family members have of dealing with other differences can be applied to cultural differences as well.

Because of the nature of the practice situation, the assessment process with couples and families is somewhat different from the process with individuals. The concepts of couple and family developmental tasks and family structure, discussed in earlier chapters, delineate personal, family, institutional, and community tasks. The intertwining of different lives, stories, and meanings, as well as the coexisting presence of conditions such as depression, anxiety disorders, posttraumatic stress, and substance abuse, brings complexity to the assessment. The passion of a family's struggle with differences, the needs of its members for justification and control, and the possibility that a relational structure may become unsafe for its members can create concern. Such problems are perceived by family members as *mystifying*: they appear to be too complex to understand and beyond any personal or family influence. On the other hand family members, individually and with others, men and women, have their own, unrecognized capabilities of action, more than their belief systems allow. For the social worker, it is easy to get lost in the details without knowing what to look for and without seeing this potential. Or the social worker, often reflecting the social agency, could take over what appears to be unresolvable complexity and try to resolve it "from above" with the power of the social institution. As with the Hmong clan, when the outside, non-Hmong community takes over, the family and clan has to retreat into dysfunction or prepare to resist. The possibility of a productive process would then no longer exist.

Functional family assessment demands a purpose. Assessment, done with family members and continuing throughout the helping process, is first of all the determination *with the family* of a workable present purpose. Family members need to become active enough to decide what they can and want to do in the light of internal and external realities. There needs to be a focus on the present, with the past as background. The most important part of such assessment is assessing conjointly the conditions and tasks a couple or family face, whether they are willing and able to do something about the problem, and how they might do it. What balance needs to be struck between personal and family tasks? How would the social worker work with different units of attention, both within and outside the family, to make a difference?

Since family structures and family needs are so diverse, initial assessment should provide just an emergent general picture in the social worker's mind of what needs to be done if the family is to regain and maintain its balance. What units of attention in the family and in the environment would be most workable? The social worker might work with one member, such as Armand (case study 4.3), a couple such as Miguel and Juana (case study 3.2) or Brian and Lisa (case study 3.3), or a parent and a child. Or the social worker might work with the whole family in session (Mario, Renata, and Marisa Antonelli in case study 8.4), a mix of family members in different configurations, as in the case of the J. family (case study 5.7) or the Hong family (case study 5.5). Or the social worker, as in all the case studies in chapters 10 and 11, might work with an institution, such as the court or the school. With the case of Jack and Jung (case study 5.6), there was work with the couple, with Jack's family of origin, and with a sectarian assistance agency. What tasks are most important for what the family needs to do? Where can they begin, and what might they aim for?

For example, the first family function—developing and ensuring safety (outlined in table 1.1)—will involve a complex of personal and family tasks. For example, individual persons may have to deal with depression and anger and an inability to communicate effectively; couples have to work out boundaries, understandings, ways of communicating, and mechanisms of anger control and may have to agree on a truce until key issues are worked out. Rather than talking about communication or history, or overwhelming family members with all the aspects of what needs to be done in the abstract, the worker begins by helping family members test out, with each other and in session, their picture of the problem of safety and their ability and willingness to do something: to communicate, to develop and respect boundaries, and so on. The worker begins with the family member who is given the most authority in the culture and then moves to other family members until a picture, with all of its differences, emerges. When this takes place, the assessment and the history usually fall into place as well. In any case, when assessment takes place in this way, it is hoped that the couple or family will remain in charge of what needs to be done. Each can reinforce each other's efforts without intruding on or taking over the personal work of the other.[1]

---

[1]With the complexity of tasks in the first interview, the authors have found that when possible, a two-hour first interview often works better and keeps the family appropriately in charge of its realities.

On the other hand, some family members may decide that in the final analysis, they are unable or unwilling to do what it takes to resolve the problems. This is in itself a most valuable finding, not ultimately undesirable because it frees other members to take appropriate steps for the new and different family structure that then needs to emerge. None of this can be fully predicted. In this sense, rather than a diagnosis, which assumes some sort of fixed, underlying reality that needs to be rooted out and displayed, functional family assessment is an ongoing and active testing of possibilities in the context of tasks to be done. The social worker becomes a collaborative coach for the family's active exploration of what it can or cannot do, what it is willing or unwilling to do, and who wants to be involved in the process. Although the worker may first have to make a very rapid tentative assessment to establish a direction for focus and exploration, most of what follows will not be known by anyone in the beginning. Trying to fit everything in at once in a feverish hunt for the problem is the wrong focus. This only overwhelms the family with what it could not do so far, and it prompts the worker to take over. What family members most need is a sense of where they can begin and what they can do, as well as some realistic hope of improvement coming from their own actions with each other. Often the worker becomes a gentle referee for communication about difficult issues—communication that in many cases may not take place at home. When this does take place in the interview context, the next task is for the couple or family to bring it into their ordinary dealings with each other.

This means that the social worker must actively structure the assessment process and provide a frame of reference, thus normalizing family members' understandings of what is happening while setting boundaries on any possibility for destructive communication, self-harm, or harm to others. Such structuring is done without explosive and dysfunctional exchanges. The couple or family members remain in control of their interaction with each other, can participate in the initial assessment of the issues and meanings, and can foresee doing something together about the situation.

MULTICULTURAL PERSPECTIVES

What does the family social worker need to know to practice competently in a society that is already multicultural and struggling to develop transcultural frameworks? A variety of approaches to practice with families have recognized and built on the specifics of culture (Fong & Furuto, 2001; Ho, 1987; Lee, 1995; McGoldrick, Giordano, & Pearce, 1996). Man Keung Ho (1987) suggests that cross-cultural family practitioners need first of all to have general knowledge about specific ethnic groups. The understanding of persons in specific cultures and the way the cultural themes may be processed by different persons in different cultures are basic to the education of every social worker. There are classic common cultural patterns and themes that arise in any comparative analysis of families in a particular context. Among these classic patterns and themes, themselves changing in the face of a dynamic society, are mate selection and marriage, gender and family roles, child-rearing patterns, acculturation, adaptation and change, and religious practices

(Ingoldsby & Smith, 1995; Locke, 1992; Mindel, Habenstein, & Wright, 1998). Ho expanded these to include nine further patterns that can be applied to each cultural group: extended family ties, the spousal relationship, the parent-child relationship, sibling interactions, intermarriage, divorce and remarriage, immigration and acculturation, and help-seeking. The social worker can apply these patterns to develop a deepened understanding of any particular cultural group.

However, in the face of a complex postmodern society, the interactive and relational patterns of ethnic families are themselves changing. Recent research and practice with cultural dynamics point out this variability. For example, there are effective alternates among Hispanic men to dominant cultural types, such as *machismo* (Falikov, 2010). Cultures that believe parenting to be an almost exclusively female role have also found ways to accommodate shared parenting while still respecting cultural pathways and traditional values (Sotomayor-Peterson, Figueredo, Christenson, & Taylor, 2012). Geographic shifts into another dominant culture are accompanied by profound value changes (Santiesteban, Coatsworth, Briones, Kurtines, & Szapocznik, 2012). The growing diversity of society also creates greater diversity and complexity of spiritual perspectives as persons from different spiritual traditions find other traditions and marry people from other traditions (Walsh, 2010). In different countries of Asia, families have experienced tremendous changes in cultural norms with the growth of divorce, rapid economic growth, urbanization enhanced education and employment opportunities, loosening of social control over marriage, a growing individualism, a decline of arranged marriages, and the rise of romantic love (Huang, 2005, pp. 162–163).

In this worldwide situation family members are often faced with adopting new roles that conflict with their traditional cultural norms, and the practitioner can experience confusion regarding what should be supported. A beginning answer to the question of what to support is to build on the strengths and resources that ethnic minority families bring with them. Very often the family itself is a captive of its own fears and restricted beliefs. It may not be aware of its own capabilities and strengths. It may not be aware of how it can grow and develop within its own cultural track, within its own cultural language, and within its beliefs. How should families and their members cope with these challenges in a dynamic, multicultural society? Again, the family itself resolves the dilemma. With the assistance of the social worker, the family arrives at and tests out its own best balance. The greatest danger is the worker's taking over, using prescriptive and reductionist approaches (Ho, 1987; Lee, 1989), and making assumptions about the family's experience without checking with them.

The family therapy field has long been characterized by divisions into different approaches. The major emphases of these approaches are related to components of family functioning, as illustrated in our discussion at the end of the previous chapter. A focus on one component of family functioning with the related methodology (see table 4.1) implicit in many conventional approaches to family therapy narrows the field of focus. It often elevates the worker as an expert in the method, shutting down the family's efforts to manage the problems. Surveying conventional approaches to family therapy, Man Keung Ho (1987) pointed out that many of these approaches are insensitive to the indigenous cultural values and structures of ethnic minority families. A family therapy method framework, which divides family functioning into parts, can narrow the focus of assessment. Some family therapists, whose major method focus is personal development, reflect this in their assessment. Others emphasize communication, or narratives, or family structure, and reflect that particular emphasis in their assessment (Cocozzelli & Constable, 1985). A more dynamic and inclusive framework needs to take in all the aspects of family functioning, with intervention geared to the problem. The integrative frameworks of Bruenlin, Schwartz, and Mac Kune-Karrer (1992) and Pinsof (1995) are meant to do precisely that. Accordingly, these frameworks are major steps forward.

In the field of social work, systems theory has been the source of theoretical integration of method theories dealing with individuals, families and family networks, neighborhoods, organizations, and institutions (Hearn, 1969; Von Bertalanffy, 1968). Ecological systems frameworks, which model relations of person to the family and the outside environment in an effort to explain complexity, have been developing since the early 1970s (Auerswald, 1971; Gordon, 1969; Germain, 1973; Hartman & Laird, 1983; Stein, 1974). These assumptions, detailed in chapter 1, frame our discussion of social work with families.

The Importance of Cultural Transition Today

Moving from a focus on a single culture in itself, it is important to account for the dynamics of cultural transition, particularly in the diverse North American society and in many countries of Asia. Using Asian American families as an example, and recognizing that there are many intra-ethnic differences, Evelyn Lee (1996) develops a typology of transition, summarized in table 5.1, which has broad applications.

The families described in table 5.1 are in transition from patterns that emphasize stability and family connectedness to other patterns with more individualistic perspectives. The same contrast can be seen in table 2.1, which contrasts British and Japanese families using the same values. Families who emphasize connectedness and de-emphasize individual preferences are often reluctant to discuss personal issues or to seek help from someone outside the family who might have a different perspective. They are reluctant to believe that any assistance could be derived from those contacts. The case of the J. family later in this chapter (case study 5.7) is a good example of dilemmas faced by these families. An external structure, generating relational tasks, was necessary for the family to make real changes.

Discussions of culturally competent practice in a North American context have acknowledged four basic assumptions essential for practice:

1. There is no single North American culture.
2. Diversity is to be acknowledged and valued.
3. Members of each cultural group are diverse.
4. Acculturation is a dynamic process. (Caple, Salcido, & di Cecco, 1995).

Table 5.1
Five Patterns in Asian-American Families

Family Types	Common Characteristics
Traditional Families	Consist entirely of family members born and raised in Asian countries. Family members hold strong beliefs in traditional values. Speak regularly in their native languages and dialects. Still practice traditional rituals and customs.
Cultural Conflict Families	Have American-born children. Arrived a decade ago, when the children were young. Intergenerational conflicts and role confusion are common problems. A husband may have lived in the United States for many years, gone home, and brought back a wife who is not familiar with American culture.
Bicultural Families	Consist of well-acculturated parents who grew up in major Asian cities and who were exposed to urbanization, industrialization, and Western influence. Some were born in the United States but were raised in traditional families. These parents often hold professional jobs and come from middle-class or upper-class family backgrounds. The power structure has moved from a patriarchal to an egalitarian relationship between parents. Family discussions are allowed between parents and children.
Americanized Families	Consist of parents and children born and raised in the United States. Have become largely Americanized. The roots of the traditional Asian cultures have begun to slowly disappear. Communicate in English and adopt a more individualistic and egalitarian orientation.
Interracial Families	Currently comprise about 10% to 15% of marriages, a figure that is increasing rapidly. Japanese Americans lead in this trend, with more than half marrying outside their group, followed by Filipino, Chinese, Vietnamese, and Korean Americans. Some are able to integrate both cultures with a high degree of success. Others often experience conflicts in values, religious beliefs, communication style, child-rearing issues, in-law problems, and so forth.

SOURCE: E. Lee (1996, pp. 231–233).

Our focus on family brings two further basic assumptions:

1. Families (and individuals in family units) adapt to their contexts and to their outer environments as well as to their internal relations (Ho, 1987).
2. No single current family therapy model of how families function can account for cultural complexity. Nor can a single model of family therapy adequately account for and treat the complex content of family interaction (Bruenlin, Schwartz, & Mac Kune-Karrer, 1992).

A TRANSCULTURAL PERSPECTIVE

The realities and complexities of cultural transition in a diverse society demand a transcultural perspective. The transcultural perspective assumes that culture is diverse, active, and adaptable, building on its own core assumptions, rather than being static and monolithic. Looking for patterns in isolation from their dynamic contexts does not deal fully with the fact that social workers operate in contexts of change, of *becoming*. Cultural values are themselves in process of change. The transcultural perspective uses functional family assessment, an emphasis on action, and relational tasks as powerful ways to assist family members to make changes. From a systems perspective, changes in any part inevitably affect the whole. People's perceptions are part of this assessment. In the case studies presented in this chapter, Jack and Jung have to learn that getting a Christmas tree should not conflict with an infant's need for food. Mr. J. needs to find better ways to deal with a disrespectful adolescent than violence and intimidation. Mrs. J. needs to learn that her implicit acceptance of gender dominance can interfere with her dignity, her worth, and her potential contribution to the family and to society.

As the world gradually becomes a global community, its dynamic and inexorable logic is to rethink ethnocentric, regional, or national membership boundaries. This trend toward a global community is inevitable as technology, trade, communication, civilization, and spirituality become common points of reference and as migration of peoples across geographical, racial, and religious lines inevitably occurs. Although the trend is inexorable, the particulars of what will emerge are still unclear. The general picture is of many families moving toward enriched relational and community contexts where development is a possibility for every person—a picture of many rivers flowing into the sea. The spirit and principles articulated in the Universal Declaration of Human Rights set some standards for this transition.[2] As such, the declaration is a tremendous resource for social workers because it concretely states values that we are all striving for but may not yet have achieved. It sets standards for a transcultural perspective.

---

[2]Adopted and proclaimed by General Assembly Resolution 217 (111) of December 10, 1948 (United Nations, 1948). See www.un.org/nghts/50/decla/htm.

A transcultural perspective focuses on the possibilities of developing connections between and among family members of diverse cultural experiences and socioeconomic backgrounds. It reaches out toward a vision of what is common to all cultures, as well as what is different and the communication necessary to manage differences. It assumes that people construct relationships with the hope of securing fulfillment of similar basic needs and relational goods but that they may have different understandings and may interact with each other in somewhat different ways. A transcultural perspective also assumes that family members can decide how much they want or need to modify their roles, as well as how much personal and feeling-oriented communication they want or need. Rosalind (in case study 4.3), for example, did not want to talk about her vulnerable feelings, which prevented her from accepting Armand. Armand respected that until she finally was able to tell him about them. This was a crucial moment in the helping process. When Armand listened, they resolved the issue for a time.

The key to a transcultural understanding can be found in the helping process itself. The helping process involves a search for the substantive, the overarching meaning of *being with* each other, despite many perceived barriers. This transcultural perspective assumes that barriers and differences do exist. However, the values that best undergird family life, the goals sought by family members because they are human, and the relational tasks needed to carry out these goals can inexorably bring members to radical choices: to encounter differences, to resolve them, and to look for appropriate change. The alternative is to face dissolution of functional communication, connectedness, and support for appropriate personal differentiation. This was the concrete choice that Rosalind and Armand had to face.

Social workers, working with change processes and differences, can assist family members to deal with the demands of these change processes within the context of transcendent human values and transformed relational systems. Family practice is beginning to assume that there really are commonly shared meanings of our family existence and that there is a mutual healing process in the context of these emergent common meanings. Paradoxically, these assumptions emerge mainly through encounters with difference and through some sort of communication. These differences, including cultural differences, demand some resolution if any unit is to grow. The transcendence over differences that emerges in any bonding process can also be present in helping relationships. Social workers can help members to create mutual healing processes, with the goal of maximizing the capacity of persons to care, to grow, to choose, and to change—and thus to transform a relational system.

Working from a Transcultural Perspective

A young couple may experience cultural differences with a surrounding environment, or they themselves may come from different cultures. In either case, their tasks are somewhat similar. They need to construct a common family culture, different from its surroundings. In this sense, the normal relational tasks of early marriage also become transcultural tasks. Armand and Rosalind (case study 4.3) combine East Indian and Greek American cultural backgrounds. Both reconstructed their relationship, blending both personal and cultural patterns into a common relational culture of its own.

Class differences can also operate in a way similar to cultural differences. In the following example, Catherine comes from a middle-class, African-American background; Dwain from a working-class, African-American background. Some of the difference in their patterns can be traced to social class of the families of origin.

CASE STUDY 5.3:
CATHERINE AND DWAIN

Catherine and Dwain are an African American couple who are having difficulty dealing with the differences emerging in their first years of marriage. Catherine, the daughter of two physicians, uses medical concepts to talk about her ups and downs; Dwain, raised "on the streets," thinks Catherine is just not tough enough. She uses general concepts, like "passive-aggressive," that from Dwain's perspective seem to implicitly criticize him. Dwain understands these concepts, but when he wants to get to her for being "uppity," he responds concretely to her abstractions and makes fun of her. She "doesn't get the joke" and responds with disappointment and hostility. For Dwain, it is a funny compliment to tell her that she is getting a little plump; Catherine feels that he rejects her when he does that. Both have trouble dealing with the polarities of their own communication. Abstractions on one side are met with concreteness on the other. The game maintains the distance between them, and they feel a vague lack of intimacy in the marriage. They need to develop common languages and patterns of communication. With help, they begin to work on developing a common understanding, uniquely their own.

Intergenerational Patterns

Relational tasks are not simply experienced on a single generational level. There are clear intergenerational patterns and precedents, as indicated in the following case study.

CASE STUDY 5.4:
DWIGHT AND BECKY

A woman from north China, an upper-middle-class Catholic refugee with a family fractured by war and resettlement, married a man in Taiwan of peasant stock, a Buddhist with a strong, intact Taiwanese family support system. With her encouragement, he became a highly educated professional and she adopted his Buddhism, but with her own reservations. Throughout their marriage, they experienced massive shifts in Taiwan toward a more open society. They moved to the United States for a time, both practicing professionally there, and then moved back to Taiwan.

Their oldest son, Dwight, was educated in the United States from his early adolescence through his PhD. He remembers with some pain his struggle as a Chinese American teenager to become "one of the boys" in the Seattle schools. Dwight married Becky, a North American Catholic woman of Irish, English, and German extraction with her PhD. Becky comes from a large, well-educated, and equally complex family. Despite ethnic differences, their educational backgrounds made them very similar in orientation. Becky grew up in an interracial family in a very diverse, well-educated urban community. As a child, she devoured books. As a teenager, she traveled and participated in international exchanges. By her university years, her friendship network was international. They now live in the United States, but their feeling of membership is broader. Together, now with their first child, they bridge massive cultural issues, developing their common family culture.

Relational Tasks in a Transcultural Perspective

When relational tasks break down, they can be recomposed and rectified in the context of a helping relationship with a social worker. Social workers bring their own experience and their ethnicity, as well as the orientation of the sponsoring agency (school, court, family service agency, or hospital) to the transcultural mix. The challenge of such transcultural family work is to channel complex understandings and specific practice approaches into a flow of couple or family energy toward the development of "we-ness" and simultaneously toward a deeper experience of self as a person.

Transcultural Assessment

To aid the transcultural assessment process, social workers need first of all to gain an understanding of the experiences of each cultural group as they have assimilated and adapted to a diverse society while at the same time retaining a distinct identity of their own. It is important to avoid stereotypical and biased generalizations about any particular group. The interaction of culture and personality is complex and difficult to differentiate. The social worker therefore needs to resist looking for simple cultural categories to explain behavior. The following list of strategies, drawn from one social worker's experience with transcultural assessment, brings together research findings with social work practice experience.[3] These strategies provide guideposts to discern both differences and commonalities across cultures:

- Consider all clients as individuals first, then as members of a minority status, and then as members of a specific ethnic group.

---

[3]These strategies were developed by Helen Brown Miller (personal communication, 1995; not otherwise published).

- Never assume that a person's ethnic identity tells you everything about his or her cultural values or patterns of behavior.
- Treat all "facts" you have heard or read about cultural values and traits as hypotheses, to be tested anew with each client. Turn facts into questions.
- Remember that all minority group people in this (US) society are at least bicultural. They have had to integrate two value systems that are often in conflict, and these conflicts may override any specific cultural content.
- Some aspects of a client's cultural history, values, and lifestyle are relevant to your work with the client. Others may simply be interesting to you as a professional. Do not prejudge what areas are relevant.
- Identify strengths in the client's cultural orientation that can be built upon.
- Help the client identify areas that create social or psychological conflict related to biculturalism. Seek to reduce dissonance in those areas.
- Know your own attitudes about cultural pluralism, particularly whether you tend to promote assimilation into the dominant society values or to stress the maintenance of traditional cultural beliefs and practices.
- Engage your client actively in the process of learning what cultural content should be considered.
- Keep in mind that there are no substitutes for good clinical skills, empathy, caring, and a sense of humor.

Transcultural Intervention

The helping process is a search for the overarching meaning of being with each other despite many perceived barriers, and so the key to a transcultural understanding can be found in the helping process itself. Helping is a process of encounters that themselves can generate energy for change. Through communication, the couple or family learn to redirect the energy from these encounters toward the transformation of the inevitable impasses in their relational systems. With the assistance of the social worker, the couple or family's own resolution of these impasses challenges stereotypes; implicit assumptions of dominance; and patterns and beliefs of race superiority, gender inequality, power abuse, and the personal and institutional exploitation of vulnerable people.

Let us begin with four basic principles of transcultural practice:

1. *Take the position of the other.* The basic understanding of each person as a subject interacting with others (intersubjectivity) underlies family work, particularly in a transcultural perspective. In real relationships differences already exist. To model understanding and working with differences, the social worker needs to put himself or herself in another's shoes and help members of the family do the same. In communication, this skill means reflecting accurately the other's meanings (accurate empathy), clearing one's mind of one's own reactions and for the moment becoming the other in feeling and thought and in dialogue. This powerful tool of communication and

mutual understanding is used collaboratively and with the permission of the other. The worker helps each person to communicate, sometimes even filling in the gaps in communication with another, and doing the same for the other when necessary.

2. *Discover and use the healing power of relationships.* Persons who come to a helping process have often experienced discrimination and inequality in the larger society. There are many persons who have never experienced their own worth and dignity, their radical equality, and the self-responsibility that goes with being a person. They do not really expect to be treated or accepted as persons. The alternative experiences of inequality, of dominance and being dominated, and of nonacceptance are carried into family relationships and even into the helping relationship. Domination is expected to continue. The remedy for the experience of nonacceptance, inequality, and exploitation is not a technique but a more personal approach to relational tasks. Relationship building needs to be rich in values that respect personhood. It must address issues of appropriate process and personhood when they emerge. The approach cannot be value-neutral.

3. *Language and communication are the media of the healing process.* Language and communication are the first elements to suffer from undeveloped or dysfunctional relationships. When cultural and relational difference intrude on personal development and understanding of roles, language can become impoverished and communication impersonal. There can be a struggle around a common personal language, the vehicle of communication, that they have yet to achieve. Catherine and Dwain (case study 5.3) fenced with each other in abstract and concrete languages respectively. To communicate appropriately, they had to learn each other's verbal and nonverbal languages. In large part, this involves listening, taking in what the other is meaning, and reflecting it accurately back to the other. A smaller part of this learning involves expressing one's self in a way that the other can listen and understand.

4. *Agency and communion resolve themselves more quickly in joint relational work.* The couple or family unit, the "we," formed out of difference, learns to act and support each other's agency through communication and relational work. However, a mentality of colonization by what is perceived as the more powerful culture can shut off a person's ability to act as an agent of one's own development. Joint relational work, with each other and with the social worker, can heal some of the mentality of colonization. The social worker/mentor helps the couple or family unit deal with these issues, which come from both inside and outside the unit.

Working across these cultural divisions within the family and with the outside world, transcultural practice inevitably involves one's own cultural integration. One cannot help others deal with a mentality of colonization if one has the same mentality. These processes of cultural integration, taking place simultaneously with the worker and with the family, deepen the river of the universal emotional system. They move toward higher and more complex resolutions of the developmental needs of persons and family units. When people find genuine connection with each other, the superficial layers of preconceived notions, preconditioned reflexes, and patterns of emotional reactivity lose their disruptive power. The shared energies (synergy) of effective dialogue flow into the core of the relational system, validating the worth of every member of the family. Appropriate communication moves toward the goal of empowering and revising family functioning and dealing with its own generational differences. When it comes together, the family system discovers its ability to deal with its own community of belonging and the outside world.

Froma Walsh (1999, p. 24) points out that the journey into different patterns and meanings has much in common with a spiritual journey. More than symptom reduction, problem solving, or communication skills, people are seeking meaning and deeper connections with others in their lives. There is often spiritual distress at the core of physical, emotional, and relational problems. Making space for spirituality—encouraging spiritual connections in family and community life—adds to the transformational power of the helping process. Making this space can begin a process of healing and overcoming barriers, whether the barriers are socioeconomic, linguistic-symbolic, racial-political, or cultural realities of dominance and discrimination.

Working with Families with Children

Moving from the couple relationship, transcultural family practice has additional dynamics with the family with children. There is now a culturally conditioned, generational divide. As they encounter another culture in school, children often feel caught between cultures. The transcultural focus needs to include both generations of the family as well as the school or other salient institutions. With the Hong family, in the following example, there was work both on the outside and the inside of the family relational system.

CASE STUDY 5.5:
THE HONG FAMILY

Myong Hong, age 16, had just moved with his family to a newly developed Detroit suburb. Myong had consistently been a good student until his sophomore year. His parents were hoping for better education for their children. Soon after he had been transferred to his new school, Myong faced peer pressure to join an ethnic gang group.

He was suspended by the school on suspicion of gang membership and activity. The school had a no-tolerance policy for any apparent gang involvement. Myong's suspension brought the Hong family to a crisis that needed professional intervention. His father, a first generation Korean American radiologist, was very disappointed to find out about the suspension of his eldest son. Myong's mother was also very upset. She was concerned about Myong but had trusted that her son's longstanding "big brother" relationship with John, the son of mutual friends, would help him avoid these problems. Both parents were also disturbed by their recent moving process. They moved from an ethnic enclave into a multicultural neighborhood with few members of their group available to them. Myong lost his old neighborhood friends. His contact with John had become occasional. Myong has a brother, Hoon (age 12), and a sister, Sunyoung (age 9), who both seemed to adjust better to the family's recent move. They liked their new house and had made some neighborhood connections at a park center. Both parents are very active volunteers in services to the ethnic community and church life. They have maintained their good connections within the Korean American Community. Nevertheless, the incident was a terrible blow to them.

After an initial meeting with Dr. and Mrs. Hong, a home visit, follow-up family counseling sessions, and individual session with Myong, the social worker sought a joint conference with the school social worker, the academic dean, and the parents over Myong's situation. Out of this collaborative process, Myong returned to school under a set of guidelines established to strengthen his self-esteem and to reduce his level of anxiety associated with peer pressures and alienation. Myong eventually recovered his sense of belonging when the family spent more time together. The school took a more proactive role in accommodating Myong with extracurricular activities, where he was able to find success.

When a child of a recent immigrant family enters the mainstream school system, he or she is at risk of experiencing both anxiety and low self-esteem unless the family, school, or neighborhood provides some support and connections. This anxiety can become unresolved emotional reactivity. It can spread to interactions in the family and the larger society (Bowen, 1966). Intervention with Myong, within the family system and with the school, was aimed at reducing anxiety and validating self-worth while promoting a secure environment, relational justice, cross-cultural accommodation, and intercultural connections in the family and school community. These goals were accomplished through tasks. Tasks for Myong would help his family and the school manage the relationship better. In this way, they would help Myong adapt appropriately to his new school and what it was asking from him.

We develop the principles of transcultural practice further through two cases. The first case involves an escalating crisis for Jack and Jung. The crisis could have led to child neglect and breakdown of the bicultural relationship.

CASE STUDY 5.6: JACK AND JUNG

Jack, a Caucasian, nonpracticing member of the Church of Jesus Christ of the Latter Day Saints (Mormon), married Jung while he was serving in Korea in the armed forces. They moved to his hometown, Ogden, Utah, after Jack's period of service had ended. Jack, taking college courses in accounting, had been laid off from his job. The couple, now with a six-month-old baby, was experiencing severe financial pressure. Both were very preoccupied with their daily difficulties getting adequate subsistence for the family.

A family crisis was precipitated over whether they should buy a Christmas tree or purchase food for their baby. For Jack, celebrating Christmas without a Christmas tree was inconceivable. He grew up with many fond sentiments associated with the tree during the Christmas season. Jung grew up in a small rural village where her parents worked hard to survive as a family. She feared that Jack's spending habits had not considered her concerns for basic needs. She could not comprehend Jack's sentimental interest in such "a luxurious decoration" during the holidays. Nor was Jack able to attend to the urgency of obtaining essential food (i.e., milk) for the baby. Jung had recurrent memories of traumatic experiences of hunger and hardship, growing up in a poor family when Korea was suffering from a destructive war. She was increasingly feeling anxious.

These issues and the couple's frustrations and disappointment led to frequent arguments with verbal abuse. Jack's parents had disapproved of their marriage and were unsympathetic to the couple. Jack refused to seek any help from them. Jung had been cut off from her in-laws from the beginning. Jack, going through a period of transition and doubt, was not at all interested in his family's faith tradition. Jung, from the time she had emigrated to the United States, had been emotionally cut off from her family of origin. Although she began taking language courses and showing some interest in involvement in the Church of Jesus Christ of the Latter Day Saints, the birth of her child and the severed relationship with her in-laws made it difficult for her to connect to supportive social networks. Additionally, Jung's limited English skills and her dependency on Jack for transportation further complicated her ability to access needed support and resources.

The social worker worked with Jack and Jung to help them develop safer and more effective communication patterns, develop problem-solving skills, clarify their goals as a couple, and eventually receive assistance from Jack's church and from his family. Helping Jack reconnect with his family was a defining moment that opened up both systems to shift in their beliefs and their structure and accommodate each other. It became a metaphor for their changed perceptions of themselves as a family. It took a good deal of work with Jack, with Jung, and with the family to develop a reconciliation so that Jung could feel real membership in Jack's family and so that Jack could come to terms with enough of his anger to reconcile with them.

Five Further Practice Principles

We now examine the helping process in this case study to elicit further principles of transcultural practice. The external crisis forced Jack and Jung to begin to deal with parts of their marriage that were profoundly incomplete. The social worker began by exploring with them what their experience was and how they were able to express what they experienced. The social worker needed to avoid imposing his views on them—judging who was right or wrong or explaining why something was taking place. Listening to their inner voices as well as their bodily messages, the worker focused on being together with them as a couple and also with each of them separately as distinct persons. He facilitated the construction of a dialogue between Jack and Jung to bring together their separate energies. Where connections were needed, he helped them make those connections, reaching out where they could be found and reframing and redirecting them. Jack knew his own mind and his preferences, as did Jung. Paradoxically, as this understanding of who they each were and what they valued was mutually accepted as part of a dialogue, they began to free themselves from their own ethnocentric and self-centered rigidity. This rigidity was causing the relationship to lose energy and connectedness, when they fell repeatedly into dehumanizing cycles of evaluating and judging each other, which had become their relational pattern.

5. *Begin where the client is.* This is the starting point for cross-cultural understanding and culturally sensitive approaches to families. It helps practitioners avoid any rigidity stemming from their own preconceived notion about who the family members are, and thus it liberates both clients and therapists from victim-blaming preconceptions or assumptions that their interaction is in any way linear. To begin in this way demands an open position. The open position allows participants to explore authentically the core of who they are, as agents of their own development, to discover the true meaning of what they seek to construct, and to discover strengths and resources, in themselves and in others to resolve the challenges of their struggle.

6. *Respect individual perspectives and choices.* Respect for the other's perspectives and choices helps participants to develop a joint perspective: Although the worker put this principle into action at the onset of his practice with the couple (case study 5.6), it became even more important when it was incorporated into the sequences of family work. The couple realized that both psychological and physical needs were essential to the healthy individual and to family development and social functioning. They decided that the main challenge was not so much deciding who would be right or wrong in a marital dispute. Rather, their problems involved lack of resources in meeting both sets of needs at the time of their crisis, an inability to mobilize available external resources as well as their limited family relational framework. From one perspective, the problem was to choose between a Christmas tree or baby milk. Both were timely and appropriate. If they had enough resources to satisfy both, each could be simultaneously pursued without conflict. When they realized this, the couple began to see more clearly their baby's needs and rights. These had been pushed aside in their tug of war about who was right and who was wrong. The baby's needs took on urgency as the couple determined to seek out the needed resources from both his extended kin

and other social service agencies. They would begin to develop their relational and cultural connections.

7. *Promote social belonging: Without belonging, there is no survival.* Social work is committed to promote social belonging for clients. Belonging is necessary for group survival. Cross-racial integration has always been a source of tension in North American society, and Jack and Jung (case study 5.6) felt it. Many immigrant families with school-age children and youth encounter and experience hostility when they settle in a mainstream neighborhood. There is a well-known Korean proverb: As fish must live in water, so people must live in a society where they find acceptance. Jack and Jung had experienced social and cultural isolation during courtship and after marriage. Their way of coping with uncomfortable social attitudes toward their interracial marriage was to wall themselves off from the outside world, from Jack's family of origin, and from each other. This self-imposed isolation prevented any meaningful contacts with friends and kinfolk. Jack and Jung needed to expand their sociocultural boundaries. These included other interracially married couples, Jung's ethnic people, Jack's kin, faith communities, and other friendship groups.

8. *The ultimate goal of family intervention: To achieve an optimal balance of integration.* In the beginning, Jack and Jung's crisis (case study 5.6) appeared to focus on a conjugal dispute over the resources to satisfy two different needs. However, the problem is more complex and goes beyond any particular individual boundary. It is interwoven with the integrity of family system. The cost of a Christmas tree cannot outweigh the child's needs. Nor can Jung's concerns for the baby obscure the more complex relational issues of her needs, Jack's needs, and their joint concerns and responsibilities for the baby. This total picture would demand more resources and expand the boundaries of the nuclear family system. To integrate each member's needs, one can also move beyond the immediate family toward the boundaries of the community, until an optimal balance between demands and resources is reached. In this case, Jack, Jung, and his family of origin overcame their initial reluctance to rediscover their connections with each other and the resources of the community where they now have their cultural and religious affiliations.

9. *Change and adaptation is an ongoing process.* Jack and Jung (case study 5.6) also needed space to accommodate the child of their bicultural bonding. Jung had to adapt herself to her new country: its laws, language, and expectations. Jack and his family needed to facilitate the acculturation processes for Jung by creating a more friendly holding environment of cross-cultural acceptance. Both Jack and Jung needed to provide their child with cross-cultural opportunities to enrich their child's bicultural identity and to integrate the strengths each culture brings to their marriage. The family on both sides needed to develop more supportive roles to bridge the emotional gulf and social distance between the generational lines. Healing the wounds of the past can take place therapeutically through the efforts of a faith community as well as through work with the social worker. Working between

different units of attention, social workers also need to help the outside units increase their cultural competence and, for example, avoid a potentially negative experience with Jack's family of origin or faith community.

TRANSCULTURAL ASSESSMENT AND INTERVENTION: A CASE

Assessment, as an active and ongoing part of the helping process, assists the practitioner to understand the complexity of a situation and provide a framework for intervention. Tools for such assessment include genograms, ecomaps, inventories, home visits, and contracts, among others. The relation between assessment and intervention is illustrated in the case of the J. family.

Mr. J., 45 years old, born in Singapore of an overseas Chinese family and living in Berkeley, California, was referred by his attorney for individual counseling in relation to a recent episode of child physical abuse involving his 13-year-old son, Kwak. At the time of the episode, the police and child protection worker had intervened, responding to a neighbor's complaint. While under an order of protection from the county court pending further hearings, he had contacted a social worker of his ethnic background in private practice for professional help.

The J. family has to develop a safe environment, shift in its ways of communicating expectations and in the socialization process with adolescent children, and rebalance the relationship between father and mother. Members have to resolve their anxiety stemming from Mr. J.'s probationary status and the consequent delay in having their immigration status changed to permanent residents.

During the assessment period, Mr. J. was seen at the social worker's office three times. Then he was joined, in weekly couple sessions, by his wife, also from an overseas Chinese family in Singapore. Following these initial sessions, a combination of the conjoint family sessions, couple, sibling, and individual sessions were synchronized according to the needs of the therapeutic process and family members' circumstances. Additionally, during the interim intervention period, two home visits were made. Their initial purpose was to assess both the living environment and family atmosphere; later it was to share the therapist's interest in engagement with the family in their own natural family space. The case narrative details work on the inside with the J. family to recompose themselves and then meet the expectations of the court. On the outside, the social worker worked with the court, sending reports to the family and the court.

CASE STUDY 5.7: THE J. FAMILY

The J. family is composed of the biological parents and two adolescent children, Chen, a 16-year-old girl and Kwak, a 13-year-old boy. They were living in Berkeley, California, with a preimmigration status, waiting for approval of their permanent residency. Both parents completed university education in Singapore. Mr. J came to the United States several years ago as an overseas business assistant manager of a leading transportation company. He moved his family from Michigan to California to manage the area branch office. Their families of origin still live in Singapore, except for Mr. J's younger brother and his wife, who now reside near the J. family. Mrs. J. is a housewife, devoting herself to the care of her family and occasionally helping neighbors with art projects. Chen, the elder child, is in her third year in a private high school with boarding facilities. Her academic achievement is very high. With support from her high school and from her family, she looks forward to admission and scholarship assistance in the best universities in the country. She lives in a school dormitory during the week and spends her weekends with her family. Kwak, the younger child, who is in the eighth grade, had been the victim of his father's severe physical punishment. In the J. family constellation, Mr. J. is closer to his high-achieving daughter, and Mrs. J. is closest to Kwak, who resembles her physically. In the family triangles, Mr. J. was the outside member of a tight bond between Kwak and Mrs. J. Mrs. J. was the outside member of Mr. J's and Chen's bond.

Mr. J. was arraigned under the state child protection law by the police and a child protection team upon a report of child abuse by a neighbor. The son had been severely punished with a broomstick for talking back to his father, and this led to a family altercation. Mr. J. was put on an order of restraint. Subsequently he was forced to separate himself from his family for a period of nearly eight months, until the court order was lifted. The court involvement would severely delay the family's application for permanent resident status.

The issue had begun around Mr. J's concerns that Kwak be ready for college. The parents are very much concerned about the education of their children, particularly as the time for college application approaches. Chen was planning her college application. Mr. J. began to worry about his son's academic performance. He believed that Kwak was not making enough efforts to improve, instead appearing obsessed with computer games. Usually Kwak is quiet in family gatherings. However, he became quite verbally reactive when he was forced to join a family gathering where Chen would consult with a university professor to develop a study plan to strengthen her essay skills. The father thought this would encourage Kwak to develop some motivation and skills for his future education. In Mr. J.'s youth, "talking back" to his parents or elders would not have been tolerated in any way, nor could Mr. J. tolerate his son's disrespectful behavior. Mr. J. had experienced severe physical punishment from his father. That evening, after the family dinner, he chose to confront and punish his son. As their verbal interaction became more intense, Mr. J. lost his temper and punished his son with a nearby broomstick. Kwak had been defiant to his father and disregarded the cultural norm of obedience. For Kwak, his father's action with the broomstick was unacceptable in their new country. Mr. J. lacked any other means of resolving his anger and his son's behavior. This conflict between cultural expectations in a country of origin and the child protection law takes place with many recent immigrants from many Asian countries. In these countries, corporal punishment is still widely tolerated as the parents' right to discipline their children. Kwak's injury was mild enough. The bruises, cuts, and a fractured finger were treated and healed quickly. However, the image of Mr. J., the father and husband, needed rehabilitation with family members. The family also needed to be able to manage issues without intimidation and violence. Psychological residues of the incident remained in the memories of each family member. The guilt, the resentment, and the secrecy, as well as other residues of the incident needed to be examined for cleansing and healing. There were strained relationships both inside and outside of the family system.

The family also experienced the institutional constraints on Mr. J. The court's expectations had been humiliating and imposed public shame on the family. The application process for their permanent resident status had to be temporarily suspended on the advice of their immigration lawyer. The family court had demanded concerted efforts from the family members toward accommodating each other. In this sense, the court was reconstructing their interactive patterns and their sociocultural realities. The court was concerned that the healthy growth and development of the J. family members be promoted. Chen, in particular, who had more quickly assimilated North American values, had a heightened sensitivity toward family violence but also a strong connection with her father. She reacted to the incident more profoundly than others in the family.

Both genograms and ecomaps are used in ongoing assessment with the family.

Genogram Assessment

A genogram is a generational family map that allows a person to see a family system historically.[4] Assessing previous life cycle transitions, the social worker can present issues in the context of the family's evolutionary patterns. The genogram includes at least three generations of family members, as well as nodal and critical events in the family's history as related to the life cycle. When family members are questioned about the present situation in relation to the themes, myths, rules, and emotionally charged issues of previous generations, repetitive patterns become clear. Genograms suggest possible connections between family events over time. Patterns of previous illness and earlier shifts in family relationships brought about through changes in family structure and other critical life changes can easily be noted. The genogram provides a framework for reconstructing what may be currently influencing a crisis in a particular family (McGoldrick, Gerson, & Shellenberger, 1999, p. 3).

The J. family genogram is constructed in figure 5.1 to demonstrate a transcultural perspective toward assessment and intervention within intergenerational family emotional systems. It provides a model that can be generalized to other multigenerational family situations. Circles denote females; squares, males. An X in the figure denotes a deceased family member.

---

[4]For a more detailed discussion of genograms, see Marlin (1989); McGoldrick, Gerson, and Shellenberger (1999); Nichols and Schwartz (2001, pp. 160–162); Goldenberg and Goldenberg (1996, pp. 181–183); and Hartman and Laird (1983).

Figure 5.1
Genogram of the J. Family

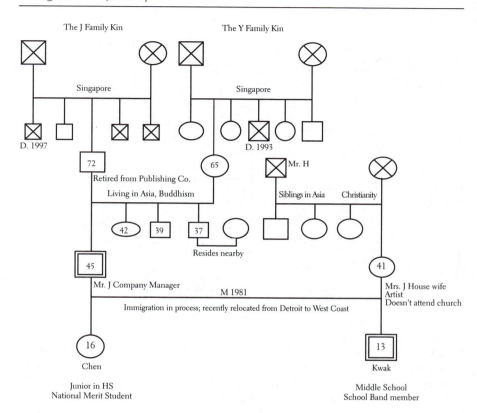

Ecomap Assessment

An ecomap is widely used as a tool to assess the level of social support inherent in family members' transactions with possible environment resources and connections. Hartman and Laird (1983) and others have elaborated the ecomap's clinical use in assessing environmental resources, including significant others, social institutions, and spiritual resources available to families. The quality of resource mobilization, external to the immediate family structure, is diagrammed according to the connective lines. These lines symbolize various types of connections (see figure 5.2).

On the basis of the initial assessment, Kwak had stressful relations with his father and was overly close with his mother. He had positive relations with his paternal uncle and the school band. He had tenuous relations with school and stressful relations with the court. Chen had positive relations with her father, her friends, school, and camp; tenuous relations with college admission offices and her uncle; and stressful relations with court. Mr. J. had positive relations with his company and

Figure 5.2
Ecomap Assessment of the J. Family

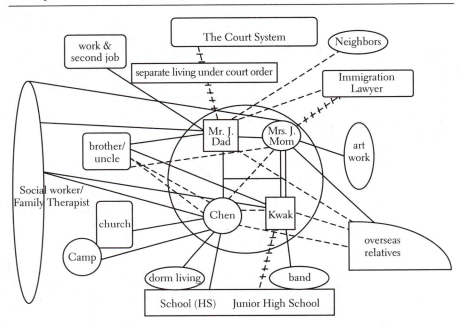

his brother; tenuous relations with neighbors; and stressful relations with the court, his separate residence, and the immigration lawyer. Mrs. J. had positive relations with her art work; tenuous relations with her brother-in-law; and stressful relations with court, her husband's separate residence, her neighbor, and the immigration lawyer. All family members had positive relations with the social worker. The ecological sources of stress for this family came directly from the court, the separate living arrangement for Mr. J., and the immigration lawyer.

Despite these strained interactions between the family and the legal system, they were able to maintain some positive relations with their school and work situations, the exception being Chen's concern with college admission and Kwak's academic progress at school. Mr. J.'s younger brother is the only close relative available to the family members.

Other than her art work, Mrs. J. has few social outlets. Both of Mrs. J.'s parents had died recently. She was unable to be with them in their illnesses or attend the funerals. Additionally, she had deferred to Mr. J. and stopped practicing her religion. Mr. J. has tended to downplay her sadness.

Chen finds her friends and opportunities to volunteer at camp satisfactory. Kwak had a limited amount of social interaction with his band group. Mr. J. finds his social outlet in his contact with colleagues at work. Both Kwak and Mrs. J. seem to lack much of a social support network. Kwak seemed to understand his mother.

She felt close to him, defending him against his father. During the incident, they both gained more weight than they would like to keep.

The Intervention Phase

Sessions with the J. family were arranged jointly. During the initial phase, the sessions were scheduled more regularly. Later they were scheduled less often, according to their needs and the time demands experienced by family members and by the social worker.

Most standard clinical procedures will work for culturally diverse families. It is important, however, for practitioners to respect the readiness (or lack of readiness) of these families for clinical intervention. Recent immigrants from non-Western countries may perceive professional (and psychological) intervention in their families as intrusive. Depending on their pretherapeutic history and the circumstances leading to professional intervention, they are often suspicious. Research on help-seeking behavior and premature termination indicates that the initial period of intervention is the most critical. Transactions with the family need to be sensitive and carefully monitored from a transcultural perspective. For those who can benefit from psychoeducational approaches, clinical procedures should be explained in linguistically and visually understandable ways. In the process of early engagement, spiritual and symbolic ways to integrate trust, humor to break the ice, or other tested ways to build relationships are useful. When necessary, mutually trusted persons may be utilized as buffers and mediators for the purpose of connecting and development of a contract with the family. Sometimes working through the context of a church, school, or another trusted institution makes a big difference in the family's receptivity to the helping process.

Goal Setting and Intervention Strategies

From the onset of the helping relationship, clients are responsible for taking part actively in the tasks leading to the expected outcomes. For the J. family, there were specific therapy goals for individual members and general goals for the entire family system. The overall context of these goals was of the need for safety and relational justice. From Mr. J.'s perspective, Kwak's talking back demanded of him the same measures his own father had used. However, Mr. J.'s act failed to accomplish its intent. It made the family unsafe for Kwak and in different ways worrisome for the others. It cemented Kwak's anger, disrupted Mr. J.'s relationships with the others in the family, and diminished Mr. J.'s stature. If he were to defend his actions, he would have had to develop further a culture of dominance and ineffective communication patterns in the family. The result would have been that members would become afraid. Communication around certain realities would go underground or break forth in uncontrolled outbursts. Mrs. J. would be further diminished in her alliance with her husband. Chen would look elsewhere to satisfy her hunger for relational justice. The family would become less effective for its members.

The J. family needed to restore its own safety and harmony. It needed to develop the means and patterns that could accommodate the different needs, possibilities, and aptitudes of each of its members. It needed to release itself from court supervision and move on with the process of application for permanent resident status. Mr. J. needed to repair and restructure his damaged relationship with his wife and children, as did each family member with each other member. Following the ecomap, each family member needed to work out a change process in relation to each of the other members of the family. With the information already presented, a list of concrete goals and the process needed to meet these goals can be established.

Intervention strategies become the definitive means to achieve these goals in the course of the helping process. Although communication techniques and cognitive-behavioral strategies have a proven effectiveness in resolving many family problems, transcultural practice principles serve as general guideposts in using intervention methodologies and techniques.

The social worker for the J. family was bilingual and bicultural, known for his expertise in such situations. Mr. J. had initiated his contact for social work services on the referral of a lawyer who had confidence in this social worker's work. Mr. J. was tense and reserved in the beginning. He faced unknown possibilities of professional engagement for himself and his family. It was important for the social worker to centralize Mr. J.'s control of his destiny, even under the constrained circumstance of receiving assistance and being under court supervision. Individual, couple, and family sessions were charted out with specific goals and a specific agenda. Contacts involved homework between sessions, periodic reviews of therapeutic progress, court hearings, home visits, information/referral services, and consultation. Mr. J. and his family became central to the hoped-for movement from a state of vulnerability and dysfunctionality to a more defined and renewed level of social functioning. All the assessment data, including the genogram, the ecomap and other inventories—journal essays and professional progress reports—were made transparent to the clients as means of ensuring that transcultural principles would be realized.

The goals for the J. family in the helping process were tied to clinical procedures and intervention strategies as well as to principles of transcultural practice. These goals were achieved not merely by means of techniques, but also by the mutual engagement in co-creating new realities of effective living and parenting.

When Mr. J. reexamined his traditional patterns of control and came to a new understanding of relational justice, he became more open to a developed appreciation of the meanings inherent in parenting and individualization in growth and development. He saw himself changing and realized that he could regulate his stress and impulses. Seeing more options for himself, he became more open to meeting the challenges of life differently. Mrs. J. also began to free herself. She moved away from her earlier depression and began to regulate her activities to strengthen family cohesion and to reduce the stress generated by her own anxiety. Although Western values might have expected even more independence, these were enormous moves for Mrs. J. Chen began concentrating her energy on her college admission. She involved herself in volunteer services and began to expand her extracurricular activities. She reconnected with her father and brother. Kwak began healing the physical, psychological, and relational wounds caused by his father's punishment. He gained back his self-esteem and was able to reach out more to his father, his sister, and his friends. Both Kwak and Chen felt comfortable enough to contact the social worker voluntarily; Chen even brought her close friends to be introduced to the social worker. Kwak would use e-mail now and then to share his feelings with the social worker. Mr. and Mrs. J. regained their balance as they were reunited and freed from the restraining order. Mr. J. began to listen to his wife's feelings and encouraged her to practice her religion. They had learned to support each other. This support could help heal Kwak's and Chen's pain associated with their father's abusive episode. It also would help heal the family crisis resulting from court supervision. The family's reactive emotionality (anger), their anxiety, and their stress-producing patterns were eased. Intergenerational cultural conflicts—family members' struggles to adapt to the expectations of society—were eventually alleviated.

The Use of Metaphors and Culturally Congruent Approaches

Metaphors and maxims are very helpful for directing a family's attention to emerging phenomenological realities that cannot easily be articulated in cross-cultural transactions. Family therapists frequently use metaphors to communicate about current family dynamics without taking the risks that may come with more direct language. Well-known maxims and metaphors, handed down from sages through many civilizations over the course of time, attest to their lasting effects on problem solving. Strategic, paradoxical and solution-focused brief family therapists, among others, often use these intervention strategies. Transcultural therapists often find parables and metaphoric messages either from a particular culture or more universally known sources (such as Aesop's fables). These parables have useful, culturally transcendent, and generative meanings. Their use could bring more congruence to therapeutic interaction. There are rich sources of stories and parables in the Talmud, the Bible, and other religious texts. There are sayings with similar meanings across cultures. The Western saying "There is a shadow under the lamp" and the Eastern saying, "A monk can't cut his own hair" are understood similarly. They can be metaphorically used to explain that both clients and therapists have blind spots and need help at different times. Edwin Friedman, a family therapist and rabbi, has made extensive use of metaphoric stories (Friedman, 1990), as has Carl Whitaker. These stories become useful in moving families beyond their impasses and in unlocking cognitive and emotive issues deeply veiled with covert, secret awareness. These issues could involve extramarital affairs, rumors of incest, and so on. Hawaiian ways of resolving family illness often necessitate calling their ancestral ghosts or spirits to reveal the secrecy hidden in the family circle (Hurdle, 2002).

In case study 8.7, of John, Mary, and Stephen Maxwell, the story of Pinocchio was used to deal with the attachment issues created by Stephen's running away. Also, certain aspects of a case can become metaphorical. Sarah's back (case study 3.1) becomes a metaphor for issues to be resolved in her relationship with Phil. Jack and

Jung's reconciliation process with Jack's family becomes a metaphor for the acceptance of their marriage in their society. Joseph and Paula (case study 7.3) construct a temporary "wall" to protect each from the other's verbal abuse. Ashford and Louise (case study 7.6) take a trailer trip through the West, a metaphor for their growing comfort with each other in their empty nest.

Mr. J. did not realize, except through discussion, that he was projecting his unresolved hostility toward his own abusive father onto his son, Kwak, and using the issue of academic performance to do so. The metaphor that helped him see his own projective anger came from a familiar saying: You can burn down your entire house to kill bugs. When the roots of his hidden anger were externalized, Mr. J. was able to differentiate Kwak's needs from his own emotional reactivity. He began to see other ways to deal personally with his projections from his father and to develop effective parenting skills. Many of the individual sessions with Mr. J. were focused on these issues. Similar to the ego-oriented approach with Gloria in chapter 2 (case study 2.1), they assisted him to deal with anxiety and achieve differentiation. Here the social worker drew from the family systems perspective of Murray Bowen (1966). At the same time, family sessions were used to reinforce structural boundary making and effective communication, using both structural family therapy and narrative perspectives. Different techniques were used in different formats to achieve related goals.

Home Visits

In their earliest work with families, social workers were "friendly visitors." Home visitation is one of the most distinctive outreach activities in social work. Although for safety and other reasons, home visits are challenging to do, they can provide many therapeutic advantages. Family members can be better accommodated in the natural setting of their daily lives. Home visits make an assessment of the ecological contexts of client's neighborhood environment and dwelling quarters possible. They widen the scope of clinical observation by making the home atmosphere and living arrangements a part of the work. They often allow clients both flexibility and control. Family pictures and other significant cultural icons can be more readily accessed for assessment and intervention. They also help social workers become more aware of human geography and space from a cross-cultural perspective. Young people and children often have more open space for therapeutic engagement when they are given opportunities to participate in a more creative way.

The worker made a home visit in the middle phase of work with the J. family. The purpose of this visit was to understand their family's ways of accommodating familial needs and to celebrate their efforts to develop a certain quality of life and relationships. He found that the J. family was living in a modest, three-bedroom rental apartment in a large racially integrated complex in Berkeley. The family atmosphere was hospitable. Their daily life was largely and noticeably centered on the children's educational achievements. They believed that this affordable location could best help them to accommodate the children's education. Chen and Kwak each had their own private room, and the parents occupied the master bedroom. Their dream is to someday own their own single-family home. A noise factor, due both to the building structure and nearby traffic, disturbed some of its peace and created some anxiety.

The family session was informally conducted and free ranging. This informality allowed a great variety of themes to emerge. There was some focus on the roles each member takes with others; the television programs they watch together; their levels of inclusiveness, control, and affection; intergenerational linkages; their ethnic support system; and their daily schedules. There was also discussion of questions of neighborhood attitudes, public facilities, public transportation, religion, social contacts, health and dietary care, and cultural and family heritage, among other things. Mr. J., although actually living outside, took part comfortably. They were relaxed, interactive, and eager to share personal things of interest to them. The experience and understanding from this visit helped the worker focus more on family cohesion and developmental tasks of each family member from each one's own personal and cultural points of view. Thus the family's strengths and their sense of control were accentuated.

Between-Session Activities

Much of the actual family work takes place outside of the formal sessions. Assignments and between-session activities are arranged around the goals and progress of the work with the family. These activities are a real test for family members' level of commitment to and competence in taking control of their situation and making their therapeutic engagement work effectively. A variety of therapeutic homework assignments can be used. Journal or letter writing, inventories, behavioral tasks, genogram construction, drawing, and communication exercises are most frequently used, in addition to a host of creative activities. These activities help both social workers and clients stay on a forward track toward the goals of family work and toward implementation of their initial agreements. They reinforce and fortify therapeutic and healing processes. They strengthen the family's control and competence in mastering the social functioning skills and tasks connected with meeting needs, solving problems, and resolving conflict. These activities should be linked to the phases of family work, including diagnosis and evaluation.

For the J. family, there were a number of between-session activities and individualized assignments for each member of the family. At the initial stage, Mr. J. was asked to provide preliminary data for genogram construction. He also got involved in writing his own reflective, bilingual letter. In this letter, he assessed his role in the family crisis from both narrative and cultural value perspectives. These two assignments, the genogram and the reflective, bilingual letter, enriched family intergenerational assessment data. Even more important was their reinforcement of the new concepts and new language that he incorporated in his narratives. They helped him to construct a more holistic meaning of the change taking place.

Mrs. J. began writing a journal, focusing on her thoughts and feelings about different things. She needed to be able to recognize her feelings and thoughts, find a language for them, deal with each of them, and find a way to balance and accommodate both to each other. Her journal was meant to increase her awareness of depressive ways of thinking, feeling, and reacting. In the face of these older ways of thinking, she would search for constructive connections and linkages, changing her feelings of helplessness and her self-blaming communication patterns. This helped her focus on her strengths. It began to rebalance her functioning with Mr. J. and with the family toward equilibrium.

Chen continued focusing on her college admission process, volunteer work, outings with her mother, dialoguing with her father, playing with her brother, and so on. As a more competent bilingual person, she was asked to take a more proactive role in representing the best interests of her family in dealing with the court system and in reaching out to colleges and universities for a scholarship. She attempted to serve as a role model for her brother in achieving academic success while recognizing his own unique strengths. She successfully wrote a very convincing letter to the judge requesting that the restraining order for her father be lifted.

Kwak was asked to send e-mail messages to the therapist as frequently as he felt he needed to express his inner struggle in dealing with his recent experience of abuse and its associated mixed emotions of guilt, anger, confusion, and low self-esteem. He got involved in school extracurricular activities, including band, and watched his eating habits carefully. He set priorities, balancing the demands of his schooling with family needs, personal health care, recreational and social activities, and computer games. He made greater effort to express himself in both verbal and written communication with his father. He appreciated what his sister was going through and learned from her success. He visited his paternal uncle on his own and maintained a close adult relationship with him. These activities were reported verbally and through telephone contacts, written letters, and e-mail messages. Each family member made an inventory of conflict tactics, using an instrument already developed. They also made their own progress reports during this period.

Linkage to Cultural and Spiritual Resources

It is critically important for social workers carefully to attend to a contextual understanding of clients' cultural resources, including spirituality, ethnic support systems, historic patterns of assimilation and adaptation, and formal and informal social service structures of the host or majority community. Ethnic families need to maintain linkages with their own cultural and spiritual resources. Such linkages often bring healing and social support. They buffer the stresses of acculturation. They help family members recover their sense of wholeness, purpose, and meaning. They become sources of synergy, enriching the family's transcultural meanings. These meanings are particularly important with interracial married couples.

Although the J. family did not belong to any particular faith community, Chen actively linked herself to a local Chinese church as a summer camp volunteer, helping the adoptive families of Asian-born children. Mr. J. involved his family with his

Singapore-based transportation company staff and their families during a Chinese festival. He maintained contact with his family of origin back home by phone and letters. Mrs. J. maintained contact with her relatives in Singapore through her art work. Kwak had a few friends of Chinese ancestry at school. The family had sought therapy from a bilingual person who could relate to their cultural roots.

THE ENDING PHASE

In the ending phase, normal clinical procedures should be followed in working with families in a multicultural setting. When they have achieved the goals of therapy, it is important that clients be set free to advance their life course with a sense of empowerment and completion. In this process, feedback and validation are directed to affirm their readiness to terminate, and an evaluation checklist can be used as a tool to facilitate the ending process. As clients depart from one's office, metaphors of their own changes can be developed to celebrate their achievements.

In some cultures, the ending needs to be stretched out with some relationships continuing. Asian American families often believe that "once you become connected as friends, your friendship should prevail in good faith over all other circumstances." They tend to maintain their relationships far beyond the time and space of therapy. Nevertheless, the focus of the ending is on ending, showing the social worker that they have changed and are able to handle new realities. They are grateful for all the social worker has done. In the family members' minds, he or she has become like a member of the family. The ending phase with the J. family, discussed in greater detail in chapter 12, was not an ending in the Western sense, but rather was a continuation. Over the next two years each member of the family "checked in" with the social worker in different ways to point out that they were maintaining their gains.

What Brought About Change in the J. Family?

Considering that Asian families often are quite reluctant to talk about personal and familial issues, the J. family had made considerable lasting personal and relational changes while still retaining their cultural identity. It was not so much communication in itself, but relational tasks and then some communication, that assisted the J. family to accomplish a major relational shift. There are a number of reasons for this:

1. *External Necessity*: There was a difficult external situation with which to deal. The court had set expectations that the family could not accomplish without help. Their immigration application was also dependent on a resolution of the court's expectations.
2. *Focus on Relational Tasks*: The focus of the worker remained on the relational tasks connected with dealing with the demands of a concrete situation. This was reinforced by the use of assignments and a mentoring relationship with family members in relation to their relational tasks. When this took place, their understanding of themselves and the others gradually also changed, and they were able to talk about it to a certain extent.

3. *Culturally Congruent Meanings*: The social worker's use of culturally congruent metaphors established a framework of meanings that made sense to the family but was not personalized.
4. *Internal Shifts Depend on External Work*: The internal forces in the family—the unstable triangles of Mr. and Mrs. J., Kwak, and Chen—were pressing for resolution. However, considering the cultural situation, these internal forces alone probably would not have brought the family to seek help.

SAME-SEX RELATIONSHIPS

The ten practice principles discussed in this chapter fully apply to same-sex relationships, as does much of the discussion of this book. Same-sex couples are easily as diverse as heterosexual couples, making it difficult to generalize about them without writing another book. In addition, there is a fully developing literature, listed at the end of this chapter, that this book cannot approximate. Although bisexual and transsexual people tend to be lumped with gay and lesbian couples, they are by no means the same (Blumenstein, 2014, p. 3). The following discussion applies to gay and lesbian couples.

Research suggests many similarities of gay and lesbian couples to heterosexual couples. For example, regardless of the partners' sexual orientations, the same set of factors tends to predict relationship quality and relationship longevity across all types of couples:

- Placing more value on security, permanence, shared activities and togetherness
- Placing lower value on having separate activities and personal autonomy
- Higher expressiveness
- More perceived intrinsic rewards for being in the relationship
- Fewer perceived attractive alternatives to the relationship
- More perceived barriers to ending the relationship
- Less belief that disagreement is destructive
- Higher trust in the partner—viewing the partner as dependable
- Greater closeness and flexibility
- Better problem-solving and conflict-negotiation skills
- Higher shared/egalitarian decision making
- Greater perceived social support from sources outside the relationship (Green, 2012, p. 181)

There are also differences. Because these couples are not as bound to gender-based roles, particularly in the case of lesbian couples, there is a greater equality in their negotiation of roles (Gotta, Green, Rothblum, Solomon, Balsam, & Schwartz, 2011). In general, they also seem to do better at resolving conflict situations (Gottman, Levenson, Gross, Frederickson, McCoy, Rosenthal, et al., 2003; Gottman, Levinson, Swanson, Swanson, Tyson, & Yoshimoto, 2003). Nevertheless, same-sex relationships tend not to last as long as heterosexual marriages (Green,

2012). Whereas monogamy is highly valued by lesbian and heterosexual couples, nonmonogamy agreements and behavior have been more accepted in gay male culture traditionally (Gotta, Green, Rothblum, Solomon, Balsam, & Schwartz, 2011). The estimated rate for gay men of nonmonogamous sexual behavior ranges from half in some research to two-thirds in other research (Gotta, Green, Rothblum, Solomon, Balsam, & Schwartz, 2011, p. 355; Shernoff, 2006, p. 407). In gay male couples, most of the nonmonogamous behavior is by prior mutual agreement (Green, 2012, p. 183), a "negotiated nonmonogamy" (Shernoff, 2006).

This can lead to a very different use of words and meanings. For example, to heterosexual couples, *fidelity* has a complex set of meanings around exclusivity, intimacy and monogamy, and their own sexual communication. It may denote relational security beyond their sexual communication, relational continuity transcending personal changes (Grisez, n.d.). Its loss may be seen as a reason to end the relationship. If the male couple has explicitly agreed to be sexually exclusive, then *fidelity* has the identical meaning for them. For other male couples, *fidelity* simply means honesty. Although not referring to sexual exclusivity, it often refers to the emotional primacy of the relationship. *Infidelity* means breaking the rules set by their agreement for how sex outside the primary relationship is to be conducted (Shernoff, 2006, p. 412). With this understanding, negotiating an explicit couple's agreement around monogamy/nonmonogamy is particularly important for the stability of the relationship.

Accounting for differences and similarities within a heterosexual culture, some commentators (Johnson & Collucci, 1999, pp. 347–348; Laird, 1993; Lukes & Land, 1990) conclude that lesbians and gays are bicultural. Reared in the same dominant culture, they have internalized many of the same sets of norms, values, and beliefs. They belong to mainstream families and use some of the same premises of family life as their heterosexual kin. Yet because of their unique experiences and special circumstances created by same-sex pairing, they are part of a complex multigenerational family system consisting of a family of origin, a multigenerational lesbian/gay community, and a family of choice that consists of friends, partners, and children. For some, the family life cycle construct may not apply in the same way. For many lesbians and gays, the couple relationship or the network of relationships with close friends constitutes a complete family unit. There is a lack of language or norms for various aspects of lesbian and gay life in the context of the family of origin (Johnson & Collucci, 1999, p. 347; Slater, 1995; Siegel & Lowe, 1994; Slater & Mencher, 1991). Although the traditional life cycle format may still be useful, it is necessary to see it from a different set of lenses, some of these very much in process and development (Johnson & Collucci, 1999).

The very diverse GLBTQ population is still in process of defining themselves for their singularities, for their connections with each other and with a broader, and very diverse, culture. There are similar aspirations for relational stability, and similar relational tasks to the already diverse heterosexual population, but there are somewhat different foci—different lenses for experiences and community. And these are still in process of development. Although the discussion and concepts developed here would encapsulate many essential concepts, the authors would prefer to respect these developing understandings of relationships, not presume to attempt to encompass this diversity within this book, nor attempt to speak for what is still in development. Rather, there is a resource list at the end of the chapter in which the reader can get acquainted with these developments more directly.

SUMMARY

Family work allows for an opening for every member to greater possibilities. The social nature of family relationships may allow members to move from the outside in, each transcending some of the limits of their situations. An ethnocentric worldview broadens and the rivers move inexorably to the sea. The following Buddhist parable tells the story:

> If you take a tablespoon full of salt, put it into a glass of water, stir it and drink, the water will taste quite bitter because of the salt. But take the same tablespoon of salt and stir it into a large, clear, pure mountain lake, then take a handful of that water and drink it. You won't taste the salt at all. (Wolin, 1999, p. 126)

The lake is the living, cultural environment of the outside world—complex, full of difference, full of stories, a precious heritage for each person. It is also the world of common understandings and meanings and the functional patterns that can emerge from the productive interaction of differences. How may persons and family units retain cultural uniqueness in a diverse and changing society? The transcultural perspective addresses the relational task of managing personal meaning and difference in a situation of diversity and change. The following chapters take the task perspective further into life cycle tasks faced by couples and elaborated families.

RESOURCE LIST FOR WORK WITH GLBTQ COUPLES

Bigner, J. J., & Wetchler, J. L. (Eds.). (2012). *Handbook of LGBT-affirmative couple and family therapy*. New York, NY: Taylor & Francis.

Firestein, B. (Ed.). (2007). *Becoming visible: Counselling bisexuals across the life-span*. New York, NY: Columbia University Press.

Fox, R. (Ed.). (2006). *Affirmative psychotherapy with bisexual women and bisexual men*. Binghamton, NY: Haworth.

Gotta, G., Green, R.-J., Rothblum, E., Solomon, S., Balsam, K., & Schwartz, P. (2011). Heterosexual, lesbian and gay male relationships: A comparison of couples in 1975 and 2000. *Family Process, 50*(3), 353–376.

Green, R.-J., & Mitchell, V. (2008). Gay and lesbian couples in therapy: Minority stress, relational ambiguity and families of choice. In A. S. Gurman (Ed.), *Clinical handbook of couple therapy* (4th ed., pp. 662–680). New York, NY: Guilford.

Greenan, D., & Tunnell, G. (2002). *Couple therapy with gay men*. New York, NY: Guilford.

Laird, J., & Green, R.-J. (Eds.). (1996). *Lesbians and gays in couples and families: A handbook for therapists*. San Francisco, CA: Jossey Bass/Wiley.

Lev, A. I. (2004). *Transgender emergence: Therapeutic guidelines for working with gender-variant people and their families*. Binghamton, NY: Haworth.

Lev, A. I. (2010). How queer! The development of gender identity and sexual orientation in LGBTQ-headed families. *Family Process, 49*, 268–290.

Shernoff, M. (2006). Negotiated nonmonogamy and male couples. *Family Process, 45*(4), 407–418.

Stone Fish, L., & Harvey, R. G. (2005). *Nurturing queer youth: Family therapy transformed*. New York, NY: Norton.

REFERENCES

Auerswald, E. (1971). Interdisciplinary versus ecological perspective. *Family Process, 10*, 202–215.

Blumenstein, R. (2014). LGBT umbrella excludes some bi and trans people. *NASW News, 59*(1), January, 3.

Bowen, M. (1966). The use of family theory in clinical practice. *Contemporary Psychiatry, 7*, 345–374.

Bruenlin, D., Schwartz, R., & Mac Kune-Karrer, B. (1992). *Metaframeworks: Transcending the models of family therapy*. San Francisco, CA: Jossey-Bass.

Caple, F. S., Salcido, R. M., & di Cecco, J. (1995). Engaging effectively with culturally diverse families and children. *Social Work in Education, 17*, 159–170.

Cocozzelli, C., & Constable, R. T. (1985). An empirical analysis of the relation between theory and practice in social work. *Journal of Social Service Research, 9*(1), 47–64.

Falikov, C. J. (2010). Changing constructions of machismo for Latin men in therapy: The devil never sleeps. *Family Process, 49*(3), 309–329.

Fong, R., & Furuto, S. (Eds.). (2001). *Culturally competent practice: Skills, interventions, and evaluations*. Boston, MA: Person Custom Publishers.

Friedman, E. (1990). *Friedman's fables*. New York, NY: Guilford.

Germain, C. (1973). An ecological perspective in casework practice. *Social Casework, 54*, 325–330.

Goldenberg, I., & Goldenberg, H. (1996). *Family therapy: An overview*. Pacific Grove, CA: Brooks Cole.

Gordon, W. (1969). Basic constructs for an integrative and generative conception of social work. In G. Hearn (Ed.), *The general systems approach: Contributions toward an holistic conception of social work*. Newbury Park, CA: Sage.

Gotta, G., Green, R., Rothblum, E., Solomon, S., Balsam, K., & Schwartz, P. (2011). Heterosexual, lesbian and gay male relationships: A comparison of couples in 1975 and 2000. *Family Process, 50*(3), 353–376.

Gottman, J. M., Levenson, R. W., Gross, J., Frederickson, B. L., McCoy, K., Rosenthal, L., . . . Yoshimoto, D. (2003). Correlates of gay and lesbian couples' relationship satisfaction and relationship dissolution. *Journal of Homosexuality, 45*, 23–43.

Gottman, J. M., Levenson, R. W., Swanson, C., Swanson, K., Tyson, R., & Yoshimoto, D. (2003). Observing gay and lesbian couples' relationships: Mathematical modeling of conflict interaction. *Journal of Homosexuality, 45,* 65–91.

Green, R. (2012). Gay and lesbian family life. In F. Walsh (Ed.), *Normal family processes* (4th ed., pp. 172–195). New York, NY: Guilford.

Grisez, G. (n.d.). *Fidelity today.* Privately published.

Hartman, A., & Laird, J. (1983). *Family-centered social work practice.* New York, NY: Free Press.

Hearn, G. (Ed.). (1969). *The general systems approach: Contributions toward an holistic conception of social work.* Newbury Park, CA: Sage.

Hurdle, D. H. (2002). Native Hawaiian traditional healing: Culturally based interventions for social work practice. *Social Work, 47*(2), 183–192.

Ho, M. K. (1987). *Family therapy with ethnic minorities.* Newbury Park, CA: Sage.

Huang, W. (2005). An Asian perspective on relationship and marriage education. *Family Process, 44*(2), 161–175.

Ingoldsby, B., & Smith, S. (1995). *Families in multicultural perspective.* New York: Guilford.

Johnson, T. W., & Colucci, P. (1999). Lesbians, gay men and the family life cycle. In B. Carter & M. McGoldrick (Eds.), *The expanded family life cycle* (3rd ed., pp. 346–361). Needham Heights, MA: Allyn & Bacon.

Laird, J. (1993). Lesbian and gay families. In F. Walsh (Ed.), *Normal family processes* (3rd ed., pp. 282–328). New York, NY: Guilford Press.

Lee, D. (1989). Book review. [Review of *Family therapy with ethnic minorities*]. *Social Casework, 70,* 517–519.

Lee, D. (1995). The Korean perspective on death and dying. In J. Parry & A. Ryan (Eds.), *A cross-cultural look at death, dying, and religion* (pp. 193–214). Chicago, IL: Nelson-Hall.

Lee, E. (1996). Asian-American families: An overview. In M. McGoldrick, J. Giordano, & J. Pearce (Eds.), *Ethnicity and family therapy* (pp. 227–248). New York, NY: Guilford.

Locke, D. (1992). *Increasing multicultural understanding.* New York, NY: Guilford.

Lukes, C. A., & Land, H. (1990). Biculturality and homosexuality. *Social Work, 35,* 155–161.

Marlin, E. (1989). *Genograms.* Chicago, IL: Contemporary Books.

McGoldrick, M., Gerson, R., & Shellenberger, S. (1999). *Genograms: Assessment and intervention* (2nd ed.). New York, NY: Norton.

McGoldrick, M., Giordano, J., & Pearce, J. (Eds.). (1996). *Ethnicity and family therapy* (2nd ed.). New York, NY: Guilford.

Mindel, K., Habenstein, R., & Wright, R. (1998). *Ethnic families in America: Patterns and variations* (4th ed.). New York, NY: Prentice Hall.

Nichols, M., & Schwartz, R. C. (2001). *Family therapy: Concepts and methods.* Boston, MA: Allyn & Bacon.

Pinsof, W. (1995). *Integrative, problem-centered therapy.* New York, NY: Basic Books.

Santiesteban, D. A., Coatsworth, J. D., Briones, E., Kurtines, W., & Szapocznik, J. (2012). Beyond acculturation: An investigation of the relationship of familism and parenting to behavior patterns in Hispanic youth. *Family Process, 51*(4), 470–482.

Shernoff, M. (2006). Negotiated nonmonogamy and male couples. *Family Process, 45,* 407–418.

Siegel, S., & Lowe, E. (1994). Uncharted lives: Understanding the life passages of gay men. New York, NY: Dutton.

Slater, S. (1995). The lesbian family life cycle. New York, NY: Free Press.

Slater, S., & Mencher, J. (1991). The lesbian family life cycle: A contextual approach. *American Journal of Orthopsychiatry, 61,* 371–382.

Sotomayor-Peterson, M., Figueredo, A. J., Christenson, D. H., & Taylor, A. R. (2012). *Family Process, 51*(2), 218–233.

Stein, I. (1974). *Systems, theory, science, and social work.* Metuchen, NJ: Scarecrow Press.

United Nations. (1948). *Universal Declaration of Human Rights.* Adopted and proclaimed by General Assembly Resolution 217 (111) of December, 10, 1948. Accessed at www.un.org/overview/rights/.

von Bertalanffy, L. (1968). *General systems theory.* New York, NY: George Braziller.

Walsh, F. (Ed.). (1999). *Spiritual resources in family therapy.* New York, NY: Guilford.

Walsh, F. (2010). Spiritual diversity: Multifaith perspectives in family therapy. *Family Process, 49*(3), 330–348.

Wolin, S. (1999). Three spiritual perspectives on resilience: Buddhism, Christianity, and Judaism. In F. Walsh (Ed.), *Spiritual resources in family therapy* (pp. 121–135). New York, NY: Guilford.

CHAPTER 6

Beginning Phases with Couples in Early Marriage

KEY TOPICS

The Newly Married Couple
Love and Fidelity: The Construction of a Secure Relational Base
Personal Tasks and Couple Tasks
Beginning with Couples
What the Worker Does: Skills
Creating a Holding Environment
Unrecognized Gender Inequalities
Problems in Developing Commitment
Marriage and Relationship Education with Couples

In this chapter, we focus on the tasks and developmental issues of early marriage. We explore the creation of boundaries and intimacy through communication as well as the concept of projective identification in couples as developed by object relations family therapists. How does the social worker begin with one couple? In the transition to couplehood unresolved issues of commitment and gender inequalities become particularly important. Building on this, we broaden our discussion to marriage and relationship education (MRE) with couples, now in a couples' group, at early stages of their relationship process.

The couple is the executive subsystem at every stage of the family in formation. For this reason, our discussion of work with couples is also applicable to work with elaborated family units in later chapters. With elaborated family units the social worker addresses the couple first of all, and then the other parts of the family complex, whether these comprise children or extended family structures, such as grandchildren, in-laws, and so on. As the family structure elaborates itself, relational tasks connected with the couple's beginnings repeat themselves in different ways. The couple may find themselves having to develop further what brought them together in the first place.

THE NEWLY MARRIED COUPLE

All the tasks of the engaged couple apply to the newly married couple as well. To understand the newly married couple, we need to imagine Brian and Lisa (case study 3.3) now experiencing the *actuality* of a committed relationship. Brian and Lisa experienced the need to communicate and develop common patterns of managing their relationship. Now they need to manage everyday decision making about issues such as family of origin, money, and their intimacy. They need to further establish their communication and relational patterns. Once they are actually married, many of the issues put off in the engagement period can no longer be put aside. They now need to develop common patterns of dealing with their common life and still preserve differences and appropriate ways of managing personal issues. These personal issues are no longer private and cannot be walled off, away from the other; nor are they common property. Rather, they are somewhere in between.

Some of the most profound issues faced by the newly married couple have to do with the couple's need to develop compatible patterns of managing their common living situation, while at the same time they are becoming a separate unit from their families of origin. This raises all sorts of personal and relational issues. Each person learns relationships and patterns of living from their family of origin, even if they learned to oppose what was expected of them. There is a certain transfer of these learned patterns and remembered relationships from each person in the marriage to the new couple as a unit, but there is not an orderly or predictable way for this transfer to take place.

In Western culture, there is a demand that the marital friendship be stronger than earlier connections with parents and siblings. However, the process of actually becoming the "number one friend" to the other and melding particular patterns is at best a lifetime process. At the same time, the son or daughter, with some secondary assistance from the spouse, needs to redefine the relationship with his or her own family and with others. This can happen only at the point where the new couple has really developed their relationship and their ownership of their common patterns. This redefinition of relationships with families of origin demands some development of the marital friendship, but the reverse is also true. The development of the marital friendship demands some relational redefinition with the families of origin.

Long-established patterns from the family of origin get right in the middle of the couple's own experiences and perceptions of things. Learned from their own families, the patterns are taken for granted until something comes up where they may be questioned. One example would be Sarah and Phil's unprocessed assumption of Phil's family patterns and beliefs in relation to household chores and other issues (case study 3.1). When Sarah's back went out, they had to develop different, compatible, and balanced patterns of managing household chores and making decisions about money and family resources. Armand and Rosalind's (case study 4.3) different cultural and familial ideas of intimate relationships, together with the immediate pressure of salvaging their relationship from their respective affairs, brought them to attempt to work out their boundaries and the patterns of intimacy and trust in their relationship. In an earlier period, when they were single, they had personal tasks of making decisions and managing resources. In early adulthood they may have struggled with depression or anxiety as they redefined their relationships with their families of origin. As they become a couple, these remain personal tasks, because they have to do with personal agency, but also, to some extent, they become relational tasks, because they have to do with connectedness (communion). Part of the problem is distinguishing between the personal and the relational. Each needs to deal with one's own feelings around money, one's own experiences, and one's own developed patterns from one's family of origin. At the same time, each needs to strive to develop some commonalities of approach. Two individual and personal patterns need to be made compatible in the development of a third pattern. These commonalities should also preserve individual initiatives and decision making. Such tasks continue throughout the couple's relationship.

All these relational tasks demand the development of common communication patterns. Communication involves a balance of listening and expressing. The majority of the effectiveness of communication comes from the ability to listen. However, in many cultures this skill may be poorly developed. Also, the skill may have been poorly developed in the family of origin—"We always yelled at each other in my family. What's wrong with that?" "My mother always nagged at my father. It was the only way anything got done." "I never learned how to talk back." These patterns often take place at lightning speed, so that the protagonists are scarcely aware of them. In any case, the shift in communication demands more than skill. It often implies profound relational shifts. Learning to communicate as a couple demands the development of the reciprocal ability of ego to express feelings and perceptions and of alter to listen and reflect appropriately and helpfully. In turn, alter needs to express and ego to listen and both to come to some resolution. The two processes should lead to a common understanding and a common vocabulary of accepted meanings. Often this needs to be done in slow motion before one can get to a normal decision-making speed. This is more than a development of expressive and empathic skills on the part of the couple—it demands recognition of and care for the other *as other*, as someone different—that is, as not quite yet part of one's expected narrative.

In contrast to a romantic myth of expecting to find one's needs, one's desires, one's preconceptions in the other, John Gottman's (1999; Gottman, Driver, & Tabares, 2002) research suggests that happily married couples have learned to embrace a realistic philosophy of persons and differences. Happily married couples and unhappy couples had about the same number of differences. Happily married couples were able to manage these differences better. When change occurs, this can temporarily upset the previous relational equilibrium. Many differences can be deep and enduring—indeed, they may be necessary. Happily married couples were able to manage them, for the most part, without a downward spiral.

Love and Fidelity: The Construction of a Secure Relational Base

What needs to be learned if a relationship is to endure through all of the changes and developmental stages that family members will encounter in each other over a lifetime? How can the relationship continue as a secure base for both members while change is taking place? What is needed if the relationship is to develop to accommodate two (and more) persons and their needs?

Most couples seek some sort of relational permanence. Yet they may have quite different ideas of what this involves. There are different fears and sensitivities; there are different levels of skill and mutuality. There are different ways of dealing with inevitable changes within and outside the relationship. In any case, although there may be a general romantic attachment to some sort of permanent commitment, it is the work of many years to become fully related to *this* person, to become a transcendent "us" (Hargrave, 2000). It is a profound realization to come to the understanding that this vulnerable person has become attached to *you*, needs you, and loves you. In this sense, such a mutual relational commitment, reinforced by the actual relationship, can be profoundly formative. It is never automatic.

A first couples' task, if their relationship is expected to be permanent, is to adopt some common understanding of love and fidelity. In much of Western society, the sentiment of love, initially fueled by romantic beliefs, nevertheless is expected to become something intrinsically permanent. While that process is taking place, the social institution of marriage could remain a safe harbor.

Marriage, Considered as a Covenant With many couples their strong, mutual understanding of commitment, keeps them going while circumstances are changing and they are still developing skills to accommodate each other. Across cultures and religious beliefs, commitment is often expressed publicly. Some couples would not make such a public commitment and are simply comfortable with their mutual loyalty. Some would make the public commitment with minimal awareness of its implications. For others the mutual expectations are a protective framework amid the inevitable changes life brings. In any case, there needs to be a secure base—an understanding, implicit or not, that may (or may not) develop as the couple develops. What specifically would this commitment be? One example can be found in the sample of a marriage exhortation below, used for many years in a public marriage ceremony before making the promises (Grisez, n.d., pp. 23–24).

Figure 6.1
Marriage Exhortation

I
"As you know, you are about to enter into a union
which is most sacred and most serious,
a union which was established by God himself.
By it, he gave to man a share in the greatest work
of the continuation of the human race.
And in this way he sanctified human love and
enabled man and woman to help each other live as children of God
by sharing a common life under His fatherly care.
Because God himself is thus its author,
marriage is of its very nature a holy institution,
requiring of those who enter into it a complete
and unreserved giving of self . . .

II

The union then is most serious,
because it will bind you together for life
in a relationship so close and so intimate
that it will profoundly influence your whole future.
That future, with its hopes and disappointments,
its successes and its failures, its pleasures
and its pains, its joys and its sorrows—
they are hidden from your eyes.
You know that these elements are mingled in every life
and are expected in your own.

III

And so, not knowing what is before you,
you take each other for better or for worse,
for richer or for poorer, in sickness and in health, until death.
Truly, then, these words are most serious.
It is a beautiful tribute to your undoubted faith in each other
that, recognizing their full import, you are nevertheless
so willing and ready to pronounce them.
And because these words involve such solemn obligations,
it is most fitting that you rest the security of your wedded life
upon the great principle of self-sacrifice.

IV

And so you begin your married life by the voluntary
and complete surrender of your individual lives
in the interest of that deeper and wider life
which you are to have in common.
Henceforth you belong entirely to each other;
you will be one in mind, one in heart, and one in affections.
And whatever sacrifices you may hereafter be required to make
to preserve this common life, always make generously.
Sacrifice is usually difficult and irksome.
Only love can make it easy; and perfect love can make it a joy.
We are willing to give in proportion as we love.
And when love is perfect, the sacrifice is complete . . .

V

No greater blessing can come to your married life than
pure conjugal love, loyal and true to the end.
May, then, this love with which you join your hands and hearts
today never fail, but grow deeper and stronger as the years go on.
And if true love and the unselfish spirit of perfect sacrifice
guide your every action, you can expect the greatest measure
of earthly happiness that may be allotted to people in this vale of tears.
The rest is in the hands of God . . .

SOURCE: Adapted from the Catholic Nuptial Ceremony prior to 1968 (Grisez, n.d.).

When one considers the implications of a covenant relationship such as this, it seems to illustrate the amazing step from membership in a family of origin to forming a new unit. On the other hand the explicit commitment can be a road map protecting what actually will take many years to develop. Such explicit commitment is seen by some as gradually unfolding in a relational process over a lifetime, despite inevitable change, growth, and the vulnerabilities implicit in any personal relationship (see Rousseau, 1995; Shivananden, 1999; 2001; Wojtyla, 1981). In any case, commitment becomes a gradual process, unfolding (or deteriorating) through life circumstances and necessities, similar to Armand and Rosalind's experience (although perhaps less dramatic). In this sense, fidelity would not simply be the avoidance of infidelity. From the philosopher, Germain Grisez's (n.d.), point of view, fidelity becomes a willingness to accept the reality of the other as a different and changing person while that person emerges and changes over time. As implied in the covenant, this emergent self is partially unknown, even to the person. To restore the trust broken after their affairs, Armand and Rosalind (case study 3.2) had to reconstruct concretely and test a relationship that could eventually become a secure base for each other. Armand had to wait to accept Rosalind's hurt and anger before she could discover she had any positive feelings below the anger. Only then could mutual trust gradually and tentatively emerge.

The reality is that couples struggle to know each other all their lives, through their changes and often through the fog of their projections onto each other. Not all couples are able to understand relationships very well. In every case example in this chapter, the couple may have imbued some romantic ideas but really do not know each other well enough yet to become a couple in this personal sense. In the best of circumstances, it would take time for them to get to know each other better and form the personal bonds needed to develop a couple relationship. Each person starts from a different point on this journey into a personal relationship. When relationships become distressed, these starting points—what each thought was their commitment, what each aspires to, what each expects to be different, what each believes concretely he or she or they would be willing to change—is most important.

Object Relations   Object relations family therapists understand that an ossified fog of projections could be at the base of a relationship.[1] Operating from a psychodynamic orientation, they contribute concepts, originally from Melanie Klein, of introjective identification and projective identification. In *introjective identification*, the image of the other is introjected—that is, assumed whole and entire by ego—which then identifies with some or all of the other's perceived characteristics (Segal, 1973, p. 126; Scharff & Scharff, 1991). In *projective identification*, marital partners unconsciously project or externalize certain split-off or unwanted parts of themselves onto their partners, who in turn are manipulated to

---

[1]For further discussion of this school of family therapy, see Nichols (2013), Nichols and Schwartz (1998, ch. 7), Goldenberg and Goldenberg (1996, ch. 6), and Scharff and Scharff (1991).

behave in accordance with this projection. One partner might discover (and then reject) a once-denied and unacceptable part of the self in the other. As a consequence, each person attempts to reestablish contact with missing, repudiated, or unwanted parts of themselves through the other (Dicks, 1967). The other person is accepted or rejected on this basis. Much of their work with couples is helping them sort this out together (Scharff & Scharff, 1991). The well-known family therapist Carl Whitaker trenchantly commented on a couple getting divorced: "Find out who's getting divorced." A partner may be divorcing an unwanted part of the self, or even a part of the other, without ever taking in the otherness of the real spouse. In this case, the person has never made the personal and relational shifts involved in "getting married."

The normal relational tasks of early couplehood provide some escape into reality from initial constructions of the relationship envisioned and induced by one or both partners. Built into the relational tasks is the demand for some recognition of the other. Recognizing the reality of Sarah's back (case study 3.1), if nothing else, can bring Sarah and Phil to let go of patterns from Phil's family that both had taken for granted. When we begin to form a relationship with the other as other, not as a reflection of the self, it has to include both individuals as persons and thus transcend the initial expectations. Ideally, a couple, such as Brian and Lisa (case study 2.5), could transform unneeded parts of themselves in the light of their emerging relationship. All this takes time.

The heart of the work of the couple with the social worker is the couple's work with each other. Using couple communication as the medium for change, this work ranges from a focus on themselves as persons, to the relationships they have now as a couple, to the worlds of their families of origin, to their friends, to their work, and to other social institutions, all of which they may now confront together. As they restructure communications, little by little the couple can reconstruct the understandings and behaviors on which on which the structure of their relationship is based.

Personal Tasks and Couple Tasks

Personal tasks and couple tasks have a reciprocal, recursive relationship with each other. Working to develop communication, to develop compatible relationship patterns, and to become a functional couple (or family), each member works on personal tasks and couple tasks at the same time. Often the focus on couple tasks is also the most effective way to work on personal tasks. Jerry (case study 6.1) decided to do something about his drinking in hopes of saving his marriage. It is possible to help a member to work directly on personal tasks in the context of the relationship, and with the other member(s) assisting, as Armand did with Rosalind (case study 3.2), but the focus needs to be both on the personal task and the relational task—that is, for Jerry, the implications of his ceasing drinking for his relationship with Kathy and hers with him.

Personal work and relational work is essentially a two-step process. First the focal member needs to take charge of what he or she has to do to deal with a personal problem or concern. Then the relational effects of the decision need to be discussed; this discussion often leads to modification of the personal task or goal, as seen in the following two case studies.

CASE STUDY 6.1: JERRY AND KATHY

Jerry decided to do something about his drinking in hopes of saving his marriage. Jerry had to take charge of this problem and do something about it. Kathy, his wife, couldn't intrude in this and, in her anxiety about his drinking, take charge of it. Jerry had to learn to manage his problem without inappropriately involving Kathy; Kathy had to learn to support Jerry's efforts to become responsible without taking over by nagging him when he fails or absorbing the consequences for him. In their ongoing work over a number of sessions, the social worker started by helping Jerry, in Kathy's presence, make resolutions and a concrete plan to deal with the drinking, as well as to find a group and sponsor. Then the worker encouraged Jerry to talk with Kathy about how she could help him with this without taking over. Over multiple sessions, the couple worked on communication and other problems while Jerry's changes and Kathy's support went on in the background. Kathy, for her part, struggled with depression, but she developed a plan, worked with a therapist, and got medication. As she took action on her depression, Jerry supported her. Both continued to deal with the implications of these personal changes for their couple issues.

CASE STUDY 6.2: BILL AND JANE

All of his life Bill had patterns of attention deficit disorder. As an adult, he found it very difficult to remain focused, to work consistently, and to achieve in work as well as in other areas. His wife, Jane, a super-organized planner, struggled with other, very different issues. She was very self-critical, had low self-esteem, and tended toward depression. She relied on Bill's sense of humor and constant energy to cheer her up. When she was unhappy with his inconsistency or when he failed, however, she became an overly responsible parent figure to him and took over his work. When Bill was marginalized in this way, he would withdraw and become less adequate. This confirmed Jane's concerns about him. In a joint session with Bill and Jane, the worker helped Bill identify his patterns (without giving them a name), and asked him how he had compensated for them when he was in school. He responded that he always did better when the parameters were clearly set. Building on this, Bill developed his own five-point plan to deal with his patterns. When he had come to the point of taking charge of this, he was able, with the worker's help, to ask Jane to help keep him on track without taking over his tasks. They talked about this in detail and agreed. The remaining sessions were focused, among other issues, on helping them to carry this out, with Bill in charge of his personal tasks and Jane beginning to involve herself in a different way. The circular patterns began to reverse themselves.

None of this work is easy. Jerry may not succeed in doing something about his drinking, and Bill will continue to struggle with his difficulty in remaining focused. To persevere in the framework of the relationship demands a second step. Jerry will need Kathy's support and Bill will need Jane's, and vice versa. The tasks that come out of this work will last a lifetime.

COUPLES WITH FAMILY OF ORIGIN AND COMMUNICATION ISSUES

We can examine an overview of the helping process with couples by looking at the case of Rafael and Angie Vega.

CASE STUDY 6.3: RAFAEL AND ANGIE VEGA

Rafael and Angie Vega, married four years with no children, have experienced increasing arguments, particularly about Angie's perceived rejection by Rafael's family. Rafael is the oldest of a large and boisterous Mexican American family. His mother constantly involves him as the problem solver with this or that family situation as if he were not married at all. Rafael is spending many of his weekends and evenings on these missions. Also, when Rafael's family gets together, he is the center of rather loud interchanges with his brothers and his mother. Angie is feeling rudely ignored, left out, and lonely on all counts. Rafael is vaguely aware of Angie's feelings. He feels caught between loyalties to his wife and to his family and helpless to change the situation. Angie is the youngest and only girl of three children of a middle-class Polish-American family with very little verbal communication. Initially she was vague in depicting her family of origin, saying that everyone got along and they were certainly not like Rafael's wild family.

Rafael and Angie have different ways of communicating with each other. There is a demand/withdraw quality to their relationship. Angie pursues Rafael with her complaints, and Rafael responds by being full of words and generalities. Rafael has great difficulty getting to the point of his feelings and thoughts. Angie doesn't really engage with Rafael, except in terms of what she expects of him. She seems to have "married marriage" in Rafael but has not yet married Rafael as a person. She has few words to say to Raphael, but usually comes directly to the point. Her trenchant criticism is totally devastating to him. She is frustrated that she must be the demanding one and that Rafael isn't direct with her and that he tries to avoid her feelings. She is feeling trapped in a family she never married, without a relationship with Rafael, whom she did marry. The problems they have around communication reflect themselves also in their discussions around money. They have not worked out an agreement about money. Rafael wants above everything to get a home, and so he saves everything he can. Angie wants a home also, but not at the sacrifice of a good life now. She usually wins any discussion, since she is more direct and fluent with communication. Rafael is starting to resent this. Their marriage has been in this holding pattern for four years. In a pervasive climate of tentativeness, neither is able to make any plans for the future. In many ways, they have not yet gone through the process of "getting married."

Relational Tasks

Personal Tasks
- Rafael needs to come to terms with the fact that he has married Angie and that he will need to become more active.
- Rafael will need to make changes in his accustomed relations and patterns with his family of origin and with Angie to make the marriage work.
- Angie needs to disengage from the rigidity and abstractness of her own expectations of her relationship with Rafael, from her chronic disappointment and comparison of Rafael's family with what she expects a family should be and what she feels entitled to.

Couple Tasks
- Rafael and Angie need to develop different patterns of listening and expressing and of communication with each other.
- They both need to discuss productively their expectations of their own marriage and arrive at some conclusion that both can support.
- Rafael needs to disengage from his family and reengage with them in a way that includes Angie as his "best friend."
- Rafael and Angie need to develop the uniqueness of their own relationship as different from either of their families of origin.
- Angie needs to join with Rafael, putting herself into the picture in a different way; she needs to find a "third way" with Rafael that can be their own.
- They both need to work out a common pattern in relation to managing money.

Rafael and Angie did attempt these tasks in marriage counseling. The process took about six months of weekly sessions. Rafael did listen to Angie's concerns, and he agreed with them. He decided that he had married Angie and that she would have first place in his life. He had an opportunity to demonstrate this when one of his brothers got married and he was to be the best man. A bachelor party was scheduled on the weekend that he and Angie had planned to take a short and much-needed vacation. He felt an obligation to attend, but this would violate his understanding that he wanted to put his relationship with Angie in first place. After discussing this with Angie in their weekly counseling sessions, he told his family that he would not attend the party unless they rescheduled it at a better time. They did reschedule. Rafael did rework his relationships correspondingly with his family. Over time, they gradually did accept Angie's position in his life and thus in theirs. In their sessions, Rafael was discovering that he could be much more direct with Angie. Rafael's pursuit of Angie reversed the pattern, and Angie began to withdraw. Angie at first felt unable to respond immediately and personally to Rafael's new directness. Instead she kept raising her expectations of him, passing the task baton back to him. This was discouraging to Rafael, and there were times when both wondered whether it was all worth it.

Eventually Angie began to let go of her expectations of an abstract person in a spousal role and to commit herself to Rafael as a real person, and Rafael to her. As this took place, they were able to develop a different and mutually compatible communication pattern. Paradoxically, what Angie would never reveal previously came out only as she became more confident in her relationship with Rafael as a person. She had been deeply disappointed by her father's alcoholism, rarely discussed in her family except for recriminations. In many ways, she had placed Rafael in the impossible position of having to be the person that her father never had been to her. When she could let this go, she discovered Rafael to be a lovable, fallible human being who loved her and needed her. She found herself now able to respond to him as never before. When she did this, she became aware of her disappointment with her father. She was able to unburden herself about it to Rafael. As they completed the helping relationship, many of their issues were well on the path to resolution. At this point, they were in the process of buying a home and thinking about children. For both families of origin this became a concrete way for the couple to establish themselves as a new unit.

For Rafael and Angie, their early period of marriage eventually became a choice of each other in preference to images left over from other experiences. These would pass away as their relationship became personal. They could then begin to plan and think of next steps.

BEGINNING WITH COUPLES

Nowhere is the struggle of the social worker and the couple to find a collaborative stance clearer than in the beginning phase of the helping process. The time needed for the beginning phase may vary from one session to many more than one. The process can be quite difficult, both for the couple and for the social worker, partly because of the obvious uncertainties inherent in it. It is important for the social worker at least to have some sense of the overall process, of what may be possible to help the couple (Rafael and Angie) make a beginning. Although couples make very different uses of the social worker, and thus the process differs greatly in each case, the social worker needs first of all to help the couple develop a sense of what needs to be done and a sense that, with some direction and help, they can do it. The couple often feels utterly defeated. They keep coming back to their old adversarial and withdrawn patterns. They feel as if they are in a "mess" that only some expert can sort out. The social worker, little by little, begins to help them see this "mess" as a problem—that is, something that is not necessarily out of control. One can deal with a problem. Then in a more concrete way, in the initial and ongoing sessions, the problem becomes "tasks" to work on. These tasks inevitably involve communication, since without communication it is difficult to make other changes.

An assessment is made with the couple. The problem is partialized with tasks. There are session-by-session objectives—otherwise, the social worker is reinforcing the couple's sense of loss of control. It would be as if they were walking together through a strange and uninhabited forest with no map or trail, with no idea of where they are going or what they are trying to achieve. To bring back the sense of control, the social worker normalizes the problem. That is, the social worker puts it into the context of what could be expected in light of the circumstances, then places it into the framework of personal and relational tasks and places the tasks in some initial time framework.

Understanding and identifying personal and relational tasks will help a good deal. Tasks clarify goals, sort out what each needs to do, and clarify what each needs to do with each other to reach them. Such goals give direction to the couple's beginning, to the tasks of each session and between sessions, and to the later, middle-stage content of sessions with the couple. They clarify what the work will be. They indicate where to start and what the process might be like. Working together on the tasks, it is hoped that the couple's communication changes as well.

Couples in the beginning stage are usually not ready to begin. There is often too much hurt. They are afraid that if they risk openness, they will be hurt again. They wait for the partner to fulfill their expectations of change before they will venture out. Furthermore, communication patterns have usually become quite dysfunctional. To avoid the needed personal and relational work, each will often attempt to shift the onus to the partner and argue about who is to blame, setting the social worker up as a judge. To avoid this, it is best to help them immediately get focused on and discuss what they think can or should be different about their relationship, including what they bring to it. The social worker can help them to structure the communication so that each is able to listen to the other. The social worker can reframe the communication from an initial blame of the other to a more workable focus on what is possible and what needs to be done. A premature focus on trying to understand the problem as a problem can take the couple away from the prior question of what they think they can and want to achieve through their work together. It also can take the social worker away from a strengths-based beginning. In any case, the question of their goals is the key to the assessment process. Social workers can quietly gather history as they listen to the couple discuss what they want to deal with and observe their communication.

The following case study is an example of a beginning.

CASE STUDY 6.4:
SHERRY AND BILL

Sherry and Bill, both successful, high-powered lawyers, were experiencing increasing conflict around finances, their search for a house, and plans to accommodate their third child, due in four months. They "review options" with each other as if talking to a client. Their discussion is almost devoid of feelings until there is a sudden explosion and breakdown. Five months pregnant, Sherry is tired. She wants to participate, but shuts down quickly. At the same time she resents the fact that she is implicitly giving the power to Bill. Bill feels shut down, cut off from Sherry, and in a dilemma. Buying a house will demand that one of them take control of their finances. Bill will be wrong to take over without Sherry's consent, but he wants to get a house to accommodate their growing family, and he is not certain how long he can wait.

It took Sherry and Bill two sessions to make a beginning. Both needed help to listen to each other. When they cleared the air, both discovered that it was easier to communicate. They then moved on to deal with finances and their basic issue of how they as a couple together were to accommodate their third child.

As a result of the beginning session, the couple should have together developed some common understanding of the problem, seen it as something they could work on with each other, made a joint beginning on it, and agreed to continue to work on it in a specific way at home and in their sessions. The social worker's role is to help the couple do this—that is, to move from the phase of beginning and contracting to the next phase, the work phase. To do this, there is a joint process of assessment and actively testing out possibilities. The beginning place for this assessment is in the here and now—the tasks confronting the couple where they are—although the past is important and also needs to be addressed.

A great deal needs to take place at once within the agency's regular intake procedures. This can be enormously confusing to the social work practitioner and can be indirectly confusing to the couple, especially when the intake, often dictated by insurance regulations, focuses on individual symptoms and disorders, rather than the couple issues which brought them to seeking help. A focus on individual disorders also fits well into the blame cycles, as the couple wonders who of them is responsible for the problem. (Who is sick, disturbed or "irrational"?) A focus on individual disorders tends to "mystify" the problem. It keeps the professional in control of this exotic problem which only the therapist understands fully. In couples' and in family counseling, the control of the process is quite different from working with individuals. The social worker is helping two people to begin on something together: to come to an understanding, develop an agreement, and begin a process together, and do this in the context of the agency's procedures. To do this, they need to give up even an implicit focus on who is sick, disturbed, or to blame for all of this. Sometimes the process of doing this can take two sessions. One author routinely does a two-hour intake, which generally works very well. Both assessment and the process of beginning can then take place with the couple (not the therapist) firmly in control. The couple or whole family finishes with a fairly clear idea of what they need to do to remain in charge of their situation and what the next steps with the social worker would be.

Let us imagine the process of Rafael and Angie's beginning (case study 6.3).

The Very Beginning

The Phone Call   Angie calls the family agency after going around in circles once more with Rafael about his family. She is getting tired of it and feels trapped and not hopeful. But at least she could try. Lynn, a social worker, calls back. After hearing briefly about the situation, she makes the initial assessment with Angie that she is not asking for help with individual problems (her anxiety or sadness about a situation). The problem could best dealt with in a couple's counseling format. Could Angie and Rafael come in together to look at the possibility of working on this? Angie agrees to talk with Rafael and confirm whether they were interested. Lynn is very careful to ask Angie to come in with Rafael for the first session, since if Angie came in alone, Rafael might later feel an alliance between Lynn and Angie and be reluctant to come in. Lynn knows that she can't accomplish much without the two starting together. Later she may want to see one or the other alone, but they need to begin the process together and eventually come to a similar understanding of things.

The Opening   The room is set up comfortably, with two large chairs a quarter-turn toward each other and a small table with a lamp and a clock on it in the middle. There is a small swivel chair facing the two chairs. Lynn greets Rafael and Angie in the waiting room, introducing herself and shaking the hand of each. She makes brief personal contact. They go into her office, and she asks them to sit in the large chairs so that they face each other and Lynn. Some workers make small talk at this point to get the couple relaxed. Lynn is actually fairly relaxed already, and she finds that when she helps them to get to the issues in her own relaxed, but focused style, the couple also relaxes reasonably well. She reviews some of the face sheet information with them that provides the concrete details that one of them has already provided over the phone. She may set a fee at this time if it has not been already discussed over the phone. They will have to set an agreement by the end of the session. Acknowledging with Angie that they talked over the phone, she moves briefly to Rafael and joins with both about whether they have talked about some of these marriage issues in counseling before. She asks them to pretend that she is a distant relative who doesn't know much about their situation. This is a mutual inquiry process. In spite of her long experience as a couples' counselor, with each new couple Lynn has learned to be curious about what has been taking place; eventually she wants them to become curious also, rather than come with fixed assumptions or explanations (Anderson, 2012, pp. 15–16). In the beginning, they will have fixed assumptions, so this will take time.

Creating a Holding Environment   As the couple is beginning and the worker is assisting the beginning process, it is most important to create a holding environment where they can work on the problem. Michele Scheinkman has eight practical suggestions for doing this:

1. Position yourself with the couple in a balanced way, giving each partner equal time, empathy, and consideration.
2. Lend hope actively, reassuring the couple that there are ways of resolving the problem and that the process of change is incremental. It occurs step by step.
3. Suggest a time-limited period to suspend making decisions about the future (possibly six weeks). Encourage a systematic review process, looking at when and how they got off track and how they might try possible solutions. The review process and the set time limit gives the couple time to become less reactive and more reflective.
4. Help the couple manage communication in session, keeping a balance, not allowing interruptions or automatic defensive responses. They will talk about things that they were never able to discuss at home.
5. Acknowledge the strengths of the relationship, celebrating and amplifying the positive steps each partner makes and encouraging the other to do the same.

Sometimes Lynn may feel blocked and may need personal consultation to deal with the relation between her personal issues (feelings, vulnerabilities, family-of origin dynamics and those of the couple. She has learned to use consultation and supervision well (Scheinkman, 2008).

Getting Them Started and Making an Initial Assessment   Lynn wants Rafael and Angie to take control of the situation as quickly as possible and to get in communication with each other. She doesn't start by taking down a lot of details, thus centralizing herself as the expert responsible for solving the problem. Instead, she helps them start their story with the question of what changes they would like to see take place through marriage counseling, as well as of what they think in reality could take place. It is important that they start by focusing on possible changes. As they talk about the situation, she will ask them about it, and they will fill in the details for her.

In asking them to communicate with each other, she is asking them to do an *enactment* of their relationship. This is a face-to-face-couple interaction, in which they are carefully guided to successfully reenact their relationship in its real-life totality. Lynn will provide coaching for their process and attempt to assist them to achieve secure interaction around core issues. An enactment takes the focus away from Lynn and toward Rafael and Angie working on their issues. It is generally more effective than therapist-centered approaches, characterized by interaction channeled through the therapist, use of interpretation, and direct instruction. A therapist-centered process may temporarily contain and structure interaction for volatile couples, yet it may be counterproductive and disempower couples in their progress toward successful, self-reliant interaction (Butler, Harper, & Mitchell, 2011, p. 205). Rafael asks Angie to go first. Angie tells her story about Rafael's family. They are talking to each other, while Lynn listens carefully. She reflects what Angie is saying and normalizes the family-of-origin issues, asking Angie a few questions about her point of view. Rafael then tells his story, talking about how he feels caught in the middle and pointing out his difficulty communicating with Angie. Lynn reflects that, normalizing it for Rafael and asking him some questions, filling in a concrete picture of the couple with them. She is beginning to get a picture of concerns about Rafael's family and about their communication. She identifies this to them, and they agree that these are real concerns they need to work on. They have been talking to each other in the presence of Lynn. She is ready to help them go further into an enactment of their relationship so that she can help them communicate and gradually make some changes.

Sampling Communication Lynn starts by getting Rafael and Angie to start talking with each other. They have real difficulty communicating, so Lynn works directly with them on this, coaching them on positive communication, listening techniques, and so on. Lynn knows how easily she can get pulled into their adversarial or withdrawn cycles, but she cannot be aloof from their interaction either: it is a difficult balance. She actively works with them, setting enough structure so that each is able to express their different perceptions as well as their agreement, and the experience moves in a positive direction.

Agreeing on Personal and Relational Tasks and Defining a Possible Focus Lynn asks Rafael and Angie how the communication felt and gives some feedback. Out of this they identify some overall goals dealing with family-of-origin and communication issues. They feel they can work on these and want to get started.

Reaching a Contract, Agreeing on Next Steps, and Ending Reflecting some of their communication work, Rafael and Angie contract for further sessions with these goals. They now have some sense of what it is going to be like. Lynn gives them some communication tasks to try the first week, together with some ways of repairing communication when it breaks down. She points out that the first time they try these they will have difficulty and they shouldn't get discouraged. They set an appointment for the next week, and Lynn shakes the hand of each as they say goodbye.

Rafael and Angie's case is not particularly complicated. Because of that, it allows us to identify a couple's process of beginning. What is important here is that Rafael and Angie take charge of their process together and Lynn helps them to do it. They make an assessment together, and it comes out in a language of tasks and goals—what they may need to work on. Rather than steering the couple toward some goal of the worker, Lynn helps them find what is doable and gets them started. There is a real parallel with what she would do with an individual client in the beginning. The difference is that her focus is on the couples' beginning work primarily with each other rather than primarily with her. She intervenes in the couple's work to facilitate it, and in this sense the work goes much faster than work with individuals.

What the Worker Does: Skills

Using a classic listing (Shulman, 1992) of beginning and contracting skills for working with individuals, we may reframe these skills in relation to working with couples.[2]

- *Clarifying Worker's Purpose and Role.* The skill of clarifying purpose and role is essential with couples, but the worker is more decentralized in work with couples than in work with individuals; the focus for activity and the work is that of the couple with each other with the worker as coach.
- *Reaching for Feelings.* The worker reflects thoughts and feelings of each partner in the beginning and when they get stuck but as soon as possible helps the partners do this themselves with each other.
- *Putting a Client's Feelings into Words.* This is the skill of articulating feelings in response to tuning in to indirect and direct communication. The couples' social worker works actively between the partners, helping them recognize implicit messages without becoming too centralized and shutting down their communication.
- *Reaching Inside of Silences.* Silence in couples' work can be an extremely powerful tool, used to "wait out" the couple's struggle to deal with some of their issues. With certain cultures, such as Native American cultures, silence may be an indication of personal work, rather than a diversion from work or an indication of difficulty. When silence seems to feel uncomfortable to the couple, the worker may ask them to talk about their uncomfortable silence and actively help them reach into that.
- *Partializing Concerns.* Partializing concerns is very important in couples work. The key to this is to move from a "mess" to a problem, to relational tasks, and to specific session-by-session objectives. Helping the couple set goals, differentiating personal and relational tasks, and setting specific assignments all help the couple to do this, but the primary means of partializing concerns is that the communication of the couple is skillfully focused by the worker.
- *Assessment.* The goal of assessment is for the couple and worker together to understand the problem and then to set objectives and plan the intervention. It is important that assessment be focused on possible change rather than on all that went wrong. The beginning assessment should generate some ideas from the couple for personal and relational tasks: ideas of what *should* be

---

[2]These skills are developed in greater detail in Shulman (1992) and, in a slightly different format, in Hepworth, Mooney, and Larson (1997).

changed and of what *can* be changed. The process takes place through reflective communication by the couple, with the social worker actively moving back and forth between them.

- *Contracting.* Contracting is an effort to establish the purpose of the work, to establish appropriate roles, to give feedback, and to deal with issues of authority. Out of a tentative assessment, an initial agreement with each other and with the social worker should emerge. In couples work, the purpose and contract is established first of all *with each other*, and then with the social worker and agency. What the worker needs to do is to listen carefully, reflect, and help the couple when there is hesitancy or ambivalence about the process. Identifying hesitancy often opens up issues they were afraid to bring up: doubts, concerns, reluctance to get involved, or a need to have the social worker take charge of the problem. What do they think they can do to accomplish these changes?

Rafael and Angie's situation is useful for its simplicity as a clear illustration of beginning work on the couple relationship. Most situations are more complex. Social workers may work with many couples where there is stress on the bond from several fronts at once, depending on the beginning perception of the problem(s). Perhaps there is a new child and one of the parents is very ill. Perhaps the husband has an addictions problem, or there has been an affair, or one of the grandparents dies. Perhaps the parents are age 16 and 17, without good employment, unable to support themselves, and with a very uncertain relationship. Perhaps one of the parents becomes severely depressed, or a baby—expected to be "perfect"—is born with a disability. One begins where the clients are.

The Miracle Question   When the beginning is difficult, several solution-focused techniques are often quite useful to get the process moving in a good direction (deShazer, 1985; 1988; 1991). One technique is a variant of the miracle question. The miracle question is: "Suppose one night when you were asleep, there was a miracle and the problem was solved by morning. How would you know? What would be different?" This question switches the focus from negative to the positive. It also asks each partner to think about what differences would tell them the problem was solved. Another similar approach is the exception question. Rather than focusing on the problem, this focuses on the times the couple didn't have the problem when ordinarily they would. By exploring the differences (exceptions), they can discuss how these exceptions can be expanded. This also makes the problem seem less overwhelming, and it can lead from an initial agreement to beginning work together on the problem. We will see an example of middle-stage use of some of these techniques in case study 7.6, Bonnie and Andy Kowalski's case.

Unrecognized Gender Inequalities   Developing effective communication means reciprocal and equitable recognition of the other as a person. Communication about relational tasks thus often automatically demands an internal rebalancing of inequitable relationships. In examples given so far, Sarah and Phil (case study

3.1), Miguel and Juana (case study 3.2), Brian and Lisa (case study 3.3), and Rafael and Angie Vega (case study 6.3), the couples developed their own balances. Often, as with Miguel and Juana and also with Sarah and Phil, the internal rebalancing needed in relation to family of origin, roles, or other issues also rebalanced gender inequalities without much discussion other than recognizing what had happened. This is because if they are going to work effectively on a relational problem, nothing constructive will happen without some rebalancing. The social worker can help them with this as she coaches the enactment. Sometimes, however, the inequalities so profoundly influence the couple's relational work that the automatic rebalancing does not seem to be taking place, and the social worker may need to get more active. Nichols and Schwartz (2002, p. 97) point out the single most useful question to ask about gender inequality: "How does each partner experience the fairness of give-and-take in their relationship?" Built on this question, all of the relational tasks can be reconfigured in a way compatible with the couple's perceptions and with a more balanced relationship.

PROBLEMS IN DEVELOPING COMMITMENT

Frequently the social worker's involvement is sought to shore up a failing structure where the unacknowledged problem is basic commitment to the relationship as a relationship. In the following case, personal tasks and issues have overshadowed any desire or ability of the couple to construct love and fidelity in a relationship.

CASE STUDY 6.5:
JOHN AND EILEEN

John and Eileen were referred to a family service agency by the court, which was supervising John for substance abuse. The couple, married for four years and with a 3-year-old child, has been separated for a year. Their marital history has been stormy. Eileen, a "perfect" child with an opinionated mother and a weak, silent father, married John as an act of rebellion and moved out-of-state with him. John's heavy drinking and drug habits were evident from the beginning of the relationship. Their relationship never developed further or dealt effectively with this problem. During the first years, there were numerous separations

and instances of violence, culminating in an incident in which John threw a knife at Eileen and severed a tendon in her arm. John was periodically unemployed. Eileen, who has had very little experience managing for herself, finally was able to leave after three years of "hell." Eileen, now living on her own, with the support of a local church, family members, and a part-time job, is managing a precarious independence with her child. John came back two months ago with the expectation of a reunion. He stopped his drug use two months ago and his heavy drinking two weeks ago. He gets about twelve to twenty hours of construction work a week, and his family continues to take care of him. He attends AA now, but isn't sure he is ready for either the program or a sponsor. He doesn't seem to be too concerned about his probation. He rejects the idea of doing work on his addictions program, but doesn't understand why Eileen is fearful and uncertain about getting back together. In the joint interview both talk about themselves, but there is very little mutual communication. Eileen withdraws quickly when he makes a demand, and that only draws out his incredulity. He openly questions why Eileen is so fearful, but it seems as if he knows the answer already.

In this case, the social worker heard Eileen's grave doubts and concerns about working on the relationship and reflected them back to the couple. They decided not to initiate work on their relationship until and unless they had done something about their pressing personal issues. Eileen decided to work individually on her issues. When offered further help with his concerns, John said he would think about it and call back, but he never did.

Sometimes the problem is that the couple has not yet made a commitment to each other. They haven't really "gotten married." In the following case, only one partner was seen. Although having both available might have been likely to be more effective, in this case, one person became anxious around communication and the possibilities of relational change. He would not be directly available to participate in the helping process. Nevertheless, the tasks remained if they were to construct a secure base for the relationship. The social worker did work with the other partner, helping her to deal with the situation as best she could. As in the case of Armand and Rosalind (case study 4.3), Sandy's systematic work helps Sheldon make a commitment. While less obvious than John and Eileen, they might have otherwise discovered that the commitment was nothing that could be built upon.

CASE STUDY 6.6:
SHELDON AND SANDY

Over their year of marriage, Sheldon, an engineer, has been chronically uncertain about his commitment to Sandy, a nurse. They have had severe marital conflict whenever the question of his commitment is raised. He says he married only because he felt he couldn't call off the ceremony, but he never made a permanent commitment. He is uncertain that he wants to stay married and has excluded any thought of children. He was particularly shaken when he heard that Sandy had briefly used drugs in college. He felt that she was "damaged goods" and on "probation" with him. He will decide whether they should continue their marriage or not. His life patterns of chronic ambivalence suggests obsessive compulsive disorder (OCD) and depression, but he keeps delaying getting help. He terminated marital counseling after two contacts because he was overwhelmed with the idea of talking to Sandy about his feelings and listening to her feelings.

Sandy continued using counseling. She decided to work on her part of the relationship with the aim of giving six months for them to either make a permanent commitment to each other or break up. As she learned to manage the situation better, conflict did drop off. They got along fairly well as long as the issue of his commitment didn't come up. He decided to let go of his concerns about her past, but he remained uncertain about commitment. In her work alone with Sandy, the social worker coached her to help Sheldon test out his commitment to her without demanding that he put feelings into words. Their communication took place in a more concrete way, through what was taking place in the relationship. With Sandy's patience, Sheldon eventually resolved his chronic ambivalence. They jointly recognized these changes in his feelings about trust and relationships and decided to recommit their marriage promises to each other in a private ceremony.

In the beginning of the case, Sheldon had not yet made a commitment to Sandy. There seemed to be only a slight chance that Sheldon would ever make a commitment. Sheldon could have been asking for individual help, but he refused any initiatives in this direction. Sheldon has great difficulty communicating. He found tasks of communicating with Sandy about feelings and changing their relationship overwhelming. Similar to Armand and Rosalind (case study 4.3), Sandy decided to work individually on the relationship. With Sheldon's anxiety around communication and explicit change, the emphasis had to be on tasks and emergent implicit understandings.

The paradox is that when it came to day-to-day issues with very limited communication, their relationship did work. Sandy asked for Sheldon's commitment within six months as the price for hers. She worked on being available to him in his limited efforts to communicate, without pursuing him. This put Sheldon in a situation in which Sandy touched on what both needed if their relationship was to grow. There would be a certain amount of time for Sheldon to respond. In any case, the work with Sandy continued with personal and relational tasks. She remained available to him, but she would not merely accept Sheldon's lack of commitment. She expected more. When Sheldon did take the step of recognizing his real commitment to her, she was able with help to support him without making her decision his decision.

COUPLE COMMUNICATION AND MRE IN SOME ASIAN COUNTRIES

In some Asian countries (Korea, Japan and Taiwan, mainland China), experiencing rapid economic growth, urbanization, and changing cultural norms, the traditional Confucian family ethic coexists with enhanced choices for women, growing individualism, the rise of romantic love, and a rapidly rising divorce rate (Huang, 2005, p. 162). While the understanding of "family" changes rapidly between generations, its importance remains and even grows. Communication can be particularly difficult for couples when the traditional norms are that problems are not to be directly addressed, only indirectly. In the past women often faced issues of control with their spouse and mother-in-law. Many quietly endured extramarital affairs and abuse. Many believed they might face retribution if they would speak their minds (Huang, 2005, p. 171). From a Western perspective, the relationship might seem to be out of balance. In this context, there is a remarkable study of Asian couples' communication involving videotaped recordings of fifty couples from Korea, Japan, Taiwan, Hong Kong, and mainland China. Couples were asked to discuss "an unresolved disagreement"—"things they had not yet reached an agreement about" (Lee, Nakamura, Chung, Chun, Fu, Liang, & Liu, 2013, pp. 499–518). Because they had not reached agreement, and because they were communicating in front of the camera, a "crisscross of monologues" would be an unsurprising result (Lee, Nakamura, Chung, Chun, Fu, Liang, & Liu, 2013, p. 500).

The article found systematic differences in communication. Communication ranged from polite, conflict-avoidant, but less direct communication to the more direct communication of the following couple with an unhappy wife whose husband had withdrawn into the kitchen (vignette 1). Nevertheless, in that vignette, in seven succinct sentences, the couple expressed what they wanted from their marriage and from each other, as well as their dilemmas in achieving it. However the vignette is still less of a conversation than a crisscross of monologues. Each statement provides a context for the other, but there is very little reflection or response to what the other is saying. Paradoxically, they did say it, and quite directly:

Vignette 1
Wife: All I ever wanted is to be like a little bird resting on my husband's chest.
Husband: I never see you acting like one. You only scold me for failing to please you.
Wife: Cooking is not your strength, and teaching the children homework is not mine. Why can't we switch our roles?
Husband: The children only listen to you. Since you don't think that I am any good, they have no respect for me, either (Lee, Nakamura, Chung, Chun, Fu, Liang, & Liu, 2013, p. 500).

Vignette 2 is more of a conversation. This couple takes longer to get to the point than Vignette 1, but not much longer. Although both husband and wife can be ironic with each other, it is a blend of conversation, with both listening and reflecting the others' points, and monologue at other times. It breaks down into a crisscross of monologues at the point when the husband says, "I don't hit you":

Vignette 2
Husband: I am under a lot of pressure. When my mood fluctuates, I still smile and act silly.
Wife: I gave you a lot of room. I am tolerant of you. I don't argue with you.
Husband: Yes, you have. But it's not as easy as you think. That's why I don't want to bother with the two kids.
Wife: I know. So I take care of them. Then I tell you how they behave.

Husband: But you can't always be the good mother and me the bad father. Now when I explain things to the daughters, they think I am nagging them.

Wife: I know when you are pouring your heart out, but you don't consider the situation.

Husband: I don't hit you.

Wife: Do you consider it an honor because you don't hit me?

Husband: Of course. There are so many domestic violence cases. I want to tell you that actually I am very respectful of you.

Wife: I want to tell you that I appreciate it. I want to do all the chores before you get up. I will not demand my kids to do the housework.

Husband: This is what I want to tell you. I think you spoil our kids, (Lee, Nakamura, Chung, Chun, Fu, Liang, & Liu, 2013, pp. 510–511)

These vignettes of couple communication, some less direct, sometimes speaking mainly in metaphor, eventually express efficiently what each wants from each other and from their relationship. They want far more than a formal arrangement. This type of communication in a Western context could be quite explosive and defensive, with recriminations and accusations—in some ways a bit more dangerous. In both examples there is an eventual need for focus and reflection, setting goals and working on chosen issues. But here there seems to be somewhat of a holding system if the couple is willing to work on their issues. A family therapist or family educator with ears attuned to couple communication and an ability to teach them to listen and respond to each other could work with them to build a more secure relational base, but in a different way and with a different speed than with some of the other cases in this book. Transcultural assessment and intervention is necessary. On the other hand for a single couple the pressure of communicating with each other systematically and in the presence of a counselor weekly over a three- to six-month period could be very difficult.

MARRIAGE AND RELATIONSHIP EDUCATION WITH COUPLES

Marriage and relationship education has become an extremely popular approach to working with some of the common issues young couples face. By the late 1990s, between one-quarter and one-third of couples contemplating marriage in the United States, Australia, and Britain were attending some form of relationship education. The focus of MRE has since broadened to include couples at all points of the family life cycle and families with a member having special needs. The distinction between family education, group work, and family therapy is now becoming more fluid, since all three forms of intervention develop somewhat similar skills in somewhat different ways. In some ways these groups combined aspects of education and individualized family intervention, so that, in what they aim for, they could be best seen along a continuum. Educational approaches provide space for couples who might profit from learning skills but who might be more comfortable in a group format.

While there is a great need for counseling, Asian couples seem to prefer education to "therapy" (Huang, 2005, p. 169). Marriage and relationship education, discussed hereafter, may provide more space for couples to experiment with change on their own, leaving them in control of how much of the problem they make public. At the same time the "all in the same boat" experience in the group serves to normalize their experience without public shame or blame. A group experience also may make them less reluctant to attempt individual relational work with each other. Many countries, such as Singapore, Taiwan, and China, actively promote MRE. For example, all Taiwanese couples are required to receive four hours of relationship education before marriage. In China, 600 two-and-a-half minute programs on marriage and parent-child relationships have been translated into Mandarin and broadcast on the 400 stations of China National Radio. They deliver spot messages such as: "love requires learning," "commitment matters," "no apology: true love waits," and "forgiveness" (Huang, 2005, pp. 165–167).

There has been a broadening of the target groups for MRE. There is more involvement of married couples or couples living together, and experiencing issues at every stage of the family life cycle: with newly married couples, with parents with young children, with parents with adolescents, with couples dealing with their aging parents, or with particular problem situations, such as death, widows groups, families facing divorce, illness, stepfamilies and families with children with disabilities, or women who have had abortions. More recently, there has been movement into using MRE with low-income and highly distressed couples, couples who normally were served with a more individualized approach.

In a review of MRE done to date, Halford and Moore (2002) classified three major approaches to relationship education with couples. The most popular approach aimed at *information and awareness*. This approach emphasized the transmission of information about relationships and marriage, helping the couple clarify expectations, and increasing awareness of key relationship processes that influence outcomes. There might be a demonstration of relationship skills, but there was little training in these skills (Halford and Moore, 2002, p. 400).

In another approach, often used with couples considering marriage, the prospective partners completed *self-report inventories*, which assessed a broad range of dimensions of couple functioning. The couple was then provided with systematic feedback about the results of these inventories (Halford and Moore, 2002, p. 401). These results led to discussion, but there was no systematic training in skills, such as communication or conflict management.

A third broad category involved *skill training*: communication, solving problems, managing negative expressions of feeling, development of commitment to the relationship, dealing with the family of origin of the couple, etc. (Halford and Moore, 2002, pp. 401–402). In any case, the concept of learning moved from information to analysis to a rich and deep sharing of experience with the goal of change. At the same time, the expected involvement of a couple or family members varied from one session (information) to three months (fifteen sessions) of work, together with between-session work. The support of the larger group helped individual family participants to put their situation into perspective, make assessments of their situations, develop their own resources, reach out to each other for help, and so forth. There is practice in good communication, listening, "I-messages" and problem resolution skills, attitudes and behaviors associated with marital success or failure. Studies showed that these relationship factors were amenable to change by educational interventions (Hawkins, Blanchard, Baldwin, & Fawcett, 2008).

At present, the most popular emerging approaches are longer-term (more than one session) combinations of all three emphases. There is a deepening of focus toward skills in communication, problem solving, attitudes and learning to manage their emotions better in conflict conversations. Many programs also help couples learn and practice good listening and problem solving skills and discuss and resolve different expectations about their relationship. For example, an engaged couples' group would work on learning to communicate appropriately and resolve problems, dealing with issues coming from their own families of origin, personal and shared goals, money, discerning their degree of commitment to a permanent relationship, discussing differences and similarities, and so forth. Some programs also emphasize the importance of marital virtues such as commitment, loyalty, fairness and forgiveness. Some address specific topics, such as balancing work and family demands, managing finances, or sexuality (Hawkins & Ooms, 2010, p. 5). In any case, the group gets to know each other, forming a group bond and developing group norms. These combined approaches last longer and use group discussion, individual couple role plays and exercises, use of inventories, with individual participants' keeping journals on particular themes. Leaders often act as mentors for individual couples as they go through the exercises.

In a recent review of MRE, Jay Lebow (2013, p. 351) commented that most of these programs incorporate the best of the modernist view of the value of teaching skills to families and the postmodern view of supporting families in their local knowledge about themselves. There have been a variety of studies of the effectiveness of diverse family education in a North American and western European context. These programs have generally proved to be quite effective for the investment of time among participants who complete the program and the evaluation research instrument (Fagan, Patterson, & Rector, 2002). An early study of twenty different marriage preparation programs found that an average couple completing any one of the programs would be better off than two-thirds of other couples who did not participate (Giblin, Sprenkle, & Sheehan, 1985). Later evaluation studies have replicated these results (Hahlweg and Markman, 1988; Hahlweg, Markman, Thurmair, Engel, & Eckert, 1998). Reviews showed that MRE programs were effective in improving relationship quality and even more effective in improving communications skills (Hawkins & Ooms, 2010, pp. 12–13). Program gains seemed to be generally maintained, although longer-term studies have not yet been done. In any case, most of the earlier studies predominantly involved middle class, well-educated, nondistressed couples. There is some early evidence that MRE programs targeted to more distressed couples can have small to moderate effects in improving couple relationships. Other populations at risk, and parental relationships might also benefit

(Hawkins & Ooms, 2010, p. 14). In the face of the popularity of these programs and the enormous emphasis on family in North America, would the same results be found in other parts of the world? In North America, there is often a great cultural readiness to trust the group process enough to talk with strangers about personal issues and problems. What adaptations and what sponsorship would make this promising tool work elsewhere?

Individual work with individual couples is far more focused on the particular situation of a particular couple, such as Rafael and Angie. Thus Lynn could act as a mentor to Rafael and Angie's halting attempts to communicate well, Rafael's work with his family of origin, Angie's with hers, developing a common pattern of managing money, and so forth. For some couples, this is too intense. It may demand too much prior commitment or exact too great an emotional cost. They may not be ready for this more personal approach, which lasts for Rafael and Angie as long as they are willing to work on their relational tasks with Lynn. Marriage and relationship education is a more fixed format with a predetermined set of sessions with other couples who are at a somewhat similar stage of learning about their family life cycle situation. It has a fixed ending. Here the group leader may skillfully use the experience of the group to teach and learn about relationships. The leader may assist the couples themselves, going through similar life cycle challenges, to use their own experiences so that couples develop a deeper understanding of their own life cycle tasks. To the extent this is done, the MRE group can be in many ways a more powerful stimulus for learning than either an abstract discussion and presentation, or even a more individualized focus with Lynn as a mentor.

Let us imagine Rafael and Angie now in a group. Within the powerful context of a group bond, Rafael and Angie may also experiment with different ways of communicating and developing other skills appropriate to their situation. The experience of communicating better and of developing other relationship skills could lead them to a deepened commitment to each other. The first powerful contribution of couples groups to Rafael and Angie's learning would be that the experiences, dynamics, personal and relational tasks of a particular stage of their family life cycle can be *normalized* through the shared experience of other couples in the group.

CASE STUDY 6.7:
A FISHBOWL DISCUSSION OF FAMILY-OF-ORIGIN ISSUES

A young, married couples group for couples in their first one to five years of marriage was sponsored by Rafael and Angie's church. Taking place over fifteen sessions, the group topics covered couple communication, managing finances, balancing work expectations, dealing with family of origin issues, the onset of children, and so on. By the third session of the group Rafael and Angie had gotten to know a few other couples. Previously, there had been some general presentations on early marriage. The second session was on communication, with volunteer couples role playing a discussion of planning a vacation and learning skills of focused listening, "I-messages," and problem solving. Then they broke out into five "buzz groups" of four couples each. Each couple was able to experiment with the skills and get feedback from the other couples. Rafael and Angie saw other couples struggling with the same communication issues they were struggling with—some doing better, some not as well. When Rafael and Angie's turn came up to discuss planning a vacation, Angie was full of suggestions, and Rafael was uncertain whether he could schedule anything until he had checked with his family. Exasperated, Angie flatly asked him why he ever got married in the first place. In the buzz group's subsequent discussion of their communication, a woman told Angie, "Honey, if you talk like that to your husband, you're on your way to a split." Angie responded, "That's the only way they did it in my family." A Mexican man from the buzz group told Rafael that he wasn't giving his wife enough respect when he put his original family ahead of Angie. The buzz groups then had a reporting session to the group as a whole. A lively discussion ensued about the many communication difficulties. They all resolved to slow down communication and work on listening and responding skills.

The third session was on family of origin issues. This time, the format was different. In the beginning the facilitator spent ten minutes discussing shifting and balancing loyalties from the family of origin to the spouse. They then used an open fishbowl technique with two volunteer couples, two empty chairs, and the facilitator in the center, the

other couples surrounding the "fishbowl" (see figure 6.2).[3] Angie was ready to talk about family of origin and volunteered with Rafael willing to go along, although somewhat reluctant. Each couple took fifteen minutes in the fishbowl group to discuss what they encountered with family of origin. This was followed by general discussion within the group, and other couples could join the fishbowl to comment or discuss their experiences. Twenty minutes of general discussion involving the fishbowl, the facilitator, and the observers concluded the exercise. When it was Angie and Rafael's turn to discuss in the fishbowl, Angie initiated by talking about the last New Year's party, where she felt isolated with Rafael the center of attention, discussing how he would fix the brakes on his brother's car. Rafael agreed that they had gotten into too much man-talk. But he was frustrated that Angie just can't hold her own with the family at all. His family was loud and fun, and frustrating; Angie's family was quiet and tense until someone misspoke, and then they all came down on that person. Angie agreed that her family was difficult as well. She wouldn't want to have a family like either of theirs. Rafael agreed, but wondered how they could combine some of their good points. The other couple in the fishbowl, when it was their turn, talked about different issues, but both couples were puzzled about what they wanted their own family to be like. When the time came for broader group discussion, there were a number of volunteers from the observers for the empty

---

[3]There are good discussions of the Fishbowl Technique available. The Intermediate Training Group of the International Labor Organization has one at http://itcilo.wordpress.com/2009/2/16/facilitate-a-fishbowl-discussion/.

fishbowl chairs. Some, sharing their own experience, could understand Rafael's point of view; some Angie's. All appreciated that Rafael and Angie would need to work out something together that would preserve their connections but that didn't allow either family of origin to take over.

Figure 6.2
The Fishbowl

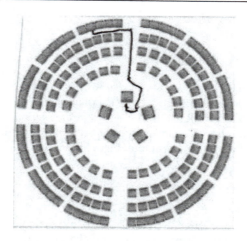

The arrangement of chairs in a fishbowl session. Four concentric rings of chairs surround a smaller group of five chairs. The arrow indicates how any member of the audience may enter the middle section. As depicted in figure 6.2, four or five chairs are in an inner circle. This is the "fishbowl." The remaining chairs are arranged in circles around the fishbowl. A few participants are selected for the center fishbowl, and the remainder of the group sits around the fishbowl. In an open fishbowl, one or two chairs are left empty to be filled by someone from the audience, wanting to respond to the discussion. With a good discussion, a number of members of the audience will join the fishbowl. In a closed fishbowl, all chairs are filled. The group leader introduces the discussion, and the fishbowl members start discussing the topic as the audience listens. As time runs out, the group leader will summarize the discussion.

Source: United Nations, International Labor Organization, http://itcilo.wordpress.com/2009/2/16/facilitate-a-fishbowl-discussion/.

Rafael and Angie learned from their third-session experience. The following twelve sessions covered other topics. Outside the group, they experimented with different ways of communicating but still tended to get into a demand/withdraw style. Rafael was able to set some boundaries with his family, which made things somewhat better, but the big job was still to work on their own communication and to attempt to develop a better understanding of what sort of family they wanted for themselves. The fifteen-session group had helped them a great deal. Angie is certain they would have split otherwise. They decided together to initiate marital counseling with a very focused request—to work on their communication, on their family-of-origin issues, and on the family they wanted to be in the future.

There are many variations of MRE, depending on the objectives, the common issues to be dealt with, the time available, and the participants. Any type of family education requires careful planning. The key to planning is defining learning tasks clearly in relation to the family developmental stages and needs of the participants and the time available. After defining the learning tasks appropriately, there are a variety of group learning and sharing processes that can be employed and combined, such as direct instruction, group discussion, buzz groups, fishbowl, and the like (LeCroy & Wooten, 2002; Pawlak, Wozniak, and McGowan, 2002).

SUMMARY

Beginning with couples is complex because the tasks of gaining an understanding of the problem (assessment) and helping the couple make their own beginning may seem to be in conflict. However, as the social worker assists the couple to make this beginning, so will the middle stage go. MRE provides another way to help couples develop skills. It also, as with Rafael and Angie, may be a springboard for more direct work in marital counseling. The following chapter looks at middle-stage work, relating social work practice theory at middle stages to the developmental and personal issues of couples.

REFERENCES

Anderson, H. (2012). Collaborative relationships and dialogic conversations: Ideas for a relationally responsive practice. *Family Process, 51*(1), 15–16.

Butler, M. H., Harper, J. M., & Mitchell, C. B. (2011). A comparison of attachment outcomes in enactment-based versus therapist-centered therapy process modalities in couple therapy. *Family Process, 50*(2), 205.

Dicks, H. V. (1967). *Marital tensions.* New York, NY: Basic Books.

deShazer, S. (1985). *Keys to a solution in brief therapy.* New York, NY: Norton.

deShazer, S. (1988). *Clues: Investigating solutions in brief therapy.* New York, NY: Norton.

deShazer, S. (1991). *Putting differences to work.* New York, NY: Norton.

Fagan, P. F., Patterson, R. W., & Rector, R. E. (2002). *Marriage and welfare reform: The overwhelming evidence that marriage education works.* Backgrounder # 1606. Washington, DC: The Heritage Foundation. Accessed at www.heritage.org/research/welfare/bg1606.cfm.

Giblin, P., Sprenkle, D. H., & Sheehan, R. (1985). Enrichment outcome research: A meta-analysis of marital, premarital and family interventions. *Journal of Marital and Family Therapy, 11*, 257–271.

Goldenberg, I., & Goldenberg, H. (1996). *Family therapy: An overview* (4th ed.). Pacific Grove, CA: Brooks-Cole.

Gottman, J. M. (1999). *The marriage clinic.* New York, NY: Norton.

Gottman, J. M., Driver, J., & Tabares, A. (2002). Building the sound marital house: An empirically derived couple therapy. In A. S. Gurman & N. S. Jacobson (Eds.), *Clinical handbook of couple therapy* (3rd ed., pp. 373–399). New York, NY: Guilford.

Grisez, G. (n.d.). *Fidelity today.* Privately published.

Halford, W. K., & Moore, E. N. (2002). Relationship education and the prevention of couple relationship problems. In A. S. Gurman & N. S. Jacobson (Eds.), *Clinical handbook of couple therapy* (3rd ed., pp. 400–419). New York, NY: Guilford.

Hahlweg, K., & Markman, H. J. (1988). Effectiveness of BMT: Empirical status of behavioral treatment in families in alleviating marital distress. *Journal of Consulting and Clinical Psychology, 56,* 440–447.

Hahlweg, K., Markman, H. J., Thurmair, F., Engel, J., & Eckert, J. (1998). Prevention of marital distress: Results of a German prospective longitudinal study. *Journal of Family Psychology, 12,* 543–556.

Hargrave, T. (2000). *The essential humility of marriage: Honoring the third identity in couple therapy.* Phoenix, AZ: Zeig, Tucker & Theisen.

Hawkins, A. J., & Ooms, T. (2010). *What works in marriage and relationship education?* National Healthy Marriage Resource Center. Accessed at www.healthy marriageinfo.org/resourcedetail/index/aspx?rid=2861.

Hawkins, A. J., Blanchard, V. L., Baldwin, S. A., & Fawcett, E. B. (2008). Does marriage and relationship education work? A meta-analytic study. *Journal of Consulting and Clinical Psychology, 76,* 723–734.

Hepworth, D. H., Mooney, R. H., & Larson, J. A. (1997). *Direct social work practice* (4th ed.). Belmont, CA: Brooks-Cole.

Huang, W. (2005). An Asian perspective on marriage and relationship education. *Family Process, 44*(2), 161–174.

Lebow, J. (2013). Programs for strengthening families. *Family Process, 52*(3), 351–354.

Lee, W., Nakamura, S., Chung, M., Chun, Y. J., Fu, M., Liang, S., & Liu, C. (2013). Asian couples in negotiation: A mixed-method, observational study of cultural variations across five Asian regions. *Family Process, 52*(3), 499–518.

LeCroy, C. W., & Wooten, L. (2002). Social skills groups in schools. In R. T. Constable, S. McDonald, & J. P. Flynn (Eds.), *School social work: Practice policy and research perspectives* (pp. 441–457). Chicago, IL: Lyceum Books.

Nichols, M. P. (2013). *Family therapy: Concepts and methods* (10th ed.). Boston, MA: Pearson.

Nichols, M., & Schwartz, R. (1998). *Family therapy: Concepts and methods* (3rd ed.). New York, NY: Allyn & Bacon.

Nichols, M., & Schwartz, R. (2002). *Family therapy: Concepts and methods* (4th ed.). New York, NY: Allyn & Bacon.

Pawlak, E., Wozniak, D., & McGowan, M. (2002). *Perspectives on groups for school social workers.* In R. T. Constable, S. McDonald, and J. P. Flynn (Eds.), *School social work: Practice policy and research perspectives* (pp. 404–421). Chicago, IL: Lyceum Books.

Rousseau, M. F. (1995). Fairest love: John Paul II on the family. *Anthropotes, 11*(2), 167–183.

Scheinkman, M. (2008). The multi-level approach: A road map for couples therapy. *Family Process, 47*(2), 200.

Scharff, D. E., & Scharff, J. S. (1991). *Object relations family therapy*. New York, NY: Jason Aronson.

Segal, H. (1973). *Introduction to the work of Melanie Klein*. London, UK: Heinemann.

Shivananden, M. (1999). *Crossing the threshold of love: A new vision of marriage*. Washington, DC: Catholic University of America Press.

Shivananden, M. (2001). Subjectivity and the order of love. *Fides Quaerens Intellectum, 1*(2), 251–274.

Shulman, L. (1992). *The skills of helping: Individuals, families and groups* (3rd ed.). Itasca, IL: Peacock.

Wojtyla, K. (Pope John Paul II). (1981). *Love and responsibility*. New York, NY: Farrar, Straus, Giroux.

CHAPTER 7

Middle Phases with Couples

KEY TOPICS

Middle-Stage Couples Work
Development of the Couple's Problem-Solving and Relational Capacities
Intimacy, Boundaries, and Communication Processes
Communication, Empathic Accuracy, and Relational Reconstruction
Middle-Stage Skills: The Work Phase
The Use of Tasks and Assignments
Decision-Making Processes and the Family
The Post-Parental Stage
The Needs of Families, the Social Worker as a Person, and the Helping Process

This chapter relates social work practice theory and personal issues of couples at the middle phase of the life cycle to development of their own problem-solving and relational capacities. The discussion of middle-phase skills focuses on intimacy, boundaries, communication, decision making, and task prescription. These themes are developed through cases. The chapter ends with focus on the qualities needed in the social worker to sustain middle-phase work.

MIDDLE-STAGE COUPLES WORK

In some cases, the beginning goes slowly, by fits and starts, beginning again and again until the couple is able to make headway together. The middle stage is more accurately called the "work phase" (Shulman, 1992), because this is the phase when the couple is actually engaging in the work promised by their beginning. The beginning and contracting work should contain all the necessary tasks and issues that might prevent the couple from reaching their goals. Obviously, the better the beginning, the better the middle stage and the better the possible outcome. The authors have often encountered situations in which the couple made such a good beginning in one or two interviews that they moved to the middle stage quickly. They were able to take ownership of the situation and continue on their relational tasks by themselves without further help, or with the social worker available just as a "consultant" if they ran into trouble.

DEVELOPMENT OF THE COUPLE'S PROBLEM-SOLVING AND RELATIONAL CAPACITIES

In the middle stage, the couple's unresolved issues become clearer and repeat themselves time after time. The social worker is often tempted to impatience or despair at what appear to be the couple's failing efforts. The polarization seems as if it will never end. It is important not to get discouraged at this time, and also to keep the couple in ownership of the problem and the tasks, not to take over the problem. The stage sometimes seems interminable when actually a good deal of work may be taking place.

The first process of middle-stage work is the development of the couple's problem-solving and relational capacities. When the couple is actively working on relational tasks with the social worker as coach, some of the most demonstrably powerful and effective tools of therapeutic change are being used. The conversation of the couple focuses on life problems, core personal relationships, and feelings (affective responses to) these problems and relationships (Orlinsky, Grawe, & Parks, 1994, p. 359). The conversation is direct and experiential as the couple, together in the session, alter their relationships. It is supportive and reassuring, drawing on the therapist's qualities of empathy, genuineness, and warmth. The therapist teaches this response to the couple in their transactions with each other. The conversation of the couple involves learning (cognitions) of different points of view and new skills. It involves action—that is, couples' managing their behavior and responses, facing fears with support, modeling behaviors, taking risks, testing new realities, and working through issues (Lambert & Bergin, 1994, p. 163). As long as the social worker has a clear professional focus on persons acting in relationships, and as long as the couple is in charge of the problem, the social worker can use a wide range of tools to help the couple accomplish these goals. There is no confinement to a particular method or tool of helping, since the worker is only, like a good coach, discovering resources in the couple and bringing out ways to help *them* accomplish something with each other (Lazarus, 1981).

Intimacy, Boundaries, and Communication Processes

The theme of the following case studies is the development of relational closeness (connectedness) and boundaries (separateness) through communication. The relationship of a couple in the early phase of marriage is expected to be close and intimate, but it is most difficult to achieve this—to know the other as other, to be known by another, to feel respected and to respect, and to solve problems without fear in a trusting relationship. Although sex is a form of communication, intimacy means more than sex.

The key to this growth in intimacy will be found in the relationship developed between the couple. Few theoretical approaches capture the complexity of the closeness-distance cycling in adult intimacy. A major task in work with couples is to help the couple build and maintain empathy with each other. Each needs to understand the other well enough to discern transactional cues signaling desired distance or intimacy. They need to be able to communicate productively about these cues. They also need to be able to maintain a necessary distance without losing the relationship and without one of the couple losing the ability to function and cope adequately. To build and maintain emotional intimacy, the couple must be able to approach each other without feeling anxious. Spouses must be able to be empathically attuned to each other without losing self and becoming enmeshed (Kheshgi-Genovese & Constable, 1995).

In a concrete sense, this can take place in two ways. Relatedness to the other and differentiation of self take place, first of all, in the process of appropriate engagement with the other—the processes of communicating, making decisions, and performing relational tasks. Second, this takes place in the mutual learning of empathic accuracy in couples' counseling sessions. A variety of tools have been developed to do this (Snyder, 1995; Wile, 1992; Guerney, 1977).[1] As couples communicate, each is taught in turn to take different communicative roles in relation to the other. The couple slows their communication and learns to distinguish an expressive mode and an empathic mode of communication. When I am in the expressive mode, I can give "I" messages to the other—that is, express how something affects me without placing the other on the defensive through the "you" message (you do . . .). The other then responds by reflecting what I said without adding further input. As soon as I am accurately reflected (this takes time), the other goes into expressive mode and I go into empathic mode (Guerney, 1977). The therapist moves back and forth between the two, coaching and facilitating communication. When things get stuck, the therapist will, with permission, reflect the other or, again with permission, even speak for the other, when necessary. (Snyder, 1995).

The point is not simply an exercise in communication. In a profound way, it is taking the attitude of the other (Mead, 1932; 1934) and teaching partners to do that with each other. One "becomes" the other for a moment, suspending disagreement in favor of accurate reflection. It then can become a mutual process of accurate empathy. Maryhelen Snyder (1995) draws from experiential-humanistic family therapy to define this mutual process. It is not simply a matter of being understanding and benign. To take on the life-world of another (Grunebaum, 1990; Habermas, 1987), to take on his or her lived experience in a particular social and psychological context, is a very special skill. Nor is it simply a matter of reflecting what has been said. Without this form of empathy, no real meeting between human beings occurs (Snyder, 1995, p. 318). In the presence of adequate empathy as Snyder defines it (1995, p. 242), "typically . . . the empathizer as a person 'disappears,' and both persons are simultaneously in the same experiential world."

Communication, Empathic Accuracy, and Relational Reconstruction

The following case is adapted to illustrate the power of empathic accuracy to help the couple reconstruct itself (Ables, 1977).[2] Nicholas and Johanna are a couple with

---

[1]Communications theory and experiential theory are discussed in Nichols (2013, p. 116), Nichols and Schwartz (2002, ch. 6), Goldenberg and Goldenberg (1996, ch. 7), B. Guerney (1977), and Snyder (1995).

[2]This example of couple communication, heavily adapted by the authors, is taken from an example suggested by Ables (1977).

a great deal of anger toward each other. Their hurt feelings and their ways of dealing with problems have become very much a part of them. During the first part of the session, Nicholas has been complaining that he feels "left out" from the family, unappreciated, and unimportant. We pick up with the social worker in the middle of the third session as they are beginning to get to the relational tasks they face.

CASE STUDY 7.1:
NICHOLAS AND JOHANNA

Social Worker (to Nicholas): And you're telling Johanna that somehow you feel you're not included in things.

Nicholas: Johanna, I'm not. . . . I'm not.

Johanna: When you go through that routine, Nicholas, you don't know how much it annoys me. I give you every chance to be a part of things. You don't take the opportunity, and someone has to make a decision. So I do. Does anyone have a problem with that? We'd be out on the street if I didn't.

Social Worker: Wait. Nicholas and Johanna. Is this what happens at home when things get tense? (They nod to the social worker, but don't look at each other.) Johanna, I know you have a lot of things that get you upset, and you have a tough job. And Nicholas, I know you get upset too, and you need to hear each other. But Johanna, let's just stay with this a minute. Because I hear something coming from Nicholas constantly as if he's neglected. And what I'm asking you, Nick, now, is would you like Johanna to include you more in decision making—to pay more attention to your point of view?

Nicholas: It doesn't make any difference. There's no way it'll ever happen . . . ever.

Social Worker: Would you like it?

Nicholas: Yes! But I might as well wait for the next millennium.

Social Worker: Could you ask Johanna now what she's willing to do now to help you with this?

Nicholas: I could, but . . . it'll never work.

Social Worker: Well, let's try it.

Johanna: What are you willing to do? The checks?

Nicholas: Well, it's not a matter of the checks. You're in control and I'd like to just have a vote on some things.

Johanna: I'd give you a vote on anything you wanted if you just didn't fly off the handle. I can't even talk to you, so I just do what I have to do.

Social Worker: Johanna, would you like to be able to talk with each other?

Johanna: That's why we're here.

Social Worker: I'd like to try this with you, if you're both willing. (Nicholas nods, Johanna shrugs. Social worker gives a ceramic floor tile to Johanna.) Johanna, you have the floor for the moment, so I want you to talk to Nick. Start with something positive, and use only "I" messages after that. Nicholas, I want you to just walk around in Johanna's head and reflect what you think she is trying to say. Don't add any of your own thoughts or reactions. Just what she is thinking. You'll have your chance at the floor as soon as you have reflected what she is saying. Okay? [Both nod.]

[Johanna starts by saying that Nicholas never listens to her anyway. The social worker goes to where she is sitting and sits next to her. She helps Johanna start with a positive ("Nick, I'm really happy we're working on this, but I don't have a lot of hope") and make the message into an "I" message. Eventually after a few false starts, where the social worker reflects her thinking as an "I" message, she says, "It's hard for me, Nick. I never see you when I need you, so I have to take over." She looks away because a tear is starting down her cheek. She quickly regains her composure. "See what you do to me!"]

Nicholas: [at first Nicholas doesn't take in the tear] What you do to me!

Social Worker: [she moves next to Nick's chair] Wait, Nicholas. You need to reflect what she's saying. [to Johanna]: Could you say it again, Johanna? [Johanna says it again, but in a slightly hurt, angry tone, and adds, "There we go again."]

Nicholas: What you're saying is I'm not around, and that's just not true! (The social worker coaches Nicholas to wait on his own response until he gets the floor and to try to reflect what Johanna is feeling.)

Nicholas: You're feeling that even when I'm around I haven't been there to help you when you need me.

Social Worker: That's real good, Nick!

The couple begins haltingly to express and reflect feelings. When the floor tile comes to Nicholas, he talks about how left out he feels, but also acknowledges that Johanna does do a good job when she does take over. Bills get paid. Johanna starts to cry and blurts out, "That's the first time you ever said that."

The rest of the session, they both start talking about how left out, isolated, and lonely they feel. They feel stuck in the roles that they generate for and with each other. When things slow down or get stuck, the social worker reaches into either's feelings and develops each one's feelings of loneliness, of being trapped in their anger, using reflection, sometimes speaking for one or the other when they feel stuck. She works out with them a between-session task of having dinner together at a favorite restaurant, with Nicholas paying, and planning a weekend at Lake Delavan with each other. They will save the intense talk for their next session next week.

This was a good session. It is probable that Nicholas and Johanna will revert for a time to their old, hurtful patterns. However, both now see other possibilities, and with lots of repetition, they begin to develop different communication patterns, different behavioral patterns, and, finally, reflecting together on these changes (which neither anticipated), a different relationship. As long as they have developed some level of communication skills and willingness to engage positively with each other, all of the relational tasks—whether they revolve around developing new patterns of money management, family-of-origin work, issues around children, and so on—can be processed by many couples in a manner somewhat similar to that used by Nicholas and Johanna.

MIDDLE-STAGE SKILLS: THE WORK PHASE

For the middle stage—or, more precisely, the work phase—we can use approximately the same framework for helping skills that we had developed in relation to helping the couple begin. The difference is that in the middle stage there is a focus on relational work with each other. The process can easily get stuck, and so the skills are used to help the couple remain on task and get unstuck when needed. The worker needs to tune in, contract for each session, and help the couple elaborate a focus. This is active work in the first sessions, but when the couple becomes more accustomed to the helping process, they begin to take more responsibility for beginning the session. Johanna and Nicholas are ready to focus, but they are utterly lost in the complexity of their relationship when they start trying to communicate. Here the social worker becomes very active, helping the couple to

- Elaborate a focus
- Express feelings and thoughts so that they can be heard and discussed
- Listen to the other and reflect the other's thoughts and feelings
- Take the viewpoint of the other
- Respond to the other's needs
- Separate personal from relational tasks
- Solve problems together

To do these things, the social worker is constantly clarifying focus and tasks, partializing this focus in relation to time and resources (what can be done in this interview), and helping the couple elaborate their direction in relation to these tasks and goals. She is sharing data from her observations of the couple, from her understanding of good relational skills, from research, and from her experience, but she is sharing it in the way the couple can use it at this point in their process. She is reaching for feelings and putting feelings into words (Shulman, 1992). She is often actively teaching relational and communication skills. She partially manages the process until the couple is ready to manage it for themselves. When this takes place, she assists them in identifying and summarizing what has taken place. She will help the couple generalize their learning to other situations and begin to manage issues by themselves.

A key question at this time is how much understanding the couple needs to have about what is happening, the roots of their problems, their attachment styles, issues passed down through families of origin, and so on. The answer to this question gets more complex and nuanced as practitioners draw from a variety of family therapy approaches, some of which emphasize insight as the major goal and some of which emphasize behavioral and relational change. Workers have traditionally tended to emphasize either one or the other (Constable & Cocozzelli, 1989). However, it seems clear that both reflection (meanings) and action (behavior change) are necessary and interrelated the one to the other, similar to our concept of process and content. Successful change is a matter of developing the connection, in theory and in practice, between the two.

Let us use our example of Nicholas and Johanna (case study 7.1) to clarify the relation between reflection and action. Clearly Nicholas and Johanna have a very complicated relationship. Both feel trapped in it, but both are beginning to see the position of the other. To some extent, both are beginning to see their own patterns. The social worker teaches them different skills of communication, expression, and empathy, and as they operationalize this learning, they see more. Learning and insight proceed along with interaction. As their relationship changes, understanding changes and vice versa. Some couples will immediately see relational and attachment connections and use them to sustain and reflect on their work. Others will be mainly interested in the changes that take place. The two are interdependent. The social worker works concretely with the tasks of relational change, helping clients come to a deepened understanding in order to sustain the process and to maintain gains. Understanding cannot be effectively reached without the experience of interaction, and interaction cannot take place without some level of understanding and ability to reflect on the process.

The Use of Tasks and Assignments

When relational tasks are central to the helping process, then understanding, reflection, and the helping process are no longer removed from the realities with which the couple is dealing. Personal and couple tasks are what they need to work on in any case. However, this is precisely where the couple is often stuck. The use of a natural focus (relational tasks) helps them experience themselves and each other differently. The tasks, once identified, sustain and help the couple take ownership of the work. Tasks provide the criteria, the bases for ongoing evaluation. These criteria make it clear and evident when it comes time to end. The tasks already exist; they are simply there to be done. It is a question of partializing the tasks, helping the couple to perform the tasks and then identifying and sustaining what they have accomplished with each other. They are in charge, and the social worker is a coach to help them do this in their own way.

The tasks already exist, but they need to be identified. The more complex question is how the worker handles these already-existing tasks. Does the social worker prescribe tasks for the couple to do in session or out of session? Does the social worker take control of the process in this way? What would be a reason to prescribe a task? What theory would justify it? How would it work?

In our case studies so far, the social worker is continually prescribing tasks both in session and out of session. The social worker prescribed communication tasks for Nicholas and Johanna (case study 7.1) and taught them to use empathic accuracy as a powerful tool of relational understanding and change.[3] The worker prescribed

---

[3]The use of a concrete focus on behaviors and tasks is well developed in behavioral approaches. See Nichols (2013, pp. 194–197), Nichols and Schwartz (2002, ch. 9), and Goldenberg and Goldenberg (1996, ch. 12).

a between-session task (take her to dinner and pay the bill, plan a weekend, and so on) that had a slightly paradoxical flavor to it (save the intense talk for our next session).

The first principle behind task construction is that the most powerful tool of learning is doing. The rationale for this approach is similar to the rationale in the discussion of "working from the outside-in" in ego-oriented casework (chapter 2). The difference is that some of the doing takes place in session with the partner, and so it can go relatively quickly in comparison with the longer time frames often associated with individual work. As with the J. family in case study 5.7, family members often work on these tasks between sessions. Doing the well-constructed task both recognizes the basic relational realities and also changes them slightly in the process. Thus Johanna and Nicholas are seeing their relationship and the position of the other differently through their communication. They are also seeing themselves differently, and this can be a source of profound personal change. Nicholas shows a more active side of himself, Johanna a more thoughtful, vulnerable side. The worker extends this into their everyday week through the assignment.

Family therapists have often prescribed that the couple or family carry out certain tasks. In some family therapy traditions, these are called directives. There are four types of directives in cascading order, going from prescribing the tasks inherent in the situation to reconstructing the relationship (Haley, 1976):

- *Straightforward Directives.* These are directives inherent to the situation. The relational work the couple has to do is simply assigned. Most directives are like this. Nicholas and Johanna should go out to dinner. If a straightforward directive will achieve its end, it's not necessary to go further.
- *Remedial Directives.* The remedial directive is the first of three reconstructive directives—that is, its intent is to reconstruct a relational pattern. Remedial directives prescribe doing something different from the normal pattern. Nicholas will pay the bill when they go out for dinner. If Mother is customarily the disciplinarian, she will take a well-deserved "vacation," and Father will take charge. One version of this was developed by Steve deShazer (1988) in the "solution-focused" approach. The worker looks for exceptions to the dominant pattern and prescribes the exception.
- *Metaphorical Directives.* These directives assign a metaphorical task for the relational issue. A boy, having issues around adoption, adopts a dog. The adoptive father (a mailman) knows a lot about dogs, and the two share this project together.
- *Paradoxical Directives.* These directives essentially prescribe the problem, the way the family has been acting to date, or restrain the couple from change.

Nicholas and Johanna should not talk intensely about their problems over dinner. By prescribing that they *not* talk intensely about their problems over dinner (a mildly paradoxical instruction for them), the social worker is doing several things at once.[4] She is first of all urging that they have an enjoyable dinner and weekend without falling into their destructive patterns, which come when they get intense with each other. Second, she is restraining them from change, thus indirectly encouraging change but in a way that they can control, and in a way that is related to their sessional work. Finally, if they do have some intense conversations (as they well may) and these break down into recriminations (also probable at this early stage), she is giving them a way of interpreting what happened in a benign way (we went too fast). For this to work, the social worker needs to be comfortable with paradox as a truthful communication, because the paradox identifies the reverse side of Nicholas and Johanna's actual intentions. By urging that they avoid intense discussion, she is siding with their real denial until their relationship becomes more manageable. Social workers should never prescribe a paradoxical directive they are uncomfortable with and should never prescribe one without a clear understanding of how the relationship (and the reverse side of their intentions) operates. For the most part, working with straightforward tasks and directives may well be enough to accomplish their goals.

Middle-Stage Work

The following three case studies are examples of middle-stage work with relational tasks of couples at different stages of the family life cycle. In the first case study, Rita and Joav Green are a young couple struggling with the decision of whether to take their child with Down syndrome home. The couple is having a great deal of difficulty deciding. The worker uses a variety of techniques to help them to make a decision.

A Couple Decides to Accommodate Their Baby with Down Syndrome

The theme of the case focuses on tasks and assignments, now with a couple dealing with their newborn baby with Down syndrome. They can't make a decision. How does the social worker help them break the impasse? What is the relation of process, understanding, and task? What is the relation of the decision-making process to the use of paradoxical tasks?

In the months of anticipation before the arrival of a baby, couples are usually beginning to think of how they will accommodate their life and work patterns (and their living unit) to what they anticipate of the baby's needs. The unfolding process of accommodation and change continues through all of the child's developmental stages. The dance of the couple is paralleled by the dance of the broader family and relatives as they work at the expected accommodation. However, it is usually also

---

[4]The use of paradoxical directives is well developed in Haley (1976), Stanton (1981), Goldenberg and Goldenberg (1996, ch. 10), and Nichols (2013, pp. 107, 109), Nichols and Schwartz (2002, ch. 11).

expected the baby will be "perfect"—that is, not have a disability. When the baby has a serious disability, the expectation of the perfect child vanishes. It is the loss of the expected "perfect child" who never came, a loss that needs to be mourned. When these tasks of coming to the reality of their child are not accomplished, the couple may be dealing mainly with hidden disappointment or fears. They may never know the child who actually comes for the person who he or she is. Furthermore, complex and lifelong care-giving responsibilities can create heavy stress on the marital unit. If the couple does not share this responsibility, one person can become the "expert" on the child. The more one parent is absorbed by this role, the less the other may be involved, creating a serious fissure in the marriage (Beckman, 1991; Bernier, 1990; Davis, 1987; Seybold, Flitz, & McPhee, 1991). Consequently, as Voysey found in her research on a British sample, the child may be constructed as "a constant burden" (Voysey, 1975) rather than as a person who can bring something to his or her surroundings. When a baby is born with a disability, the couple has much to struggle with and the event can derail their normal processes of anticipation and acceptance.

CASE STUDY 7.2:
RITA AND JOAV GREEN

Rita and Joav Green, a creative, well-educated Israeli couple in their thirties, came to a child welfare agency in Jerusalem. Three weeks earlier their second child had been born with Down syndrome. The baby was now in temporary care, and the Greens could not decide whether to bring him home or to give him up. The Greens had already developed a comfortable, respectful relationship with each other. They had one other child, a bright 8-year-old girl. Joav had a limited and unsteady income, but his business was growing. Rita, a professional, provided the primary income and had begun to move up the career ladder. She had tried to nurse the baby in the hospital, but he had poor sucking reflexes. She then left his care to the hospital staff and some of them hinted at the possibility that she might refuse to take him home. Family members advised them to leave the baby. They

knew social services would find a foster home if they abandoned the child. They feared that if they took the baby home and decided not to keep him, they would have a hard time placing him on their own. They were paralyzed with the decision they had to make, and if one of the couple indicated a decision in one direction, the other would take the other side. In some ways, the idea that this was their decision, a decision they could control, made it all the more difficult to make. In one way or another, the couple could see difficulties: professional and economic limitations, the energy the child would draw from the whole family, their other child, and pressure from their families and even the hospital staff. All of the options were so painful that it immobilized the Greens' ability to make decisions. As long as the baby did not exist in their perceptions as a couple, they didn't have act on their perceptions and their values. The work they needed to do and therefore the impossible decision could be forestalled.

The work of the couple was to make a decision and a commitment at the same time. If they took the baby home, they would only want to do it mutually. When they couldn't do this, they became paralyzed. The social worker took an approach that emphasized familiarizing the parents with the child and getting information to help them make an informed decision. She said they could do that only through some hands-on experience with the baby and through supportive involvement of the temporary care facility presently caring for the baby. They had to know what they were losing, but part of each of them didn't want to know this, because they would then feel obligated to take the baby home, and so on.

The worker encouraged them to explore the implications of both possibilities; to visit the child with an experienced child care worker, who gently helped them with certain details of care; and to discuss the situation with the social worker over the time the agency allowed. She encouraged the couple to evaluate their ability to bond with their child. She directly confronted with them the problems of caring for him. She asked them about other special-needs children in their respective families and asked about family beliefs and legacies about such children. How did they ordinarily react to crises? How would their parents react if they decided to keep their baby? She encouraged them to grieve, normalizing for them the grieving process for the perfect child, whom they expected, but who never came. When they still made no decision after several weeks, she paradoxically tested the possibility with them of letting the child go but also reviewed the supportive and special services that would be available if they took him home. She said that it sounded as if they had already made the decision to let the child go, and the worker was only recognizing it. They cried with the worker as they resisted the idea of abandoning their child. They then visited the child and in two more sessions decided to take the child home. They came to the next session like two changed people. With a warm and mischievous smile, the husband told the social worker his baby was "ugly as hell." In their final session they brought the baby, now three-and-a-half months old, dressed in bright, new clothes, the parents relaxed and attractive. They were getting specialized help and had even succeeded in making arrangements so that, in the end, neither of them had to sacrifice his or her career to care for the baby. (Adapted from Bardin, 1992, © The Psychotherapy Networker)

Decision-Making Processes and the Family

There is a direct relation between decision-making and bonding processes. After all, the decision-making process has to reflect already-existing bonds. Additionally, the product of the decision-making process may be a commitment to change, a changed structure, an altered bond, a different way of viewing another person or network, or a different way of acting with the other. These are continuous processes leading to assent and commitment. Commitment is the irrevocability of consent (Turner,

1970). Sandy and Sheldon (case study 6.6) had made somewhat different decisions when they went through the marriage ceremony. It took them much longer to reach a mutual commitment. John and Eileen (case study 6.5) apparently never did.

Decision making ideally moves toward a consensus—that is, all giving equal assent and all feeling equally committed, without private reservation or personal resentment. This level of consensus is infrequently achieved, particularly across the dividing lines of generation and gender. Members usually give assent in order to allow a decision to be reached, and not because they are privately convinced that the decision in question is best. This assent is an *accommodation*. Agreement is achieved by the adjustment of some or all of the members to the irreconcilability of their views (Turner, 1970).

Rita and Joav (case study 7.2) see clearly that they could have a lifelong commitment to their son that could unbalance everything they had planned. They also see that they could easily control this possibility by placement of the child. They were pressured to do so by relatives, nurses, and hospital staff. It took them time to resolve the conflict between an underdeveloped, disregarded status bond with their son, the obligations going with it, and the question of whether they wanted to recognize it. Fortunately, in the short time the agency allowed, the social worker helped them go through this decision-making process and arrive at the consensual decision that they needed to go forward with such a serious commitment.

Their beliefs about their relationship demanded that they pursue consensus rather than accommodation. From their perspective, if the decision was simply an accommodation, it would be a decision reflective of a type of dominance of one partner over the other. Drawing from this discussion, Turner builds an intriguing hypothesis on this very point:

> The more extensive the common values of family members or the more extensive the understanding that members have of one another's values, the less often will decision making contribute to unequal domination in the family, the less often will commitment to group decisions be conditional or ambiguous. (Turner, 1970, p. 104)

Their love and respect for each other and the undeveloped bond with their child made the decision difficult. As they began to deal concretely with this with the paradoxical help of the social worker, their common values eventually brought them to a consensual decision.

Personal Tasks: Joseph and Paula

The major themes of the following case study are *personal work* and *genograms* (see figure 5.1) in the context of relational work.[5] Joseph and Paula have a lot of personal work to do. In the beginning, their personal work keeps getting enmeshed and con-

---

[5]For a more detailed discussion of genograms, see McGoldrick, Gerson & Shellenberger (1999), Nichols (2013, pp. 85–87), Nichols and Schwartz (2002, pp. 160–162), Goldenberg and Goldenberg (1996, pp. 181–183), and Hartman and Laird (1983).

fused with their relational work and vice versa. On the other hand, they cannot do personal work without dealing with their relationship. Redeveloping their relationship will presuppose the accomplishment of personal tasks. In Joseph and Paula's case, they agreed to reduce dysfunctional communication (to "construct a wall") so that they could deal with personal tasks and then reconstruct their relationship. Every couple faces a dilemma between the pull of personal and relational tasks, although Joseph and Paula expressed it more dramatically than most.

Several things helped them do this work. First of all, rather than opening up the possibility of communication as with Nicholas and Johanna (case study 7.1), the social worker prescribed a partial shutdown. The shutdown was a somewhat paradoxical task that also allowed both to separate their respective issues of near-alcoholism, and depression from each other. As they dealt with these problems personally and apart from each other, positive communication could be relearned and cautiously resumed.

Joseph and Paula have chronic marital problems. In addition, Joseph is on the fringes of alcoholism, and Paula has struggled with depression most of her life. They will return for help periodically in their lives. The example is useful to see a couple with serious problems fully using the opportunity to make changes in what appeared to be an impossible situation.

CASE STUDY 7.3: JOSEPH AND PAULA

When they came to their first interview together, Joseph and Paula presented as a chronically contentious couple in their late thirties who were disagreeing sharply in almost all of their communication, to the point of verbal and some physical abuse. Paula tended to criticize Joseph incessantly for everything, making him responsible for anything that went wrong or even her fears of something going wrong. Joseph, who had good verbal skills, would respond by making fun of Paula. Everything was going wrong in their relationship. The only positive points were that Joseph held down a very good job as a factory manager. Despite their conflict, they were able to agree on their parenting of their twin 13-year-old girls. They were both ready for divorce, and marriage counseling was to be their last step.

Both had previous marriages that had ended in divorce. An immigrant from Romania, Joseph began his first marriage shortly after his immigration to the United States. Both had married hastily the first time. Paula had had a three-month marriage to a man who was alcoholic, constantly physically abusive to her, and unable to leave his family of origin. Joseph was on the fringes of alcoholism. When drinking, he would explode in verbal abuse of Paula, and she would respond in the same way. Paula had struggled with depression all of her life. When she was depressed, she would become extremely blaming, and Joseph was an obvious target. Both would trigger each other's responses and fence with each other until the communication became explosive. Both, on the other hand, had a heavy investment in their marriage, partially because their first marriages had failed. They needed, however, to separate their individual problems from their relational problems and begin to work on individual problems without making the other responsible for those problems. They needed radically to change their communication patterns so that the patterns became supportive of the other rather than hostile. If they made and stabilized these changes, they could begin to think of developing a forgiveness process between them. The negative communication patterns, however, were strongly established.

After making an assessment together of the situation, they decided on an initial threefold focus:

- Joseph would take responsibility for his binge drinking and its effects on the relationship. This was a disease as fatal as cancer unless he did something about it. He agreed to stop drinking entirely and go to Alcoholics Anonymous for help.
- Paula would take responsibility for her depression and its effect on the relationship. She would go back to her medication, begin a journal where she differentiated her thinking from her feelings, and do some other things that could be effective against depression.
- Both were to limit communication with each other to things that could be managed: the children, the news of the day, describing what happened at the factory or home, and so on. They should save the serious or contentious issues for sessions together with the social worker. They needed to construct a "wall" around any issues that would create problems.

They agreed to this and in fact did do all these things. During the following sessions, they kept up the wall of communication, with Joseph and Paula communicating with each other only through the social worker. In the beginning each took turns talking about their situations to the social worker in the presence of the other. There was a focus on genogram work at this time. They found it very interesting to see the flow of their lives and their very different heritages. The focus of the work on individual genograms was on the roots of their problems as they had experienced them in their families of origin. Paula came from several generations of very strong women who took over for husbands who were somewhat dysfunctional alcoholics. The failure of the first marriage was a deep shock to her, which made her all the more fearful that her second marriage would also fail. She would not be taken advantage of again and would remain on the defense against this. Joseph also came from a family of very strong women, who had complete control of their sons but whose husbands paid no attention at all to them. The shift from Romanian to North American society was very difficult, but he was proud that he had always been able to work and be well paid. Work was his route to success, and in his previous marriage, he was hardly aware of a relationship. He had his work, so he could thus fit into North American society. The first marriage had deteriorated over several years, and he hardly was aware of it when it ended.

Over the following months Joseph and Paula listened to each other's stories. Each took personal responsibility for working on their own alcoholism and depression. They began to attribute these problems less to each other and to take action on them themselves. The physical and verbal abuse stopped completely. Joseph did maintain complete sobriety, even when pressed by his Romanian friends to drink. Paula's depression began to lift as she took more responsibility for working on it. They each then could gradually let some of the wall down, and they began communication with each other in a completely different way—no criticism, no mocking. It was like learning to communicate when they had never communicated before. A warmer relationship emerged to the extent that during the Christmas holidays, their twin daughters showed mock disgust that their mother and father were now treating each other so well. With their ability to maintain better communication stabilized, Joseph and Paula were able to manage to their satisfaction without further help.

The task model allows us to differentiate personal from relational tasks. In Joseph and Paula's case, it allowed personal work by both to take place in the presence of the other with some protective barrier to destructive communication in the meantime. As both would progress in personal tasks, they eventually could move to relational tasks. A balance then would emerge between personal and relational work.

Boundaries Protecting Personal Work

Communication is obviously important and is a major tool in helping couples reconstruct relationships. However, we have already seen a number of cases in which verbal communication remained very limited (Armand and Rosalind [case study 3.2] and Sandy and Sheldon [case study 5.6]) so that the social worker worked only with one partner with the focus on relational tasks and communication, not with words but with action. In several cases (Jack and Jung [case study 5.6] and the J. family [case study 5.7]), cultural values put communication of feelings and meanings in second place to relational change. Joseph and Paula (case study 7.3) created a "wall" so that they could work on personal tasks and then shift to relational tasks. In the following case study, Edward and Joyce also needed a "wall," but for them the purpose was to stabilize their respective areas of competence from interference.

CASE STUDY 7.4: EDWARD AND JOYCE

Edward is much older than Joyce, very bright, thoughtful, and not verbally aggressive. In some ways, Edward's consistency anchors Joyce's unpredictability, but this unpredictability keeps Edward on the alert with Joyce, ready to take over. He will tell her only what he feels she can manage to deal with. This shuts down much of what he would want to say and keeps him patronizing Joyce. Joyce shows symptoms of bipolar mood disorder, and she is getting psychiatric help and medication for this. She oscillates between reasonableness and becoming overwhelmed and explosive with him and with the children. Her unpredictability in her treatment of the children is a source of constant concern to Edward, so that he is losing a great deal of time in his home business. Edward tries to compensate when she is upset, taking over with the children, but this feels paternalistic to Joyce. In some ways, she feels free to explode when Edward is so available. She shuts down when he goes into his long, quiet explanations. Edward feels that he is a hostage of the situation.

In their work with the social worker, Joyce gradually took more responsibility for managing her outbursts. When she did that, they would construct a partial "wall." Joyce was more comfortable when she was in charge of her role and herself, but she had to work to achieve this internal balance. Her care for Edward and for the children motivated her as nothing else could. Edward's involvement and communication was taking over her responsibility, felt "touchy-feely" to Joyce, and didn't always help. They agreed to communicate on a regular basis on practical issues. Each could be in charge of their own area but available to the other when needed. They were both relieved to operate in their own spheres, check in with each other on a regular basis, and arrange immediate communication if there was a need. Further relational goals would depend on their stabilizing their own areas.

Reconstruction: Societal Narratives and Couple Narratives

Social constructionist intervention focuses on changing contexts for meaning. In some cases, the target is the couple's context of meanings. This context needs to be reconstructed so that appropriate, relational tasks can proceed. Changing culturally constructed words and language makes way for the family's appropriate constructions. Words derive their meanings from the contexts in which they are produced or constructed. Language emerges from the cultural practices that give shape to human interaction. It constructs the means by which thoughts, feelings, and behaviors are produced (Gergen, 1999; Monk & Gehart, 2003). Foucault (1972; 1979; 1980) discusses how a society's dominant narratives and discourses marginalize some groups and empower others. Michael White took Foucault's discussion of dominant societal narratives and translated it into an approach to changing the way the family processes these narratives. The narratives were often the basis for the family's own current balances or status quo (Nichols, 2013, pp. 274–288; White, 2007; White & Epston, 1990). Many of these dominant narratives are narratives of political oppression that people internalize, but also there are narratives of ideal beauty, of physical attributes, of gender, of age, of able-bodiedness, of success, of children, of mental health, of sexuality, and so on. These narratives are often taken for granted by the couple. However, when they are used for comparison, they can be oppressive and denigrating to the real people experiencing them. Rather than drawing from the effects of dominant narratives, social constructionists focus on construction of local meaning. Freed from the effects of dominant narratives, the construction of local meanings can release the couple to focus on workable and appropriate relational tasks rather than being drawn into impossible narratives drawn from the broader society. Because social workers represent many of the societal institutions that create some of these dominant narratives, they are in a good position to assist both the institution and the family to manage their part in them. Rita and Joav Green (case study 7.2) had to develop a discourse with each other and with society's dominant narratives around disability. The Kowalskis had to let go of a variety of societal scripts that had emptied their relationship.

CASE STUDY 7.5:
BONNIE AND ANDY KOWALSKI

Bogoslawa (Bonnie) and Andrzej (Andy) Kowalski both are second-generation Polish Americans whose parents arrived as refugees, having experienced enormous losses to their families in World War II. Bonnie and Andy were the next generation, retreating from very painful family experiences and conforming to their new society. In their university experiences, they found their identities and each other as antiwar rebels of the generation of 1968. Extended intellectual conversations were interlaced with considerable alcohol and marijuana consumption. They eventually married, struggled with their addictions and let them go, and settled down to a middle-class existence. Somehow their own relationship, the conversations and the addictions, were replaced by work, children, and other things propagated by the media.

Bonnie became absorbed by her jobs as a freelance computer consultant and, more recently, by their son, Paul, age 4. She finds it very difficult to say "no" to him. When Paul is not sleeping, he controls Bonnie. Lately she has had difficulty working because of Paul's increasing demands. Bonnie sees herself as seriously overweight, is preoccupied about eating and dieting, and

shows symptoms of major depression. Andy has been similarly absorbed by his job as an accountant. They are civil to each other. There is little overt conflict, but both feel that the relationship, after eighteen years, is "nearly dead." Now they find only emptiness when they look at their relationship, and they plan to divorce if nothing else happens. Both feel trapped by their work, and Bonnie by their son, Paul. Sex has become a non-occurrence. Their communication and the overall relationship are extremely undeveloped. They have to work hard to make their interaction personal. Bonnie tends to talk about herself in a somewhat impersonal way and has very little "voice" to ask anything from Andy. When Bonnie and Andy do try to make contact, Bonnie remembers past hurts and becomes very impatient and reactive so that Andy is discouraged. Andy is quiet, feels it is difficult for him fully to comprehend Bonnie, and feels lost for words with her but actually does reasonably well in their discussion. Bonnie has great difficulty responding to Andy in any way. Bonnie feels entitled to more sensitive behavior on Andy's part. She becomes hyperalert to any evidence of his insensitivity and tends to depreciate his efforts to be more sensitive to her: "You are sensitive only because I pointed out your insensitivity." Andy, feeling trapped by her logic, acknowledges that he has been insensitive but feels that he can never win and wonders whether it is worth trying. Bonnie does, however, appreciate his willing and competent help with Paul. He does prevent her from losing herself in Paul. Both feel close to hopeless about their relationship but are willing to work on it "for one last time."

Bonnie's depression was identified in their first contacts. She started working on it with an individual therapist. The marriage problems were connected with her depression (and vice versa). She continued to work with Andy on the marriage. Their emptiness and hopelessness was partially being fueled by outside investments of themselves and outside criteria governing their meaning systems, on their (local) experience of each other. Both had lost important parts of themselves and were colonized by work and standard images of success. Bonnie had lost herself in Paul, in her feelings about her weight and dieting, and in her depression. Could Bonnie deal with her depression without medicalizing her life? Andy found some success only in his work. Both had little hope their sexual relationship would be "successful" and were very reluctant even to try. The more they focused on their present relationship, the emptier they felt.

Their first step was to reestablish communication, particularly around their most pressing immediate concern, Paul. They did this. Andy enjoyed taking over with Paul as soon as he came home. Bonnie had some time to let go and recover, and Paul got better and less demanding. Building on that improvement, the social worker coached them to look for the exceptions to the negative picture of their relationship they had adopted. They could find these exceptions only in their past. Bonnie loved the heady, intellectual conversations they once had with each other, and Andy remembered them fondly as well. Could they bring them back again? They began to see how external definitions of work and success, societal ideas of some ideal weight, and Bonnie's concerns about being a" perfect" parent had robbed them of their care for each other as unique persons, of their real priorities, and even of their time with each other. Indeed, this was shutting Paul down from his own struggle to develop. The worker encouraged them to write their own stories of their relationship, set their own priorities, and develop these stories together in the way they wanted. Removing their relationship from the partially self-imposed oppression of societal criteria became a key to the unique relational tasks of rediscovering the friendship and their appreciation of each other, which did eventually emerge.

THE POST-PARENTAL STAGE

The post-parental stage is sometimes called the empty nest, dramatizing a loss of active responsibility for children as parents gradually become independent. Actually, the nest is not always empty. Often, there is still the need to care for elderly parents as they become less able to care for themselves. Adult children also have a way of returning from a divorce or some other difficulty. Increasingly often these days, there may be a grandchild living at home. In addition, the relationship with adult children often remains quite active. Shorn of their responsibility to socialize, make decisions and carry responsibility for them, the family often becomes quite a bit more comfortable. In any case, much more couple work than child-oriented work is done. The post-parental couple remains quite active as long as they remain healthy. They are often the center of a very complex network of children, grand-children, their own parents, and friends, and now they have some leisure time. The shift from a work role to retirement could be a crisis if work has been the only source of identity and pleasure. It is the season of life to call upon one's inner resources to appreciate art and beauty, and often to be a support to a very complex network of friends and family. This needs to be well understood. When this personal shift has not occurred, or where there are losses or relational absences of the people with whom one would ordinarily share this, there can be bitterness, loneliness, and despair. Older men with losses, cut off from family, sometimes with drinking prob-lems, can be at risk for suicide.

The major shift inside the family is that the couple needs to move some way back toward its original structure, prior to the arrival of children (as long as that structure was functional)—but now with a very different history and outlook on the future. They may prevent this from happening out of fear of intimacy. They may try to remain in an earlier, child-centered stage. Although there are many distractions of a complex network, the couple needs to rediscover the dyadic relationship and its potential for them at this point in their lives. Another danger is enmeshment with each other. The loss of work and of direct parental roles could throw them much closer into each other's orbits than they may have been accustomed to. They may become quite critical of each other, dabbling in each other's affairs, or explosive, as the Caldwell family (described in the following case study) experienced. Another extreme, if they have never really developed a relationship with their spouse, is the loneliness and feelings of hopelessness that come with recognition of their disen-gagement. Illness is always a real possibility at this time. Illness can cut off any pos-sibilities of development. It can lead to loss and be a great source of stress. In addi-tion, there can be an accumulation of real losses that leaves the older person bereft and detached from life. Older men are one of the most suicide-prone groups of all, partially because losses of work and those closest to them may leave them less able to create new networks.

CASE STUDY 7.6: ASHFORD AND LOUISE CALDWELL

Ashford and Louise Caldwell, a retired African American couple in their late sixties, are a study in contrasts, although they do have some common values and beliefs. Ashford is a retired ironworker, a foreman. He did his job well, "managing men," as he puts it. It was a source of great pride to him, and he misses it greatly. Although he hasn't changed his waking habits, he has less to do. Louise manages his senile mother, something she is very willing to do, but it is a full-time job, and sometimes she wonders how she ever got into this. On the other hand, she considers it *her* work and hardly lets Ashford in on any of it. When she has time at all, she loves her garden, although with her arthritis she needs Ashford's help to manage it. She will get help only grudgingly, and so she doesn't ask any more. It is one of a number of issues that bring her to the "slow burn" she carries into many relationships. Both are very religious, but they have affiliated with different Christian denominations. Ashford constantly criticizes Louise's religious practices as if they were his own. He has also become quite critical of Louise's housekeeping. Louise's slow burn seems to be constantly with her these days, and she appears to be depressed. Ashford takes the slow burn seriously, because he (somewhat correctly) sees that it comes from a long list of Louise's disappointments with him. Louise has never easily forgotten things.

They have very different communication styles. Louise is quite verbal. She easily overcomes Ashford with her words. When Ashford feels overwhelmed by Louise or by a situation, he becomes quite explosive. This occurred when he was working at the mill, with their children, and with Louise. There have been increasing explosions between Ashford and Louise. Ashford never was subtle in his relations with their four children. Louise says that he would tell you to do it and how to do it, and you would do it that way, or else. He managed to alienate all three sons when they were in their late teens or early twenties. They left home prematurely and with controversy. They couldn't take his constant direction. Louise always had the stronger relationship

with the children, and this somewhat undercut Ashford's relationship with them. It irritated Ashford, and he felt isolated from his children. At one point many years ago, when his 15-year-old second son, Chad, talked back to him, Ashford exploded and beat him. Chad ran away to a friend's house, but quietly returned after a week. Louise "let him in the back door." Ashford was embarrassed about his behavior with Chad but never dealt with it. Neither apologized to the other, and there are lasting, uncomfortable feelings between the two. Louise, concerned about an explosion, has taken pains never to remind him of it.

Louise was the oldest girl in a family of five. She has always been placed in something of a caretaker role, and has long had mixed feelings about the role. When she was 16, she found herself pregnant. Without much discussion, her mother made her place the child, a boy she named Joey, for adoption. She considered abortion, is happy she didn't have one, and is happy that Joey is alive somewhere. She remembers his birthday and wonders how he is doing now, at age 50. When she looks quiet and sits away from him sometimes, Ashford knows she is talking to Joey, and respects that. Other than Ashford, no one knows this family secret.

Louise and Ashford came to Lutheran Family Services for help after a particularly explosive week. They were increasingly uncomfortable with the constant arguments, and now, after forty-two years of marriage, threats of divorce. Ashford was still reactive from the last argument, and Louise carried her slow burn, so it was difficult to get the couple talking with each other at all. They seemed simultaneously to occupy different universes. At the same time, they appeared overinvolved with everything the other was doing. From Ashford's perspective, the problem was religion and Louise's involvement with a Pentecostal group (he is Lutheran). From Louise's perspective, the problem is Ashford's need to control everything she does, even things of which she was previously in control. On the other hand, she would pursue him incessantly whenever a difference came up until he exploded. She didn't seem to be able to stop. She was also showing signs of some mild to moderate depression. In the initial contract, they identified Ashford's need for anger management and Louise's depression, together with what were problems in communication and differentiation of one from the other's areas. Their in-session communication with each other bore all this out. They set personal and relational goals dealing with anger management, depression, and "time out." They identified their mutual patterns of pursuit, withdrawal, and explosion. They needed to find different ways to communicate and set boundaries on some of their involvement with one another.

There were a total of fourteen sessions over a total of five months, with the social worker's vacation in the middle. During the first six weekly sessions, they identified patterns of communication, set boundaries on things that lead to explosions, helped Ashford deal with his anger and Louise with her slow burn, depression, and tendency to pursue. Ashford got a job cleaning the church and began to do some volunteer work. Louise, with Ashford's more willing help, got involved with her garden again. Both began to "date," partially to rebuild their relationship and partially to get respite from the constant chore of caring for Louise's mother-in-law. Louise gradually permitted Ashford to take more care of his mother, something Ashford was quite willing to do. Arguments began to lessen, although they still occurred. Ashford began to say positive, loving things to Louise. Louise was surprised, but wondered whether it was just because of their counseling. Most of the sessions involved communication between the two. It was difficult, but getting somewhat better. One of the things they were able to talk about was Louise's continued hurt and slow burn, something she was totally unaware of. She began to use this insight to deal with it as a personal task. This made a great difference when she began to get some grasp of it.

When the worker returned from a one-month vacation, they had gone back to many of their older patterns but had also held on to some gains. After three weekly interviews, they had recouped their earlier losses and were making further progress. In addition, Ashford was beginning to be able to repair the relationship with his son, Chad. There was a potential point of controversy between Ashford and Chad at a family picnic. Ashford took him aside, and they were able to talk it out, something they had never done previously. Ashford was surprised that Chad was so willing to accept his relationship and implicit apology. His eyes filled with tears as he described the incident. Louise talked about her recollections of her early life and of Joey. She made some connections of these incidents with her slow burn, while Ashford listened respectfully. Louise was feeling far less depressed as she began to unburden herself and as she saw concrete improvement in her relationship with Ashford.

In three more weekly interviews, they came to the point where they were ready to go on a biweekly and then monthly maintenance schedule. They were close to termination. In the meantime, they had bought a travel trailer and were fulfilling a lifelong dream of touring the West. Someone was taking care of Ashford's mother at home. The worker received a postcard from them. They were having a wonderful time but they noted that they still argued once in a while. They used the techniques they had learned and were mostly enjoying a new freedom and closeness they had never dreamed of before. They thanked the worker for the help. In one further session on returning, they talked about their new patterns. Louise had gone back to her garden, Ashford to his church work, and both in their own ways were including their adult children in their lives. They were excited about all of this and felt comfortable in what they had achieved.

The case of Ashford and Louise, though not a complicated one, is an example of all the principles we have been discussing in this chapter. The couple learned to reconstruct their relationship through communication. Although the relational tasks are typical of the post-parental stage, there is a parallel with the case of Joseph and Paula (case study 7.3) in that both were overinvolved with the other in some ways, and very separate from the other in other ways. They needed to separate personal from relational tasks. If they were to be successful, work had to proceed on both levels at once

THE NEEDS OF FAMILIES, THE SOCIAL WORKER AS A PERSON, AND THE HELPING PROCESS

In the first chapter we examined a model of the interaction between human needs of people in families, such as safety, belonging, communication, and so on; the response of the social worker; the response of the family; and general principles of practice. The theory reviewed in this chapter on middle phases of the helping process can be summed up in the Caldwells' story (case study 7.6). Families are assisted at different stages of development to carry out relational tasks. Techniques that help them do this have similarities to each other. The differences in the content and process of helping are contained in the stage of development, the personal realities of family members, and to some extent the process.

The family becomes a place where identity bonds are respected and can develop, where members can act appropriately in relation to others' needs and in relation to self. Knowing this, the social worker assists the family to develop this moral unity through the repairs needed in carrying out personal and relational tasks. The response of the social worker generates values in the performance of tasks. The family responds by carrying out these values in their communication, in their relations and in their action. The practice principles, listed in the fourth direction column of table 1.2, are essentially complex values placed into specific action by the family through the worker's response.

In the Caldwell family (case study 7.6), Louise and Ashford learned to differentiate themselves from each other, to respect each other's uniqueness, and to reconnect with each other as they are now, with their own respective developmental issues. They had something on which to build from the beginning. Louise was able to trust Ashford with the secret of Joey, knowing that it would not be violated. Ashford's guilt and delicate relationship with Chad was never used by Louise to hurt him or harden him. In the sessions, they learned to communicate, to express feelings and thoughts, and to respond in entirely different ways. They carried over these new patterns into their relationship. They learned to repair areas of difficulty. Both Louise and Ashford did different things for themselves, knowing that they had the other's support. Ashford took on a part-time job and did volunteer work. Louise spent time with her beloved garden. They also were able to do things together, such as their dates and finally their trip west. In the end, their relationship became a relationship in which they were each free to be the person they are with the other—and to choose this comfortably.

The principles generate a picture of the social worker's not simply carrying out effective techniques, but actually becoming these techniques in his or her interaction with the family, and thus helping the family to carry them out. These principles become qualities of the worker, and from these there come qualities, in their own way, of the family, to the extent that the family is willing to process them. They generate a type of "virtue orientation" to practice. In light of this model and the discussion of the book, what qualities of the worker result?

- The ability to take the role of each family member in relation to the other(s)
- The ability to visualize the possible good connections of family members with each other
- The ability to develop the listening language of empathy as a tool for growth and to teach others to use this tool according to their needs and capabilities
- The ability to express feelings and needs, respecting the other(s) and without being hurtful
- The ability to accept and value the other(s), including their potential to contribute, of which they themselves may have been unaware
- The ability to use this acceptance and good vision of the possibilities of the other(s) as a teaching tool
- The ability to help people in families to choose appropriately, respecting themselves and others, without being swayed by external pressure
- The ability to maintain safety and discretion, protecting the fragile identities of others, and to teach others to do so
- The ability to be honest with oneself and with others

These qualities are qualities of the social worker that underlie techniques. There is a strong research tradition that connects therapist qualities, such as empathy, genuineness, and warmth, with therapeutic effectiveness (Orlinsky, Grawe, &

Parks, 1994; Truax & Carkhuff, 1967), far more than allegiance to a particular school or technique (see discussion of the common factor components of the helping process in chapter 12). The relationship is, at least in part, created by the beliefs and values to which the social worker has come and that he or she is willing to help the family learn through coping with personal and relational tasks, with all of the implicit values contained within these tasks if they are to be done well.

SUMMARY

Work with couples is important. Research points out that clinicians work with about twice as many couples as elaborated families—that is, families, where the focus is on taking care of children or elderly persons (Doherty & Simmons, 1996). Moreover, work with the couple within the elaborated family is also the key to working with the elaborated family. The following chapters develop the themes of middle-stage work with elaborated families, work with families reconstructing themselves, and work between families and social institutions. Because the couple is the center of the family, the principles from work with couples in this chapter can be carried over into work with elaborated families.

REFERENCES

Ables, B. S. (1977). *Therapy for couples*. San Francisco, CA: Jossey-Bass.

Bardin, A. (1992). Less than perfect: A couple's struggle to accept their Down syndrome baby. *Family Therapy Networker*, November–December, 75–76.

Beckman, P. (1991). Comparison of mother's and father's perceptions of the effect of young children, with and without disabilities. *American Journal on Mental Retardation*, 95, 585–595.

Bernier, J. (1990). Parental adjustment to a disabled child: A family system perspective. *Families in society*, 71, 589–596.

Constable, R. T., & Cocozzelli, C. (1989). Common themes and polarities in social work practice theory development. *Social Thought*, Spring, 14–24.

Davis, B. (1987). Disability and grief. *Social Casework*, 68, 352–357.

deShazer, S. (1988). *Clues: Investigating solutions in brief therapy*. New York, NY: Norton.

Doherty, W. J., & Simmons, D. S. (1996). Clinical practice pictures of marriage and family therapists: A national survey of therapists and their clients. *Journal of Marital and Family Therapy*, 22, 9–25.

Foucault, M. (1972). *The archeology of knowledge*. New York, NY: Harper & Row.

Foucault, M. (1979). *Discipline and punish: The birth of the prison*. Middlesex, UK: Peregrine Books.

Foucault, M. (1980). *Power/knowledge: Selected interviews and other writings*. New York, NY: Pantheon Books.

Gergen, K. (1999). *An invitation to social construction*. Newbury Park, CA: Sage.

Goldenberg, I., & Goldenberg, H. (1996). *Family therapy: An overview*. Pacific Grove, CA: Brooks-Cole.

Grunebaum, J. (1990). From discourse to dialogue: The power of fairness in therapy with couples. In R. Chasin, H. Grunebaum, & M. Herzig (Eds.), *One couple, four realities: Multiple perspectives in couple therapy* (pp. 191–228). New York, NY: Guilford Press.

Guerney, B. L. (1977). *Relationship enhancement*. San Francisco, CA: Jossey-Bass.

Habermas, J. (1987). *The theory of communicative action*, vol. 2, *Lifeworld and system: A critique of functionalist reason*. Boston, MA: Beacon Press.

Haley, J. (1976). *Problem-solving therapy*. San Francisco, CA: Jossey-Bass.

Hartman, A., & Laird, J. (1983). *Family-centered social work practice*. New York, NY: Free Press.

Kheshgi-Genovese, Z., & Constable, R. T. (1995). Marital practice in social work. *Families in Society, 76*(9), 559–566.

Lambert, M. J., & Bergin, A. E. (1994). The effectiveness of psychotherapy. In A. E. Bergin & S. L. Garfield (Eds.), *Handbook of psychotherapy and behavior change* (pp. 143–189). New York, NY: Wiley.

Lazarus, A. (1981). *The practice of multimodal therapy*. New York, NY: McGraw-Hill.

Mead, G. H. (1932). *The philosophy of the present*. Chicago, IL: University of Chicago Press.

Mead, G. H. (1934). *Mind, self and society*. Chicago, IL: University of Chicago Press.

McGoldrick, M., Gerson, R., & Shellenberger, S. (1999). *Genograms: Assessment and intervention* (2nd ed.). New York, NY: Norton.

Monk, G., & Gehart, D. R. (2003). Sociopolitical activist or conversational partner? Distinguishing the position of the therapist in narrative and collaborative therapies. *Family Process, 42*(1), 19–30.

Nichols, M. (2013). *Family therapy: Concepts and methods* (10th ed.). Boston, MA: Pearson.

Nichols, M., & Schwartz, R. C. (2002). *Family therapy: Concepts and methods*. New York, NY: Allyn & Bacon.

Orlinsky, D. E., Grawe, K., & Parks, B. P. (1994). Process and outcome in psychotherapy—noch einmal. In A. E. Bergin & S. L. Garfield (Eds.), *Handbook of psychotherapy and behavior change* (pp. 270–378). New York, NY: Wiley.

Seybold, J., Flitz, J., & McPhee, D. (1991). Relation of social support to the self perceptions of mothers with delayed children. *Journal of Community Psychology, 19*, 29–36.

Shulman, L. (1992). *The skills of helping: Individuals, families and groups* (3rd ed.). Itasca, IL: Peacock.

Snyder, M. (1995). "Becoming": A method for expanding systemic thinking and deepening empathic accuracy. *Family Process, 34*(2), 241–253.

Stanton, M. D. (1981). Strategic approaches to family therapy. In A. S. Gurman & D. P. Kniskern (Eds.), *Handbook of family therapy*. New York, NY: Brunner-Mazel.

Truax, C. B., & Carkhuff, R. R. (1967). *Toward effective counseling and psychotherapy*. Chicago, IL: Aldine.

Turner, R. (1970). *Family interaction.* New York, NY: Wiley.

Voysey, M. (1975). *A constant burden: The reconstitution of family life.* London, UK: Routledge & Paul.

White, M. (2007). *Maps of narrative practice.* New York, NY: Norton.

White, M., & Epston, D. (1990). *Narrative means to therapeutic ends.* New York, NY: Norton.

Wile, D. B. (1992). *Couples therapy: A nontraditional approach.* New York, NY: Wiley.

CHAPTER 8

Beginnings and Middle Phases with Families of Two or More Generations

KEY TOPICS

Families Comprising Parents and Children
The Skills of Beginning with Families
One-Step or Two-Step Beginnings
The Family with School-Age Children
The Family with Adolescents
Parent Training
Family Tasks and Structure in Later Adulthood

The focus of this chapter and the following one moves from working with couples to working with more complex family units involving two and three generations. These families are families of parent(s) and children and possibly an older generation. Such families may have already experienced disruption and loss, but this is another level of complexity. We deal with this further complexity in the next chapter—families where parents are divorcing, families blending through remarriage, and underorganized families. The task framework is particularly useful amidst complex and disrupted arrangements.

ELABORATED FAMILIES

Families Comprising Parents and Children

We will examine beginning and middle-stage social work practice with families with school-age children and with adolescents. These families involve two or more generations: the parents, the children, and grandparents and other relatives in the picture. There are several stages of family development here. In Rita and Joav Green's family (case study 7.2), we have already seen a glimpse of the decision-making process used to accommodate a child with apparent severe disability. The emergent structure demands a strengthening of the couple relationship in a new set of tasks. As the child grows, the relationship of socialization and responsibility for the child demands inequality of power between parents and children. It demands a functional hierarchy. The parents need to be in charge.

In adolescence, there is an unstable shift in the hierarchy as the adolescent brings in reference groups other than the parents and challenges the family structure. On the other hand, the risky behaviors of which adolescents are capable (but often blissfully unaware) still demand some external controls. These behaviors are also often seen by the parents as a challenge by the adolescent to the perceived structure and a move toward power. The challenge for both parents and children is how to move from power and control to a more functional relationship, a relationship that respects the adolescent's growing self-responsibility. This movement is what much of the discourse between parents and adolescents is about. There needs to be a qualitative change in communication, which may become less formal to the extent that power may be less frequently called upon by both generations. Ideally, the transition in adolescence moves from a power struggle to a cooperative effort. Ultimately, friendship, attachment, membership, and belonging should operate more frequently than power. Parents remain secure attachment figures, and the adolescent explores his or her appropriate competency and autonomy. When this transition appears to be impeded, the frequent result is family conflict and negative developmental outcomes (Diamond & Liddle, 1999, p. 9).

Families Where Parents Are Divorcing and Families Blending through Remarriage

In chapter 9, we will examine practice with families in the process of divorce and its aftermath. In the case of the divorcing family, there are two structures, often at war or in conflict. One is the family as it was (with two parents), and the other is the family as it now must be if the custodial parent is to take charge. Because a transition from one to another structure takes time and needs to be tested, these family forms (divorcing or blending families) can be chaotic and full of confusion, with members having different or mixed allegiances, now to one parent, now to another (Montalvo, 1982). Remarriage brings in another set of allegiances.

Underorganized Families

Families that are underorganized often have experienced poverty and societal neglect, but they also may be chronically stuck in a transition. These are families of two or more generations, unable fully to carry out the socialization of children and other family functions. In chapter 9, we rely on Harry Aponte's (1986) developed discussion of this type of family structure, together with a case study illustration of work with these families.

Couples with Children

The couple is the executive subsystem of the family with children. The basics of working with couples, of course, are still important. Many of the basic issues within elaborated families are still couple issues. The parents of the young child need to come to an agreement around socialization and what they should expect of the child and of each other. They need to preserve and develop their own relationship at the same time. If one spouse's alliance with a child is stronger than his or her alliance with the other spouse, parents will not be able to manage relational tasks of socialization or of couple formation. They will be undercutting each other, with one parent experiencing greater closeness to the child, and one experiencing distance. Their conflicts come to be played out through this triangle.

As the child reaches adolescence and encounters a more complex world, the couple will need to shift their relationship again to the adolescent's changing needs and world. They need gradually to encourage responsibility on the youngster's part. Even if they privately disagree, the couple needs to support each other. Adolescents are legendary in their skills at gaining power by setting up cross-generational triangles, pitting one parent against another. This is stressful for the couple. Such triangles generate failure in the parenting role, as well as testing the couple relationship. Paradoxically, the triangulated structure, when it does foster problems with an adolescent, can also provide the couple some short-term distraction and relief from their own issues as a couple. They now focus on the adolescent rather than their own issues. To cope with this potential double dysfunction, the couple needs to form a united front while dealing appropriately, lovingly, and firmly with the needs of the adolescent. Such circumstances force parents to come together or face chaos. Eventually the adolescent we knew, with all of his or her creativity, will disappear, replaced by a young adult with different relationship and attachment needs. The problem is that some of the damage to the adolescent, as well as to the couple, may remain as both move on into a next phase. The young adult may remain as an adolescent. The couple may remain stuck in repetitive, relational triangles.

BEGINNING WITH FAMILIES WITH CHILDREN

Work with families with children is different from work with couples. The task focus is no longer primarily a search for boundaries and intimacy in the couple relationship. Instead, there is a twofold focus on managing the needs of the child and the couple relationship at the same time, retaining solidarity at both levels. In the Peterson example (case study 8.5), involving a 10-year-old child, the focus was mainly on the child and secondarily and implicitly on the couple's relationship. The Maxwell example (case study 8.7) involved an adolescent. Here the focus on the chronic marital problems of the couple alternated with the focus on Stephen Maxwell, who was running away from home. In the throes of their chronic marital difficulty, the parents had great difficulty relating to his needs.

Beginning with two-generation families can be somewhat complex. Coexisting couple and parental problems create different agendas. Often the agendas are conflicted or hidden. It is possible that the couple may find it more acceptable to work on a problem with a child than to acknowledge marital tension and deal with that. It may be hard to admit that the marriage is feeling tension. The couple may perceive less shame in having problems with their children than in having problems with each other. A perceived threat of losing the relationship may seem drastic.

There are several related sets of tasks for family members. One set is inherent to the couple as a couple. The other set is inherent to the couple as socializing agents with the youngster. And the youngster is developing as well. Multiple sets of relational tasks generate a complex picture. From a systems perspective, each set of tasks is implicit in the other. The couple's work on socialization issues also means working on their couple issues at the same time. This means that working with the couple on socialization issues with an adolescent, there is an implicit focus on their own marital relationship. In the same vein, by working with the adolescent, helping him sort out his issues of closeness and disengagement with either or both parents, one is also setting up the conditions for a possible reaction on the part of the couple to these changes in each parent's relationship with the child. On the other hand, the couple might have difficulty working on their own relational realities without the distraction of a cross-generational coalition with their son or daughter. The adolescent may be supplying the distraction, which prevents them from working on their own relationship. However, without the distraction, there is now an opportunity for the couple to resolve their relationship issues. If the couple does appropriately unite in the face of the problem, this developed unity may help resolve some of the couples' issues as well.

The Skills of Beginning with Families

Many of the skills of beginning with these families are quite similar to the previous discussion of beginning with couples. The family's perception is that things are out of control. It sees itself in a mess. It is important that what family members perceive as a mess be transformed into a problem, then into workable tasks. It is important that the family sees the process as hopeful, as something in which they can engage. A focus needs to be defined; a contract needs to be reached, and some personal connection needs to be made with the social worker as a possible helper. As with couples' counseling, this may be reached through a phone contact and two to three interviews. The difference is that there are now more people involved in the process and thus more contingencies. Although the process may take longer, the steps are similar. The dance needs to start with those who should be involved (given the tasks). Whether to begin through sessions with the couple or with the whole family is itself a complex question. The parents and others need to agree on tasks, define a focus, reach a contract they can trust, and agree on next steps. The skills listed for beginnings with more elaborated families (Shulman, 1992) are similar to the skills of beginning with couples. The social worker needs to do the following:

- *Clarify the social worker's purpose and role*, now with two generations.
- *Reach for the feelings* of a more complex network with multiple perceptions, interests, and tasks.

- *Put feelings into words*, acknowledging that there is in the nature of the situation an unequal relationship of parent and child; that there is a different language of feelings between the generations and different reference groups.
- *Reach inside silences* when the silence has been set up on both sides by fears of revealing parts of self.
- *Partialize concerns* when concerns get distorted and are translated into privileged demands on both sides, or when some concerns are unrevealed.
- *Contract* under conditions of generational inequality.
- *Assess* more complex structures and more complex tasks, often involving other societal institutions.
- *Respect the normal parental hierarchy* without aligning with it.
- *Join the family* enough to experience and describe the interaction without getting caught in it.

"Joining" the Family   To "join" the family, I need to temporarily suspend whatever responsibility I may have and any accompanying judgments which go with it, so that I might listen to the family. I do have responsibilities, but if I let mine take over, they could prevent members of the family from appropriately carrying out theirs. I know how easy it is to become over responsible for a family. The family then joins together to resist this unwanted influence. Or, more subtly, they quickly abandon their own efforts to cope and their own resources for change in favor of following the plan of this knowledgeable professional. Of course, the plan will fail, because they fall into dysfunction when they give up their own rough ability to act. I often need to take a "one-down" position to the family to help them discover how they, as individuals and as a family, can remain agents of their own development. Taking this position, I have learned to preserve a certain distance for their benefit and mine as well. I can temporarily listen to the music of the family and of each member. I can take part in their dance, but I cannot lose myself in the family. If I do, I will lose my unique, outsider, "one-down" perspective.

Respecting Hierarchies   In working with families with children, the major difference from working with couples is that, rather than a focus on equals, the *hierarchy* of the family needs to be respected. The parents need to be in charge. How does the social worker avoid taking over the process and thus displacing the parents? When what is happening in the family appears dysfunctional, as it will, the temptation will be very strong for the social worker to enter the family as an "expert" and undercut the already tottering parental power. When the "expert" takes over, both parents and child(ren) either move into dysfunction or fight the agency and social worker in order to remain in control. It may be better for them to disagree with the agency and the worker, since moving into dysfunction eliminates any possibility of betterment. Energy is then simply invested elsewhere.

Safety   Safety is particularly problematic where there has been abuse or the threat of abuse. Nothing can proceed if there is violence in the family or if people, including parents, don't feel safe. The only solution to problems with safety is to start with an enforceable agreement with the parents, and parents with the children around their tasks of creating safety. There should be a well-understood safety plan. These tasks, worked out in detail, will be the key to any other tasks that follow. The social worker is there to help the parents as well as children carry out these tasks. This, then, is the basis for the contract. The social worker will need to use all of the beginning process skills listed above to help the family assess the problem, contract on this basis, and begin. Their efforts to create safety need to be supported, but if safety cannot be created and maintained, then the community and the legal system will have to intervene. In situations where safety is not an issue, the social worker still must work delicately to preserve the hierarchy of responsibility of parents and children. This is particularly a problem when parents or child(ren) would prefer to hand over the power to the social worker.

One-Step or Two-Step Beginnings

Beginnings with the entire family are often quite complex. For this reason, it might be quite effective to work with the parents as a couple on developing a united approach to the needs of the child (and implicitly to their own needs) without the child or adolescent being involved at all. If this is a possibility, the process can go much faster. In any case, the issue of focus and who should be included needs to be resolved, even if it is necessarily tentative. Is this to be a one-step beginning—that is, the social worker sees the parents and not the child(ren)? Or is this to be a two-step beginning—that is, the social worker has one session with the parents, then a family session with parents and child(ren)? This can be determined with the client either at the stage of the initial phone inquiry or in a first session with the parents alone. As with couples' counseling, it is important to listen to the request and determine with the person calling whether it is (1) an individual problem that can best be dealt with individually, (2) a problem best dealt with by beginning with the couple alone, the one-step beginning, or (3) something best dealt with in the whole family, with parents and child(ren) together in a session.

Beginning with Parents

When the problem has to do with parenting issues, it is generally best to start with the couple together to decide whether the children should be included. Usually, if the couple can be helped to agree on specifically what the problem is and how to deal with it, they can be a support to each other and their approach to the problem can be more effective. Naturally, a parent with a spouse obdurately opposed to coming in for help, or a person clearly identifying a personal problem or need, will need an approach tailored to the situation. Although it is generally preferable to start with both parents, it may not be possible to do this. If beginning with both parents is not possible, working with one parent still can have impact on the total system. For single parents, sometimes it is better to begin without involving the child(ren). The following case study is an example of the social worker working with single-parent issues.

CASE STUDY 8.1:
A SINGLE PARENT

Joan, a single parent, is dealing with a chaotic home situation immediately after her divorce. She had never wanted to be a single parent and has difficulty accepting the implications of the role. No one—not her children, her mother, or her former spouse—takes her seriously, and she is having great difficulty exerting any control at all. The social worker works with Joan over four months, helping her to differentiate herself in relation to her family so that she can meet the demands of this new role. With her children, she eventually takes charge. With her former spouse, she sets limits. With her mother, she clarifies that she will manage her problems. She is in control, but she would accept help from her mother. She strengthens her approach with her children, her mother, and her former spouse. These respond by changing their own expectations and relationship with her, eventually allowing her to take her role. In this particular case, it was unnecessary, and would be dysfunctional, to see any person other than Joan for working with her parenting issues. With support and extensive work, she became strong enough to manage the situation.

A One-Step Beginning with a Couple

A parent may call with a problem. When the social worker returns the call, she briefly helps the parent clarify the problem and arrange to come in with the partner to see how she might help them to manage the problem. To avoid an implicit alliance at this stage, she doesn't spend a lot of time over the phone. They both come in and, as a result of the session, resolve together to try a different approach to the problem. The worker keeps them in charge. The approach works to the point of resolving the issue without further involving other parts of the family. The couple may come in a number of times with different issues. The focus is always on helping them to clarify their roles and strategy in relation to the problem—that is, on empowering the parents as parents while helping them to respond in a differentiated way to situations where their normal responses seem to fail. The approach takes some experience on the part of the social worker to make the assessment, to deal with parents' problems with relational tasks, and to begin the process of coaching parents on dealing with these tasks without the children present.

The Kim family was able to manage without bringing in their teenage son, Justin. From the parents' perspective, bringing him in would have empowered Justin (with his verbal skills in English) and undermined their delicate sense of control in a different culture.

CASE STUDY 8.2:
THE KIM FAMILY

Mrs. Bernice Kim called Methodist Youth Services on the advice of their minister at the Korean Methodist Church about the problems she and her husband, Dr. Peter Kim, were having with Justin, age 15. She had some reluctance to come in with her husband but assumed that an expert from the agency could just tell them what they should do better. Both were born in Korea and had emigrated as employees of a multinational company. All their kin on both sides of the family are in Korea. Recently there has been a problem between Justin and his father. Dr. Kim feels that Justin, born in the United States, no longer respects his father as a Korean boy should. He spends a lot of time with his American friends, even sleeping at their houses when he can. He is not doing as well in high school as Dr. Kim thinks he could. He will not study more than a few hours a night. He refuses to go to Korean Saturday school and spends his weekends watching videos with his friends. Dr. Kim has been restrained with Justin. His father would have used a degree of physical punishment on Justin for being lazy that he knows he cannot use in the United States. Mrs. Kim tends to see Justin's side of the problem, saying that he is growing up as any other American boy. As long as they live here, they must adapt. Justin is adapting more than they are. They can expect nothing more from Justin.

The previous night, Dr. Kim and Justin had an argument. Rather than Justin's listening to his father, he left home to spend the night with his best friend, Kerry, and his family. Kerry's family seems to be a rather disorganized American family with no clear hours or well-defined relations. For example, they never have any meals together. Kerry tells Justin how unfair and repressive Justin's family is. Justin told his father this. His father was so angry and ashamed of him that he told him to go and stay with Kerry. Justin left to stay with Kerry. Dr. Kim now regrets his outburst. Justin may be getting tired of being a long-term guest, but neither of the two will back down.

The social worker suggested that this couldn't be resolved over the phone and suggested that Dr. and Mrs. Kim come to the agency to discuss it further. They need to develop a plan. They made an appointment to get together in a few days. In the session, the social worker was fairly formal, addressing them as Dr. and Mrs. Kim, and asked Dr. Kim to identify his concerns to see whether they could develop a strategy together. As Dr. Kim described the situation, she responded by reflecting his narrative and commented that that "It sounds as if you feel that you are losing your son." Dr. Kim's chin quivered as he said "yes." Mrs. Kim, seeing Dr. Kim's emotion, moved in to say that she doesn't think they are losing Justin, but that he is like an American boy now. It is a shame, but what else could we expect? We have done it (looking at her husband). The social worker encouraged them to talk about how they saw the problems. Summarizing their discussion, she reflected the point of view of each, the concerns about loss of cultural heritage and connections with family, some of the reality of Justin's present high school and friends. Both saw their common point of view in this, together with some of their different perceptions, and agreed with the picture. The problem was how to help Justin to rejoin the family without either his father or him feeling shame.

They worked out a plan for his mother to call Justin on the weekend and invite him for dinner with them in a good Korean restaurant. The worker coached Dr. Kim on helping Justin to tell his story, just as they had just done, this time about how things were at the house of his friend. She coached him on how to invite Justin back without criticism. They agreed to follow the strategy. At the same time, how could Justin learn more about his Korean heritage? The outcome of this discussion was that Dr. Kim would wait for Justin to settle comfortably at home again. When things had settled, he could take a two-month vacation from the company and invite Justin to come back with him to Korea to spend some time with his relatives. At the end of the session, they agreed to try this strategy and to stay in contact. They would get together with the social worker again, but this would get it

started. The dinner was initially somewhat tense, as Justin expected his father to reprove him for his behavior. When this didn't happen, his mother wondered if he was ready to return. He said he was. His father welcomed him and Justin apologized to his father on his own. His father accepted his apology. Later his father invited him to take a trip with him to Korea, and Justin accepted the offer. The Kims had more sessions with the worker discussing some of their own differences with North American culture, and some of Mrs. Kim's issues to which she had not previously been able to give voice.

As communication got better between Justin and his father and the tension lessened, Justin's grades improved somewhat. The Kims stayed in touch with the social worker and had a final couple's session before Dr. Kim left with his son for the two to make connections with Dr. Kim's family again. She gave them a genogram assignment to do when they were visiting his family, and they agreed to come back, when they returned, to share the genogram and what they had discovered about their families.

The Kims did not have a cultural expectation of extended work with the social worker, particularly around their feelings. Clarifying purpose and role, partializing concerns, assessing and contracting were skills that helped develop the framework of the worker's approach to the Kims. Feelings were mostly implied, evident to everyone, but not centralized in the discussion. Dr. Kim's quivering chin as he spoke of possibly losing Justin, and Mrs. Kim's move to protect him from sharing feelings further were understood by everyone. Later Mrs. Kim could express some of her own feelings about herself, which up to that moment she was living out through Justin. The worker does not need to reach out aggressively for these feelings. They are already understood, and they will emerge through further process. To go faster would be to frighten the Kims away from the work. They responded well to the worker's coaching and task approach, which kept them fully in charge of their concerns.

In other cases, the one-step approach may involve extended work with the parent(s) without the children. This may be particularly useful where the major focus is marriage counseling or individual counseling, and any issues between the parent(s) and the child(ren)can be managed by coaching the parents alone.

CASE STUDY 8.3: DAVE AND BECKY AND THE BOYS

Dave Harrison, a recovering alcoholic, worked with his wife, Becky, on issues stemming from his years of alcoholism. She had become the central support and director of the family during those years. It was difficult for both to move to a more balanced position. At the same time, their four boys were out of control. Their out-of-control behavior was implicitly supported by the posi-

tion Dave had taken with them as "one of the boys" and against Becky during his drinking years. Dave and Becky worked for nine months on these issues. They were able to do most of the work with the boys on their own, talking about it in their weekly couple's sessions. It was not necessary for the boys to take part in family sessions, but the boys responded well to the rebalancing of mother's and father's relationship, which went on at home.

A Two-Step Beginning

In many cases there is a two-step beginning. Sometimes the patterns are very entrenched and there are reasons for eventually involving the youngster(s) in family sessions; or the parents may expect and want the youngster to be involved. In the following case, in the initial phone contact, the worker determines that this is a possible direction and schedules an initial session with the parents with the goal of having a family session following the initial session. As in the Antonelli family situation, originally cited in chapter 2 (case study 2.2), the social worker sets this up from the first phone call.

CASE STUDY 8.4: RENATA AND MARIO ANTONELLI, MARISA

Renata Antonelli called about her only child, Marisa, who is two months short of 18 years old. Marisa was originally a compliant child, the center of attention of her parents and extended family. For three years, she has been rebelling against the family strictures, particularly around dating and boyfriends, but this has intensified with the approach of her birthday. Her

mother, Renata, has taken responsibility for discipline. Renata's husband, Mario, a bookish man absorbed in his small business, is not as definite as she is with Marisa. Renata learned of Marisa's sexual activity with her boyfriend about five months ago by listening to and tape recording her phone conversations with her girlfriends. The parents had previously been quite restrictive of her activity, but now the restrictions and Marisa's rebellious response have escalated to extreme positions on both sides. Marisa could not make a phone call. Marisa avoided any of her mother's restrictions at school, and her mother found herself, in her own words, "micromanaging" all Marisa's affairs, going through her purse regularly and engaging in a cat-and-mouse game with her. Marisa has run away for a day at a time but was brought back by the police. Marisa was winning the game in any case, and the parents were very concerned that she did not seem at all to be aware of the risks she was taking. She will be 18 in two months and firmly plans to move out on her birthday.

The situation had moved to a point of seriousness. Parents' and child's positions had rigidified. Marisa was close to emancipation. The parents wanted whole-family work. For all these reasons the social worker opted for a whole-family approach. Over the phone, the social worker promptly set up an interview for Renata and Mario to discuss the situation and plan for a family session that week. Renata seemed to be aware that she had trapped herself into a cat-and-mouse game with her daughter, that both were now at extreme positions, and that her daughter seemed so invested in the game that she was unaware of some of the risks she was taking. She knew that there would have to be some change in their approach but couldn't find a safe alternative to what they were doing. Marisa's rebellion and the corresponding restrictions had escalated to the point where she was permanently grounded. Marisa had little to lose.

The initial interview with Mario and Renata started a working relationship and confirmed the initial assessment that parents and daughter were caught in the cat-and-mouse pattern. It was decided to change the pattern by

shifting the primary responsibility of working with Marisa to Mario. Renata would be Mario's closest adviser. This was discussed in some detail. Mario was willing to do this, and Renata was willing to step back, since she had borne the bruising conflict until now. She could see that she had lost effectiveness. They also needed to shift from their extreme restrictiveness, if the daughter could make a corresponding shift toward a degree of self-responsibility. Her privileges could come back gradually, but she had to merit them in some way also. It was decided that they would ask her to write down what she should do to regain privileges, and work out an agreement with her in their next family session with her included. They would also be thinking about her thinking systematically about her planned emancipation in two months. Mario agreed to talk with her. They would remain in touch by conference call prior to the family session in two days.

Mario took Marisa out to dinner, where they talked over the situation. Eventually he asked her to write down what she could do to remedy the situation. Instead of writing what she would do, Marisa wrote what they should do for her, including buying her a car and providing an allowance of $300 each month, so that she could manage her upcoming emancipation. It was decided by phone that this was a place to start and that it would all be worked out at the family session. Rather than getting caught up on Marisa's concrete expectations of $300, the process of beginning would be more important.

In the family session, the room was comfortably set up with seven chairs arranged in a circle around a low table. The family sat so that they could have eye contact with each other, with the social worker sitting in one place or moving next to one or another family member to facilitate communication between them. The social worker began by connecting with each family member, then setting the focus; the purpose of the meeting was to help Marisa and the family to deal with the difficult situation they were all in, with all of its risks for Marisa. He started sitting next to Mario and helped him to get things started with Marisa. Mario started reasonably well with concern for Marisa but tended to preach a bit as soon as he sensed Marisa's resistance. Without undermining Mario, the social worker supported Mario's efforts to reach out to Marisa and her concerns. The mother, as agreed in the previous session and over the phone, made a heroic (and successful) effort to sit back and let the father take over. The social worker moved to sit next to Marisa as soon as he sensed that Mario was comfortable with what he was doing and that Marisa was responding. Initially she threw obstacles up to her father, but eventually softened her position with some support. Several times later in the discussion she began to cry as she continued softening her stance in the face of her parents softening their own stance.

They worked out a beginning agreement under the terms of which privileges would be restored under certain conditions. The family agreed to meet weekly to monitor this and move to the next restoration of privilege. The social worker warned that there would be difficulties on both sides and shifted the focus to Marisa's plans to emancipate in two months. At a certain point, the social worker moved in and began a dialogue with her in the context of her discussion with her father. When the social worker reached for her feelings, she really opened up about her uncertainty about her planned emancipation. When this came from Marisa, it was accepted by all without any preaching. It had become obvious to all, including her, that her plans were unclear. If she emancipated, Mario and Renata would continue to care about her but would not support her financially, providing a car and so on. She would have to get a job, possibly at Kmart, to manage things, and it would be hard to manage that and college at the same time. After some further discussion, Marisa admitted that she had been "just as stubborn as her parents" and that she might want to defer this plan a bit. Renata joined in at this point, supporting the direction the family was taking. The ending task was for Marisa to work out on paper a plan for what she should do to get her privileges back. On a separate piece of paper, she was to write her dreams and aspirations for the time in her life following high school. She agreed with that. As the family was ready to leave, the Renata rejoined Marisa in an accustomed enmeshed position when she reminded her that Marisa ought to go to the bathroom before they went on the road. Marisa dutifully complied. During the following sessions, Mario remained in charge, now with Renata sharing his position. Marisa relaxed somewhat and was able to show a softer side of herself. The family became able to discuss their concerns with each other without an explosion and without punishment. Marisa is beginning to take a longer-term perspective and talk of her dreams of further education and a career working with teenagers in trouble in a school.

The Antonelli family still has a good deal of work to do. The focus of the work of the interview was clear, and all were engaged in it. The worker could decentralize himself and help the family to engage with each other. They did come up with an agreement and a shift in the structure. There was a good deal of work with Marisa, reaching for her feelings through some of her silences and helping her to bring them into her discussion with her father. By the end of the interview, the contract had a more specific focus on the immediate arrangements at home, on her planned emancipation, and on her dreams. She may be sacrificing her dreams for an emancipation, but she also needed to know how her parents could appropriately support her reaching for her dreams. This would then be some of the work for the following sessions. Using all of the skills listed, a beginning had been made sufficient for the family to move on to middle-stage work.

MIDDLE-STAGE WORK

The Family with School-Age Children

The family with school-age children is now accommodating the reality that another agent of socialization, the school, will share in their responsibility. When the child is having difficulty in his or her psychosocial functioning in school, school social workers will work with child's teachers, the family, and the child so that, on an individual basis, the difficulty is alleviated. At the same time, the child is growing and his or her relations with the siblings and parents are becoming more complex. Within the couple relationship, the arrangement has to shift to make space for the developing needs of their children. They need to take on appropriate parental roles. On the other hand, they also need to maintain their spousal roles. Sometimes, as in the Peterson family in the following case study, the child feels cut off from one parent and begins to develop problems that demand a shift in the family relations. In the case of Jerry Peterson, he wanted more connection with his father as he was growing up.

CASE STUDY 8.5: LARRY AND JENNIFER PETERSON, JERRY

Larry and Jennifer Peterson, a couple in their early thirties, are concerned about their oldest son Jerry, age 10. Jerry is having daily screaming tantrums when he is frustrated about anything. These occur mainly at home in the presence of his mother. He presents no problem at school and is doing well academically. The mother feels she has lost control of him and brings in his father from his work to deal with him. Jerry has always been very close to his mother, who has elected to remain at home with her children. He particularly appreciates his mother's cooking and can name every dish she has cooked over the past several weeks, describing each with great relish. His younger brother, Craig, age 8, is close to his father; the two brothers have differentiated themselves in this way. Both Craig and his father spend a lot of time together and love outdoor activities, such as hunting and fishing. The family now has a baby girl, Karen. Jerry now has less time with his mother, and he is growing up into a boy's world. Larry feels trapped in his job in the family business. He had been a rebellious son as a teenager and now feels the need to make up for his past mistakes. Larry's relationship with Jennifer, although it appears somewhat unconflicted, also appears undeveloped. They carry out their roles as they individually conceive of them, but they are not necessarily close in their friendship. They were eager to get help with Jerry, but their own spousal relationship was not part of the bargain.

The initial interview was a family session with the mother, the father, and Jerry. It was clear that the first task was for Jerry to get control over his tantrums. Both the mother and father needed to support that control with a positive approach. Jerry needed a better relationship with his father. Jennifer and Larry needed to accommodate that relationship shift without upsetting the balances of their own marital relationship.

The first task was for Jerry to begin to manage his own tantrums. In the first session, he talked about them. He agreed to keep track of them on a calendar, which he would fill out every night before going to bed. With a focus on his good days, his father would reward him when he had a good day. Also Larry and Jerry would spend time together doing activities that Jerry enjoyed. These days with his father were not to be used as rewards. The mother would stay out of the arrangement between Larry and Jerry, but would encourage it. If Jerry caused her problems, she would deal with him herself rather than call in Larry to punish him. Mother and father

would communicate on a regular basis about how things were going with the children, including Jerry. They would also use their weekly sessions for this communication, with Jerry taking responsibility for how he was managing his tantrums.

The first session had begun with the family. The social worker made an assessment, developed a plan, worked out the agreed arrangements, and began with Jerry so that Jerry could take charge, as much as possible, of his part in the situation. A plan emerged and was agreed upon in the first session. As they moved to the following sessions and the middle stage, the father and Jerry would need to communicate with each other in the sessions about how things were going with these arrangements. The mother would encourage them, but not interfere. Jerry was immediately responsive and loved the opportunity to have some access to his father. Larry had much greater difficulty finding ways of relating to Jerry, finding words to say, being consistent with his rewards, and finding ways to have a relationship with Jerry that was different from his relationship with Craig. Jerry didn't seem to mind or to notice that his father was having difficulty. For the sessions following, as they had previously arranged, Jerry brought his calendar with the good days and bad days marked on it. The first week he had more good days than bad days. Jennifer tended to get overinvolved with this, and the worker had to help concretely shift the focus from the mother to the father and to Jerry. The father tended to focus on the bad days, and so he needed help to focus more on the good days. As Jerry recounted the days in the family sessions, he also would recount with great relish every meal his mother had cooked that week. He had noted them on the calendar. The sessions following had fewer and fewer bad days until they completely disappeared over the period of a month. The parents also began to notice that Craig, formerly the good boy in the family, did some things to get himself in trouble, and that Jerry had some really helpful qualities in these situations. However, the majority of the time together was focused on the time spent between the father and Jerry, encouraging their developing relationship. This was again more difficult for the father than for Jerry. The whole process took place over six weekly sessions, and, with change stabilized, the family was able to end the process.

The focus on Jerry's taking charge of his tantrums was elaborated throughout the middle stage. For him to accomplish this, the family shifted; the mother let the father get closer to Jerry, and the father discovered that he could have a relationship with his oldest son. There was not the framework of intimacy one would have in couples' counseling. There was a certain level of focus on feelings, but in accordance with what the family wanted, there was a primary focus on behavior. The social worker was continually clarifying the focus and partializing it in relation to what could be done within the space of a week. The social worker shared data, provided support for Jerry's good response, and helped the family deal with problems when they occurred. The worker was actively teaching communication and relational skills as the structure changed. When Jerry could maintain his changes and begin to generalize them, the process could end.

Three-Step Processes

If one strategy is not working, the worker may need to go to another within the same framework of relational tasks. Jerry's problem could have proved to be unmanageable, or the parents could have begun to show couple issues. The process with Jerry would then have to take one further step, becoming a three-step process. What was started with the family would continue, but in this context, it might also be necessary to see Jerry alone for him to process further his work on his tantrums. Another possibility is that the parents could have become aware of their marital issues behind the focus on Jerry. What if the cross-generational coalition of mother and son is so strong that, when they try to change it, it becomes stronger? Then the third step would be to work with the couple. In the Maxwell case discussed in case study 8.7, this is what happened. At different times, the social worker did family work, couple work, and individual work with the son and with the father.

What would trigger the further steps is that from the social worker's assessment, the simpler one- and two-step alternatives do not work. Parts of the family begin asking for a more individualized approach. The social worker needs to decide whether this can be done without losing the family work that has already been started. Since the tasks are embedded in one another, the same family work can be done in different ways, now working with a couple, at another time an individual. In any case, a good assessment will determine the direction taken. Whatever options seem best, there needs to be a good understanding of the dynamics of the family as a whole and of family tasks.

The Family with Adolescents

The adolescent usually challenges the family system. The family with adolescents needs a combination of firmness, ability to communicate, flexibility, and the wisdom to know when to be firm and when to be flexible. The couple must be able to resolve any differences around childrearing, since any perceived division can be fatally exploited by the adolescent. A good example of this was seen in the Antonelli family (case study 8.4) earlier in the chapter.

As discussed earlier, personal tasks are sometimes buried in the relational tasks of the couple dealing with parental responsibilities. In these cases, there is again a two-step process: first helping the member to own the task and do something about it, then helping the partner to assist in this without taking over or reacting inappropriately to the other's efforts. Some of these issues can be profound, as in the case below of George, Marian, and 17-year-old Sean. The parental and couple relational tasks inherent in raising an adolescent become the context for some resolution of George's personal issues. Much of this particular work was done in a couple's counseling framework.

CASE STUDY 8.6:
GEORGE AND MARIAN, SEAN

George and Marian had been having great difficulty with their oldest son, Sean, age 17, who was displaying out-of-control behavior, particularly having to do with drinking and drugs. The family has a number of boys. George has been quite close with his sons, and in particular with Sean as a younger child. As Sean reached adolescence, George began to withdraw and became very inconsistent, sometimes harshly punishing him for small infractions, sometimes being indulgent. In the face of his father's withdrawal, Sean retreated into a relationship with his generally indulgent mother. In this triangulated situation, a high level of marital conflict over Sean

developed between George and Marian. Sean would either play one against the other or ignore them both. George and Marian felt helpless in the face of Sean's behavior and their emergent marital conflicts.

As part of a broader process of helping George and Marian to come to some agreement on how to treat Sean's increasingly self-destructive behavior, George pointed out that he had lost his father through divorce when he was 16. As a consequence, he feels paralyzed when he tries to be a father to a boy this age. He gets overwhelmed with the same helpless feelings he had when his father left him. The focus of the work in the couple's sessions then switched to George. The theme to be explored and developed in their work together became: you can be the father to your son that your father never was to you. George accepted this and worked on it. At the social worker's instigation, George asked Marian to help him with this, since she had had a different experience with her father in her family. George and Marian were able then to come to a common agreement on how to manage the situation with Sean.

Building on George and Marian's agreement, as in the Antonelli family in case study 8.4, one further step was to include Sean in the process. Involving Sean, the focus on George and Marian as a couple shifted to a focus on their relationship with Sean and Sean's with them. There would be an opportunity to shift from a power struggle to a discussion of themes of attachment—trust, commitment, power, protection, and love (Diamond & Liddle, 1999). With the more secure base settling some of the problems the attachment issues might bring, it was possible for Sean to begin an appropriate and real exploration of connectedness and autonomy. For parents and adolescents, this is a difficult path, accomplished in spurts, not really at once.

When Sean came to the sessions with George and Marian, there was a gradual shift in focus. Initially the struggle was over whether parents still had the power to influence a 17-year-old boy while still at home. Over several sessions, a truce was developed on this discussion. As long as Sean lived at home, George and Marian did have the right to set some standards, but ultimately Sean was in charge of his future. The social worker attempted to shift the focus to attachment and relational themes. Did George and/or Marian have regrets about the way things had gone with Sean? Did Sean know of these regrets? Does Sean have regrets? Would he have liked things to have been different? If there were a miracle and things were different tomorrow, how would he like them to be? This was difficult work, but it succeeded in shifting the focus from power to attachment issues. The social worker was particularly focused on developing father-son dialogue. Over the following sessions, George felt himself to be less responsible for Sean's choices. He was able to get more consistently involved with Sean as a friend as well as his father. In what would have to be a continuing process, Sean began to take some responsibility for dealing with his emergent addictions.

A Three-Step Process: A Case

The Maxwell family is far more complex in its needs, so the social worker found himself working at different times with every part of the family to help them carry out the relational tasks. The family faced issues similar to those faced by the Antonellis. However, the parents had a long and chronic history of marital conflict, and it was difficult for them to agree on anything. Both had previous marriages and had adult children from these marriages. Mr. Maxwell, in his late sixties, was dealing with retirement issues at the same time he was raising two adolescent boys. An uncontrolled diabetic, his circulatory problems were at the point of chronicity and possible collapse. Although often in contact with reality, at times his own private demons tended to take over and he would appear to distort reality profoundly. When challenged in a humorous way, he would cycle back into reality contact. The social worker learned to do this repeatedly, reinforcing his grasp of reality so that, at least in sessions, his outbursts of profound reality distortion receded. The family system was rigid. Paradoxically, Stephen's runaway episodes were the one thing that eventually brought his parents to find some agreement at least on how to deal with him. Both eventually learned to put away their private demons in the interests of Stephen. This eventually also reinforced a certain calmness and unity in their approach to each other.

CASE STUDY 8.7:
THE MAXWELL FAMILY

John and Mary Maxwell came to a family service agency when their 16-year-old son, Stephen, had run away from home to live with the family of his girlfriend, Jodi Smith. The Maxwell family had experienced continual conflict for many years. It was the second marriage for both. John, age 66, and Mary, age 45, had experienced conflict since the beginning of their relationship. This conflict was now aggravated by John's retirement from his position as a supervisor in a factory. John was frequently verbally abusive. He regularly related to Mary as if she were his abusive and hated grandmother, who had raised him. This association was very close to the surface in his mind and in his verbalizations. John had grown up in South Dakota with roots in the Sioux culture of his extended family. He ran away to the city when he was 16. Later he joined the Army and worked his way up to master sergeant and drill instructor before his discharge. Mary, of Lithuanian ancestry, had a drinking problem, which she would not discuss with anyone. The family living with John and Mary at the

time the case began comprised Saulius, age 30; Stephen, age 16; and Mike, age 14. Saulius is Mary's son from her first marriage. He is mentally retarded and extremely dependent on her. Mike, a remarkably resilient youngster, escaped his parents' focus as long as he could bury himself in his beloved computer. Occasionally in the process, the social worker had to protect Mike from his parents' focus when they were looking for a substitute for Stephen. From the social worker's earlier assessment, he decided that it would be better to leave Mike out of family sessions. Including him might actually unnecessarily create dysfunction by burdening Mike with family triangles he had skillfully opted out of in favor of Stephen. He did see Mike twice over two years however, and he worked with him indirectly through the parents. Mike continued to function reasonably well outside of the family triangles, and the assessment, in retrospect, seemed correct.

Stephen had been a somewhat naive youngster, a good student who was very much a focus of the family triangles. He was alternately overprotected and the object of conflict between John and Mary. He could not easily break free. When he met Jodi Smith, he met an entire family, profoundly dysfunctional, who allowed and encouraged him to have sex with Jodi on the condition that he in effect become a member of their family. This attraction was the equivalent of joining a cult with sex as a bait. He was running away from the tense, conflictual enmeshment of his own family to the loose and pleasureful enmeshment of the Smith family. Regular access to Jodi was an incentive for a 16-year-old, for whom the attraction of sex became like an addiction. Over two years, Stephen ran away four times and stayed with the Smiths for months at a time. Partially because Stephen was close to 18 and partially because the Smiths seemed to have a certain amount of power with the police, the police colluded with the Smiths in this. Finally, Stephen became able to mature beyond the attraction of the Smith family for him. He was able to discuss this in individual work when he eventually became ready to let it go.

The Maxwell family initially presented as both rigid and out of control. The relationship between the mother and father was chronically conflicted. Any communication between them was difficult and subject to distortion. The father would take over an entire interview ventilating about his earlier abuse and traumatic memories. Any focus on Stephen or Mary would be lost. The mother enmeshed herself with Stephen in the interviews, thinking for him and speaking for him. Stephen would come with a list of how cruel and unfair his parents were. None had any experience of listening to the other and so their communication tended to be reactive — acting out rather than expressing their

thoughts and feelings through words and listening to the other person. It was clear that the process would have to move slowly, and it was unclear how much the family would tolerate before they summarily ended their contact with the social worker, and how much they might be able to accomplish together. However, John, with his Native American background, understood the value of silence. In any case, words or explanations were not particularly effective. Some of the most productive work was done slowly and in relative silence. The family was eventually able to develop ways of communicating, but good, uninterrupted, sustained communication was rare. For John and Mary, Stephen's acting out tended to distract from their problems with each other. Without Stephen's dramatic problems, their marital problems escalated.

Members of the Maxwell family were seen in different combinations for approximately two years. During this period there were also contacts with a counselor from the school Stephen attended and with an officer of the juvenile court. In the initial phase, the social worker worked with Stephen and his parents together on issues of differentiation. Then, when he would run away to the Smiths, she worked with the parents alone on communication, problem-solving, and relationship building in their efforts to bring him back. When he returned home, they would work in joint family sessions on differentiation of self in the family. There was some progress in both sets of tasks, but never enough to stabilize the situation until the last six months of the case. By this time, they had made enough progress in family work to move to a third step — seeing the parents separately on couple issues and Stephen on differentiation issues. Although the situation remained unstable, Stephen did fully separate from the Smiths, graduated from high school and had a period of reworking his relationships with his parents before he joined the Army, where he did very well. Both parents were pleased and appropriately involved with this step toward emancipation. As Stephen moved toward differentiation, the parents worked on their marital issues and made some progress on them. The social worker ended with some individual sessions with the father working on personal and couple issues.

The tasks of the Maxwell parents and of Stephen are dramatically interrelated. Stephen needed to disengage from Jodi and the Smith family and reengage with his parents enough to complete schooling and eventually emancipate. At the same time, he needed to differentiate himself from enmeshed relationships with each of his parents and with their marriage. Then he needed to develop appropriate plans for his further education or his work. His mother and father needed to learn to communicate and work together in the difficult and stressful situation of Stephen's runaway episodes. They needed to begin to manage some of their chronic marital and personal issues without involving Stephen. For Stephen to let go of the Smith family and reengage with his own family enough to emancipate, there had to be an appropriate relationship at home. The mother and father could not use Stephen as a distraction. They had to manage their marital issues without Stephen.

The focus with the Maxwells was always complex. There were two sets of tasks of different generations that were interdependent and therefore needed to be worked on at the same time. Communication had to take place if they were to cope with the issues, but both Stephen and his parents had a tendency to act rather than work out issues in this way. Only toward the end did they show any ability to communicate effectively. To the extent that they did develop these skills, the problems slowly alleviated. The most important point is that the assessment perspective and intervention focus had to remain with each person in the family and at the same time with the family as a whole in its interactive processes. Based on this perspective, a three-step process could take place, with the social worker working with the family as a whole and all of its parts in different ways until there was sufficient improvement for Stephen to emancipate, the couple and individual problems to alleviate somewhat, and Mike to survive adolescence with the protections he had already ably constructed for himself. A useful metaphor for the complex transaction between Stephen, the Maxwells, and the Smiths was the story of Pinocchio, with his recruitment to and escape from Donkey Island (where boys became donkeys). This was used at different times with the mother, the father, and Stephen to give a context for their emerging story and Stephen's transformations. The metaphor became quite meaningful to all, especially Stephen. He would be in charge of his transformation. Once he was ready to take himself willingly out of Donkey Island, he could develop a different relationship with his mother and father and eventually emancipate.

PARENT TRAINING

Parent training is a popular and fairly effective way to help parents develop the understanding, skills, and relational alignment needed to cope with the needs of children at different developmental stages as well as with different levels of challenge and need. A variety of parent training programs available can be adapted to special needs of children, to different ages and to different parental situations and learning needs. While parent training programs are diverse, they are somewhat similar in format to the MRE discussed in chapter 6. The focus is on the couple learning skills which hopefully would translate into their interaction with their child(ren). The programs may run from six to twelve sessions, but sometimes fewer, depending on what they wish to achieve and on their audience. There will be short presentations of developmental information, information on special needs of particular children at particular stages as well as discussion of what parents are experiencing. There will be roleplays and skill training. The parent experience and skill development may come with fishbowl sessions and buzz groups, as in MRE. There may be mentoring of parents for further skill development, depending on the needs of the group and the resources available. Different from the couple counseling format discussed above, the primary relationships and the power of the group will not come from the facilitator as much as from seeing other couples cope, from networking with them, getting their feedback, seeing skills demonstrated in the fishbowl, and testing out new skills in the small groups and on their own. The focus is less individualized to the couple. However, some of the relational realignment needed for both parents to be involved with their child can quietly take place as long as both parents are engaged and getting implicit support from the group for a relational shift in their interaction with their child(ren). For situations in which more is needed, there may be mentoring possible. Also, the group could be a springboard for a more individualized and focused involvement with couples' or family counseling, when that is needed.

There are many approaches to parent training, some with well-developed manuals and certification programs. Some examples would be the Oregon model of parent management training (Forgatch, 1994; Forgatch & DeGarmo, 1999; Forgatch, DeGarmo, & Beldavs, 2005; Forgatch, Patterson, & Beldavs, 2009), and systematic training for effective parenting (STEP) (Dinkmeyer & McKay, 1989). What they have in common is a focus on communication, giving clear directions, setting limits, positive reinforcement and problem solving and monitoring behavior (Parra-Cardona, Domenech-Rodriguez, Forgatch, Sullivan, Bybee, Holtrop, et al., 2012). Some include reduction of parental laxness, verbosity and overreaction to behavior (Wiggins, Sofronoff, & Sanders, 2009). Others emphasize minimizing parental reinforcement of negative behavior through attention to it, together with scaffolding and shaping of positive behavior (Hektner, Brennan, & Brotherson, 2013). There is in all of them a basic focus on parenting skills through reinforcement, communication, and relationship development. These have been applied to immigrant parents of Latino youngsters (Parra-Cardona, Domenech-Rodriguez,

Forgatch, Sullivan, Bybee, Holtrop, et al., 2012), youngsters with oppositional defiant disorder, ADHD and conduct disorders (Hektner, Brennan, & Brotherson, 2013), borderline youngsters (Wiggins, Sofronoff, & Sanders, 2009) and youngsters who live with severe disabilities (Roux, Sofronoff, & Sanders, 2013).

FAMILY TASKS AND STRUCTURE IN LATER ADULTHOOD

In some ways the Maxwells, as a couple, were experiencing the same issues of the post-parental stage that the Caldwells were experiencing (case study 7.7). Retirement had brought the spouses face to face with each other without a well-developed relationship. In the Maxwells' situation, there were serious mental and physical health problems and their relationship was actually far less well developed or resilient than that of the Caldwells. In addition, the Maxwells had two adolescents. The combination of ingredients could lead to breakdown. Corrective family work was needed on all fronts.

Separating and Relating Generational Tasks

In the Ambach family, a relationship with an older child needed to be reworked in order for the structure to shift and all the family members to carry out their own developmental tasks.

CASE STUDY 8.8:
THE AMBACH FAMILY

The Ambach family is a rural family with seven children. All of the children—except for Walter, 26 years old, the second youngest—have left home to make their way in the neighboring metropolis. The family is very success-oriented. The father, John, and the mother, Loretta, have advanced educational degrees but continue farming, anticipating retirement when Walter leaves home. All of the children have at least graduated from college. Some have completed graduate school and, except for Walter, project a strong image of success. Walter has made a number of efforts to keep a steady job and to live elsewhere. He has never been satisfied with his work. He feels he is a failure compared with his brothers and sisters.

His mild obsessive-compulsive and depressed life patterns have brought him to quit the jobs he had. He is now at home, with a part-time job, that he will soon have to give up with nothing in prospect. He evidences no thought of doing anything. His mother Loretta has been his support through all his ups and downs, but she is losing her patience. John would like to travel with Loretta. They are both waiting for Walter to launch himself before they attempt this next phase in their life together. Walter is a concern for all his brothers and sisters, but they differ in what they would suggest, some urging more patience and protection for Walter and some urging that he be put on his own. Previous efforts to help him have been defeated. The helping process initially involved the whole family and then shifted to Walter.

In the initial sessions, after the social worker connected with all the family members and Walter, she moved to focus the process through Walter. Walter was able to tell his family that he did want to find a job for himself and get out on his own. The process shifted to how he could take charge of this and what certain family members could do to help him with this. With some individual sessions and group sessions, a plan was worked out involving mom and dad not getting involved, very temporary housing with a sister, a mentoring relationship with an older brother he admired, a job search plan, and a plan to get back on medication and receive some mental health services. The family should relax and let Walter do what he needed to do. Walter was then seen with his "landlady" sister and his mentor brother and briefly by himself. He needed some help coming to terms with a less-than-perfect job, with his new life in the city, and with sorting out his own direction from those of his brothers and sisters. With the family less involved with him, he did get a job, and an apartment, started taking appropriate medication and got further help, and, with some support from his siblings, gradually adapted to the city.

Breakdown in Later Adulthood

The Ambachs (case study 8.8), the Maxwells (case study 8.7), and the Caldwells (case study 7.7) still have some health and independence. They have not yet come to the point of being dependent on another generation for survival. The O'Conner family are at a later stage of family development. They are at the point of experiencing disability and the family relational shifts that come with this. They need to draw in a younger generation to help them but are having difficulty doing this, so that relations at every generational level are not working well. The family is a three-generation family that needs to become elaborated and complex in its ability to assist each other but that so far has not been able to find a way to do this. It is a good example of relational tasks at the stage of family development when the founding generation faces disability. It is also a further example of focusing both on the family as a whole and on the persons within it.

CASE STUDY 8.9:
THE O'CONNER FAMILY

Maura O'Conner, age 72, is involved in the older adults program of a community family service and mental health agency. She has recently been diagnosed with early-stage Parkinson's disease, which may not progress beyond its present point. Her mobility is somewhat limited, and she is now afraid of driving. She will be having cataract surgery soon. She was born in Ireland into a family of fourteen children, ten of whom were girls. Her mother, who lived to be 98, was cared for by the daughters who remained in Ireland. When Maura was 15, she moved to the United States with her sister, Kate, who is five years older than she is. Maura has suffered from depression and anxiety attacks off and on during much of her life. Now she is fearful of being alone. Her depression has been intensified by recent life events. She has been living alone for a year now. Her husband, Peter, was placed in a nursing home by the family, working with the agency. They had been a socially active couple. Both Peter and Maura had been teachers, active in the teachers union and committees. They would travel together to conventions, had a wide circle of friends, and had planned to retire with several of those friends to Florida. Peter had had brain surgery for removal of a tumor six years ago. Before his surgery, he had been the active one of the couple. Maura had depended on him to keep her going. When she was feeling sad, he would take her to a movie or for a drive to take her mind off things. She would then feel better. After his surgery, Peter rapidly became depressed, withdrawn, and noncommunicative. He was exhibiting inappropriate behavior, such as exposing himself in front of the window of their home. Their friends stopped visiting after Peter began to decline. He went into the nursing home a year ago. Maura visits him once a week with her only son, Jack. Now he does not carry on a conversation, responds with yes or no answers, and cries when he is visited. Maura feels Peter is "like dead." The experience of these visits immobilizes all three — Maura, Peter, and Jack.

Maura's older sister, Kate, lives in the area and stays with her periodically for several days at a time. Although Maura is grateful for Kate's companionship, she feels that Kate nags at her and doesn't understand her depression. Kate tends to ally herself with Jack by saying that Maura is asking too much of him

when he drives her every week to see Peter. She feels that Peter could have been kept out of a nursing home for longer. Maura feels Kate is resentful that she can no longer drive and be as active as she had been in the past. Kate had always depended on Maura for these things and can no longer do so. Indeed, Kate may need to take care of Maura someday.

Maura's only child, Jack, his wife Nancy, and their four children, aged 15, 13, 10, and 6, live in a suburb forty-five minutes away from her. Maura is frustrated with the relationship she has with Jack and his family, because she feels that they do not give her the emotional support that she needs. She feels they are too busy with their own lives and that she cannot really talk to them about her problems. Jack takes Maura to her monthly appointments with her psychiatrist, and he occasionally sits in on the sessions. She states that her son's presence inhibits her from being completely open with the psychiatrist, that she "isn't a strong enough person to totally tell her son everything." The relationship with Jack seems formal and obligatory. She wants emotional and "moral" support from Jack but finds it difficult to open up to him, saying "sons aren't aware of feelings and personal problems like women are." On the other hand, Maura's relationship with Nancy is also not very close. She believes that Nancy has no time for her, because she is involved with her own mother and sisters who live in the same area. Maura considers Nancy close-minded and conservative. Nancy doesn't call to see how Maura is doing and rarely invites Maura out to their home. Maura appears to have a standard as to how a daughter-in-law "ought" to behave toward her, but she is unable to communicate this openly. Maura had always wished she had had a daughter and is disappointed that Nancy doesn't fill this position as a daughter-in-law. The grandchildren are growing up in their own worlds. They are extremely busy with sports activities in their suburb, as are their parents. They rarely visit except on holidays. They have never visited Peter since he went into the nursing home. "But who would want to visit him?" Maura feels it is an obligation and a chore. It is enough for her to do it. Peter just looks at her and Jack and cries. What can they say? Nobody has the heart to say anything. "I just wonder when I will be like that. It won't be long now. What did I do to deserve this? I think God is punishing me."

To understand the O'Conner family, one needs to see the entire family in relation to Peter and Maura's situations with their disabilities. A genogram (figure 8.1) allows the reader to see the complexities of this family more clearly. The disabilities involve a role shift and a demand on each of the members for a corresponding shift. Carlos Sluzki (2000) discusses the necessary transformation of social networks of the elderly, with relational networks already attenuated by losses. The entire family needs to construct in different ways a secure base for Peter and Maura and ultimately for themselves. This is precisely what is *not* happening in this family. The paralysis of the O'Conner family toward the first generation affects the other generations as well. Family members seem afraid to care for each other, and so they seem paralyzed

Figure 8.1
Genogram of the O'Connor Family

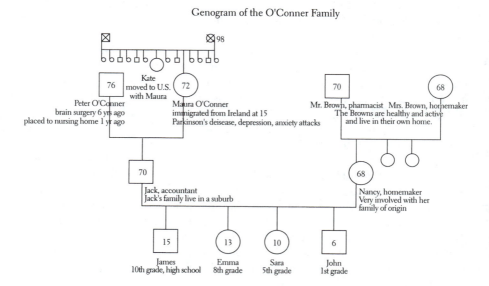

Genogram of the O'Conner Family

to act at all, to become a network in relation to the needs of the first generation. The presence in all three generations of a family network of care would prevent the burden from falling on one person. Importantly, this does not mean that the O'Conners necessarily should personally take care of Peter and Maura. Even if an institution is included in the network, the issues of connection and membership are still the same—the institution is included in care, but it is not a substitute for family membership. The first generation—Peter, Maura, and Kate—is also paralyzed in a type of denial of any ability to be a family for each other and fear that all the burden will fall upon one person. Paradoxically, the fear is realistic in a culture that values autonomous individuals and has fewer developed patterns for solidarity in the face of weakness or dependency.

The major issue is whether members can adapt to each other's needs, and thus whether a change in personal circumstances—struggling with the possibility or actuality of disability—really changes relationships. In this case it does. In the absence of an ethic of care for each other, relationships become somewhat unreal and artificial. The family becomes a collection of ice statues. Change is equated with loss. Peter is not really "dead," but he can't take care of Maura any longer. Actually, his situation is a metaphor for the whole family's inability to function effectively as a family. He now needs loving care and concern for his lost role and capabilities. He is very sad about his losses, but he is still a very important family member. Maura cannot take care of Kate in the same way as she always did, and so Kate acts as if a 72-year-old relationship, which includes emigration together, is gone. Jack is losing some of the relationship to his father that he previously had. He might try to have some relationship with him, although it would be different from what he has known. He might try to listen to his mother's feelings, and Maura might try to find a different relationship with her son. Men can often listen to feelings and understand, if asked. Maura is afraid of a relationship with Nancy, and Nancy is afraid of being obliged to Maura (of "being the daughter" and taking on the needs of the whole O'Conner family).

The children are absorbed in their sports activities and their achievement, so they are not learning the implications of family membership. Jack and Nancy's energies are absorbed in making it possible for them to pursue their activities without reference to the larger family. Everyone is missing the opportunity to change slightly and to come together around the needs of Maura and Peter. Maura and Peter need to draw in a younger generation to help them, but they are having difficulty doing this. Maura is afraid to ask them. The legitimate fear of the younger generation, as in the case of Nancy, that one person will have to take all of the burden, is preventing anyone from doing anything. For Maura and Kate, who could be beginning to face disability, the anxiety about facing disability in these circumstances, alone, may be more paralyzing than the disability itself. They know that there should be some way to manage it, as in the case of their mother in Ireland. The availability of nursing care facilities, when needed, may ease some of the difficult aspects of care, but this should not obliterate the family issues of membership and care in changing circumstances. The availability of nursing home care may only alter the way membership is managed.

Maura and Kate's implicit assumptions are that disability has to be managed alone, and that men (Jack) cannot manage relationships. Their roles are fixed on these abstract assumptions, rather than interpersonally and in relation to each other's need. The absence of adaptive roles proclaims a functional breakdown of the family *as a family*. If the O'Conner family members are to be a family at all, they need to be concerned and help take care of each other when members, such as Peter and Maura, are in need. There should be enough flexibility in roles that a role shift—that is, a functional shift in the way members are able to relate to each other, should not obliterate membership. Yet this is precisely what is not happening. The key task of the O'Conner family is to become elaborated and complex in its ability to assist each other to develop workable and balanced patterns of solidarity and caring for members in weakness and need. A whole range of relational and personal tasks would emerge from this, but so far, the family has not been able to find a way to do this.

The social worker from the community family service and mental health agency has as clients Maura and Peter O'Conner but then also, with the needs of the founding generation, has the entire family as clients. Keeping Maura and Peter central, she needs to involve Jack in a different way, and then Kate, with the needs of the situation. This could be done perhaps in family sessions with Maura and Jack and then Kate, and then possibly with Nancy. Nancy may be more willing to be involved if Jack and Kate are involved and carrying what they can. The children also have roles to play in this opportunity to learn about family taking care of one another. Much of the hard work is already being done by the nursing facility. It is basically a matter of family shifting in their roles. They need to communicate and listen to each other, to make requests and work out problems, and to support the older generation's efforts to remain independent as long as possible, but also to feel membership in the family they have fostered. With this taking place, the central focus of the family would eventually shift to Jack and Nancy.

Middle-stage work, then, would involve the social worker taking this broader perspective on family relational tasks and personal tasks that arise from disability in the founding generation. The focus needs to be elaborated and adopted by agreement of key members of the family in family sessions. There will need to be a great deal of work on communication, on helping members to express feelings and thoughts so that they can be heard and discussed, on listening and reflecting. Each needs to appreciate the viewpoint of the others. From this appreciation, they may respond to the others' needs through developing a family plan, separating personal from relational tasks, and solving problems together.

SUMMARY

The O'Conner family is a relatively simple example of work with elaborated families. It can get even more complex. The multiple focus for work on both the persons in the family and the family as a whole needs to be maintained. The basic task for elaborated families is to help them elaborate in an appropriate way. To live out her dreams, Marisa Antonelli reworks a rigid and enmeshed relationship with her parents (case studies 2.2 and 8.4). Jerry Peterson moves from an exclusive relationship with his mother to a relationship that includes his father and his mother (case study 8.5). Stephen Maxwell emancipates, but remains in appropriate contact with, both parents and his brothers (case study 8.7). His father and mother no longer need him to take them away from their couple issues, nor will they use Mike. To do this, both John and Mary will separate personal issues from their relationship. The O'Conners (case study 8.9) begin to include each other, using community resources, when needed, to keep membership bonds alive in the face of disability. In this sense, using the nursing home still necessitates a whole range of family membership work, the work of sharing the memories and dreams that keep the family alive and carry on its traditions and bonds.

In this chapter, we have reviewed the processes of helping families in a generational dance, managing relationships between generations, dealing with socialization responsibilities of parents to children and care responsibilities to an elder generation. One primary reality in family work is that its members will change—indeed, must change at every stage to meet the internal demands of development. The work of the family, the relational tasks and the personal tasks that flow from developmental needs, becomes the medium that makes these changes possible. The family continues in its essential role, supporting solidarity in the face of change and in the face of its members' needs. It would best make change possible in a way that most respects the common humanity, the dignity, and the dreams of its members. The social worker's role is to help the family and its members to do this. In the next chapter, we add a further set of tasks in middle-stage work with elaborated families, where the family structure itself has been disrupted and demands reconstruction.

REFERENCES

Aponte, H. (1986). If I don't get simple, I cry. *Family Process, 25*(4), 531–558.

Diamond, G. S., & Liddle, H. R. (1999). Transforming negative parent-adolescent interactions in family therapy: From impasse to dialogue. *Family Process, 38*(1), 5–26.

Dinkmeyer, D., & McKay, G. (1989). *The parent handbook: Systematic training for effective parenting*. Circle Pines, MN: American Guidance Service.

Forgatch, M. S. (1994). *Parenting through change: A training manual*. Eugene, OR: Oregon Social Learning Center.

Forgatch, M. S., & DeGarmo, D. S. (1999). Parenting through change: An effective prevention program for single mothers. *Journal of Consulting and Clinical Psychology, 67*, 711–724.

Forgatch, M. S., DeGarmo, D. S., & Beldavs, Z. G. (2005). An efficacious, theory-based intervention for stepfamilies. *Behavior Therapy, 36*, 357–365.

Forgatch, M. S., Patterson, G. R., & Beldavs, Z. G. (2009). Testing the Oregon delinquency model with nine-year follow up of the Oregon divorce study. *Development and Psychopathology, 21*(2), 637–660.

Hektner, J. M., Brennan, A. L., & Brotherson, S. E. (2013). A review of the nurtured heart approach to parenting: Evaluation of its theoretical and empirical foundations. *Family Process*, 52(3), 425–439.

Montalvo, B. (1982). Interpersonal arrangements in disrupted families. In F. Walsh (Ed.), *Normal family processes* (pp. 277–296). New York, NY: Guilford.

Parra-Cardona, J. R., Domenech-Rodriguez, M., Forgatch, M., Sullivan, C., Bybee, D., Holtrop, K., . . . Bernal, G. (2012). Culturally adapting an evidence-based parenting intervention for Latino immigrants: The need to integrate fidelity and cultural relevance. *Family Process*, 51(1), 56–72.

Roux, G., Sofronoff, K., & Sanders, M. (2013). A randomized control trial of Group Stepping Stones Triple P: A mixed disability trial. *Family Process*, 52(3), 411–424.

Shulman, L. (1992). *The skills of helping: Individuals, families and groups* (3rd ed.). Itasca, IL: Peacock.

Sluzki, C. (2000). Social networks and the elderly: Conceptual and clinical issues, and a family consultation. *Family Process*, 39(3), 270–284.

Wiggins, T. L., Sofronoff, K., & Sanders, M. R. (2009). Pathways triple *p*-positive parenting program: Effects on parent-child relationships and child behavior problems. *Family Process*, 48(4), 517–530.

CHAPTER 9

Radical Family Reconstruction: Toward Middle-Phase Work

KEY TOPICS

Family Reconstruction
Membership Losses and Transitions
Family Processes of Divorce
Realignment of Relational Architecture
Blended Families
Family Life Education for Postdivorce Families
The Underorganized Family

This chapter focuses on families in the process of structural change and reconstruction and helping underorganized families reorganize.

FAMILY RECONSTRUCTION

In this chapter, we move to a further level of complexity: that of the family experiencing serious relational deficits and needing to reconstruct itself in some form if it is to survive. Actually, the process of relational reconstruction takes place for all families at every family life transition. After all, this is what relational tasks for all family members are all about. However, for some families that are losing members, the changes are more radical. These families have children and are experiencing relational losses through death or divorce. Some of these become single-parent families, whereas other single-parent families, such as the Hannons (case study 9.4) have always been that way. Families who have experienced relational losses frequently remarry and form stepfamilies.

The formation of a stepfamily is a further process. But the work of stepfamily formation often gets confused with the personal work of dealing with a loss. The stepfamily could become an illusory attempt to substitute for the different losses the family members have experienced. Family members who experience losses cannot really go back to the relational structure they have known. Often family members have hardly any effective patterns for dealing with the change that has taken place. They need to understand that they are simultaneously developing a new unit and retaining workable patterns from the previous unit. Without this understanding, the relational shifts, if they are accomplished at all, will take much longer than other, expected family life transitions. They will be more difficult, and in some ways they will continue on through each member's life span (Wallerstein, Lewis, & Blakeslee, 2000). There may well be conflict and blaming. There is often less support from the extended family for members going through these transitions than in other circumstances.

Some families are simply chronically underorganized, without being able to point to any one event, such as a divorce, related to their underorganization. Over many generations, these families have been unable to deal both with their own internal tensions and with the outside world, particularly with necessary social institutions of employment, school, courts, police, the welfare system, and so on (Aponte, 1986). There is no abrupt break or loss in the family history to explain their problems relating internally or with external institutions. Often these problems are associated with chronic poverty. There is a chronic inability to influence external institutions or utilize their support for their functions connected with education and socialization, health care, security, or work and income. The loss or dysfunction of their relations with potential external supports can lead to a type of internal starvation and limited effective patterns of dealing with each other. Similarly, internal dysfunctions can generate external dysfunctions in a never-ending cycle, with profound effects on the self-image of each family member. These families are often involved with multiple social institutions, community resources, and social workers. They present problems that go much deeper than the immediate difficulties and concerns of the school, the clinic, the court, or the child welfare agency, among others. But they are often involved with all of these. The long-term job of the social worker is to interrupt the cycle and help the family reconstruct both internal relationships and external relationships with their environment at the same time. This takes considerable time and an ability to overcome the inevitable barriers within the family of mistrust coming from many encounters with social agencies. We will discuss this type of work in the later section of this chapter and in the chapters following.

In chapter 6, we saw couples whose relationships were very incomplete from the beginning. In John and Eileen's case (case study 6.5), the severe immaturity of one partner, the addiction of the other, and the constant threat of violence since the beginning of the marriage raise questions about whether they ever made a basic agreement to marry and understood what they were doing. For Eileen, it may have been more a matter of reacting to and running away from her strict and closeted family. John was already "married" to addictive substances, which were in firm control of his life. Whether he ever detached himself enough from drugs and alcohol to commit himself to Eileen as a person, to take in her needs (or Eileen his needs as a person), is questionable. In Sheldon and Sandy's case (case study 6.6), there was a question of mutuality of consent as well as of what they were consenting to. One partner essentially said, "I didn't really consent to marry, but I didn't want to disappoint people, but let's stay together for a time and see what happens." For John and Eileen — and for Sheldon and Sandy — to survive as a couple, they would not simply have to correct dysfunctional patterns and remedy serious structural deficits; they would have to reconstruct their relationship and the understandings on which it was based.

For John and Eileen, the relationship itself continued to seem full of risk. Other than John's family's pressure, there seemed little motivation to form a stable union. John's efforts to deal with his addictions did not so far seem to promise success. Eileen had scarcely become more of a person in her own right and showed no signs of wanting to revisit the relationship. For both, their own emotional processes seemed to overwhelm any possibility of accommodating the other at all, much less the complexity of the other's emotional process. For Sheldon and Sandy there was more hope. There was at least the opportunity to work things out. They did not have a dangerous relationship, and on some levels it was working. There was some time to work; Sheldon was responding somewhat, although communication of any depth was very limited. It would be a difficult challenge for everyone involved, and it would be unlikely to succeed. However, for Sandy it was worth trying for a limited time. From her perspective, the costs of not trying might be even greater.

Membership Losses and Transitions

Losses are the most serious issue faced by members of blended or reconstructed families. Families establish a network of relationships, validate those relationships through interpersonal patterns, and then lose a crucial member. These losses have multiple implications. There are families who have lost a member through death, as well as those in the process of divorce and those in the process of blending with another family or parent. Dealing with membership losses, they often experience their current relationships as incomplete. A new person bond, a new identity bond, can never replace the bonds with the person lost, no matter how problematic the original bonds have actually been. While mourning the old, persons are often already in transition to a new and untried set of relationships and a new set of interpersonal patterns of doing things with each other. Members are asked to adopt new patterns and relationships without first coping with losses from the old ones. Worse still is when a member feels asked to substitute a new relationship for an older one. From an identity bond perspective this is impossible, because any bond to a person as that *person* is not substitutable. The new bond and the older one need to live side by side. Side by side, a new relationship can still bring good things without threatening the older bonds. The problem comes when there is an expectation that the bonds be substitutable.

During the transition period there inevitably will be great confusion. Many of the older interaction and communication patterns of relationships discussed in chapter 4: socialization, boundaries, alignment and power, and so on, will have to change. Often there will be efforts to shorten the painful relational work and become "like other families" through a new marriage, as if one person could substitute for another. There may be little awareness that older patterns and preferences do not change so easily, and in some ways should not. In any case, for success, an entirely new set of relationships—not a substitute for the old relationships but a new set of relationships that does not compete with the older ones—will have to emerge side by side with the old memories and the old bonds. Families are usually quite unprepared for this complexity, especially when they attempt to measure themselves by their images of families who have not experienced losses. It is at this time that family education can be most effective when it normalizes the stresses of transition and provides support and opportunities to network. When families have difficulty they may experience breakdown and find themselves working with schools, courts, family counseling, child welfare, or other agencies. Particularly if the referral comes from a concern of the agency and is involuntary, social workers from these agencies find themselves working between the particular agency, the court, the school, the child welfare agency, and the family. Probation officers, school social workers, and so on are often focused on one family member. They do not always see themselves as doing family work, helping families to restructure their relationships and become effective again. Work with families in the context of these agencies will be discussed in chapters 10 and 11. For the moment, we can discuss families coming voluntarily to a family counseling agency or private practitioner to find some resolution for their relational difficulties.

Tom Fields's family is dealing with the recent loss of Meg, wife and mother.

CASE STUDY 9.1:
TOM FIELDS, LOSS OF MEG

Tom and Meg Fields had a very traditional but relaxed marriage. When Meg started her fight with cancer, Tom retreated into his work, which consumed him, and into his fishing, his outlet from work. The death of Meg was a double loss for the four children, because they also lost communication with their father. Eventually, as Meg got worse, they would get housekeepers, but none could manage this impossible situation. Over the course of the year before her death, Meg gradually weakened, taking on different regimens of chemotherapy. The treatments sapped her energy, but none worked. As Meg gradually withdrew, the oldest, 13-year-old Ashley, took over, becoming a link between Meg, Tom, the housekeeper, and Ashley's brothers and sisters. Power struggles centered on Ashley. Housekeepers left, some after a few days, and the family descended into chaos. After Meg's death,

Tom retreated further into his work and his fishing. Ashley would take over sporadically with the same relaxed firmness she remembered from her mother, but then she would get into conflict with the housekeeper and withdraw. Finally, one housekeeper stayed and tried with a will to shape the family up. However, the more she tried, the less successful she was. In the meantime, Ashley's grades slipped dramatically, and she started hanging out with a drug crowd. Each of the other children was also having his or her own similar difficulties, some with school, some with behavior problems, some with depression. After an explosion, the housekeeper left, and Tom went to the family service agency. The family was in chaos, and he was at a loss.

The social worker worked with Tom to bring him back to the family, first to Ashley, and later the other children. The worker helped to normalize and connect the problems they were experiencing individually and as a family, to unresolved mourning and family work that had been left undone after Meg's death. There was a need of each, especially the father, to take charge of what he or she could and to connect with the others. The family needed to develop a more appropriate set of patterns to fit the new situation. The work with the social worker took approximately a year and a half to get to the point at which they felt ready to manage on their own.

The Fields family did begin, over time, to overcome its chaotic and wounded state. Families in this situation do this best when there are spiritual resources and a supportive network, although depression, associated with loss, can prolong the healing process.

FAMILY PROCESSES OF DIVORCE

The divorce rate in the United States grew exponentially from 1960 through the late 1970s (Glick, 1979). It stabilized in the early 1980s and has been dropping slightly since then. At today's rate, the chances that a marriage contracted in 2012 will end in divorce before one partner dies has been estimated to be from 40 percent to 50 percent (National Marriage Project, 2012, p. 67; also see Goldstein, 1999; Popenoe, 2001; Norton & Miller, 1992).

Virtually all discussions of divorce point out that its effects on families and children are complex. Divorce should not be approached as a single event but as a process, and indeed often a painful and long-lasting one for children (Amato & Booth, 1997; Glenn, 2012; Greene, Anderson, Forgatch, DeGarmo, & Hetherington, 2012; Wallerstein, Lewis, & Blakeslee, 2000). Divorce always demands special coping skills on the part of every family member. Although approximately 75 percent of children experiencing divorce do eventually cope with it, the process is painful. A considerable remainder are quite damaged by it (Hetherington, 2002). A recent study of adult children of divorce indicated that persons whose parents had the highest quality of divorce (the good divorce) fell short in measures of happiness and life quality, by a statistically significant margin, of those who reported that their parents had a low-conflict but less than very happy, intact marriage (Glenn, 2012, p. 23).

Children begin to have to cope with the effects of severe marital conflict before the divorce. This coping must continue long after the split (Amato, 2000; Amato & Booth, 1997). Wallerstein and Kelly's initial findings (1980) on children of divorce were confirmed over a ten-year longitudinal study following 116 children (Wallerstein & Blakeslee, 1989). The divorce is just one step in a series of consequent family transitions: prior to the divorce, the divorce itself, the one-parent family, remarriage, the stepfamily, and so on. In one study, five years after a divorce, one-third of the children were functioning more poorly than they had been at the time of the divorce. One of three children found themselves still embroiled in the ongoing bitterness of their two battling parents (Bryner, 2001). Wallerstein and Blakeslee's (1989) ten-year follow-up found that half the women and one-third of the men studied were still intensely angry at their former spouses. Children felt caught in the crossfire. While the overwhelming majority of children do cope with divorce, the many studies of children of divorce also show that the experience of divorce doubles the risk of serious problems for children (Greene, Anderson, Forgatch, DeGarmo, & Hetherington, 2012, p. 107).

The systems principle of equifinality is well illustrated in the child's response to divorce. The child who shows little response at the time of the divorce may react quite severely many years later as his or her relational needs become different. As in the case of Alan (case study 10.1), the child who is initially quite reactive to the divorce may eventually find ways to cope and adapt (Wallerstein, Lewis, & Blakeslee, 2000).

Paul Amato (Amato & Booth, 1997) studied 2,000 married adults and 700 of their children over twenty years. There were approximately 300 divorces in the group during the study. Amato and Booth found that divorcing families could be divided into those with low-satisfaction/high-conflict marriages and those with low-conflict marriages. Amato and Booth (1997, p. 197) suggest that children for whom divorce is an opportunity to escape from a highly conflictual, hostile, and abusive home may be better off in a well-functioning single parent household. Low-conflict marriages looked very much like many other marriages in terms of satisfaction and conflict one-and-a-half years before the divorce. They were quiescent, but less than fully satisfactory. Parents might divorce for reasons of self-fulfillment or the presence of a more attractive partner (Amato & Booth, 1997, p. 197). There may have been very little discussion of the divorce with the children. Divorces in low-conflict marriages, representing around two-thirds of the divorces Amato and Booth studied, had a broad negative effect on virtually every dimension of their children's well-being. On the other hand, recent research, using a large national sample, indicated that 86 percent of people who were unhappily married in the late 1980s but who stayed with their marriage indicated five years later that they were happier. Sixty percent of these formerly unhappily married couples rated their marriages five years later as either very happy or quite happy (Popenoe, 2001; Waite & Gallagher, 2000).

The divorcing family suffers losses often without the support and the compensations available when a family member dies. When a parent is lost through divorce, the family needs to go through a realignment of relations similar to what the Fields went through (case study 9.1), only the process is often more difficult (Herzog & Sudia, 1973). Most important is the understanding from attachment theory that relationships do become parts of every person and that, although persons have the capability of adapting to relational changes and losses, they do not do it readily. When they experience such change, they often need help to deal with it. In the divorce process there is often considerable painful marital conflict. Often there are children involved on one side or the other. Conflict precedes the divorce, and it continues in different ways during and after the divorce. The voluntary separation is often taken by family members as a personal rejection of each of them. Even with joint custody, there can be a perceived loss of one parent, frequently over the years turning into a diminished relationship and a real loss. There is often loss of relationships with one side of the family, as one parent's ties weaken. This is often profoundly resented. Finally there is almost inevitable economic insecurity.

Social workers of course become a part of these processes, working with the spouses, with the children, and with schools, health care agencies, courts, child welfare agencies, and other social institutions. These agencies inevitably are drawn in different ways into a difficult divorce process and/or its aftermath. There are a number of dangers in this process.

Dangers of Triangulation   The first task of the social worker is to avoid triangulation into the family system, at the same time helping the parents discover whatever possibility there is of coping adequately and even working together on some issues. This may seem impossible. When there is sufficient marital tension for one or both partners to consider divorce, the parents are gradually moving to an adversarial role. This is supported by a legal system whose main concern will not be the complexity of relationships, but the settlement of property rights. Involvement in an affair, alcoholism, depression, a history of constant conflict, simple anxiety, and the need to self-justify all reinforce the adversarial position of the spouses. Each would try to align the social worker with his or her position in a type of rehearsal for a divorce court, with the social worker in the position of judge. Furthermore, the children are often drawn into the conflict and either aligned with one parent against another or confused. Paradoxically, the children may hold more power than either parent.

If the social worker is to be successful at all, he or she needs to support the appropriate functioning of both parents whenever possible, to the extent that they allow themselves to be involved with the helping process. The social worker should immediately avoid even a shadow of alignment with one parent over another. Unless there is a question of the protection of a vulnerable person, he or she should gently refuse to become triangulated on one side or another of the conflict. In the first interview, the social worker should redirect interaction so that the partners take responsibility for whatever each best can do about the situation and the emergent relational realignment that comes with divorce. A further problem is that a school, child welfare agency, court, or other agency often already has a particular client. Unless the social worker is able to address the whole family from the beginning and skillfully include both parents in working on the problem, a premature alignment with one or another in the family, whether parent or child, could prevent productive work from being done.

During the divorce process itself, so such energy is taken up with the legal issues that there may be very little time or energy available for a helping process. Moreover, there is always concern that getting help may be taken by the other contending party as a sign of inadequacy. The legal necessities often trump the social and emotional issues. The emotional issues are usually much broader than the divorce, so that for each partner the divorce becomes a symbol of many other issues that have nothing to do with the divorce. If this is the case, the underlying issues will not be resolved by the divorce. There is also the myth that relationships can be easily (or ever) dissolved. Attachment theory and object relations theory suggest that relationships remain a part of each person in different ways.

Dysfunctional Beliefs and Cognitions   Will the problem really be resolved by the divorce process? Family therapist E. W. Beal (1980b) suggests that subscribing to the following beliefs may indicate that the problem or dysfunction will not be resolved by the divorce:

1. A belief that the problem lies in the current relationship and is not likely to be found in subsequent relationships
2. A belief that a divorce will not produce long-term serious losses in the sense of self or sense of identity
3. A high level of denial about the possibility of loss in the divorce process
4. A belief that the only important thing is to get away from the other
5. Making a decision solely on what "feels" right or what is legally possible for the purpose of revenge (Beal, 1980a, p. 248)

Assisting divorcing spouses may be a matter of helping them to sort out the broader processes and beliefs or thinking patterns that have led to the divorce decision. Each cognition denotes an unresolved problem in the current marriage that divorce probably will not resolve. Unresolved, the cognition is faced again in the postdivorce period. It could lead to serious postdivorce problems or an attempt to resolve the divorce issues through remarriage.

The first several years after the divorce are predictably chaotic and difficult. Family functioning is worse twelve to eighteen months after the divorce than at the time immediately surrounding the divorce. Five years later, one-third of the children were functioning worse than they had been at the time of the divorce (Bryner, 2001). Eighty percent of children have severe and increasing difficulties with the process (Wallerstein, Lewis, & Blakeslee, 2000). Ten years afterward, significant numbers of former partners report intense anger (Wallerstein & Blakeslee, 1989). When there is single custody, there is the risk of a diminished relationship with the noncustodial parent. Children of divorce seem to fare better if there is a joint custody agreement, unless there is intense parental conflict or an abusive or mentally ill parent (Bauserman, 2002). However, the joint-custody agreement may be difficult for the estranged parents to manage and may demand professional intervention. Social workers may work with co-parenting arrangements. There is considerable concern for the children who do not make an adjustment to divorce. These often show difficulties, are involved with courts and child welfare agencies, or have difficulty at school and are seen by social workers or others.

Realignment of Relational Architecture

By definition, divorce creates a vacuum in the relational structure of the executive subsystem of the family and also in each member. One parent leaves; the other must take charge. A joint-custody arrangement alternately empowers one and then the other to take charge. Both must learn a new role, play it, and then, when the other's period of custody comes, turn it over to the former spouse for him or her to play.

Boundaries are inevitably confused in the beginning, with family members getting involved in areas no longer open to them. Extremes of enmeshment with one parent bring about disengagement with the other. Overfunctioning in one partner brings about either conflict or underfunctioning on the part of the other. Alignment problems are legendary. Children become triangulated into the parental conflicts and resentments. Moving from one parent to another brings about constant shifts. Power becomes diffuse. Parents can become helpless and dysfunctional. Often the children step into the power vacuum, becoming a type of guidance system for their parents (Montalvo, 1982). Sometimes there is massive confusion, compounded by the other problems of single-parenthood. The communication skills and relational investment demanded by the co-parental relationship, favored by joint-custody arrangements, may be in short supply. In many ways, the joint custody arrangement, while it may be a partial solution to some of the child-caring problems divorce brings, is quite difficult to implement. This arrangement will probably require better communication, relational and problem-solving skills, and interpersonal maturity than a marriage with a moderate amount of conflict. The only solution possible is the gradual and painful realignment of boundaries, alignment, and power in favor of the parent who mainly has custody, and withdrawal of the non-custodial parent from authority while the custodial parent is in control. There needs to be some communication, agreement, and a well-articulated shift between the parents as the child moves from one orbit to another. This could be done with good will on the part of both parents and some guidance from a disinterested party. Small wonder that families have painful experiences and that postdivorce child care appears dysfunctional, as seen in the following case study.

CASE STUDY 9.2:
EDNA FRIEDMAN AND RENEE

Edna Friedman came to Jewish Family Services with her daughter, Renee, age 15. The family had been through a very acrimonious divorce several years ago. Renee regularly visits her father, Hal, telling him about her problems with her mother. Mrs. Friedman has very little control over Renee. The number of screaming fights with each other has increased dramatically since Mrs. Friedman began talking about marrying her boyfriend, Lloyd C. At this point, the triangle of Renee with her mother and father has become quite

rigid and is aggravated by the oncoming marriage to Lloyd C. and the emergent triangles implicit in this relationship. Whatever Mrs. Friedman will say, Renee will say the opposite. If Mrs. Friedman ignores Renee, Renee will scream at the top of her lungs for hours. Mr. C's daughter, Allison, age 18, has already moved in with them. Although Allison plans to move out as soon as she can find a place, Mr. C. will be moving in after they get married in three months. Renee is opposed to all this and wants to prevent it from happening. Mr. C. is reluctant to involve himself in the problems with Renee. He believes that if Renee was nice to him, she would feel like a traitor to her father. Mrs. Friedman treats Renee like a sister and appears to be afraid of her.

Renee sat reading a magazine through the first session with her mother, Mr. C., and Allison, pointedly ignoring everyone and refusing to put the magazine down. In the process of family therapy, the social worker assisted Mrs. Friedman to defer the new marriage for a short time and begin to work on her relationship with Renee. She needed to work on taking over in issues with Renee that she considers important. There were separate sessions with Renee and her father. Her father eventually was able to encourage Renee to listen to her mother, thus beginning to resolve some of the triangle. Her mother made an agreement with Renee over issues, such as school, bedtime hours, and weekends. Mrs. Friedman agreed to spend time with her but not involve her in Mrs. Friedman's relationship with Mr. C. The social worker had considerable concern about Allison, since she seemed to have the most to lose from her father's new arrangement. Deferring the wedding gave Mr. C. some time with Allison, and they were encouraged to reconnect. There needed to be some resolution of these triangles before adding another one with the marriage. The Friedman case is a good example of the complex work of the postdivorce family and the role of the social worker in that work.

Blended Families

Blended families are one further structural shift in a family that has already experienced losses. The Friedman family (case study 9.2), with the impending marriage to Mr. C., has the problems of a blended family superimposed on the relational tasks of a divorcing family. The blended family needs to develop new traditions while preserving what may be worthwhile from its older traditions or patterns. It has to find a way to integrate itself without denying the reality of the older family relations. New alliances need to be formed while preserving the old alliances that are still important. The experience of adjusting to a stepfamily is likened to making a lasting move to a foreign country, having lived in a home country for some time (Pasley & Garneau, 2012, pp. 157–158). This all takes time and cannot be hurried. Perennial issues in blended families are issues of insiders versus outsiders; boundary disputes; power issues; conflicting loyalties; rigid, unproductive relational triangles; and unity versus fragmentation of the new couple relationship (Visher & Visher, 1982; 1996). Evidence shows that the quality of the stepparent-stepchild relationships is more predictive of marital adjustment and outcomes than is the quality of the marriage itself (Pasley & Garneau, 2012, p. 152). As was implicit in the Friedman family dynamics, the more the blended family organizes itself to deny the loss and to substitute a stepmother or stepfather for the mother or father lost, the less successful it is likely to be. Step-parents have a very difficult time being accepted. Fewer than 20 percent of young adult stepchildren feel close to their stepmothers (Hetherington, 2002). We can see all of these dynamics in the case of Rich and Marcia Jones in the following case study, even though their divorces were somewhat less complicated than the divorce in the Friedman family.

CASE STUDY 9.3:
RICH AND MARCIA

Rich and Marcia, both recovering from alcoholism, met in a treatment group. It is the second marriage for both. Rich, age 56, had been married for twenty years before his divorce. He is a successful businessman and has two married daughters, ages 25 and 36. While they were growing up, he was drinking heavily, and he regrets that he had so little contact with them. The relations with his first family are strained and full of regrets on his part. Additionally, he had a very strict upbringing, and his knowledge of teenage behavior appears to be limited. Marcia was married ten years before her divorce. She was deserted by her husband when her daughter, Julia, now 16, was a baby. Marcia and Julia have a very close relationship, "like sisters." Marcia's upbringing was much more relaxed, and she reflects that in her patterns with Julia. Since their marriage a year ago, Rich and Marcia have experienced constant arguments over Julia. This has absorbed most of their energy, so their relationship remains somewhat undeveloped. Rich, strongly motivated to be the father he never was to his own daughters, tries to take over the parenting of Julia. When Rich gets involved with Julia, Marcia gets protective of her and undercuts his authority. When this happens, Rich becomes more harsh and Marcia becomes more indulgent. Neither seem to have well-developed communication

skills, and one extreme seems to bring out the other. Moreover, when Marcia tries to become the mediator between Julia and her husband, it seems to prevent her daughter from developing a real relationship with Rich. Julia never had a relationship with a father and actually would like one with Rich. She has no idea of how to achieve it, especially in view of Rich's extreme behavior and her mother's protectiveness.

The social worker met only with Rich and Marcia in the beginning. She began by normalizing for both of them some of the stepfamily issues they were facing. They couldn't treat the family as if nothing had happened, as if Julia and Marcia did not have a long and deep relationship. Neither one would or should accept that change. Although Julia is growing older and is at a point where she can gradually assume some of her own responsibilities, Marcia ultimately needed to remain as the parent in charge. Rich could at best be second in command, with authority delegated from Marcia. With this arrangement, Rich could then develop a different relationship with Julia. The social worker worked with Rich and Marcia, guiding them through the steps of a relational shift, and then included Julia in a few family sessions until the relationships became more manageable and stabilized. However, when relations with Julia stabilized, it became clear that Rich and Marcia needed to do the unfinished work on their own relationship that the focus on Julia had absorbed. There

was a lot of hurt left over from their previous relationships and from their families of origin that the problems with Julia
had covered up. They contracted with

the social worker for marital counseling.
Working together on the issues with Julia
made their marital issues clear and gave
them a start on this process.

Family Life Education for Postdivorce Families

Educational approaches for postdivorce families and stepfamilies are particularly
useful and popular. These would normalize what appears to be an out-of-bounds
experience, giving family members realistic expectations to replace their first marriage family expectations together with permission and support to cope with the
experience appropriately. Groups can address common parenting and stepfamily
issues. They can provide a supportive network for coping and problem solving
(Pasley & Garneau, 2012, pp. 159–163). Should the group support and education
not work, they provide the opportunity for family members to get further, more individualized help. Many of the group and education methods used are similar to the
MRE methods discussed previously, except that the content needs to be tailored to
the particular situation of postdivorce and blended families.

THE UNDERORGANIZED FAMILY

If the ability of the family to function well depends on the degree to which the family relational structure is well defined, cohesive, and flexible, the underorganized
family shows deficiencies in the degree of constancy, differentiation, cohesiveness,
and flexibility of its relational structure. Family members have a limited repertoire
of relational patterns and structures to manage internal situations (their own dynamics) or external situations with community institutions, resources, and relational
structures. Family members have learned rigidity in using the relational patterns
they do possess, and they are inconsistent in their use of these patterns and structures. These patterns may be handed down over generations, resulting in considerable isolation of the family and a lack of awareness that these patterns necessarily are
problematic. Not all poor families are underorganized by any means. Indeed, it is
remarkable how resilient so many families are in the face of what appear to be insu-
perable obstacles. Harry Aponte (1986) suggests there can be a relation between the
situation of poverty, deficits in relationships with community institutions, resources
and relational structures related to poverty, and internal deficits of relational patterns
and structures. To help these families reconstruct their relationships with the inside
and the outside is to help them to learn to acquire some of the resilience that other
families somehow have managed to develop. The long-term job of the social worker
is to interrupt the cycle and help the family reconstruct both internal relationships
and external relationships with their environment at the same time. Indeed, to
reconstruct the outer relationships effectively, the inner relationships also need

reconstruction, and vice versa (Aponte, 1986). This takes considerable time and the ability to overcome the inevitable barriers of mistrust. We will discuss relationships for the most part on the inside of these families in this chapter. In the following chapter, we will discuss relationships with outside institutions, resources and relational structures for these as well as other families.

Harry Aponte uses the Hannon family case as an extended illustration of the assessment and intervention processes with underorganized families.[1] We will also use Aponte's record of one session as a way of summarizing our previous discussion of the interaction process with families and applying some of the skills discussed in previous chapters. The interview can be divided into eight phases. The helping process of subsequent sessions is built on this session.

CASE STUDY 9.4: THE HANNON FAMILY

The Hannon family is a poor African American family of nine members from four generations. Mrs. Hannon, 47, is the head of the family. She has five children, ranging in age from 22 to 11, living with her. Her oldest daughter Vera, 22, is fearful of living on her own. Vera has two children, Rita, 3, and Curt, 1½, also living with them. Mrs. Hannon's senile father also lives with them, but he is not present in this family session. Mrs. Hannon, previously on public assistance, works from 11 p.m. to 7 a.m. cleaning offices. She is exhausted and finds little energy to give to complex issues in the family. She had delegated authority to a parental child, Joan, age 17, who appeared to be the only one of her children able to take leadership. Now she is particularly concerned because Joan's leadership has become very uneven, her relationships at her high school seem to have broken down, and she is in danger of dropping out. She makes an appointment at the mental health clinic and the whole family,

with the exception of her father, comes to the session. To clarify assessment and interaction, parts of the interview are summarized. The focus rests mainly on Mrs. Hannon, Vera, and Joan.

Phase 1. Introduction   In the beginning, the family seated itself in the interview room in a chaotic manner. Mrs. Hannon remained quiet and uninvolved and Joan fruitlessly attempted to organize them. People were talking at once. Vera's two children were somewhat out of control, but the mother did nothing to manage them. The therapist introduced himself without response on the family's part. He initially tested out whether Joan's sister or brothers would be able to quiet things down. When they could not, it became clear that of the older children, Joan has leadership. He then tried to engage Mrs. Hannon, who appeared to him to be withdrawn and unhappy. Joan quickly began speaking for her, and he was not able to keep her centralized for long.

Therapist: Mrs. Hannon, everybody else looks pretty happy except you.

---

[1]Source: Aponte (1986, pp. 531–545). © 1986 FPI Inc.

Joan: She ain't got no sleep, that's why.

Vera and Mark: [speak simultaneously, inaudible]

Therapist: Did you just get home from work? [He walks across room and sits next to Mrs. Hannon.]

Mrs. Hannon: Uh huh.

Joan: Tired as a . . . [inaudible because Vera talks simultaneously and Curt yells]

Earl: [brother, age 11] I bet she is gonna go to sleep as soon as she go home.

Therapist [to Mrs. Hannon]: Where do you work?

Mrs. Hannon: Horsham, Pennsylvania.

Therapist: How far away is that?

Mrs. Hannon: On the other side of Willow Grove. [The youngsters quiet down, except for Curt, who is still fussing.]

Therapist: What do you work at?

Mrs. Hannon: Cleaning offices, 11 to 7.

Therapist: 11 to 7 every night?

Mrs. Hannon: Uh-huh.

Therapist: And you have all these children to take care of by yourself? [The children are teasing Curt, who suddenly yells as the noise escalates]

Vera: We all take care of each other.

Therapist: Are you just tired, or are you really as unhappy as you look?

Mrs. Hannon: No, I'm just tired.

Vera: She's not unhappy.

Joan: [Curt yelling persistently as Joan talks] Yes, she is unhappy. She just don't want to tell nobody. I'll tell you why she is unhappy. She is sick and tired of us. She wants me to go to school and get graduated, but I don't like school. She wants her [points to her sister, age 18] to stop

acting like a fool. She wants him [points to her brother, 16] to mind his own business and stop messing around. She wants her [points to Vera] to get an apartment and get her kids and get together. She wants him [points to her brother, 11] to get straightened out and go to school. . . And me, I got nerves. Boy I got some nerves on me!

Phase 2. Initial Assessment   The therapist got the picture of the family from the first interactions. Joan speaks for Mrs. Hannon and gives a picture of the dilemmas of everyone in the family, including herself. In the following interaction, the therapist continues to try to bring out Mrs. Hannon without Joan talking for her. During this time, the children go out of control. When the therapist asks what she does to manage it, Mrs. Hannon responds that she "puts on her gorilla suit. That's all." Curt yells and kicks. The therapist is stymied by Curt, and Vera offers no help.

Mrs. Hannon: Just ignore him. [To Curt] Sit down, boy. Hey, sit down. Down.

Joan: [Overlapping] Sit down, man.

Mrs. Hannon [To his brother]: Just ignore him. Hey, sit down. Sit down. I'll bet I'll bash you if you don't sit down. [Children guffaw.]

Brother: Sit your behind down, boy. You better sit down.

Joan: That is why he is so super mean. 'Cause he don't like nobody to tell him what to do. [Mrs. Hannon walks up with a rolled-up newspaper and strikes Curt lightly on the legs.]

Mrs. Hannon: Sit down! [Excited comment and laughter from the children as Mrs. Hannon physically takes Curt off the coffee table and sits him on the chair. Curt whimpers a bit and then sits quietly.]

Mrs. Hannon: You better shut up. [Vera laughs like one of the children.]

Mrs. Hannon: [To everyone] Now, leave him alone. It's not funny.

Therapist [to Vera]: Would he listen to you the way he listens to her?

Vera: Nope.

Joan: No, he won't listen to anybody.

Therapist: So you're kind of a mother to everybody.

Mrs. Hannon: I am the mother of them all.

The basic, problematic family patterns came out clearly. While Mrs. Hannon sought refuge for the events in the family through her withdrawal, Joan was the overriding personality. When Curt took over the session with his screaming, Joan is unable to manage it. Eventually, Mrs. Hannon took action by putting on her "gorilla suit." Everyone then settled down, but the burdensome weight of the family was totally on Mrs. Hannon's shoulders. When overwhelmed, she would withdraw and leave the family in chaos. Joan would take over, attempting to pull the family together. In the process, she became the family lightning rod. She paid a price for this role. At this point in the interview, the family had settled down and Joan was able to address her problems with school and the lack of support the family is getting from the school system. Vera was able to talk about her concerns about getting work, getting together with her husband, and getting an apartment. She was afraid

to be in a house by herself. The neighborhood was dangerous. Mrs. Hannon was able to protect the youngsters but was unable to instill in them the strength she possessed. The girls were looking to their mother for support and direction. The young men did not see themselves as having any role to play at home. With the family started on its work and a beginning assessment made, the therapist could get started, now with Joan and Mrs. Hannon only, separate from the others.

Phase 3. Beginning   The therapist began with Mrs. Hannon and then shifted to Joan as she identified her part in Mrs. Hannon's concerns. He is reaching for feelings, putting feelings into words, reaching inside of silences, and partializing concerns. What emerges will be a clearer picture of what is going on, at the same time assisting Joan and Mrs. Hannon to differentiate their concerns. The therapist began moving toward middle-stage work with them. He eventually wanted to help mother and daughter to elaborate a focus. For the moment, he drew conversation from each that was pertinent to an emergent dialogue with each other. This eventually can lead to more middle-stage work, that is, to express feelings and thoughts so they can be heard and discussed, and to listen to the other and reflect the other's thoughts and feelings. We see only a hint of that now, but the direction is clear.

Therapist: Mrs. Hannon, I don't know how you can do it.

Mrs. Hannon: Uh-huh.

Therapist: You know, you really have more than one problem at home. You know that?

Mrs. Hannon: The whole batch is a problem. [She speaks with a strong voice for the first time in the interview.]

Therapist: That's right. Why did you pick Joan to ask for some help for her?

Mrs. Hannon: This is suppose to be my sensible one.

Therapist: Yeah?

Mrs. Hannon: And when she starts goofing off, I know the whole house is crazy.

Therapist: She helps hold things together?

Mrs. Hannon: Right, and when she starts blowing her stack and falling apart, it's time to find out what's the problem.

Therapist: Okay. You need her to help you. You can't afford not to have her.

Mrs. Hannon: I can always depend on her, you know.

Therapist: Yeah.

Mrs. Hannon: But when she starts falling apart, well, shucks [shaking her head].

Joan: That's why I fell apart.

Therapist: That's why you fall apart. Because she depends on you?

Joan: Nope.

Therapist: Because what?

Joan: Because when she wants me to do something and I can't do it. [She buries her face in her hands and starts to cry quietly.]

Therapist [to Mrs. Hannon]: She's upset.

Mrs. Hannon [nodding] [long pause]

Joan: I got tears. [She giggles tearfully.]

Therapist: That's all right.

Joan: I don't like to cry. [She moves closer to Mrs. Hannon and gets tissues.]

Therapist: That's all right. That's okay.

Joan: No, no. That's all. No more. I get mad at myself when I cry.

Therapist: You don't have to.

Joan: I do [dabbing eyes quietly and recomposing herself]. Now let's talk.

Therapist: Okay.

Joan: [pause] If I get simple, then I can tell you what's wrong with my mind. If I don't get simple, I cry.

Phase 4. Middle-stage Work With this last statement, Joan clarified why her manner has radically changed when the other youngsters in the family left. Now she no longer needed to protect her mother with her "simple" behavior. But when she let go of this compelling need, she felt the hopelessness of the situation from her perspective. She was overwhelmed and began to cry. The therapist worked with Joan in front of Mrs. Hannon and Joan clarified her concerns.

Therapist: All right, okay. What's wrong with your mind then?

Joan: Boy, I worry too much. She [Mrs. Hannon] going off to work, she have an accident. [She laughs tearfully as she relates her imaginary fears.]

Therapist: Go ahead. Go ahead.

Joan: Jack [brother] gets shot walking down the street. Earl [brother] having a train accident.

Therapist: Yeah?

Joan: Rita and Curt choked to death. Vera gets shot by her husband, and me—I'm going crazy.

Therapist: Yeah, but you haven't always been this upset. Why are you getting upset? Why have you been upset lately?

Joan: 'Cause they don't do what I say. And I know I'm right.

Therapist: How long has it been? How long have you been getting so upset? Since everything's been getting so bad?

Joan: Since June, I guess.

Therapist: Since June? What happened? What happened then?

Joan: A whole lot. I can't stand it. Well, not so much, except they just get on my nerves.

Therapist: No, no, something happened. Something has changed at home since June. Why is it worse since then?

Joan: Let's see. They don't listen to what I say.

Therapist [to Mrs. Hannon]: Do you know what happened?

Mrs. Hannon: Think I do.

In this exchange, the therapist assisted Joan to explain her concerns and tracked them concretely. They were *her* concerns, rather than her mother's. Mrs. Hannon was a part of this, although she was silent, and when Joan couldn't recall some of the issues of the previous June, the therapist shifted to Mrs. Hannon. She filled in that Vera got married. She was going to move out, but she couldn't because of difficulties with her new husband, and presumably because she was afraid to become independent. Joan, her confidante, who readily takes others' burdens, seems to have been worrying about it more than Vera.

Phase 5. Focus on Joan I   In the next phase, the therapist tracked Joan's tendency to worry for others. He paradoxically illustrated her chosen role: "you're supposed to worry about the other people in the family." He continued the paradox by relating this to Mrs. Hannon's concerns.

Therapist: So Vera tells you her problems. Who else do you have to worry about?

Joan: I don't know. I just worry for no reason, I guess.

Therapist: No, but you're supposed to worry about other people in the family.

Therapist [to Mrs. Hannon]: She's really been like a part of you.

Mrs. Hannon: Uh-huh.

Therapist: To take care of things and hold them together, because you can't possibly do this by yourself, and she's been the only one you could really depend on to handle things.

Mrs. Hannon: Uh-huh. Right.

Phase 6. Focus on Mrs. Hannon   With Mrs. Hannon's agreement, the therapist now moved to a point of clarification with Mrs. Hannon of her situation and Joan's, as well as the differences between the two. In the discussion he encouraged Mrs. Hannon to take the viewpoint of the other and also implicitly encouraged Joan to identify her situation and differentiate it from her mother's. On this basis, at a later point they could begin to separate personal from relational tasks and solve problems together.

Therapist: You know, when I talk to you, when you first came in here, you looked very tired. You looked out of it. The kids have all left, and I can really see you now, and your eyes are very clear, and I think they're very clear because you see a lot. And I think maybe your nerves are as bad as they are because you see too much, and there's nothing you can do about it.

Mrs. Hannon [softly]: I'll go along with that.

Therapist: And she [Joan] is trying to carry this burden with you. [Mrs. Hannon nods.] [Pause] I can understand why she can't worry about school; she's got the worries of any woman, not a 17-year-old kid. [Mrs. Hannon nods] She couldn't have more worries if she had ten kids of her own. [Pause]

Therapist: You don't really have any help from the outside?

Mrs. Hannon: No, they don't even care.

Phase 7. Move to Tasks The last exchange between the therapist and Mrs. Hannon shifted the focus from perceptions, thoughts, and feelings to an assessment of her current situation and what could be done. Now there would be a gradual shift into sorting out tasks (personal and relational) and problem solving. With the focus on Mrs. Hannon, there was some discussion of what might be most important for the family to do. What emerged from the discussion with Mrs. Hannon was, first, the need to help Vera to become independent and then find some care for

Mrs. Hannon's father. Joan kept wanting to be a part of these concerns. The therapist acknowledged her but deflected the focus of work to Mrs. Hannon, who is beginning to be able to see herself taking charge. The following exchange reflected a longer process in the interview:

Therapist: Joan, you have so much on your mind that I think you need to forget a few things. You can't keep all these things in your head at once or you'll go crazy.

Joan: I know I'm crazy. That makes me mad [laughing], 'cause I can't do nothing about it.

Therapist: Yeah, this kind of thing would drive anybody crazy. You're crazy because you have too much to deal with. [Pause] [To Mrs. Hannon]: I guess in a way that what we should really be concentrating on first is Vera and her kids. If we can get something done for her and the kids.

Mrs. Hannon: Right, right!

The process continued with the focus on Vera and Mrs. Hannon's father. This discussion didn't need to get too concrete, since that would come in a discussion between Mrs. Hannon and Vera in later interviews. The important thing at this point was to help Mrs. Hannon to take over and to relieve Joan of some of the responsibilities she had assumed. She still feels hopeless about herself.

Phase 8. Focus on Joan II In the next phase the focus turns back to Joan.

The therapist gives a fairly clear formulation of the problem, and Mrs. Hannon, with the therapist's coaching, addresses Joan's concerns.

> *Joan*: And you know, I think things will never go my way.
> *Therapist*: Why do you say that, Joan?
> *Joan*: I don't know. . . 'Cause they *don't*.
> *Therapist*: Joan, right now you can't live for yourself. You're living for a lot of other people. At this point in your life, you're not thinking about what you're going to do for yourself or where you want to go tomorrow.
> *Joan*: Nope.
> *Therapist*: You're thinking about what you're going to do for all these other people in your house.
> *Mrs. Hannon* [to Joan]: And that will make you sicker than anything in the drug store. It will, because you can't solve everybody's problems. This you can't do. We just have to make arrangements with them and if they can't solve the problem, I can see if I can help them solve the problem and get them off your back, and maybe you can solve some of your own problems. (This is the crucial move in the interview. Mrs. Hannon spontaneously takes over from Joan, dis-

missing her from the job of worrying for the rest of the family.)

Phase 9. Support New Structure
In this phase, the therapist supported this new configuration of the relationship emergent between Joan and her mother. There was problem-solving discussion about finding a new school for Joan where she could begin again. With their jobs sorted out from one another, Joan and Mrs. Hannon were less burdened. The therapist supported this and connected this with the concrete work each would be doing in the future and in future sessions. The foundation was now set for further sessions with this family, assisting them with relational and family tasks. From the systems perspective, issues were related to each other. When the family is helped to resolve one issue, others come closer to resolution. Once the family is able to manage, the therapist may be available but may not need to be so deeply involved. In the further narrative of the Hannon family's story, Vera was reunited with her husband, who joined the Air Force. They moved to the West Coast. Joan did not return to school, but she earned her high school diploma by passing the GED examination. Mrs. Hannon's father died at home. It was rumored that as things developed, Mrs. Hannon eventually entered some form of the ministry.

From Aponte's perspective, the therapist needed to identify specific issues of the family and to assess how the dynamics of the individual, the family, and the social context converge in relation to these issues. The therapist entered the system to shift its configuration in a way that would resolve the problem. At the same time, he worked between the family and the external structures, the community resources and the agencies that have such a powerful effect on them. Resolving the leadership in the family would allow them to use these structures beneficially. Joan could let go and pursue her education. Mrs. Hannon could manage her concerns, and Vera could manage hers. It became a matter of tasks and support for the new structure. Working between the family and these institutional structures and community resources will be discussed in the following chapter.

SUMMARY

The family's experiencing serious relational loss and reconstructing itself adds another level of complexity and profoundly changes what otherwise would be classic family life cycle stages. The additional stress of the loss brings temporary underorganization and a greater threat of breakdown. Some families remain underorganized over generations, somehow carrying on with the basics of family living but with minimal external and internal adaptations. Families experiencing losses and underorganization, whether over one or more generations, frequently draw in other social institutions to support their functioning. These may be the courts, the schools, child welfare agencies, and health and mental health agencies. Social workers often work for these organizations and work between these families and the social institution. In this sense, the next chapter, which adds the dynamics of social institutions to the internal dynamics of the family, is a natural completion of the discussion begun in this chapter and in the previous one, on elaborated families.

REFERENCES

Amato, P. (2000). The consequences of divorce for adults and children. *Journal of Marriage and the Family, 62*, 1269–1287.

Amato, P., & Booth, A. (1997). *A generation at risk*. Cambridge, MA: Harvard University Press.

Aponte, H. (1986). If I don't get simple, I cry. *Family Process, 25*(4), 533–544.

Bauserman, R. (2002). Child adjustment in joint custody vs. sole custody arrangements. *Journal of Family Psychology, 16*, 1.

Beal, E. W. (1980a). Separation, divorce and single parent families. In E. M. Carter & M. McGoldrick (Eds.), *The family life cycle: A framework for family therapy* (pp. 241–264). New York, NY: Gardner Press.

Beal, E. W. (1980b). *Adult children of divorce: Breaking the cycle and family fulfillment in love and marriage*. New York, NY: Delacorte Press.

Bryner, C. L. (2001). Children of divorce. *Journal of the American Board of Family Practice, 14*(3), 178–183.

Glenn, N. D. (2012). *How good for children is the "good divorce"?* New York, NY: Institute for American Values. Accessed at www.americanvalues.org/search/item.php?id=86.

Glick, P. S. (1979). Children of divorced families in demographic perspective. *Journal of Social Issues, 35*, 170–182.

Goldstein, J. R. (1999). The leveling of divorce in the United States. *Demography, 36*, 409–414.

Greene, S. M., Anderson, E. R., Forgatch, M. S., DeGarmo, D. S., & Hetherington, E. M. (2012). Risk and resilience after divorce. In F. Walsh (Ed.), *Normal family processes* (4th ed.). New York, NY: Guilford.

Herzog, E., & Sudia, C. E. (1973). Children in fatherless families. In B. M. Caldwell & H. N. Ricciuti (Eds.), *Review of child development research* (pp. 141–232). New York, NY: Russell Sage.

Hetherington, M. (2002). *For better or for worse: Divorce reconsidered*. New York, NY: Norton.

Montalvo, B. (1982). Interpersonal arrangements in disrupted families. In F. Walsh (Ed.), *Normal family functioning* (pp. 277–296). New York, NY: Guilford.

National Marriage Project. (2012). Social indicators of marital health and well-being in *The state of our unions: Marriage in America 2012*. Charlottesville, VA: Institute for American Values. www://stateofourunions.org; marriage@virginia.edu.

Norton, A. J., & Miller, L. F. (1992). *Marriage, divorce and remarriage in the 1990s*. Washington, DC: U.S. Bureau of the Census.

Pasley, K., & Garneau, C. (2012). Remarriage and stepfamily life. In F. Walsh (Ed.), *Normal family processes* (4th ed.). New York, NY: Guilford.

Popenoe, D. (2001). *The top ten myths of divorce*. The National Marriage Project. http://marriage.Rutgers.edu/Publications/pubtoptenmyths.htm.

Visher, E. B., & Visher, J. S. (1982). Stepfamilies and stepparenting. In F. Walsh (Ed.), *Normal family functioning*. New York, NY: Guilford.

Visher, E. B., & Visher, J. S. (1996). *Therapy with stepfamilies*. New York, NY: Brunner-Mazel.

Wallerstein, J. S., & Blakeslee, S. (1989). *Second chances: Men, women and children a decade after divorce*. Boston, MA: Houghton-Mifflin.

Wallerstein, J. S., & Kelly, J. (1980). *Surviving the breakup: How children and parents cope with divorce*. New York, NY: Basic Books.

Wallerstein, J. S., Lewis, J., & Blakeslee, S. (2000). *The unexpected legacy of divorce*. New York, NY: Hyperion.

Waite, L., & Gallagher, M. (2000). *The case for marriage*. New York, NY: Doubleday.

CHAPTER 10

Working between Families and Outside Social Institutions: Schools, Child Welfare, and the Juvenile Court

KEY TOPICS

> Families and Outside Social Institutions
> Social Work Fields of Practice
> Working between Institutional and Family Systems
> Social Work in Schools
> Social Work in the Judicial System
> Social Work in Child Welfare
> Family Preservation
> Substitute Care Arrangements
> Social Work in the Juvenile Court

Families, particularly vulnerable families such as underorganized families and those in life cycle transition, could not operate without supportive connections with outside social institutions. Social workers in large part work for these institutions. They work between the family and the social institution, attempting to help both family and institutional process proceed optimally. This chapter examines this practice in schools, in the judicial system, and in child welfare. The following chapter examines practice in health and mental health systems and in community resource networks, which often work to bring together schools, child welfare, health, mental health, and the judicial system. These are experiments in different states to coordinate services. All of these are areas where social institutions have had to expand their concept of clientele to include families. Social workers have important roles in this. Each is a different field of practice in social work. In each field, social workers are mediators between the social institution and its clientele, and in each field, social work practice differs according to the different processes, concerns, and tasks essential to the institution.

FAMILIES AND OUTSIDE SOCIAL INSTITUTIONS

In these chapters we take the systems model, inherent to social work, one step further to include the relationships of families with social institutions and community resources. The social worker often works between families and these institutional structures or community resources. Social institutions are established to promote public order, to protect, to provide resources, and sometimes to set appropriate standards for individuals and family members. The institutional missions and tasks, whether of education, health care, or justice, often shape the relational tasks of the family. But the dilemma of the institutions is always how to work with the family: how to assist the family to do its work without distorting, taking over, or colonizing the family.

In all cases social institutions, such as education and health care, have discovered that their clients (pupils, patients) were more than individuals, that in reality families were essential parts of education, of health care, of the juvenile justice system, and certainly of child welfare. From the family's perspective, to say that these institutional structures are outside the family would be somewhat paradoxical. They are often outside families only in the sense that many families are unable to use them to assist in their functioning. However, if they are really outside families, that itself becomes the problem. Social institutions such as schools, health and mental health care, the judicial system, and child welfare agencies have important functions that place them on the inside of families. Families need social institutions to carry out certain functions. The more complex the situation or the deeper the need of a member, the more the institution or community resource needs to exercise an inside role with family functioning—without, however, disturbing the family's natural exercise of its own appropriate functioning. If family is vulnerable to institutions, the reverse is also true. For the most part, social institutions cannot carry out their missions without the help and participation of families.

Social workers, who can be uniquely positioned on the inside of both institution and family, can help both to carry out their respective functions harmoniously. They can facilitate the complex relationships between vulnerable families and their necessary social institutional environments. Their interventions can make a connection between the institutional mission and family relational tasks. Social workers have done this for a century in different fields of practice. They focus on the needs of vulnerable persons but also relate to the necessary work of social institutions, who deal with deep, human vulnerability.

Social Work with Vulnerable Persons in Families

Social work practice first grows out of the needs of the vulnerable persons and situations that institutions serve. Persons who most often need care and protection are children, the elderly, or those with disabilities. These persons often live in families who are their first resource for care. Thus, emergent fields of practice include the following:

- *Child welfare—work with children and their parents and/or caregivers.* Child welfare is about helping children and families sustain or reconstruct secure attachments and connections. It creates a context for children to grow appropriately as persons of dignity, worth, and emergent competence. When the family is unable to care for a child appropriately, child welfare workers may work with that family or that kinship unit to rehabilitate itself, or they may connect the child with substitute care, often another family.

- *Social work with the elderly and their caregivers.* When elderly persons decline in their ability to manage independently, maintenance in their family or placement in an assistive living unit often requires significant assistance for the elderly person and for the family. This can create profound change in different generational units of a family. An example is the O'Conner family (case study 8.9).
- *Social work with adults with disabilities and their caregivers.* Adults who have disabilities, and their caregivers, are another vulnerable population similar to the aging, Social workers in the health system and other systems often work with these situations.

Social Work in Social Institutions: Health and Education

Parallel to work with vulnerable persons is work with families in social institutions such as health care and education:

- *Social work in health care and mental health.* Many events in health care—birth, death, a difficult treatment regimen, disability, the need for more intensive care in a patient's environment—demand more than medical intervention. Often these are family events even more than medical events. In some cases, such as birth and death, medical intervention is secondary to profound human meanings and the social relational work that must be done. The social worker in the health care setting works with patients and their families, struggling with the relational issues when social functioning is affected by illness or disability. The issues for the patient in mental health are often profoundly connected with the family. Many patients could not survive without the family's ongoing assistance and support.
- *School social work.* The school social worker works to construct a workable relationship between child, family, and school that may help children carry out their developmental work of intellectual, social, and physical maturation. The family is the first educator of the child, and the school cannot accomplish its purpose without at least the implicit support of the family. When the child may be vulnerable there is need for a more developed relation between family and school.

Other institutions in which social workers are involved with families are in the world of work, in trade unions, in corporations, and in military organizations. Social workers also work in the system of justice with the courts, with the police, and in corrections.

Religion as a Social Institution   Social workers often work for religious sponsored agencies serving families and children (Kohs, 1966). Religion, culture, and
family become the guidance systems of human action and meaning. Religion, as a
social institution, celebrates the spiritual in the social and personal context of each
person's essential relationships and obligations. Although religion is very diverse, it
defines common meanings and supports and links families with each other.

SOCIAL WORK FIELDS OF PRACTICE

Social workers have a long history of working between families, social institutions,
and community resources where people and their environments are in exchange
with each other. This relationship in many ways is the underlying paradigm of
social work. It is the duality of focus on people and their environments that dis-
tinguishes social work from other professions (Joint NASW-CSWE Task Force,
1979). Social workers work between institutional resource systems and family systems to establish a match between resources, standards and needs, helping both
develop this match optimally (Gordon, 1969; 1979). Fields of practice in social
work grow from the need for mediation between persons and social institutions to
meet common human needs. Practice within each field is unique to that field. It
is defined by a particular clientele, a point of entry, a social institution with its
institutional purposes, and the contribution of social work practice. Such practice
is specified through the contribution of social work knowledge, values, and their
appropriateness to the institutional purpose and to common human needs
(Bartlett, 1971). We will use this framework to discuss practice with families and
social institutions.

For social workers, the practice problem becomes the unequal and unstable
relations of any social institution, such as a court or a school, to a family. We can
see this in the J. family (case study 5.7), the Hong family (case study 5.5), and the
Hannon family (case study 9.4). The social institution should not take over the
appropriate functions of family members or attempt to substitute for them, but
instead should support family members and their appropriate functions. This is difficult. Success demands a skilled mediator who can work on the inside of the institution and the family. The dangers are that without a mediator who can work on the
inside of both the family and the institution, the family could become paralyzed or
the institution fail its mission. In the best sense, the social institution or community
resource would become a "part" of the family for a time through the social worker
and through the individualization of policies that this arrangement might encourage. The social worker could monitor the complex relationship between institutional resources and standards and family functioning. Practice would then take
place, not simply as a transaction between practitioner and client system, but more
broadly, involving social institutional structures and community resources. In this
sense, the beginnings, middles, and endings inherent to a helping process are also
beginnings, middles, and endings with the social institution or community resource
as well as with the social worker (Smalley, 1967, pp. 3, 4). Representing the institu-

tion as well as the family, the social worker helps family members use the institution to carry out relational and personal tasks. In turn, the family helps the institution fulfill its societal functions.

When families interact with social institutions, there is a natural and continuing concern that family members will either be controlled by the social institution or lose their functions. Yet if they oppose the institution, families fear losing what the institution can offer the family—or even facing possible punishment. This is the dilemma. Schools, the police and court systems, child welfare, and health care all have different meanings to different families, meanings that are defined by the family culture and the family history. Families develop patterns and complex linkages with institutions, often handed down through generations. Generations of disappointing relationships in one's family history may be difficult to overcome. Nineteenth-century Irish Americans had great difficulty with the schools and child welfare systems, to the point of developing their own alternative religiously and culturally compatible systems. When they achieved power in the police and political systems, they had less difficulty. In the wake of Reconstruction, African Americans experienced prejudice and discrimination from all systems. They lacked the resources to develop alternate institutions, except for those having to do with religion and, to some extent, child welfare. Only in the last decades of the twentieth century has this situation changed. Native Americans have long been in the same position, although sometimes the tribe can act as a mediator.

As in the case of the Hmong family earlier in this book, institutions may be quite unaware of cultural differences and family needs. They depend on families to meet their objectives, but they need to work hard to acquire sensitivity to families. This means that the family social worker often must advocate strongly to help the institution adapt to the needs of its clientele and their families. The social worker does a great deal of work with the institution, developing resources, helping them to fit with family needs and meanings, and removing obstacles that prevent families from using these resources.

Underorganized Families

Underorganized families need particular assistance from the outside to reorganize themselves and to relate effectively with social institutions. With multiple needs, they often have multiple involvements with different social institutions and great difficulties getting what they need. These multiple involvements can be confusing. They can put the family at risk of further loss of functions and eventual collapse. Differing institutions themselves can become like contentious families, at odds with one another over a particular family. In the resulting confusion, nothing gets done, and the risk to the family grows. The social worker can bring services together to resolve issues with families with multiple needs and involvements, keeping family members appropriately in charge of their own functions and responsibilities, and keeping agencies in workable relations with each other (Constable & Kordesh, 2009). Such networks of agencies are discussed at the end of chapter 11.

The concept of relational justice, previously applied to relationships on the inside of families, can also be applied to transactions between institutions and families. The needs of families are often dependent on institutional processes. The J. family (case study 5.7) could not change without the involvement of the court. Indeed, the expectations of the court largely set its goals and defined its tasks. Ultimately, with the mediation and family work of the social worker, these expectations helped the family make changes it would never make on its own. The social worker works in schools with the multidisciplinary team, in the hospital with the medical team, in the military with the commanding officer, in the workplace with the boss, in the justice system with the judge, and in the police system with the police chief and his or her delegates. The aim of the work is to adapt the institution to the needs of the family (and vice versa) so that family members can carry out their tasks and meet appropriate institutional expectations. Family members can then support the institution's work.

Ecomaps   Ecomaps are particularly useful to illustrate the relationships between family members and institutions, for assessment and for intervention. They put the relationship of family members to community agencies in graphic form. They are also useful when there is more than one agency involved, as well as when the relationships are complex (Hartman & Laird, 1983). In case study 5.7, the J. family had a very complex relationship with the court that was supervising Mr. J. (see figure 5.2).

WORKING BETWEEN INSTITUTIONAL AND FAMILY SYSTEMS

Social Work in Schools

Social work in schools provides an extended example of the process taking place within the family, within the institution, and with the social worker. Schools and families are the crucial institutions in the socialization of children. Effective education is essential if children are to participate in a globalized economy, as citizens, and ultimately as family members themselves, raising a new generation. School has become the place where children come to participate in a common experience of membership and personal achievement within the broader society. It is their first step into society. Because of this, the school, at best, is a community of families, of teachers, parents, and others, working in partnership with one another as socializers of children. Schools have not always taken families in or individualized their curricula to the child's needs. The history of education in modernizing societies is an uneven history of a gradually increasing awareness of individual differences in ability, culture, and class, increasing inclusion of these differences as they affect learning. School has become more than simply learning language arts, social science, and mathematics. The mission and meanings of education have broadened and become intertwined with concerns that each pupil develop as a human being and realize his or her potential contribution to society. Research evidence points out that, particularly with vulnerable children, schools cannot accomplish their mission to educate any child without an implicit partnership with parents (Bailey, Blasco, & Simeonson, 1992; Bernier, 1990; Bristol & Gallagher, 1982; Frey, Greenberg, & Fewell, 1989; Hanson & Carta, 1995; Hanson & Hanline, 1990; Walberg, 2013). No amount of educational inputs, money for teachers, classrooms, and the like will be effective without the support and involvement of parents, without the school's being a partner with and an agent of the parents (Walberg & Lai, 1999). But for the most part, schools have only limited recognition of this fact.

However, many schools have gradually broadened their concepts of who their clients are to include the pupil's family as a partner in certain ways, particularly ways in which they could not succeed without family involvement. Social workers in the school are positioned at the central point in the ecosystems of child development, at the meeting point between parents, pupil, and school. They work with children at risk. The school social worker makes education possible for many children who otherwise would have difficulty coping with the educational process. For schools, the school social worker works in multiple functions within the most vulnerable parts of the educational process, where the education process can break down in its relations with the child and with the family. Accordingly, the basic unit of attention in school social work is the constellation of teacher, parent, and child. The school social worker may work with teachers, families, and children to address individual situations, or it may work as a consultant to help schools to be more effective with children and respond appropriately to them (Kelly, Massat, & Constable, 2015).

The School as a Community of Families   From the origins of public education, schools in the United States have often operated in relative isolation from their constituent families. As long as this isolation of school from the family sphere has been taken for granted, the school social worker's role has been to span the boundaries between schools and families as expeditiously as possible (Litwak & Meyer, 1966). The complexity of the challenges facing schools today has developed an alternate conception that the school is a community of families and teachers in partnership. There have been numerous recent experiments with parent-sponsored schools, and that trend is now becoming very important. The development of this supportive community is even more important when the community is off balance and in crisis, when children, families, communities and schools have special needs, when the connection between home and school is not easily developed, and when there is cultural or linguistic diversity. It is a commonplace in education for resilience in children to be promoted when the resources in the school, family, and community are united and dedicated to the healthy development and educational success of children (Christensen & Sheridan, 2001; Kelleghan, Sloane, Alvarez, & Bloom, 1993; Walberg, 2013; Wang, Haertl, & Walberg, 1998, p. 55; Webster-Stratten, 1993). This relationship of school, family, and community, central to the work of the school social worker, is becoming recognized as central to effective education, resilient children, and school reform as well.[1]

---

[1]From Constable and Walberg (2009, p. 555). Used with permission.

The Necessary Arrangement of Relations between Family and School   There is a necessary order in the relationship between family and schools. Families cannot educate their children in a complex modern society without the assistance of schools, and schools cannot educate without the cooperation of families (Walberg, 2013; Walberg, 1984; Walberg & Lai, 1999). Each can prevent the other from accomplishing its proper function. This is particularly true for vulnerable children and families. Families are the first educators of their children. When the family acts in its capacity to educate, its educational functions take place in a child's life prior to the school's function, and they remain most important through the child's developing years. The school's functions exist to help the family accomplish its prior functions in accordance with the needs and standards of society and the rights of members of the family. Children are in a recognized position of vulnerability and require protection from their environments. They have a right to receive adequate nurture and socialization, whenever possible, in their own families. The community, often represented by the school, is obligated to ensure that families have all the assistance—economic, social, educational, political, and cultural—that they need to face all their responsibilities in a human way. It is not the function of the school to take away from families the child-rearing functions that families can perform on their own or in cooperative associations. Rather, in the spirit of *subsidiarity*, the school must support and even assist what the family can do best, particularly when these functions are at risk.

The relationship of the family to the school and the community can be encapsulated by three principles:

1. The family has primary functions in the care and socialization of its children. It has rights and responsibilities derived from this function. These responsibilities include the economic, social, educational, and cultural provision for the needs of its members. As such, the family is the basic social unit of society. The work of the family is always personal. Transactions en famille are expected to be based on affection and respect for the other person. Particular types of learning would be distorted if they excluded this dimension of affection and respect for the person as a person, worthwhile in his or her own right. In families, this personal dimension is experienced and learned in work, worship, gender roles, respect for others in social relations, and respect for one's developing sexuality.
2. The school's primary functions are helping the family accomplish its responsibilities and supplying certain cognitive instruction that the family cannot take on. A partnership of home and school, particularly when the child has special needs, can be developed between parents and teachers and school social workers, when needed.
3. A secondary function of the school (and, in a broader sense, of the community) is to monitor potential abridgment of rights of children as pupils and citizens when external conditions of society or internal conditions within the family make it impossible for the family to accomplish its primary function.

This must be done, as in the first principle, without inappropriately abridging the family's exercise of those functions it is able to accomplish.

These principles involve a balance between family and school, an order, and a defined relation between their respective functions. They inevitably lead to the need for more integrated relationships between school and family. The danger is that in the face of the weakness of the family and the complexity of the child's problems, schools might attempt to substitute for family functions. This never works well. When services take over duties, rather than empowering families to carry them out, they limit the effectiveness of the partnership.

Working between Pupil, Family, and School

The school is a stage with opportunities for each child to play out the great developmental issues: separation individuation, self-esteem, social relationships, language, imagination, emotions, assertiveness, achievement, competition, productive work, and the discovery and use of one's self. If school is used well, it is a great normalizer. In many respects, the school is the basic place for services to be delivered to children in families. There are many possible approaches to social work practice with pupils and families in school. Intervention, running from consultation and multidisciplinary teamwork through individual, group, or family involvement to assisting in policy and program development, can vary with the emergent needs of children and the community situation. In an elementary school, as in the case of Alan, it is possible that the social worker might know and work with a pupil and family for up to nine years.

In Alan's case the social worker carried out a wide range of functions with different units of attention to support Alan's functioning and eventual developmental maturation. It is a good example of school social work practice with children, families, and the school as a system. Alan faced a chaotic family and personal situation in second grade. He had great difficulty. His world, as he knew it, was falling apart.[2]

CASE STUDY 10.1: ALAN

Alan, age 7, was referred for evaluation by his second-grade classroom teacher about five weeks after the start of school. The social worker found him quite withdrawn, with considerable emotional energy tied up with his parents' divorce process. He felt that his parents yelled a lot at each other, at him, and at his brother. He could also say that he felt angry when he didn't get his way. A transfer student from another school, he had difficulty following directions and concentrating on his work. He was easily distracted, and he had poor fine motor coordination and poor visual perception. He would often try to copy from

---

[2]This case is adapted from Wolkow (2002, pp. 364–370), with permission.

his neighbors or just sit, sucking his fingers and not attempting to do his work. Testing showed that his support systems were eroding and that his self-concept was rapidly deteriorating along with his academic performance. His reading difficulties could be an indicator of possible learning disabilities.

Alan lived with his mother, his 10-year-old brother, and his 3-year-old sister in a mobile home park. His mother and father had separated at the end of his kindergarten year, and the divorce became final after first grade. At this time, the family had moved to the mobile home park, where the mother's parents lived. During this time, the father would take the children on weekends. He was consistent in doing so, and both children and father seemed to enjoy the time very much. There were also contacts with the extended family on both sides.

The social worker met with the parents and recommended that Alan receive outside counseling. They did not agree to this, and so she decided to monitor him on a consultative basis until further direct work could be arranged. She provided consultation to Alan's second-grade teacher. The second-grade teacher was somewhat rigid and unresponsive to Alan and was not particularly receptive to direct suggestions. Consequently, the social worker worked closely with the learning disabilities teacher and the reading teacher, who were, in different ways, involved with Alan's situation. The second-grade teacher left on maternity leave in February. Alan's new teacher was warm, caring, and creative. She liked Alan and was responsive to suggestions. Alan was

also provided with more direct learning disabilities help. Shortly after this, Alan began to respond. On the other hand, he also drew a picture of himself with a noose around his neck and talked with the social worker about his sad feelings. The social worker discussed this with the mother. Although the mother was open and cooperative, she resisted any suggestion of outside help for Alan. The father wanted to get outside counseling. They agreed on a plan whereby Alan would check in with the social worker every day for the remainder of the year. The social worker also saw Alan in a group. She remained in contact with the parents and provided consultation to his teachers. Alan gradually became more outgoing and showed improved social skills, first in the group and later in the classroom. The social worker encouraged the teachers to support Alan's progress in class, and Alan continued to do better for the remainder of the school year.

At the end of the second-grade year, the social worker met with the parents and again recommended outside counseling help. The mother continued to be reluctant: it would not be something she would ever do. The father was able to follow through with arrangements and bring Alan to his appointments. In third grade, the social worker was able to match Alan with a male teacher who was very warm, accepting, and competent. He provided regular consultation, helping the teacher institute a behavior modification program for the whole class that was focused on positive social interaction, as a way of keeping a handle on Alan's real social progress. In fourth grade, Alan continued to show considerable improvement, with the social worker moving toward monthly check-ins except when Alan had concerns to discuss. At this time, the mother remarried. In class discussion, Alan showed his concern about this new development. The social worker met with the mother and the stepfather, and they agreed to come in throughout the year to talk about issues surrounding their relationship with the children, especially Alan. She began seeing Alan again in a social skills group. Alan made improvements in anger control, remained in contact with his father, and managed to have a good relationship with his stepfather as well. He continued his progress for the next four grades, although he continued to have learning disabilities in the area of reading. He was still shy and a loner, but he managed to have friends in his father's neighborhood. In the following grades, the school social worker remained available. Alan continued to maintain his progress academically, socially, and emotionally.

In the beginning, Alan was dealing with the changes in his family, his move from his old neighborhood, and his learning disabilities. When his school situation improved, he was able to express his depression and even suicidal ideation. His family went through profound changes—severe marital upset, separation, divorce, single parenthood with joint custody, and remarriage. While the social worker's focus remained on Alan, she was a resource for both parents and for his stepparent. The school in some ways became a type of "holding system" for the whole family during this time of turmoil. Alan was able to use the support of the school to avert possible deterioration and showed considerable change over seven years. Throughout all this change, he was working steadily on the same problems. Working between the family and school worlds, the social worker helped the teachers, the parents, and Alan in different ways to develop this holding system, to support Alan's strengths, and—as Alan grew and matured—to help him to put things together.

Although Alan's case is not particularly complex, it illustrates well several important points about school social work and about social work practice in the contexts of families and social institutions. In contrast to the cases of community-based work with families that we have discussed to this point, the relational tasks of the person and the family were related to the work of education. Alan's family situation reflected itself in the massive breakdown of his ability to cope with educational and social tasks, his thoughts of dying, and his chronic sadness. The helping process built itself on Alan's developmental thrust to adapt to school. It centered on the transaction between the pupil and the school but also included the family. The parents were open to this process at a time when they would have had difficulty using any other resource. The social worker, embedded in the school, worked at different levels of intensity throughout Alan's elementary school experience, attempting to bring all the elements of the situation together optimally. The focus on different units of attention varied according to the particular situation. She would provide consultation to all at different times. She met with Alan individually and in groups, according to Alan's current need. Mostly, she set the conditions for Alan and his family to resolve this complicated situation. To do this, she needed to know a good deal about individual development, families, schools as resources for pupils like Alan, and the ways he could use himself with all parties involved to make the process work over time.

SOCIAL WORK IN THE JUDICIAL SYSTEM

A number of fields of social work practice come from the judicial system: child welfare, juvenile corrections, adult corrections, and police social work. We will be particularly concerned with the family court, which, depending on state statutes, generally exercises jurisdiction over families and youngsters under 18, and thus with the fields of child welfare and juvenile corrections.

The law and the judicial system set standards of child protection and care for families and for children. When children are endangered by the inability of a family to care for them appropriately, or when minors are in violation of the law, it is the function of this system to help families and members of families meet these standards, to deal with the implications of not meeting them, and to help victims when possible. Social workers or probation officers within these systems work with family members to carry out these institutional purposes. In both systems, clients are mostly involuntary. For any person and for whole families as well, being referred to court is indeed a crisis. The J. family (case study 5.7) is a good example of this. Most of the time, such people are not explicitly asking for help, but if the process is to succeed, they must come to a point at which they want help and can use help to meet the standards of the law and the court.

For families, this is a delicate and uncertain transition. First, it means that energy directed to resisting the implications of the judicial process needs to be converted into energy available for a sort of self-transformation to meet the expectations of the law. In many cases, particularly when the focus is on one person alone, these transformations never occur. The energy of the court confronts the oppositional energy of the child *and* the parents. It requires a special type of skill on the social worker's part to keep the court and the family systems appropriately open and separate, in charge of their own concerns and able to transform themselves (Baker, 1999). Second, when children and adolescents are involved, this transformational process needs to be a family process as well. The J. family (case study 5.7) is a good example of the social worker working between both systems, helping the family keep its own system open so that productive work can be done. As we saw in the example of Alan (case study 10.1), the social worker is not providing some generic therapy in a school, child welfare, or probation setting. Rather, the social worker is helping family members meet the expectations of the institution—in this case, the court— while at the same time the child and family are taking crucial developmental steps. If change does not take place, the court can take custody and, through *parens patriae*, itself take on and assign the parental role. In many ways, the helping process in these contexts can be much more complex and fraught with difficulty than family therapy in the community. On the other hand, the supervision of the court and the law and its procedures can provide a framework for growth and self-transformation when the family is unreachable and nothing else may be possible. However, this level of practice would demand a level of professional skill and an understanding of the helping process not always present in many court systems.

Social Work in Child Welfare

The status of child, by its nature, demands parents. For the last several decades, the field of child welfare has been shifting from a strict child protection approach with minimal family involvement to a child-centered, family-focused approach (Leiderman, 1995). Child welfare has to be family welfare as well, whether it means working with a child's family at home or working with substitute caregivers, whether these are foster homes, adoptive families, or residential homes. The first goal of child welfare is to strengthen, support, and preserve families and keep children with their parents whenever possible and when it is in the best interests of the child. Recent studies report that only a small percentage of children reported to child protective services are ever placed in some form of substitute care (Pecora, Reed-Ashcraft, & Kirk, 2001). In six major states, about 4 in 1,000 children aged 0 to 4 and about 2 in 1,000 children aged 5 to 17 will enter foster care (Pecora, Reed-Ashcraft, & Kirk, 2001). This means that in most cases, the child welfare worker may work mainly with the family of origin. When there is a foster placement, there is a broader focus: on the family of origin, on the foster home, and on the child. The foster child has a type of membership in both families.

Family Preservation

Family preservation services have emerged as a more intensive effort to help parents at severe risk support and care for their children (Kinney, Haapala, & Booth, 1991). This is done through (1) family resource, support, and educational services, (2) family-focused casework services that address problems as they arise, and (3) intensive family-centered crisis services that seek to stabilize families when there is an imminent risk of child placement because of abuse or neglect. Sometimes these services are provided by a state child welfare agency, sometimes by a subcontracted agency. However, the process of family reorganization needs to be the same, with the state agency and the court monitoring whether the family intervention is successful. The following case of the Clark family shows the wide range of services necessary, even in an intensive, short-term intervention, to help a family respond to the needs of their children.[3]

---

[3]From Kinney, Haapala, and Booth (1991, pp. 133–135). Adapted with permission.

CASE STUDY 10.2:
THE CLARK FAMILY

The Clark family was referred by a public health nurse when their premature daughter was released from the hospital. Toby, age 3, had recently been diagnosed as hyperactive with some brain damage. Children's Protective Services and the nurse were suspicious about Toby's three concussions over the past year. Another child in the same family had died not long ago from sudden infant death syndrome. The nurse wondered whether Toby and the baby shouldn't be placed in foster care.

When the social worker arrived, she immediately noted the smell of gas leaking from the furnace. Pam, the mother, age 22, appeared very depressed and said she hadn't felt up to going to the public phone to call for help. She had no phone, although considering her premature child, the clinic advised her to get one. The social worker immediately helped the mother get dressed and call the landlord. Then they talked. She was very thin, pale, and weak, had a chronic cold, and had lost her front teeth. She said she had been very depressed since her baby's birth and had often felt that the child did not belong to her. She was also extremely upset about her Toby's "wild" behavior and wondered whether he didn't have a "bad seed" in him. She had been thinking she would rather kill him now rather than see him grow up to be a murderer like his uncle. She had had three children and four miscarriages in five years of marriage. She was very lonely. Her husband, Ralph, was usually away from the house from mid-morning to late at night, unsuccessfully trying to sell life insurance. He had not sold a policy in five months. She told me that every counselor they had ever seen had told her that her husband was "rotten" and that she should leave him. But she said she loved him and he didn't beat her. They had moved from another state last June so that they could stay married and still be able to get help from the state.

The next day they approached a local organization to secure the $50 needed to have a telephone installed. They also got two old bedsheets that could be nailed up as curtains, since she had expressed fears about sitting alone at night with no curtains for privacy. A man had been peering through her window. She had been raped before and was very afraid it might happen again.

On her next visit to the family, the mother and the social worker discussed Toby. Pam said that she did not love him and described a variety of what she described as self-destructive and wild behaviors that he engaged in. She reported incidents such as him throwing himself backward off of furniture, touching the hot stove and laughing, turning on the kitchen burners, banging his head against the wall until unconscious, and biting, scratching, and hitting other people. Although he was 3, he was not talking at all. She was concerned that Children's Protective Service would think she was abusing him because he hurt himself so much or because they locked him in his room at night. They did this because he slept only two or three hours at a stretch. When awake, he would go into the kitchen at night and eat until he vomited. She said she thought she should put him in an institution because she couldn't handle him. He would not kiss or show any affection to people. She said that he had been removed from the home by Children's Protective Services when she had a "nervous breakdown" and was hospitalized. Since that time, the parents had already voluntarily placed Toby once because "she couldn't cope" with him. She was also afraid she might harm him because he made her so angry sometimes.

Before leaving, they made a list of what Pam could do if she felt her son's behavior was so bad she would want to place him again. The social worker let her know that she felt it was a good idea to put him in his room sometimes and explained the concept of "time out." If Pam did it right, she might not have to lock the door. The list also included calling the social worker (their phone was to be installed the next day). They then made an appointment to take the son to a local children's hospital learning center to see about enrolling him in a special school program. Finally, they talked about the mother getting some free time for herself. The social worker would like to meet Toby and could stay with him for several hours later that week. Pam accepted her offer.

During the social worker's time with Toby, she got to know him and learned a lot about him. He did try some of the behaviors Pam had described. But he could respond to positive reinforcement and time out. She taught him to play a game in which he expressed affection to a cuddly bear. It was proof for both of them that Toby could change. Pam cried the first time they played the game and he kissed her.

During their second week, Pam began to talk more about her discontent in the marriage. She said she knew Ralph wasn't really working all the times he was gone. She expressed resentment over his dressing nicely when she had only one outfit, his freedom to play all day and night while she sat in their apartment, and his refusal both to get her a driver's license and to drive her places. The social worker coached her to respond, but also be appropriately assertive. She also helped her to call the public assistance office and get authorization to get her front teeth replaced.

Ralph began to be curious about what was happening and decided to stay home one day to meet the social worker. He shared his frustrations with having to be on welfare and agreed to attend the next session. In the next sessions, they moved to focus with Pam and Ralph primarily on behavioral child management skills. In the process, the social worker began to help them work on their own communication and come to some agreement about how to handle Toby. Toby had begun attending the school program, and the mother rode the bus with him every day; she later met his teachers and other staff. She began to report having some positive feelings about Toby, and she no longer felt she should send him away. With a temporary cap on her teeth, she began to smile more. She was also beginning to gain some weight.

As the end of the intervention period approached, the social worker explored ways the mother could continue counseling. Pam decided she would go to a counselor at a local mental health center. She had known the counselor from the time right after the baby was born.

A follow-up call from this family several months later revealed that although there had been many upsetting events that had occurred after the social worker left, they were still together as a family. Pam had been seeing her counselor and was working on some of her depression. Pam and Ralph were also going for marital counseling. Ralph had quit selling insurance and was in a job training program. Toby was attending a new school, and his mother was participating in a parent education program required by the school. Toby was starting to talk and did not seem as wild. The infant daughter was doing well.

The Clark family case is a good example of family preservation work. The work is often quite concrete and crisis-oriented, but the direction is the gradual restructuring of family relationships and better use of community resources, as relationships inside the family get better. Careful contracting is particularly important, because families may well at first be unwilling clients. Someone has made a complaint to the state department of child welfare about the possibility of child maltreatment by the family. The social worker needs to proceed carefully, not from a one-up position but as a consultant to the client (Baker, 1999). The contract agreement respects the fact that the parents are still in charge, and the social worker and the resources of the community are there to help them provide safe and nurturing relationships with their children, as well as care for themselves in the process.

The big danger with this type of work is that when confronted with the difficulties clients have in managing issues, such as having to call the landlord about the gas leak, the social worker could become overactive and do it for them. This would confirm and reinforce the previous patterns. Instead, the social worker helps Mrs. Clark call the landlord, put up the curtains, begin to cope with Toby, and develop communication with her husband. As new patterns develop, she encourages Mr. and Mrs. Clark to *own* them. The nature of the service—short-term, time-limited, and intensive, with an evaluation—encourages this ownership. There is an ending, with follow-up. By the follow-up, Mr. and Mrs. Clark are continuing their progress. The child welfare agency has subcontracted this case with an outside agency, focused mainly on the intensive services connected with family preservation. For this reason, the formal court referral process found in many other child welfare cases is missing. When court process is necessary, it becomes a framework for the parents to work on particular goals and to decide whether they have a strong enough unit to refrain from abusing their children and, if the children have been placed outside the family, get them back, when appropriate.

Substitute Care Arrangements

In 2009, 423,773 children were placed out of their homes in substitute care arrangements (Engstrom, 2012) in the United States. These could be a group residence for children, care by a relative, adoption, or family foster care. Adoption, a permanent placement arrangement, can be a complex process, demanding the highest level of professional skill (Rampage, Eovaldi, Ma, Weigel Foy, Samuels, & Bloom, 2012; Triseliotis, Shireman, & Hundleby, 1997). Over the previous decade, about 75 percent of all substitute care was family foster care or kinship care (Everett, 1995; Engstrom, 2012). Family foster care, intended to be temporary, is contingent on the natural parents' making improvements in their ability to care for a child. Often this does not happen. The long-term problem with foster care is that children can be left in a "temporary" arrangement that has become permanent (Maas & Engler, 1959). The temporary nature of the placement may also make it difficult for foster parents (or foster children) to invest themselves in the relationship.

Work with foster homes demands a high level of skill (Engstrom, 2012; Lewis, 2011). It is a process of helping the foster parents "make room" for the child(ren), to accommodate their special needs and the inherent uncertainties of their attachments, to provide for them and work with the school, to accept the complexities of their relationships with birth parents and with visitation, and to let them come back to their parents in a natural and comfortable way when the time comes. It is remarkable how well foster parents and children often manage these relational acrobatics! It is also not surprising when foster homes do fail to be the homes of permanent attachment that children need. In the last analysis, they are not designed to be such homes. One can only hope that children will use them as well as they can, sorting out their different attachments from each other. There is the highest need for professional input here, which is frequently left unsatisfied.

CASE STUDY 10.3: ALICE AND MICHAEL, FOSTER PARENTS

When Alice and Michael Smith decided to become foster parents, their son, James, was 9, and their daughter, Johanna, was 13. Michael is an engineer, and Alice teaches part-time in a high school. They live in a comfortable suburban development. As both children grew older, the parents wondered about taking in a younger child whom they could help. The child welfare agency was responsible for three siblings: Jane Barclay, age 10, Lisa Barclay, age 6, and Joey Barclay, age 5. The agency wanted to place the siblings together, and Alice and Michael agreed to be foster parents to them. Their mother was working to get her children back as soon as her drug problems alle-

viated. It was understood that the children would stay with Alice and Michael for at least a year. For the Barclay children, Alice and Michael's home and family was a totally strange and different world. Adapting to their routines was difficult. Alice felt the brunt of the placement. She felt overwhelmed by all of the needs she became aware of, and she felt caught between getting the children to change patterns or adapting to them. She was particularly concerned about integrating the children into school. Her old problems of depression started to come back, and she increased her medication. Michael, normally a busy engineer, wanted to support Alice, but he found himself becoming authoritarian, particularly with Joey. Jane Barclay, a parental child with severe learning disabilities in school, had been accustomed to her own control of Lisa and Joey Barclay. Lisa was highly disorganized, and Joey was defiant, both at home and at school. James Smith felt that Jane, older by a year, had displaced him and was "bossing" him. Johanna Smith remained aloof from the turmoil in the home but profoundly missed the time and attention she was accustomed to having from her mother. The judge was ambivalent about whether Mrs. Barclay was ready to take her children back. A decision about the Barclays was delayed from one hearing to another, and three years elapsed before they returned home.

The social worker worked closely with Alice and Michael and, despite initial chaos, the two older children did settle in the Smith home. Jane took over some responsibilities in her accustomed way but also developed a relationship with Alice. When Alice secured help in school for Jane's learning disabilities, she eventually found herself making progress. Lisa followed Jane closely and began to organize herself. Joey was in constant difficulty. It became manage-

able when Michael learned quietly to support the good things Joey was able to do rather than to overreact.

With their mother's improvement, the court ordered the children to return to their home. It was a difficult adjustment in reverse, with Jane feeling much of the conflict now. Their mother had been clean of drugs for six months. She had worked things out with her boyfriend to accommodate her children. He was not their father, and except for their visitations, he had hardly known the children. Visitation time was gradually increased so that the change would not be so abrupt for them. However, both mother and children felt the loss of three years of their relationship. They needed a lot of help to readjust. Michael and Alice miss the children but are ready to move on with their lives. They have no regrets about being available to them and have learned a great deal from the experience. James and Johanna, now three years older, also feel as if they learned something from the experience, painful as it was for them.

Social Work in the Juvenile Court

The juvenile court is meant to be a court that acknowledges the special status and special needs of youngsters who have violated the law in some way. Approximately one in every twenty youngsters come to the attention of the juvenile court in any one year (Barton, 1995). Somewhat more than half of all youngsters adjudicated delinquent are placed on probation. The probation arrangement usually consists of a set of conditions for the youngster mandated by the court: regular attendance at school or work, compliance at home, and perhaps community service work or restitution. If the youngster fails to meet these conditions, he or she may be placed in a more restrictive setting. The probation officer's responsibilities in each case are to monitor the youngster's compliance with these conditions through regular (perhaps monthly) meetings, as well as to act as a sort of counselor and case manager to the youngster. Because the officer has other responsibilities, such as making preadjudication reports and recommendations, there is a very limited amount of time available for work on any one case. On the other hand, many courts have recognized that some cases will inherently take more time and that, contrary to the traditional focus on the youngster alone, there is often a need for family involvement. The Moorhead case, presented in the next case study, involves a protracted struggle by parents with the juvenile court over the issue of the court's involvement in the family and its effect on parenting. Fortunately, this particular court had the professional resources to work with the situation.

CASE STUDY 10.4:
BILLY MOORHEAD

Billy Moorhead, a very bright youngster of 13, never previously in trouble, had constructed a small bomb-making laboratory in his garage. After a series of incidents, he was caught attaching a bomb to the ignition system of an auto in his wealthy suburban enclave. Fortunately, only one of the previous bombs he had attached to cars had caught fire, and the fire had been doused before it went to the gas tank. As part of the preadjudication report, the judge had asked for a psychiatric evaluation, which the parents would have to initiate. Both Mr. and Mrs. Moorhead came in as if it were they who were the subjects of the hearing. Both were indignant that they would have to be involved, refused permission for the psychiatric evaluation, and vowed to fight legal action with every resource they had. Although he wasn't really aware of much of Billy's life, Mr. Moorhead had

an evident and deep identification with Billy. In many ways, he was afraid the court would take over his parental role. This prevented his coming to terms with the implications of Billy's behavior and seeing Billy's need: It was as if he were on trial. Mrs. Moorhead supported her husband's resistance to the court process. With considerable empathy, the social worker listened carefully, reflected and clarified what they were saying, gently pointed out the danger for others, and gradually over several sessions helped them deal with the inevitable realities of Billy's situation—and, correspondingly, with theirs. Eventually they began to see Billy's needs as being separate from their own and began to work with the court, giving permission for an evaluation with their own psychiatrist. When the results suggested a deep and serious disturbance, they again went into crisis. The social worker was gradually, over time and with much struggle, able to help them to work in partnership with the court to deal with Billy's needs.

Approximately one-third of juvenile courts have initiated intensive supervision programs (Barton, 1995; Krisberg, Rodriguez, Bakke, Neuenfeldt, & Steele, 1989, in Barton, 1995). These programs may be used for youngsters who have more complex needs, or, in some serious cases, as an alternative to residential correctional placement. Intensive supervision might mean as frequent as daily, rather than monthly, meetings. Furthermore, many juvenile correctional settings are now developing a mix of residential placement and home placement with community supervision. The court, through the probation officer, then becomes a type of case manager, using a variety of approaches, such as community-based residential programs, training schools, "boot camps," and so on. Because the family is often involved in different ways with the situation, many of these approaches work with the family. Often one part of the problem is the confused parental subsystem after the loss of a parent.

CASE STUDY 10.5: JULIO CHAVEZ

His mother found Julio Chavez, age 14, impossible to control after her boyfriend, Allen Bell, moved in. When Julio got into trouble, Mrs. Chavez asked Mr. Bell to take over Julio. Julio has never accepted Mr. Bell. The trou-bles only escalated the more Mr. Bell got involved. When the police called on suspicion that Julio stole and sold some merchandise, Julio cursed Mr. Bell and refused to talk about it to him. Mr. Bell punched Julio repeatedly when he wouldn't respond to him or respect his authority.

Clearly the parental system in the Bell family is confused and ineffective. It is not difficult to imagine Julio getting into trouble, the parents responding ineffectually, and a whole host of figures from the police and the courts descending on the Chavez family, attempting to set limits with Julio where the parents have not been able. It would seem that working with the parental system as well as with Julio would be more effective—and certainly an alternative to incarceration.

Accordingly, many juvenile courts are turning to families as partners. A program that is often effective with early-stage offenders is parent training (Bank, Marlow, Reid, Patterson, & Weinrott, 1991; Patterson, 1982). In a series of group-oriented classes, parents practice and learn techniques of making consistent rules, enforcing them consistently, establishing positive and negative consequences, and effective communication. These techniques are generally effective with adolescents. Even more than learning effective techniques of responding to their adolescent, the very fact of taking a class together can assist parents to clarify an appropriate family structure and to respond to and communicate with their youngster. Similar to the Friedman example (case study 9.2) in Julio's situation, Mrs. Chavez cannot simply put Mr. Bell in charge and withdraw. Mrs. Chavez needs to take a more active role and use the support of the court to help Julio deal with its expectations and hers as well. Together, they might stabilize the situation.

In the following case study, a combined approach involving parent training, family sessions, and a community-based institutional program was used.

CASE STUDY 10.6: DANIEL AND KEVIN POLLACK, MRS. RUSH

Daniel and Kevin Pollack, aged 10 and 12, had a history of numerous station adjustments for delinquent behavior and running away. In school there were behavior problems in the classroom and poor academic performance. Most recently, the boys burned down a garage in their neighborhood. The home is "chaotic." Mrs. Rush admitted that she had not provided the structure and limit-setting that the boys needed while growing up. She attributed this to the confusion in the family surrounding her divorce five years ago from their father, George Pollack. She never was able to take over with the boys. The father has always undercut Mrs. Rush. Now he is mostly intoxicated when he visits—if at all. Mrs. Rush has felt increasingly overwhelmed and powerless. She and the stepfather needed help, as did Daniel and Kevin.

The boys were placed in a residence for ninety days for an initial study. The residence recommended to the court that long-term placement be considered. The court, the child welfare agency, and the father decided to try family treatment with the goal of family reunification. They developed a service contract with the parents and Daniel and Kevin. Parent and stepparent would go for intensive parent training. There would be visitation and weekly family sessions. The family sessions reinforced the parenting classes and encouraged Mrs. Rush to take charge with the support of the stepfather. The focus on Daniel and Kevin's issues helped her gradually to let go of some of the issues left over from the divorce. Now with the boys at home, the parents have been more consistent in setting limits and providing structure. Daniel and Kevin's running away has ceased. The school reports have been more positive. So far there has been no delinquent behavior, although the boys do test limits, disobey, and "talk back." The entire situation will be reviewed at the next court hearing.

SUMMARY

In the first of two chapters focused on family social work with the clientele of social institutions, we have briefly sketched family social work in schools, in child welfare and with the juvenile court. In each field of practice, social work is quite different, according to the field's connections with the work of a social institution. In every case, the social worker is a mediator, working both within the family and within the social institution for a better and more effective, dynamic balance. The other part of such practice, not covered in depth here, is work within the institution itself on behalf of the family and an index client, such as in the case of Alan. In the next chapter, we move to health care, mental health, and networks of agencies (health care, education, child welfare, courts, etc.) in the community also functioning as mediators with families.

REFERENCES

Bailey, D., Blasco, P., & Simeonson, R. (1992). Needs expressed by mothers and fathers of young children with disabilities. *American Journal on Mental Retardation*, 97, 1–10.

Baker, K. A. (1999). The importance of cultural sensitivity and therapist self-awareness in working with involuntary clients. *Family Process*, 38(1), 55–68.

Bank, L., Marlow, J. H., Reid, J. B., Patterson, G. R., & Weinrott, M. R. (1991). A comparative evaluation of parent-training interventions for families of chronic dropouts. *Journal of Abnormal and Child Psychology*, 19, 15–33.

Bartlett, H. (1971). *The common base of social work practice*. New York, NY: National Association of Social Workers.

Barton, W. H. (1995). Juvenile corrections. In R. L. Edwards & J. G. Hopps (Eds.), *Encyclopedia of social work* (19th ed., pp. 1563–1577). Washington, DC: National Association of Social Workers.

Bernier, J. (1990). Parental adjustment to a disabled child: A family system perspective. *Families in Society*, 71, 589–596.

Bristol, M. M., & Gallagher, J. J. (1982). A family focus for intervention. In C. T. Ramey & P. L. Trohanis (Eds.), *Finding and educating high-risk and handicapped infants* (pp. 137–161). Baltimore, MD: University Park Press.

Christensen, S. L., & Sheridan, S. M. (2001). *Schools and families: Creating essential connections for learning*. New York, NY: Guilford.

Constable, R. T., & Walberg, H. (2009). School social work practice with families. In C. R. Massat, R. T. Constable, S. McDonald, & J. P. Flynn (Eds.), *School social work: Practice, policy and research perspectives*. Chicago, IL: Lyceum Books.

Constable, R. T., & Kordesh, R. S. (2009). Case management, coordination of services and resource development. In C. R. Massat, R. T. Constable, S. McDonald, & J. P. Flynn (Eds.), *School social work: Practice, policy and research perspectives*. Chicago, IL: Lyceum Books.

Engstrom, M. (2012). Family processes in kinship care. In F. Walsh (Ed.), *Normal family processes* (4th ed., pp. 196–221). New York, NY: Guilford.

Everett, J. E. (1995). Child foster care. In Edwards, R. L., & Hopps, J. G. (Eds.), *Encyclopedia of social work* (19th ed., 375–389). Washington, DC: National Association of Social Workers.

Frey, K., Greenberg, M., & Fewell, R. (1989). Stress and coping among parents of handicapped children: A multidimensional approach. *American Journal on Mental Retardation*, 95, 240–249.

Gordon, W. E. (1969). Basic concepts for an integrative and generative concept of social work. In Hearn, G. (Ed.), *The general systems approach: Contributions toward an holistic conception of social work*. New York: Council on Social Work Education.

Gordon, W. E. (1979). The working definition of social work practice: The interface between man and environment. Paper presented at the Council on Social Work Education Annual Program Meeting, Boston, MA.

Hanson, M. J., & Carta, J. J. (1995). Addressing the challenges of families with multiple risks. *Exceptional Children, 62*(3), 201–212.

Hanson, M. J., & Hanline, M. (1990). Parenting a child with a disability: A longitudinal study of parental stress and adaptation. *Journal of Early Intervention, 14,* 234–248.

Hartman, A., & Laird, J. (1983). *Family-centered social work practice.* New York: Free Press.

Joint NASW-CSWE Task Force on Specialization (Joint Task Force). (1979). Specialization in the Social Work Profession (NASW Document no. 79-310-08). Washington, DC: National Association of Social Workers.

Kelleghan, T., Sloane, K., Alvarez, B., & Bloom, B. S. (1993). *The home environment and school learning.* San Francisco, CA: Jossey-Bass.

Kelly, M. S., Massat, C. R., & Constable, R. T. (2015). *School social work: Practice, policy and research.* Chicago, IL: Lyceum Books.

Kinney, J., Haapala, D., & Booth, C. (1991). *Keeping families together: The homebuilders model.* New York: Aldine de Gruyter.

Kohs, S. C. (1966). *The roots of social work.* New York: Association Press.

Krisberg, B., Rodriguez, O., Bakke, A., Neuenfeldt, D., & Steele, P. (1989). Demonstration of post adjudication, nonresidential, intensive supervision programs: Assessment report. San Francisco, CA: National Conference on Crime and Delinquency.

Leiderman, D. S. (1995). Child welfare overview. In Edwards, R. L., & Hopps, J. G. (Eds.), *Encyclopedia of social work* (19th ed., 424–433). Washington, DC: National Association of Social Workers.

Lewis, C. (2011). Providing therapy to children and families in foster care: A systemic-relational approach. *Family Process, 50*(4), 436–452.

Litwak, E., & Meyer, H. (1966). A balance theory of coordination between bureaucratic organizations and community primary groups. *Administrative Science Quarterly, 11*(June), 31–58.

Maas, H., & Engler, R. (1959). *Children in need of parents.* New York: Columbia.

Patterson, G. (1982). *Coercive family process.* Eugene, OR: Castalia.

Pecora, P., Reed-Ashcraft, K., & Kirk, R. S. (2001). Family-centered services. In E. Walten, P. Samdau-Beckler, & M. Mannes (Eds.), *Balancing family-centered services and child well being.* New York, NY: Columbia.

Rampage, C., Eovaldi, M., Ma, C., Weigel Foy, C., Samuels, G. M., & Bloom, L. (2012). Adoptive families. In F. Walsh (Ed.), *Normal family processes* (4th ed., pp. 222–246) New York, NY: Guilford.

Smalley, R. (1967). *Theory for social work practice.* New York, NY: Columbia.

Triseliotis, J., Shireman, J., & Hundleby, M. (1997). *Adoption: Theory, policy and practice.* London, UK: Cassell.

Walberg, H. J. (1984). Improving the productivity of America's schools. *Educational Leadership, 41*(8), 19–27.

Walberg, H. J. (2013). *Transformational innovations in K-12 education.* Chicago, IL: Heartland Institute.

Walberg, H. J., & Lai, J. (1999). Meta-analytic effects for policy. In G. J. Cizek (Ed.), *Handbook of educational policy* (pp. 418–454). San Diego, CA: Academic Press.

Wang, M. C., Haertl, G. D., & Walberg, H. J. (1998). *Building educational resilience*. Bloomington, IN: Phi Delta Kappan Educational Foundation.

Webster-Stratten, C. (1993). Strategies for helping children with oppositional defiant and conduct disorders: The importance of home-school partnerships. *School Psychology Review, 22,* 437–457.

Wolkow, H. (2002). The dynamics of systems involvement with children in school: A case perspective. In R. T. Constable, S. McDonald, & J. P. Flynn (Eds.), *School social work: Practice, policy and research perspectives* (pp. 364–370). Chicago, IL: Lyceum.

CHAPTER 11

Working between Families and Outside Social Institutions: Health Care, Mental Health, and Community Resource Networks

KEY TOPICS

Care, Mental Health, and Community Resource Networks
Social Work in Health Care
A Psychosocial Model for Illness and Disability
An Educational Workshop with Multiple Family Groups in a Health Setting
Social Work in Mental Health
Psychoeducation for Families with Schizophrenic Members
Outpatient Work in Mental Health
Working between Families and Community Resource Networks

In the previous chapter we examined the practice of social work with families working with outside social institutions that carry out different family functions, thus bringing their operations into the relational networks inside of families. These outside institutions include schools, child welfare agencies, and the juvenile court. In this chapter we examine social work with families dealing similarly with health systems and mental health care. Families and health-care systems are often wary of each other. At the same time they need each other. While health care is focused on an individual patient, in many cases health care issues are also family issues. The healing process for a family member cannot take place without the involvement of the family. While health is often viewed as a private affair, healing processes and family processes need to find an appropriate relation with each other. The implications of this relation will profoundly change both.

When an individual's situation or a family's need is complex, the person or family often needs to be served by several institutions, whether these are schools or agencies for child welfare, health, mental health, or corrections. These agencies, when they work together, can become community resource networks. But from a family's perspective it can be confusing to work with more than one agency. The family may keep them outside of their circle by manipulating them or playing one against another. From an agency's perspective, if they do not coordinate or do not keep the family's needs central, they will fail. In this chapter we will examine social work practice within the community resource network and between the resource network, the family, and an individual family member.

SOCIAL WORK IN HEALTH CARE

Social work has a century of history in health care. In 1905, Dr. Richard Cabot introduced medical social workers to Massachusetts General Hospital to help patients deal with personal and social factors that affect disease onset and recovery (Poole, 1995). Cabot believed that medicine and social work were branches split off the same trunk—the care of people in trouble (Carlton, 1984). With the stress of disease in both chronic and acute health conditions, there is often a corresponding loss of social functioning. On the other hand, problems in social functioning often result in health problems. Thus the purpose of direct social work practice in health care is to enhance, promote, maintain, and restore the best possible social functioning of individuals, families, or small groups when their social functioning is affected by actual or potential stress caused by illness, disability, or injury (Poole, 1995).

The relation of health care to family caregivers has been recognized since the time of Dr. Cabot and before, but it has taken the social institution of health care a long time to broaden its focus to its caregiving partner, the family. Birthing, dying, struggling with loss of one's family role brought on by illness or disability, caring for an elderly parent—these are all family issues as well as issues in health care. Similarly, one person's serious illness or special need can affect the entire family. Social functioning has always been intertwined with the stresses related to illness, disability, injury, or the medical processes themselves. As patients live longer with their illness, as the course of an illness can be predicted, as treatments themselves are often accompanied by disability, the caregiving circle around the patient is broadened. Genetic predictability of illness often adds to a burden carried by patients and their families. In any case the people affected by an illness and the caregiving circle are usually the family. The social worker in health care often works with families.

A Psychosocial Model for Illness and Disability

John Rolland (2012; Rolland & Williams, 2005), a physician, follows Cabot into twenty-first-century medicine to translate a medical understanding of serious illness and disability into a psychosocial model for illness with implications of illness for patients and their families. Over the period of his work, he has developed four general principles illustrating the necessary familial components in much of health care. The complex, mutual interactions between the illness, the ill family member, and the family system, when they are understood, generate their own frameworks for social intervention (Rolland, 2012, p. 453). If people are essentially relational and families are the secure bases for relations, then the appropriate treatment of many serious illnesses and/or disabilities has a family component. This means that a focus on the disease process or a disability alone, while useful, is too narrow and distorts the necessarily transactional qualities inherent to a full diagnosis and treatment, which includes the patient's environment of care. The family component might be recognized or unrecognized, either by the health care practitioners or by the family itself. Not recognizing the family component often means that it could be badly handled, leading to a problematic outcome. The problem is that there is a focus on physical medicine without consideration of the broader personal and family issues inherent in a particular condition and without consideration of the role a family unit could optimally take in its care. The case of the O'Conner family (case study 8.9) in chapter 8 is a good example of the breakdown of each one of these principles. It is useful to review the case in some detail. We can take each of Rolland's principles, define it, and illustrate it through some of the issues in the O'Conner case.

A Broadened Unit of Care   First, in serious illnesses, the *unit of care* needs to be broadened from the focus on the ill individual alone to the family and the caregiving system necessary for its treatment. This then would encompass all persons involved in the family unit and in caregiving, which in turn can influence the course of an illness and the well-being of the affected person. The effect of this idea is to revolutionize diagnosis and treatment for serious illness. In its optimal sense *everyone*—the individual, family, and caregivers—copes in individual ways with serious illness. The problem comes when the individual affected, the health care system, and the surrounding family believe that this should be the private matter of the sick person alone.

In the O'Conner case, Peter, the husband, in his seventies, functioned very well before his surgery six years ago for removal of a brain tumor. Others depended on him. After the surgery, this all changed when he became depressed, withdrawn, and uncommunicative. His functioning declined. He was placed in a nursing home a year ago (prematurely, according to his sister-in law), and his functioning declined further. He is barely communicative now. There are indications of some brain damage. He has lost his normal roles. He lives in a nursing home. His wife perceives him as being "like dead" and is seriously depressed. He spends most of their visiting time crying. Maura, his wife, age 72, has early-stage Parkinson's, which may not progress beyond the present point. Her mobility is compromised, and she is afraid of driving, but she is otherwise functional. Maura and Peter do not seem to know how to manage their relationship in the face of disability. There is a large family network around Peter and Maura—sister, son, daughter-in-law, grandchildren—but all seem paralyzed. Maura wants emotional and moral support from her son, but she can't open up to him or to her daughter-in-law. Her psychiatrist sees her as a depressed individual but doesn't seem to see the family component of this. The grandchildren are completely left out of the picture, supported by the middle generation in pursuing their chosen activities. Every problem seems to be seen as an individual problem, but no one person will be able to deal with it. Only a larger and cooperative unit can do it. However, no one in the broader unit seems to know how to be "family" to the other in need. In the face of Peter O'Conner's illness and disability and Maura's fears of her Parkinson's advancing, and the others' fears of being left with all the responsibility, neither the couple nor the broader family were able to manage their personal or relational tasks. The many possibilities of helping Peter and Maura cope seem to be lost.

Conceptualizing Illness and Care Transactionally   Second, rather than focus on pathology alone, the illness and its possible care needs to be conceptualized *transactionally*—that is, in terms of patients, their close relationships, and their close family transactions and the potential for care and coping which comes from that. In the O'Conner case, the focus is narrow, and each family member seems paralyzed from any further involvement. There is little support for Peter and Maura's coping and no focus on strengths. Rolland notes that traditional models of patient and caregiver roles can shackle families—especially a designated female caregiver in the face of protracted strains of illness and threatened loss (Rolland, 2012, p. 454). There are some cultural and gender-based beliefs in the family system about illness, disability, and caregiving, which limit them. Maura has gender stereotypes about men's capabilities. Kate remembers her older sister taking care of her but seems unable to reciprocate at this time in their lives. Nancy has enough with her family of origin. There may be (Irish) cultural difficulty acknowledging problems or asking for help (Hines, Preto, McGoldrick, Almeida, & Weltman, 1999, p. 77). And the Americanized third generation is preserved from any involvement at all. Peter and Maura appear with their physical symptoms, but not with the possible mutual support that might help them function better. There is an implicit assumption that help is given by one person, rather than the unit. An answer would be a type of coordinated partnership of available caregivers, including the nursing home. It would be difficult for any potential caretaker, whether it be Kate, Nancy or Jack, to volunteer for anything if he or she felt he or she would receive no support or help from others. In that case, better to hide behind one's age, gender, or child care responsibilities.

Predictable Illness Sequences   Third, symptoms or genetic conditions have their own predictable, time-generated effect on the person afflicted and on the caregiving family. Particular illnesses are interwoven with individual development and with family development in a somewhat predictable matrix. Rolland maps out in matrices the known time phases of illnesses (crisis, chronic, terminal), each with an expectable *onset, course, outcome,* and *level of incapacitation.* To the extent that these are predictable, the levels and needs for care are also predictable (Rolland, 2012, pp. 459–461). However, with the O'Conners, we see illness aggravated by lack of mutual support. Each family member seems paralyzed, unable to take part with each other in any sort of active coping or dealing with their situation. We are left to guess what their optimal family and health adjustment might be if they were more fully engaged with the problems and with each other.

Health Care Based on Family Strengths   Fourth, the family is usually far more capable of coping with the illness as an event than its own belief systems (or the beliefs of the pathology-focused health care system) may allow. The family can usually discover and draw on its own strengths-based, resilient beliefs after some help in identifying them. The health care system can build on these with family as partners in care. However, it knows very little about families and is habituated to excluding them.

From Rolland's (2012, pp. 471–476) perspective, family belief systems about health and illness are particularly important. Taking this general idea, there are at least five areas in which these belief systems may either help or hinder coping with the stress of illness or disability.

1. The medical *knowledge* about the conditions patients are dealing with has dynamic importance for the family. It can be shared in a way that the patient and family can use to activate their own systems. With this knowledge about the real condition, there are possibilities for a better adjustment with optimal supports. At different times, depending on the phase of the illness, this can be done individually, or even in a group with other families. In the O'Conner case illness is seen as something individual and catastrophic, rather than something the family could cope with, when they have some support from others. No one has helped them discover their strengths and coping abilities. Paradoxically, there are (Irish) family memories of families caring for an ill person. Such care could be given in a nursing home, but without the patient being alone and desolate. A nursing home can be a part of family care. The patient does not lose family membership when he is in a nursing facility.

2. The patient's and the family's responses can be *normalized* so that the situation becomes less overwhelming and more a project to work on. Sometimes contact in an educational group with other families coping with an illness can do that. Often the social worker can reframe catastrophic expectations. If patient and family believe that nothing can be done, then nothing will be done.

3. The patient and their family may not know what they can do or even understand their own *coping capacity* until they have actually tried different approaches, with support, to coping with this situation. They may carry limiting beliefs from previous experience or from culture. Again, seeing others cope can be helpful.

4. The social worker needs to help develop and maintain a belief among family and health system that *partnership* of the patient, medical resources, and the family is far better than isolation. Each has something to contribute.

5. Although some *cultural beliefs* could prevent individuals and families from coping effectively, others will give them strength to deal with difficult and inevitable situations. It is essentially a transcultural situation. They may remain in one set of beliefs about the situation and their capabilities, or they may discover their own resources and beliefs that help them cope, adapt, and accommodate themselves to the situation. Working with the family, the social worker should be aware of and draw from their healthy beliefs—for example, that God does not really want you to suffer, but wants you to use your resources together to cope with these new realities. Such beliefs as that "God wants you to suffer," that "one shouldn't need to ask for help," and that "men aren't aware of feelings or personal problems" often change when they

need to change and when that change is supported by another person who believes that change is possible. And there are family cultural memories of caring for others, even in the poverty of Ireland that brought Maura and Kate to emigrate so many years ago.

As in the O'Conner family, serious health problems faced by a family member have serious effects on the total network of family relationships. We can apply the full range of family intervention methods to respond to these changes and to develop the necessary family caregiving networks. As in the O'Conner family, major role shifts are often needed to deal with oncoming illness and disability. In the face of poor communication, guilt, rigid perspectives on role, or a poorly developed relationship, of course these shifts may not take place. Accompanying the role shifts, often lifestyle changes are needed. Illness and poor communication often shuts down a person's ability to act (agency), together with his or her ability to receive or give support to others (communion). Family members must find meaning in the illness and grieve for the many losses the illness causes. The challenge for the social worker is helping the partners do all this—accept the changing situation, communicate about it, adjust to it, and balance their needs for agency and communion with the demands of the illness (Ruddy & McDaniel, 2003). Sometimes these can be opportunities for family changes never seen before—even to rework or rediscover family legacies, as in the O'Conner case. This is the resilient way to approach issues of health and disability.

In the Jimenez family in the following case study, the needs for relational work early in the marriage were combined with the stresses of poverty, of being undocumented immigrants, of inability to speak the language of the country where they resided, and finally of the special needs and risks of their child, Teresa.

CASE STUDY 11.1:
TERESA JIMENEZ AND FAMILY

Teresa Jimenez is a 4-year-old child with a deficiency of the enzyme PAH. When this deficiency is discovered at infancy, the child will normally need to go on a very specialized and expensive diet. The diet will prevent the otherwise inevitable retardation that accompanies the lack of this enzyme. Teresa's levels have been very low, an indication that she is not following her diet. Her parents, Manuel and Victoria, can apply for a state stipend to pay the cost of this special diet, but they are undocumented

and they speak very little English. They are fearful that if they apply for the stipend, they will be reported to the Immigration and Naturalization Service (INS) and deported.

Laura, a bilingual medical social worker from the clinic, worked with the Jimenez family. As she got to know the family, more complexities unraveled. Mrs. Jimenez is so overwhelmed by the dilemmas they are facing, together with unresolved marital stress, that her first thought is to run away, to return home to her parents without Teresa. This would be effectively abandoning Teresa, because it is unlikely that Mrs. Jimenez would be able to return. She feels like a failure because she cannot feed her daughter well. They are afraid of the INS. She married in haste in Guatemala and left her family there without ever getting to know Manuel very well. She is young, close to her family, and she misses them. Manuel promised that things would be better, but he is always working. Even when he is free, he is moody, and they do not communicate well. He can't understand why Teresa needs a special diet.

Laura started the helping process in the hospital with Victoria but quickly moved to involve Manuel. This was not easy, because he was constantly working and seemed fearful and reluctant to get involved. In a joint interview, it became clear that their communication was very poor and full of confusion around Teresa's situation. The family's difficult economic conditions and the precariousness of the marriage made Teresa's needs even more difficult to face. Laura perceived that in focusing with them on Teresa's situation, she was also focusing on Victoria's loneliness and lack of self-esteem, Manuel's issues with Victoria, the fears connected with being undocumented, and their problems in communication. She worked concretely on helping them to make the application for the stipend to pay for Teresa's special diet. They checked into the implications of receiving the grant with an advocacy foundation. When they learned it would not be reported to the INS, they did apply. However, Laura realized that much more was involved. When Victoria blurted out that she might go home to her parents, Laura gently pointed out that it would be like ending the marriage and losing Teresa. Victoria herself knew she wouldn't be able to return from Guatemala. Did she really want to do that? Victoria started to cry and said she really didn't know what she wanted to do, but it all seemed so hopeless. Talking directly to Manuel, Laura encouraged him to reflect exactly what he had heard Victoria say. For the moment he shouldn't add his own feelings. He did reflect what Victoria was saying, and his eyes filled with tears. Victoria had never seen him cry before. He had always been so strong and distant. Then Laura helped him to respond without anger or defensiveness, and Victoria reflected what he was saying. Their communication got a little better. Victoria agreed to wait on any decision. They met a number of times. After they received the grant, Teresa's condition started to improve. Laura referred them for marital counseling to a Spanish-speaking worker at Catholic Charities who specialized in work with Hispanic immigrants. They are continuing to work with Catholic Charities, and they check in from time to time with Laura when they visit the clinic. They still have difficulties, but things are better, and Teresa is better. She is looking forward to kindergarten next month.

The health issues in both the O'Conner and the Jimenez cases can be understood in their psychosocial contexts. The O'Conner case faces complex family relational issues and it is a model for considering the possibilities of expanding the caregiving unit in illness and disability. The Jimenez case faces environmental issues which prevent them from dealing with their relational and health care issues. As Manual and Victoria faced Teresa's condition, complicated by other stresses having to do with culture, marital history, and their undocumented status, their ability to respond, their human agency and communion in relation to the problem and the situation shut down. In the face of health stress, they stopped functioning as an effective family. Working with both the health care situation and the Jimenez's communication about it, the social worker was able to help them take steps to get help for Teresa and for their marriage.

AN EDUCATIONAL WORKSHOP WITH MULTIPLE FAMILY GROUPS IN A HEALTH SETTING

In both cases, a major problem is that patients and their families do not understand the implications of health stress and the ways they could cope with it. They may see it as an individual problem, or something the professionals need to deal with, rather than something that they need to deal with as a family. Sometimes education can assist families to take part in the health issues of one member, which also confront everyone in the family. A good example of this process, and the use of a *multiple family group* (MFG) modality, is work with adult cancer survivors. With the advances in early cancer detection and aggressive treatment, many patients are beginning to have good prognoses for disease-free survival. With patients' living longer, there has been a shift toward concern about the long-term impact of a cancer diagnosis and treatment on family life. As families progress through acute diagnosis to active treatment to chronic rehabilitation, there is concern that the effect of cancer and cancer treatment, unexamined and unaltered by the patient and family, could threaten to take over the family's identity and interfere with (distort or inhibit) the family's ongoing development. Tracking the impact of chronic medical illness on family priorities, daily routines and problem-solving styles, one can determine the extent to which a family has lost some of its normal functioning and has become reorganized around illness, now a central family theme. One sees an inevitable interaction between "family style"—problem solving, affective style, communication, organization—and the illness, which can absorb these and paralyze the family's normal functioning. In the effort to attend to issues raised by having to live with cancer, other family goals and needs (including those of the patient) could be neglected. Family resources (financial, parental attention, time) could get increasingly allocated to illness management. Family members can experience social and emotional isolation within the family as well as with extended family and friends (Steinglass, Ostroff, & Steinglass, 2011, p. 397).

To deal with these normal family reactions to extended cancer treatment, a one-day workshop with multiple cancer patients and their families was developed. These families had dealt with head and neck cancers and were treated by Memorial Sloan-Kettering Cancer Center. However, the problem definition and the helping process could apply to a multiplicity of situations where families through education about a situation could recover their own lost functioning. The workshop sought to do the following:

- Educate families about the ways that family life is affected by cancer diagnosis and treatment.
- Normalize the experiences, reactions, and struggles that families have in attempting to cope with the post-treatment adjustment phase of cancer recovery.
- Confront and challenge the isolation that these patients often feel from their support networks.
- Explore ways that families can develop an effective balance between illness and non-illness issues in their lives. The metaphor used for this was to "find a place for the illness in the family, while at the same time keeping the illness in its place." (Steinglass, Ostroff, & Steinglass, 2011, p. 396)

The one-day workshop is a combination of group education and an opportunity for patients and their families to share their illness experiences and their coping strategies. They are encouraged to discuss their experiences as pre- versus postcancer families in a non-blaming, non-pathologizing atmosphere. Bringing together multiple families allows them to share the common elements of the effects of cancer, cancer treatment, and their coping with all this, while they remain a family. How do they develop family ways to help them separate cancer from noncancer family issues? How might they map out strategies for the future (Steinglass, Ostroff, & Steinglass, 2011, p. 397)? Figure 11.1 provides an outline of the workshop.

The "Group within a Group"   One of the important components of the workshop is the use of the "group within a group" to facilitate connections between participants' dealing with analogous family and illness roles. It is a type of "fishbowl" discussion, illustrated in chapter 6. Figure 11.2 illustrates (a) the initial and final gathering of the entire group, (b) the members of the patient subgroup communicating with each other the effects of head and neck cancer on them and their family, work, life, and friendship relationships, with the nonpatient, observer subgroup listening, and (c) the observer group communicating with each other, with the patient group listening. The observer group would discuss the ways that cancer affects *well* family members, with the patient group listening. Then the listeners (patients) respond to the well family members. In the final stage, the group as a whole discusses the issues, with the facilitators exploring and emphasizing any similarities or connections that have been noted between different members' experiences in the different discussions.

The discussion developed a new appreciation on the part of nonpatients of some of the issues following cancer treatment, particularly when patients kept symptoms and worries to themselves, particularly worries about possible cancer reemergence. These were given voice and discussed. The participants liked the groups and the connections with others that emerged. The opportunities to get others' perspectives, to see the effect of cancer on their lives would lead to the perception of better family functioning (Ostroff, Ross, Steinglass, Ronis-Tobin & Singh, 2004). Multiple family group interventions for patients and their families have been used with patients with other chronic conditions, such as inflammatory bowel disease. The

Figure 11.1
Outline of the One-Day Multifamily Discussion Group (MFDG) Workshop

---

I. Introductory component (30 minutes)
   A. Provide an opportunity for families to introduce themselves to each other and to briefly tell their cancer "stories."
   B. Have group leaders describe the goals of the workshop and the schedule for the day.
II. Illness impact component (90 minutes).
   A. Use "group within group" (fishbowl) technique to facilitate connections between participants occupying analogous family and illness roles.
   B. Identify shared experiences, and introduce metaphors to describe these experiences, especially metaphors useful in introducing the concept of creating an appropriate balance between cancer-related needs and noncancer family issues (the metaphor of "finding a place for the illness and keeping the illness in its place").

<< 15-minute break/snack >>

III. Family development component (90 minutes)
   A. Discussion of family life before versus after cancer as vehicle for "normalizing" the illness experience.
   B. Summary by group facilitators of issues raised by families and shared challenges experienced by MFDG families.

<< 1-hour lunch break >>

IV. Family–illness integration component (90 minutes)
   A. Describe and clarify current coping strategies and possible changes via construction of art montages visually representing each family's relationship to cancer.
   B. Presentation of collages to the other MFDG families for feedback and suggestions about possible changes to make to better integrate cancer and noncancer issues in family life in future coping strategies.

SOURCE: Steinglass, Ostroff, & Steinglass (2011, p. 398). © 2011 FPI Inc.

formats may vary with all day workshops becoming six ninety-minute sessions. Evaluations, using quality of life as a criterion, have been positive (Lopez-Larrosa, 2013). These findings suggest that MFG can be applied to different chronic illnesses, using Rolland's (2012) psychosocial model. It is a good example of the use of group education to help patients and their families deal with difficult, unspoken issues that affect family functioning.

SOCIAL WORK IN MENTAL HEALTH

There are few illnesses as stressful for social relationships, particularly within the family, as mental illness. This was recognized early in the history of social work. As social work in health care began, so also did social work in mental health. Presently, social workers are nearly twice as prevalent in the mental health field as psychiatrists or psychologists (Ginsberg, 1992, p. 140), a ratio that has remained for at least a half-

Figure 11.2
Seating Arrangements for Group-within-a-Group Sequences

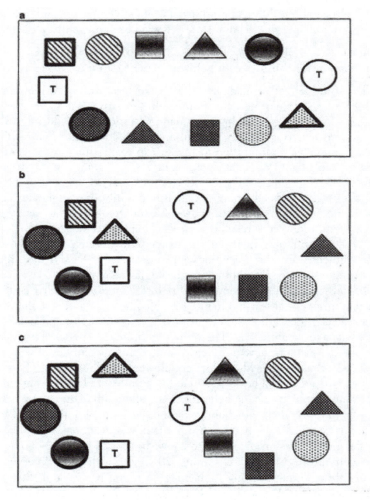

(a) Phase one: Initial gathering as whole group; (b) Phase two: Patient subgroup; (c) Phase three: Observer subgroup.

- Family membership connoted by varied within-symbol patterns (e.g., the "Polka-Dot" family; the "Diagonal-Line" family; the "Cross-Hatched" family).
- Illness role is connoted by either single (noncancer) or double (cancer patient) outlining.
- Family role is connoted by geometric shape (e.g., circles for wives, squares for husbands, triangles for children).

SOURCE: Steinglass, Ostroff & Steinglass (2011, p. 400). © 2011, FPI Inc.

century. Using an interdisciplinary approach, social workers provide direct treatment, case management, and family involvement in community mental health centers, hospitals, and residential centers. Although adapted to the particular problem, the service is not entirely different from social work in other areas. The case of Charlotte later in this chapter (case study 11.3) is a good example of this process.

Psychoeducation for Families with Schizophrenic Members

A special contribution, often made by social workers, is psychoeducation for family members of patients exhibiting schizophrenia. In the early stages of a major psychiatric disorder, decreasing social and occupational functioning and negative communication and behavior often brings out anxiety and a sense of vulnerability in other family members—amounting to higher expressed emotion than previously experienced (McFarlane, W. R., & Cook, W. L., 2007). Without assistance and education about schizophrenia, family members would often try to confront the patient in episodes of high expressed emotion, criticism, hostility, or emotional overprotectiveness of different family members. These environmental stressors, as the patient would see them, often were related to a subsequent psychotic episode (Zubin & Spring, 1977). During the 1980s and more recently, effective models of psychoeducational interventions have been developed (Anderson, Reiss, & Hogarty, 1986; Hogarty, Anderson, Reiss, Kornblith, Greenwald, Javna, & Madeira, 1986; Hogarty, Anderson, Reiss, Kornblith, Greenwald, Ulrich, & Carter, 1991) that could lower hospitalization rates or at least postpone this outcome. These interventions helped family members to develop coping strategies, lowered tensions, and increased the patient's medication compliance. These findings, initially reported among families of schizophrenic patients, have also been reported among families of patients with bipolar disorder. In any case, educating a couple about what behaviors of the ill partner or child can and cannot be attributed to the disorder, and enhancing their communication and problem-solving behavior in the aftermath of an episode, have the potential to improve their functioning and reduce the seriousness of episodes (Miklowitz & George, 2003, p. 679). Similar family educational approaches, dealing with the unique stressors of a condition, have been used with parents of children who live with autism (Solomon & Chung, 2012) and with borderline personality disorder (Hoffman, Fruzzetti, Buteau, Neiditch, Penney, Bruce, et al., 2005).

In the case of the Maxwell family (case study 8.7), the social worker helped Mary Maxwell respond to the parts of John's verbalizations that were not psychotic, but to avoid engagement with his talk when it turned psychotic. It became something of a game that John himself recognized and encouraged. He pointed out himself that he didn't want Mary to take him seriously when crazy parts took over. Because most of the time he made a good deal of sense, it wasn't difficult to recognize an abrupt switch in communication and wait for his more in-touch parts to come back. They always did, particularly when Mary didn't involve herself emotionally with the other parts.

Post-Hospitalization Work in Mental Health

Although most mental health services are carried out in the community, sometimes a patient requires hospitalization for an extended period. In the case of Jack C., part of the approach to the family was psychoeducational. Another part of the approach was to assist family members, particularly Jack's wife, Barbara, to accommodate Jack in a meaningful role upon his return from the hospital and develop a more workable family structure.

CASE STUDY 11.2: JACK AND BARBARA, DAUGHTERS ANN AND MARIE

Jack had spent several months in the hospital when he exhibited symptoms of severe schizophrenia. During the years leading up to his hospitalization, his role in the family had gradually become marginalized. His wife, Barbara, herself somewhat depressed, became centralized in the family. Having difficulty taking on a parental role alone, she acted more like an older sister than a parent to their two daughters, Marie and Ann, now 12 and 14, respectively. The girls fought all the time, and Barbara felt helpless to manage the problems. In fact, the fighting seemed to bring on Barbara's helplessness and her sense of hurt and depression, and vice versa. Before Jack returned home from the hospital to day treatment, George, their social worker in the community mental health center, suggested that Barbara attend some group sessions that George was running for families of patients living with schizophrenia. With coaching from George and help from other relatives of patients, Barbara developed a low-key approach to relations with Jack. George had been particularly concerned that Barbara's deep identity with her daugh-

ters, coming out of her own loneliness and depression, was inappropriately empowering the daughters and isolating Jack, and that it could cause an explosive situation in the future.

Jack was willing and ready to work in a family format regarding some of the shifts needed upon his return to the family. So George set up a family session with Jack, Barbara, and their two daughters, Ann and Marie. Initially, the session was chaotic. Barbara focused on her personal problems and concerns, and the girls started fighting. At the same time, Barbara tended to unite with the girls in their resentment of Jack and reinforce their rebellion. Jack and Barbara would find themselves in disagreement about the girls, and the girls ignored both of them. Jack felt disqualified as a father. If he was watching a program on television, one of the girls would simply switch the channel to her preferred program, complaining, "He always wants to watch what he wants on TV." When conflict erupted, Jack and Barbara said the girls were beginning to hit their parents at home. Both parents were intimidated by the hitting and unsure what to do.

In the initial family session, rather than focus on Barbara's complaints, or Ann and Marie's fighting, George focused on Jack and Barbara, and Jack's coming home. The family was in chaos. What could they do about it as parents? Barbara's response was to identify her resentment that Jack was away so long. What could she do? George responded by normalizing the stress they were all feeling at the time. Jack was gone. Things got very difficult before his hospitalization. Now Jack is back. We know that when parents work together, things do get a little bit better. He asked Barbara to talk to Jack about how he could help her now. The girls started to giggle as Barbara started to talk to Jack. George calmly intervened, saying that if the girls wanted to stay, they needed to let their mother and dad talk about this. Barbara was hesitant, but for the rest of the session Barbara and Jack did try to communicate and develop a tentative alliance, while the girls periodically interrupted and tried to redirect the interaction to themselves. Barbara and Jack eventually succeeded in keeping them on the sidelines while they made tentative efforts to communicate.

George was very active in supporting both parents in their very tentative communication with each other and in their efforts to keep the girls on the sidelines. This family interview set the tone for a family process that went on for several months. Much of the work was done between Jack and Barbara, with the girls coming in for occasional sessions. Barbara needed help to let Jack gently back into the parts of his role that he could handle, as well as to communicate without high emotion, hostility, or the need to control Jack. As crises alleviated, George continued to educate Barbara and Jack on communication and management skills effective when one person has schizophrenia. Although there were still conflicts, testing of limits, and a tendency for Barbara to align with her girls against Jack, there were also more and more episodes of Barbara and Jack working together on issues. There was a relation between Jack's improvement and the improvement in the family situation. Eventually Jack was able to find a job, but he continued his treatment. The family sessions became monthly check-ins. Barbara and Jack joined a couples' group.

The social worker employed two approaches with Barbara and Jack's family. He helped the family make a structural shift. Barbara, chaotically aligned with the girls and hardly able to exert appropriate parental controls, realigned with Jack with the worker's support. Barbara needed Jack's support, but couldn't place too much pressure on him. The worker also took a psychoeducational approach with both. The worker's support, the structural shifts, and the skill training would be crucial in the family managing its crisis.

Outpatient Work in Mental Health

At other times in outpatient situations, the social worker, as a key member of the psychiatric team, takes major responsibility for work with patients who are also working with individual and family issues. Charlotte des Jardins was struggling with issues connected with differentiation and connectedness with her family as she was moving toward independence.

CASE STUDY 11.3:
CHARLOTTE DES JARDINS

Charlotte des Jardins, age 23, became severely depressed and suicidal in the middle of her college experience. She is the second of three children in a prominent but somewhat emotionally disengaged African-American family, longtime residents of New Orleans. She left college, came home, and got a job in a restaurant. Charlotte's return home with failing grades was met with anger, resentment, and hopelessness by her parents. In response, Charlotte became even more withdrawn and spent most of her time at home in her room and away from her parents. Unable to continue at the restaurant job with her depression, she took a leave of absence and received outpatient treatment from the psychiatric clinic at Samaritan Hospital. Dr. Smith put Charlotte on antidepressants and checked up with her periodically. Charlotte did most of her work with her social worker, Astrid. Astrid encouraged her to talk about her thoughts about the complex situation she faced at home. She needed to deal with her isolation, develop a support system, and take steps to alleviate her severe depression. Since Charlotte had extreme difficulty with verbal expression, she was encouraged to write down her thoughts in a daily journal. Therapeutic discussion often focused on these entries. Charlotte reestablished contact with two old friends and began an exercise program at the YMCA.

Faithful in taking her medication and attending her individual sessions, after six weeks Charlotte was able to return to work. She was very confused about the direction of her life. She won-dered whether she should return to college or find a career. She felt as if she were the "failure" in her high-achieving family, particularly in comparison with her younger sister, Eloise, age 19, whom she saw as vivacious, intelligent, "successful in everything," and who was going to college. Charlotte felt emotionally isolated from her family, dependent, and unable to assert herself in both familial and extrafamilial situations. She wanted to become independent and eventually move out and establish a life of her own, but she didn't feel as if she could. She had never told her family about her problems. Only with considerable help and repeated roleplays with Astrid was she able to tell her mother and her sister about some of her concerns and needs. No one had informed her father, and Charlotte was afraid to talk to him. She would feel even more like a failure. Her mother was willing to participate in a family session, but the session was postponed until Charlotte had told her father. He was already peripheral to the family, and it would not be desirable to reinforce this.

Charlotte did tell her father, but only after she told Matthew, her 30-year-old brother who was living at home after a divorce. Matthew and Charlotte told her father together. Her father, a high-powered lawyer, did something entirely unpredictable. He started to cry and blame himself for what had happened with Charlotte and with Matthew. He should have spent more time with them. He related that there were so many things going on in this family that no one ever talked about. Charlotte was deeply touched by this entirely unexpected response. The family session took place with the mother, the father,

Matthew, and Charlotte. Eloise was away at college, but her absence also allowed a clear focus on Matthew's and Charlotte's concerns. The session was difficult, with a lot of underlying tension and blaming, particularly between the mother and father. The family had never talked to each other about these issues before. Astrid needed to be very active in framing out and setting boundaries on their communication, modeling a nonblaming approach. She would normalize feelings and issues that had been latent and undiscussed for so many years. The four sessions they had were almost too much for them. As a result, Charlotte developed a somewhat closer relationship with her father and brother. The mother and father began marital counseling. Charlotte continued to make progress on her depression. She decided to get training as a paralegal. After two years, she found an apartment of her own and left home comfortably. Her father and brother helped her move.

WORKING BETWEEN FAMILIES AND COMMUNITY RESOURCE NETWORKS

Recently, human service reforms have sought to break down barriers between categorical programs and make formal service systems more accessible and responsive to families, communities, and diverse cultures, when the patient's need is deep and wide-ranging and the caring unit needs assistance. The theme of integration of educational, health, and social welfare services now reverberates through local, state, and national dialogues. A number of experiments involve different agencies from different social institutional sectors—child welfare, health, mental health occupational disability, schools—coming together to work on the needs of complex case situations, involving multiple agencies. To some extent, these agencies share in planning, decision making, and, possibly, resource allocation. Certain basic principles run through these discussions and experiments:

1. Services are to be designed and delivered with respect for the diverse cultures of clients or, to use the term more predominant in reform language, "customers." Culturally competent practices are required by policies to ensure that human services help recipients use the strengths in their cultural traditions and institutions.
2. Services are to empower families to take active roles in the design, implementation, and evaluation of programs that serve them.
3. Services are to prevent problems from occurring, rather than to respond to problems only after the fact.
4. Services are to be accessible to people in the neighborhoods where they live.
5. Services are to be linked in comprehensive strategies, drawing on multifaceted resources from mental health, health, economic development, delinquency prevention, and other traditionally separate fields.

6. Services are to conduct assessments and provide interventions that address the problems and resources of whole families, rather than of individuals only.
7. Services are to emphasize the strengths, or "assets," of the communities in which they are located, rather than stressing the deviance and deficiencies that might be present.[1]

These shared aspirations have called forth new institutional models for services. Many child welfare services and health and mental health services have positioned themselves in schools, both as individual agencies and as parts of broader, communitywide efforts.

Many schools are experimenting with programs that keep them open into the evenings, on weekends, and during summers, allowing them to function as community centers for a wide range of populations with a wide range of services rather than only as sites for classroom-based teaching. Family centers create places in schools for whole families to receive services, to deliver mutual support to one another, and to deepen the involvement of parents in the school itself. Complex prevention initiatives take advantage of the fact that the school provides the best setting in which to reach the greatest numbers of children who are at risk of failure or have serious health or social problems. Brokered service networks reposition human services into schools in order to keep children in school and to allow teachers to focus on basic education. These are particularly important when there are multiple needs and underorganized families.

The family is central to the process that brings together family and child with school and community resources into an interagency team (Coffey, 2004) or "wraparound" ("wrap") team. The following cases illustrate work with the family of a 10-year-old boy in school, agency systems, and two young adults in transition out of schools.

CASE STUDY 11.4: DANNY AND HIS GRANDMOTHER

Danny is a 10-year-old African American boy with pervasive developmental disorder. In class he was disruptive, showed poor attention to tasks even with assistance, showed very poor academic performance, and was aggressive with other children, otherwise tending to isolate himself from them. Danny seemed strange to other children and they were afraid of him. Having come recently from living in Germany, with his father in military service, he spoke a mixture of English and German that wasn't easily understood by others. According to his paternal grandmother,

---

[1]See Kordesh & Constable (2002a, p. 87). Adapted with permission.

with whom he lived, he had been developing reasonably well in early childhood, and he walked and talked normally. Both parents have a history of severe drug and alcohol abuse. When Danny went to Germany, he experienced severe physical abuse by his mother and neglect by his father and was heavily involved in the military social service program for children. At the time of referral, his mother was in a residential substance abuse program; his father was still in the Army. Danny was being raised by his grandmother. She had given up her business of twenty years to care for him. The following agencies and individual services were involved with the case:

- The state child protection agency
- The state department of mental health
- Adair School
- A big brother program
- A homemaker services agency
- Karate lessons from a community volunteer

- In-home therapy from a contract therapist especially trained in pervasive developmental disorders
- Tutoring twice a week

The state child protection agency sponsored the transagency team through the school and paid for the services provided through its LANS (local area network services) program. The grandmother was overwhelmed with all the services involved. The placement needed to be stabilized, particularly if either parent would return. There were differences within the team about whether Danny should remain in this placement or be hospitalized. The main goal at the moment was that Danny maintain himself at school and that the home continue to provide appropriate parenting, belonging, and security for him. This was beginning to happen, although the situation both at home and at school, was very delicate. The team, including the grandmother, met monthly to discuss and work out issues.

The team's major tasks were to support the grandmother's parenting of Danny and to work out agency issues with each other. These were both difficult and time-consuming. The tasks had to be done without overwhelming the grandmother and bringing her to give up on Danny. When the grandmother did strengthen her coping, Danny did somewhat better. However, at this time the father came back from Germany, and the mother came out of her residential substance abuse program. The grandmother became uncertain of her role again, and Danny regressed. When it was decided that the grandmother would remain in charge, with the father supporting and the mother visiting, the grandmother strengthened her coping again, and Danny did better in his long-term process of development.

The following two cases involve the transition out of school of young adults with severe disabilities.[2] They imply a possible continuation of the transagency team, this time for adults with disabilities.

---

[2]Adapted from Kordesh and Constable (2002b, pp. 400–401). Used with permission.

CASE STUDY 11.5: DORIS AND HER MOTHER

Doris was an 18-year-old with severe psychological disturbance. Her reactivity to a symbiotic conflict with her mother and the resulting self-destructive behavior had led to several hospitalizations. Whenever there was a possible separation from mother, she showed increased disturbance. The school had found itself reacting to the behavior and programming for Doris alone, rather than getting the mother and daughter into contact with help. The mother and daughter began with a social worker in private practice. The school brought Doris into a one-hour-per-day class in ceramics with only the instructor present. When this was even-

tually established without incident, Doris became involved with a pet zoo run by another agency. Because the situation between the mother and daughter was potentially explosive, a shelter arrangement with a relative to be used in a crisis was worked out. It was used occasionally. This arrangement kept Doris in the community. The social worker worked with Doris and her mother, supporting each as separate persons with separate problem-solving abilities. When the social worker made further gains with the mother and Doris' school adjustment stabilized, the next step was to develop a program with the state department of vocational rehabilitation. The state agency was involved in the plan and agreed to give special consideration to Doris' needs.

CASE STUDY 11.6: MICHAEL RETURNING HOME

Michael was a 21-year-old severe and barely stabilized diabetic, legally blind, who lived in a nursing home because his single working parent was unable to care for him. He was about to graduate from his special education program because of his age. A plan was developed in the wrap team to make it possible for Michael to return home by using public assistance, Medicaid, and homemaker and home health care ser-

vices to support him when his mother was working. Some further medical and vocational assessment was done. The social worker from the school worked with Michael and his mother, coordinating with other agencies. She kept Michael and his mother involved and responsible while the many agencies were working out a plan with them. When the two had solidified their own direction and connections with other services, the social worker passed case management responsibilities onto another agency.

Although such cases present complex needs and will take work over a span of years, they are not particularly unusual. A combination of resources could prevent institutionalization or make movement from an institutionalized setting possible. Furthermore, none of the "hard" service provision, no matter how flexible, could have been effective or even possible without the "soft" services to parents and children that helped them deal with the situation and link their processes and needs with programs and resources. To make complex plans for families without their choice, involvement, and participation—indeed, not to make the individual-in-family unit the center of the decision process—is to court disaster and set up an unproductive struggle around power and control. In addition to being highly skilled at family-oriented work, the social worker is a member of the interagency team, a colleague, and a consultant to others on the team.

SUMMARY

Our discussion of the helping process with families and outside service institutions, such as schools, courts, and health care institutions, is necessarily brief. It illustrates the general parameters of practice with families in the context of social institutions. There are other sources that adequately illustrate social work in particular fields of practice (see, for instance, Carlton, 1984; Kelly, Massat, & Constable, 2015). These sources develop the nature of a particular field of social work practice. The systems concept and the concept of relational justice are extended to the family's relationship with outside social institutions. Without these internal and external connections, families could not maintain themselves.

REFERENCES

Anderson, C. M., Reiss, D. J., & Hogarty, G. E. (1986). *Schizophrenia and the family: A practitioner's guide to psychoeducation and management.* New York, NY: Guilford.

Carlton, T. (1984). *Clinical social work in health settings: A guide to professional practice with exemplars.* New York, NY: Springer.

Coffey, E. P. (2004). The heart of the matter 2: Integration of ecosystemic family therapy practices with systems of care mental health services for children and families. *Family Process, 43*(2), 161–173.

Ginsberg, L. (1992). *Social work almanac.* Washington, DC: National Association of Social Workers.

Hines, P. M., Preto, N. G., McGoldrick, M., Almeida, R., & Weltman, S. (1999). Culture and the family life cycle. In B. Carter & M. McGoldrick (Eds.), *The expanded family life cycle.* New York, NY: Guilford.

Hoffman, P. D., Fruzzetti, A. E., Buteau, E., Neiditch, E. R., Penney, D. Bruce, et al. (2005). Family connections: A program for relatives of persons with borderline personality disorder. *Family Process, 44*(2), 217–226.

Hogarty, G. E., Anderson, C. M., Reiss, D. J., Kornblith, S. J., Greenwald, D. P., Javna, D., & Maderia, J. J. (1986). Family psycho-education, social skills training: One year effects of a controlled maintenance chemotherapy in aftercare study treatment of schizophrenia on relapse and adjustment. *Archives of General Psychiatry, 43,* 633–642.

Hogarty, G. E., Anderson, C. M., Reiss, D. J., Kornblith, S. J., Greenwald, D. P., Ulrich, R. F., & Carter, M. (1991). Family psycho-education, social skills training and maintenance chemotherapy in the aftercare treatment of schizophrenia: Two year effects of a controlled study treatment on relapse and adjustment. *Archives of General Psychiatry, 48,* 340–347.

Kelly, M., Massat, C. R., & Constable, R. T. (2015). *School social work: Practice, policy and research* (8th ed.). Chicago, IL: Lyceum.

Kordesh, R., & Constable, R. T. (2002a). Policies, programs and mandates for developing social services in the schools. In R. T. Constable, S. McDonald, & J. P. Flynn (Eds.), *School social work: Practice, policy and research perspectives* (pp. 83–100). Chicago, IL: Lyceum.

Kordesh, R., & Constable, R. T. (2002b). Case management, coordination of services and resource development. In R. T. Constable, S. McDonald, & J. P. Flynn (Eds.), *School social work: Practice, policy and research perspectives* (pp. 385–403). Chicago, IL: Lyceum.

Lopez-Larrosa, S. (2013). Quality of life, treatment adherence and locus of control: Multiple family groups for chronic medical illnesses. *Family Process, 52*(4), 685–696.

McFarlane, W. R., & Cook, W. L. (2007). Family expressed emotion prior to the onset of psychosis. *Family Process, 46*(2), 185–198.

Miklowitz, D. L., & George, E. L. (2003). Couple therapy complicated by a biologically based psychiatric disorder. In A. S. Gurman & N. S. Jacobson (Eds.), *Clinical handbook of couple therapy.* New York, NY: Guilford.

Ostroff, J., Ross, S., Steinglass, P., Ronis-Tobin, V., & Singh, B. (2004). Interest in and barriers to participation in multiple family groups among head and neck cancer patients and their primary family caregivers. *Family Process, 43*(2), 195–208.

Poole, L. (1995). Health care: Direct practice. In R. L. Edwards & J. G. Hopps (Eds.), *Encyclopedia of social work* (19th ed., pp. 1156–1167). Washington, DC: National Association of Social Workers.

Rolland, J. S., & Williams, J. K. (2005). Toward a biopsychosocial model for 21st century genetics. *Family Process, 44*(1), 3–24.

Rolland, J. S. (2012). Mastering family challenges in serious illness and disability. In F. Walsh (Ed.), *Normal family processes* (4th ed., pp. 452–482). New York, NY: Guilford.

Ruddy, N. B., & McDaniel, S. H. (2003). Couple therapy and medical issues: Working with couples facing illness. In A. S. Gurman & N. S. Jacobson (Eds.), *Clinical handbook of couple therapy.* New York, NY: Guilford.

Solomon, A. H., & Chung, B. (2012). Understanding autism: How family therapists can support parents of children with autism spectrum disorders. *Family Process, 51*(2), 250–264.

Steinglass, P., Ostroff, J. S., & Steinglass, A. S. (2011). Multiple family groups for adult cancer survivors and their families. *Family Process, 50*(3), 393–409.

Zubin, J., & Spring, B. (1977). Vulnerability: A new view of schizophrenia. *Journal of Abnormal Psychology, 86,* 103–126.

CHAPTER 12

Ending Processes with Families and Evaluation

KEY TOPICS

Social Workers and the Ending Process
Case Study Endings Revisited
Indications for Ending
Endings with Couples
Endings with Families
Difficult and Complex Endings
Endings and Transitions Involving Social Institutions
Incomplete or Premature Endings
Evaluation
Research Outcomes and Effectiveness of Couple and Family Work
Research on Components of the Helping Process
The Research Effectiveness of Couples' Work and Family Work

The ending process can be understood as the completion of all that has gone before. Endings are made by couples, by families, and by institutions with the assistance of the social worker. The most important part of ending is that it is first of all done by the client or client system, with social workers assisting the client(s) to finish their work for the time. The ending process is a final review with all of these of the content and process of the work, a letting go and a moving on. Evaluation is part of this ending. It is a review with the family of what has taken place in relation to the objectives set with the client system in the beginning and later. The objectives set in the beginning and throughout the process set the tone for the formative and summative evaluations that take place. A further context for evaluation is the scientific foundation for family work that, within the limits of research, provides a general understanding for what effective intervention should be and some context for the agreements made.

SOCIAL WORKERS AND THE ENDING PROCESS

The social worker is like a temporary steersman who for a time helps crews guide a ship through difficult waters or to harbor, and then moves on, no longer needed. For the family, an ending is first of all a milestone marking a transition, and then it is an ending with the guide who has helped them steer through the shoals. It is only for the social worker that an ending process is fully an ending. In the best of circumstances, family members begin to invest themselves in coping together with a problem that up to this point has mystified them. They may have felt hopeless about any possibility of change. Perhaps some changes did occur, and now they face different circumstances. It may be that the hoped-for changes did not occur and they have to modify their expectations—even give up on what they hoped would take place. Whether or not they have achieved a change, they face an altered set of possibilities.

A chapter on ending processes presupposes and builds on all that has gone before. The ending processes with a family also are a test of all that has gone before: of whether family members, and the family as a unit, have been able to take charge of their experience and make changes together. This is the relational work of the family. The work of the social worker is mainly to help them do it in a way that reinforces their ability to function relatively independently and recognize the new unit that has emerged in the helping process. In the best possible circumstances, the family has sufficiently accomplished the tasks in the work they started so that they can move on. They have been able to finish their tasks with the social worker. The social worker assists the family to do this and begin a new phase in their lives together. The family holding system, formed out of their communication and agreements, is ready to set sail. The experiences and memories of communication, the agreements, the altered patterns and structures become the maps and the charts. They are the points of reference to deal with the fog and the inevitable storms without a collision and without sinking. Often endings may be tested over time. In preparation for an ending, the family may meet every month, then every two months, then as needed. In some cases—such as a family with a member with long-term problems such as schizophrenia or bipolar disorder—there are many endings for a time, but there will be other beginnings as well.

Other endings are abrupt and unplanned, and the social worker has to work quickly to help the family system establish closure. In other situations it is not possible to establish closure (Walsh, 2003). In these situations, the concept "ending" becomes a relative term, an ending for a time. In any case, the family unit continues in one way or another. Nothing has changed except the social worker's part of it, now a memory. Although there is a sense of loss in every ending, there are few total endings. Other tasks quickly emerge in the transition.

In many Western cultures, endings take place in a fairly structured way. With relationships closer to each other than with the social worker, family members are ready to move on and out. In other cultures, such as with the J. family (case study 5.7) discussed in chapter 5 as well as in this chapter, the relationship with the social worker could be expected to stretch over a longer period. The family had made tremendous changes while it maintained itself in a new and strange culture. The social worker had helped family members reorganize themselves. They reinforced these relationships, and the changes they had made, through periodic check-ins with the social worker.

Ending with the social worker may take place when family members have achieved "good enough" growth in the areas specified in the initial contract. It is useful to return to table 1.2 to examine the basic human needs that the family can support: safety; belonging; communication; the capacity to choose, to be concerned for self and others; and the capacity to grow, to interact, and to take care of self and others. In a particular sense, these areas become themes of every interview, set and revised by the social worker and the family unit. They are the work of the interview. They are also goals to accomplish through the whole of the social worker's work with a family. They are briefly evaluated every time the social worker asks the family how the previous week has been. They indicate whether things are moving in the right direction, whether a modification of course is called for, and whether it is time to wrap up. In this sense, a certain ending process that establishes closure takes place at the end of each session—a formative (session-by-session) evaluation in preparation for the summative evaluation.

Case Study Endings

Endings with individual clients are quite different from endings with family groups. For Gloria, the Philippine nurse in case study 2.1, the ending was very difficult with the intensity of a long-term, individual helping relationship.

CASE STUDY 2.1 REVISITED

For Gloria, ending with the social worker meant coming to terms with the impossibility of her obsessions and forging a satisfying life for herself in her circumstances. For a long time, the social worker had been her cognitive steersman, and now she was ready to go on without this relationship. As Gloria developed her own cognitive functioning, the ending took about six months of direct planning to establish closure. Her new realism and her good feelings about her achievements were circumscribed by her feelings that she was losing a good friendship. She questioned whether, if it had to end, it was a real friendship at all. When she came to the understanding that in the heart and mind friendship doesn't end even when people don't see each other, she was able to let go and move on.

Endings with families are different because, if successful, the temporary intensity of the friendship with the social worker has now been absorbed by other family members with each other. The focus on relational tasks and family interaction, with the family in charge and the social worker as a mentor/coach, makes it easier for the family to let go and move on. In Gloria's situation, the depth of the relationship demanded a great deal of work to let go and establish closure. In contrast, the social worker who works with families is from the beginning assisting them to test what they can do with each other through between-session tasks. As family members discover the possibility of improved relationships, the ending is placed in the context of their growing affirmation with each other. The social worker is no longer as necessary.

Indications for Ending   There are a variety of indications for ending. The first and most obvious indication for ending is that the changes agreed upon in the first session have been sufficiently accomplished for the family to be able to operate on its own. Family members are ready to try these relationships on their own, and they are both fearful and excited about this prospect. There may be a loss of the relationship with the social worker, but there is a gain in their relationships with each other. As in the J. family (case study 5.7), these changes don't have to result in a total revision of the family's relational structure, only enough to go on effectively and continue the process.

Endings with Couples

Among couples we have already discussed were Brian and Lisa (case study 3.3), Joseph and Paula (case study 7.3), and Ashford and Louise (case study 7.6). These couples, stuck at different family life cycle stages, moved on to resolve conflicts inherent in the demands of the stage. There was a natural ending when the work could likely be completed on their own.

CASE STUDY 3.3 REVISITED

Brian had made progress sorting out personal issues with a previous life style, an old girlfriend, and patterns of binge drinking. Lisa had made progress with her tendency to depression and to spill the depression over to the relationship, and progress with her need to control. Both found their own relationship with each other reinforcing and invested themselves in the work they had to do to get married. In the last session, both were excited about planning for an apartment and their common life together.

CASE STUDY 7.3 REVISITED

Joseph and Paula continued to work on personal issues of drinking and depression. Each found energy for their relationship with each other as long as they could work on personal issues and there was a little wall of protection. Their twin daughters, now young adolescents, wondered what was happening with their father and mother now that they seemed to be enjoying each other's company.

CASE STUDY 7.6 REVISITED

Ashford and Louise took a trip West together. This was for them the honeymoon they had never had. They argued at times, but they were able to use what they learned about communication to work out some of their issues. When they returned, they had one further session. Louise had gone back to her garden and Ashford to his church work, and both in their own ways were including their adult children in their lives. They were excited about all of this and felt comfortable in what they had achieved.

Endings with Families

When children become one focus of help, a shift and realignment inevitably occurs over two generations and the realignment involves both parents and children. The ending reflects this realignment.

CASE STUDY 12.1: BECKY

Becky, a 16-year-old girl, the oldest of an Orthodox Jewish family of four, is a very talented violinist. Becky resembles her father in many ways—in intensity, in his love for music, in quiet temperament. The two have always been close without needing to acknowledge this with words. Last year she moved from a private, religious school to a new public high school to get better music instruction. Her mother and father felt that she changed profoundly that year. She had begun to go with a very different crowd, some of whom were acting out sexually. She began to lie to her father and mother. Her mother, an intense, loving, but somewhat controlling person, had an explosive reaction to Becky's lying. The more explosive and controlling the mother became, the more Becky withdrew. Becky's withdrawal drew out the extreme reaction from her mother, and things went from bad to worse. Becky's father quietly withdrew, disappointed by Becky. He felt helpless, having been actively excluded from her mother's problem solving. In couple sessions, the mother and father developed better communication and were able to agree on a strategy about Becky. In family sessions, the mother learned to become less intrusive, and the father became more involved with his daughter. Becky learned to be more candid with her mother and father about her concerns and fears of school. Becky was growing up, but that did not mean that their basically strong relationships would be diminished. She also learned to take charge of her own choices of friends and gradually became less fearful of school. Ending took place over the first months of school when Becky, although anticipating that she would be afraid, found some friends. Her mother managed her anxiety about Becky and found a better relationship that she could trust. Her father became a close resource for Becky when she had certain things to talk over. Their ending sessions were a "recital" and acknowledgment of what had happened. They were an affirmation by Becky that she could handle high school, though not without difficulty.

In some cultures, the ending needs to be stretched out with some relationships continuing. Nevertheless, the focus of the ending is on ending, on showing the social worker that they have changed and are able to handle new realities. They are grateful for all the social worker has done. In family members' minds, he or she is like a member of the family.

CASE STUDY 5.7 REVISITED

It has been approximately two years since the J. family and the social worker said goodbye to each other and the court released Mr. J. from supervision. Over the span of two years, every member of the J. family individually communicated appreciation of what the social worker had done for them collectively as well as personally. Chen brought the letter of reference forms to the social worker for her applications to several Ivy League schools. Kwak kept the social worker's e-mail address and sent him an additional progress report some time after the ending. Mrs. J. prepared a jar of health food as a token of her appreciation. Finally, Mr. J. called the social worker on a Chinese holiday, wishing him the very best.

Difficult and Complex Endings

Some endings and transitions are difficult and complex because the relationship itself is complex and multifaceted, and the worker has had to be very active. The deeper the relationship, the more the ending may need to take place over a longer period. Here the understanding of endings, developed in work with individuals (Walsh, 2003), is most valuable. The ending with difficult situations becomes similar to the ending with Gloria.

CASE STUDY 12.2: MICHAEL AND ALYSON

Michael and Alyson are an African American couple who have had a tumultuous first ten years of marriage. There have been numerous separations. Both have been involved in infidelities. There has been near constant conflict. Alyson's oldest child, Trisha, had been born when Alyson was 14 and about five years before she had married Michael. With the birth of Trisha, Alyson never was really able to differentiate herself well as a person from a tight triangle between her mother, Anna, and Trisha. This triangle dominated her relationships during the early years of her marriage. She remained her mother's daughter, and her mother took care of Trisha. Trisha had always had a claim on Alyson prior to Michael. Consequently, Alyson had little real relational space for Michael. Indeed, she felt pulled between her relationship with Trisha and with Michael. As Trisha grew older, this got worse, and the marriage was threatened. Alyson clearly could not handle Tricia and attend to her marriage at the same time. Eventually Alyson's mother, Anna, became the caregiver for Trisha. Alyson took care of her three younger children and tried to reconstruct a relationship with Michael. Anna herself had been raised by her grandmother, and she did not object to raising Trisha, although Trisha gave her lots of problems. On the other hand, Trisha wasn't sure where she belonged. She actively shifted back and forth between her mother and her grandmother, depending on her desires and the level of conflict in the situation. The competition and the constant issues between Alyson and her mother created difficulties with Trisha. There was a deep and conflictual identification between mother and daughter. Trisha had many of the problems Alyson remembers having had herself as a teenager.

Michael had grown up as a foster child. He has no contact with his family of origin and regards his foster parents as his parents. He found Alyson's struggle to differentiate herself from her mother and from Trisha confusing. He never sensed that he had a stable relationship with Alyson as a real person, but rather only one as someone reacting to Trisha, or her mother, or at times overusing addictive substances. Very loyal to Alyson, he was never certain what to expect from her. He often became impatient with her difficulties, taking them on as his own. He had a tendency to become over responsible for Alyson's problems, and this would leave Alyson in a position of a rebellious child.

The social worker worked with Michael and Alyson for two years, helping the family unit respond appropriately while Alyson was able to shift and rearrange her complex network of allegiances without losing herself. During this time, the social worker did marital counseling, counseled individually with Michael and Alyson when necessary, and worked with Alyson's parents. The sessions with the grandparents took place with Alyson and Michael. In these two-couple sessions, Alyson, with Michael's support, worked out child care arrangements for Trisha and did family-of-origin work with her parents. She worked closely with Alyson's psychiatrist and with Alyson when Alyson went through a severe depression with some psychotic features. Trisha had a long-term relationship with her own therapist and actually managed reasonably well when not subjected to the push and pull of Alyson's relationship with Anna or her relationship with Michael. The social worker coached Alyson in her relationship with Tricia. In the process, Michael and Alyson showed considerable improvement. Alyson gradually learned to deal with her complex triangulated relationship with Trisha and her mother, and also to invest herself in her relationship with Michael and with their other three children. She became very consistent in taking her medication and became predictable to Michael. Michael felt able to respond to her. Their relationship, now much better, was reinforcing to Alyson, so that they began talking about buying a home. When Trisha had problems, Alyson would no longer get caught in a triangle with Anna. Trisha did better with this. She learned to remain close to her mother and Anna in different ways.

The ending process took several months. The relationship with the social worker had become a holding system for everyone. Alyson was able to take steps to manage the relationship with her mother over Trisha so that joint sessions were no longer necessary. At first neither Alyson nor Michael, nor Anna, believed they would ever succeed on their own as a couple. The act of settling their chaotic financial affairs and looking for a home became a way of testing the steadiness of their relationship. They moved to interviews every other week and then monthly. In their final contact it was understood they could return when needed. They had developed communication and problem-solving skills and were able to recognize what they had done together.

In some cases, the ending is complex because some of the issues remain and will remain, and the family continues to come to terms with these continuing realities, as with John and Mary Maxwell's situation, discussed in case study 8.7.

CASE STUDY 8.7 REVISITED

John and Mary Maxwell and Stephen's situation had a natural ending over about five months. This took place during the summer after Stephen's graduation, before his entry into the army, and extended several months after he entered. During the summer, he got a job and gradually learned to take responsibility with their pickup truck. As he waited for a September induction, there was a reduction of conflict. However, John and Mary were more anxious than Stephen until he was inducted. Their relationship remained quite tense. After Stephen was inducted, their concern and anxiety shifted to Mike, his younger brother. This time, however, their experiences with Stephen and the assistance of the worker helped them manage their concerns about Mike without provoking a destructive reaction

from him. As the boys' problems became less pressing, John and Mary then had to deal with the natural limitations and possibilities of their relationship and their empty nest issues. Facing gradually the limitations and possibilities of their own relationship, they began to feel they had accomplished all they could in couples counseling. It wasn't heaven, but they would manage with each other. Later John's physical condition became life-threatening. He stayed in occasional touch with the social worker as needed to discuss his marital issues and his serious health issues. Mary had saved his life when he was found with a blood clot in his leg, and this began a new relationship with her. He began to see her differently from his grandmother, whom he had feared and hated. His contacts with the social worker became the completion of the life narrative he had begun long ago.

Often, the closer the relationship of the social worker with particular members of the family, the more difficult the ending. With individual relationships of some depth, it is fairly normal to experience termination reactions. This is well discussed in the literature (Hepworth, Rooney, & Larson, 1997, pp. 597–615; Shulman, 1992, pp. 164–169). In a one-to-one relationship of some depth, ending inevitably is experienced as a great loss. In these circumstances, it is not unusual for clients to regress, to display anger at the social worker, to deny that an ending might take place, and to deny that they have accomplished anything. The social worker needs to normalize these feelings, give the persons a chance to express and deal with them, and help clients recount what they have accomplished, as well as help them realize that they can take all of what they accomplished with them. Family work is different, because their relationship itself becomes the holding system. If this system, although problematic, gets better, a loss of the social worker's relationship may not be so devastating. When strong regressions, anger, or denial are characteristic of family sessions, it may be a signal that they are not yet ready to end or that they need to be more in control of the ending process. It may mean that occasional checkups should take place. It may also mean that the social worker should continue with one member of the family, as with Mr. Maxwell (case study 8.7). If the family appears ready to end but is blocking on it, sometimes an effective approach is to ask them to review carefully and discuss in detail with each other, in session, what each of them would need to do if they were to bring the problem back (Tomm & Wright, 1979).

ENDINGS AND TRANSITIONS INVOLVING SOCIAL INSTITUTIONS

Other endings are built into the structure of the social institution. A school term ends in the summer. The beginnings and endings of school terms set a certain rhythm, and the availability of the social worker when needed during the school year makes a difference for pupils and parents. The respite of the summer is often an opportunity for children and parents to make further progress, built on what had been begun during the school year. In Alan's case (case study 10.1), from second grade through the elementary years and eighth-grade graduation there was an ending each June, but then a new beginning of gradually diminishing intensity the following September. In any case, an outside therapist was available to provide continuity when it was needed. Finally, all that was needed was for the social worker to continue to be available and interested in a relationship that had continued seven years from their first meeting.

Time as the Medium of the Helping Process: Institutional Time

In schools, and also in other institutions, time, when attended to by the social worker and the family, can become the medium of the helping process. This phrase of Jessie Taft (1949) means that in many respects, the work of the helping process, if used well and within reasonable limitations, can fit itself into the time available.

School is perhaps the easiest example of this. School is an institution with expected ebbs and flows of work. Time extends itself through eight years of elementary school and four years of secondary school. The rhythm of the school year is in many ways the rhythm of families, and the two institutions have accommodated themselves to each other over many years. There are beginnings and always endings, but the long-term process takes place over many years of development and many episodes, as in Alan's case. Families, even very difficult and troubled families, readily work with social workers in schools, and accommodate goals of the school as developmental goals for the child. Families often will accept assistance from the school when they will accept it from no other agency.

Other agencies, such as child welfare and juvenile justice institutions, have shorter and more intense time lines. There is only so much time before the hearing. The probation officer with the Moorhead family (case study 10.4) used the time before the hearing, together with preparing the family for the hearing and preparing a report, as a means of helping the family to clarify their perspectives and realign themselves in relation to Billy's problems. They would have never been able to do this clarification and realignment work on their own and without the deadline of the court hearing.

The Clark family (case study 10.2) had ninety days with their social worker to recompose themselves to take care of their children. This time frame served as a stimulus both for the family and for the worker. Family preservation work, detailed in chapter 10, was limited to three months. During this time, the social worker was very active in helping the Clarks recompose almost all aspects of their relationship. As with Alyson and Michael (case study 12.2), the danger of such an active relationship on the social worker's part is that if it took place over a longer time, the social worker would become like a member of the family. She would become essential to continuing to stabilize the situation, and the family would not be able to function without her. She could become "overadequate" in relation to the Clark's progress, and the Clarks could become "underadequate." Paradoxically, with the three-month limit of the relationship, the enforced ending could operate as an external safety valve to motivate the Clarks and the social worker. A ninety-day relationship with an external evaluation sets boundaries. The family can enjoy the temporary infusion of the social worker's energy but will have to take over their own situation and relationships fully in three months. When they consent to an agreement with the worker for ninety days, the ending is inherent in the beginning. The ending gives them hope that they can eventually manage by themselves. It can motivate them to make the changes necessary to preserve their family unit. As it did with the Moorheads, the institutional boundary helps social worker and family do what otherwise would be very difficult under other circumstances.

Incomplete or Premature Endings

Another possibility is that members of the family have not accomplished what they had hoped to achieve and have decided not to continue with the work. These are often very difficult endings, because the initial agreement has not been accomplished. There are unfulfilled expectations and feelings of frustration: a different outcome, a different social unit, had been hoped for. The social worker, particularly the new social worker, who has also an investment in their goals, may feel a personal sense of loss and personal failure and may draw in that feeling from family members also. A sense of loss and personal failure can impede the work that must be done in ending, but there are fewer illusions. The hoped-for direction will not be possible. What was uncertain, confusing, and challenging may now be less so—or at least it may be different.

CASE STUDY 12.3: ROBERTA AND SAM

Roberta and Sam Piotrowski had sought marital counseling at Evangelical Family Services (EFS) over Roberta's suspicion that Sam was having an affair with a mutual friend. Sam denied all this in the beginning. Roberta accepted Sam's denial. However, their relational work in session seemed flat and ritualistic. Increasingly, under pressure from the communication tasks themselves, Sam admitted to the ongoing affair. Although he adored their 3-year-old son, Jake, Sam came to some clarity with himself: he had no intentions of continuing with the marriage or with marriage counseling. The couple worked out an in-session understanding over Jake's custody and the house. Given the circumstances, they ended couples' work as amicably as possible. Sam did not want to do any further work individually. Roberta continued individually for several months, sorting out her concerns and issues over her next steps, the concrete goals in her life situation, and some of the loneliness, depression, and anger with which she was struggling. When she felt clearer and more able to deal with the emergent tasks in her life situation, she ended the individual sessions. She continues to be a major source of referral of others for help at EFS.

In Sam and Roberta's situation, the social worker was able to help them deal with a potentially explosive situation and to individually help Roberta with her disappointment, anger, and depression, as well as the challenges facing her. The social worker, who had dealt with similar situations before, was not taken aback nor drawn into the conflict personally. He was able to help them manage the situation as well as possible. Much as in the situation with the Maxwells, he switched comfortably to individual work when it was necessary to complete some of the personal tasks generated by the couples work.

Evaluation

With endings and transitions comes evaluation. In a particular sense in practice, the process of evaluation takes place in every interview and is a formative evaluation. This continual process governs the direction chosen and the feasibility and speed with which certain goals may be attained. In a cumulative sense, again in practice, evaluation takes place in the ending and is summative. In fact, together with the energy and hope of family members, it becomes a major stimulus for ending. What have been their goals? Have they achieved them? What has changed about each person's understanding of family relationships since they have begun? What can they live with now? Are they ready to end the process of helping? Are they able to use the social worker as a resource in the future? The ending discussion is tailored to the understandings and agreements arrived at in the beginning and through each formative evaluation. The evaluation process should suit the situation. Not every question is asked in the same way. In some settings and in some approaches to practice, there is a formal instrument to measure symptom reduction or movement from a baseline established in the beginning (Corcoran, 2000). In others, the measurement is less formal, more individualized, and more geared to the family's understandings and control. In every case, the practice process is the same. It is governed by the needs of the couple or family to end—to wrap up and to move on—and by the accountability needs of the social worker.

RESEARCH OUTCOMES AND EFFECTIVENESS OF COUPLE AND FAMILY WORK

Often the question of research outcomes and effectiveness of intervention methods is approached from the simple logic of a drug trial. Does the intervention reduce a named symptom for an index client within a matched population? This would not work well with individual persons in their complexity. Persons have choices to make. Persons have uncertain goals. The systems involved in family work are complex and full of contingencies. Couple and family work generally does not hinge on whether certain symptoms have been alleviated in an index client. It focuses on relational systems as a primary intervention point. It considers individual, couple, and family functioning from multiple perspectives. It often works with multiple systems (e.g., individuals, couples, families, schools, medical providers) (Gurman and Knishkern, 1978; Sexton, Coop Gordon, Gurman, Lebow, Holtzworth-Monroe & Johnson, 2011, p. 379). Yet there is much to be learned from the research that does seek to compare the processes and outcomes of helping. Let us first examine the outcomes of the cases cited in this chapter, letting them stand for the moment for the complexity and the choices involved in any case situation the social worker would encounter:

> Case study 2.1. Over many years, Gloria gradually let go of some of the obsessions that paralyzed her, but others remained. She moved to a new professional productivity and gradually was able to function well without the helping relationship.
> Case study 3.3. Brian and Lisa's progress in their relationship was paralleled by progress with the personal issues which held them back. They would never have been able to make these personal changes without their developing relationship motivating them.
> Case study 7.3. Joseph and Paula found energy for their relationship as long as they could do their own work on personal issues. Their discovery of a possible relationship after such difficult personal histories made things worthwhile.

Case study 7.6. Ashford and Louise discovered a comfortable relationship with each other and their children as they each worked with their personal life cycle issues.

Case study 12.1. Becky rediscovered a somewhat better relationship with her father. The slight relational shift from her anxious and centralizing mother allowed her to take better charge of her coping with her new school. Mother's holding back on her anxiety and need to put herself in the center of a process helped Father get more involved and opened the possibility of a better relationship with Becky.

Case study 5.7. The J. family dealt with their own cultural issues and with the court's expectations; the father was released from supervision, and the family rebalanced itself. Each of the family members continued receiving the worker's support through informal check-ins, although these diminished over two years.

Case study 12.2. Alyson shifted her complex relationships with her mother and oldest daughter so that she was able to deal with her own personal demons as well as accommodate Michael and the relationships with their three other children. Michael supported Alyson through this and found their relationship was developing. Their ability to deal with their chaotic finances and look for a home was a significant step in their developing relationship.

Case study 8.7. As John and Mary Maxwell were able to form a responsive, united front, Stephen's situation gradually resolved itself. With Stephen in the Army, doing well, and no longer a distraction, their old unresolved marital issues reasserted themselves. John faced rapidly deteriorating health issues, but Mary was there for him. They never would be close, but a certain stability emerged in their relationship as John coped with his dying process and Mary began to cope with this inevitability.

Case study 12.3. Roberta Piotrowski discovered the truth that Sam was having an affair and was definitely planning to marry his friend. After this revelation was made in session to Roberta, Sam moved out of the relationship and made himself unavailable for further work with her. Roberta continued individually with the social worker. Over a period of time, she was able to deal with the issues of becoming a single parent, getting a job, finding a network of relationships, and taking care of their son. She still feels the relational loss—but less and less so as her energy and intelligence go to other things.

Successful outcomes in practice are not imposed from the outside, but rather are relative to what is possible and to the choices made in a situation. The units of attention and the focus eventually emerge at the beginning of the process from this understanding. In each case, the client(s) chose their desired outcomes depending on the emergent situation. Some outcomes would not be foreseen. Prespecifying one possible outcome would have cut off other even more likely outcomes. The cutoff would have created for each person a climate of unreality and loss of control. It would have obliterated the choices that each family member had to make and the actions they would have to take with all of their uncertainty. It was assumed that

Sam and Roberta initially came to work on their marriage until Sam revealed that he was unavailable for this: he had already chosen another relationship. Roberta now had to deal with a different situation, one not of her choosing. Her best outcome would be that she would discover her strengths and deal with the situation.

In the other situations, without intervention the likely outcomes would have been negative: John and Mary would not have formed a united front; Alyson, her oldest daughter and her mother would still be relationally stuck, and thus Alyson would be unavailable for a relationship with Michael. It was likely that the J. family would remain paralyzed between two cultures and in conflict with the court. Becky would remain stuck with her mother's anxiety, unable to cope with high school. Ashford and Louise would likely remain at loggerheads, giving preference to their personal life cycle issues over their relationship. Both Brian and Lisa and Joseph and Paula would choose to marry alcohol or to marry depression rather than discover a better relationship with the other.

But none of this actually happened. The surprising result was that the couples, for example, did discover something in their relationship powerful enough to let go of alcohol and depression. In many cases, their newly discovered relationship with each other allowed them to deal with personal issues and better attend to each other as well. When they found that they could cope better and that the relationship might last as a holding system, they no longer had the same need for the social worker. The social worker could let go as soon as balances were restored and they were able to cope on their own and with each other. Of course, not every case works out well or can be seen so simply. Each follows its own course with the social worker assisting persons to cope better and to find relationships with others, when relationships become possible.

Thus, in practice clients choose the outcomes in the beginning with the worker. Social workers are free to draw appropriate techniques and skills for what becomes necessary in the situation to achieve these agreed-on outcomes or, failing that, to achieve another chosen outcome. Research, however, requires that processes and outcomes be comparable. When this control can be set, there is much to be learned. In the following discussion, we can look at research for what we can learn about the helping process and on the relative effectiveness of techniques and skills that would aid this process.

RESEARCH ON COMPONENTS OF THE HELPING PROCESS

There are common factors of psychotherapeutic effectiveness. From Hubble, Duncan, and Miller's (1999) review, it is likely that the beneficial effects of intervention result largely from the combination of four therapeutic factors that research has estimated as the principal elements accounting for client improvement:

1. Client extratherapeutic factors (strengths and needs, risk and protective factors, intrapersonal resources and deficits, interpersonal social network involvement, and reflective skills the client brings) account for 40 percent of the outcome.

2. Relationship factors account for 30 percent of the outcome. These are the interpersonal connectedness and expressive attunement of the therapeutic alliance or relationship. They include Rogers's (1957) classic core therapeutic conditions of a healing relationship—empathy, genuineness, and unconditional positive regard.

3. Placebo, hope, and expectancy factors—that is, the belief that change can occur, agreement with the rationale of a treatment approach, and "confidence in and mastery of a chosen method (that) ultimately works by enhancing the client's belief in the potential for healing" (Snyder, Michael, & Cheavens, 1999, p. 183)—account for 15 percent of the outcome.

4. Model-specific factors (the philosophical underpinnings, rationale, theory base format, goals, tasks, techniques, treatment processes and anticipated outcomes of the intervention model) account for 15 percent of the outcome.

Social Work Outcomes   Applied to social work practice, Cameron and Keenan (2010) build on the common factors framework to include five general sets of factors associated with positive client outcomes:

1. *Social network factors*. These have to do with support for positive functioning. They are supportive values, supportive knowledge, supportive funding, policies, procedures and practice guidelines, client social support, and whether the client's social support views social work practice as credible.

2. *Social worker/helper factors*. This includes the social worker's well-being, acceptance, genuineness, and empathy.

3. *Client factors*. This includes distress, hope or expectation of change, active help seeking, and a view of the social worker as credible.

4. *Relationship Factors*. This includes engagement in the relationship, engagement in the change work, productive direct and indirect communication, mutual agreement on problems, tasks roles and goals, and collaboration.

5. *Practice Strategies*. These include developing a rationale for change, modeling, feedback, ventilation, exploration, awareness and insight, emotional learning, interpersonal learning, knowledge, information, development and practice of new behaviors, success and mastery of these, reinforcement, desensitization, suggestion, and advocacy (Cameron and Keenan, 2010, p. 64; Drisko, 2004; adapted from Grencavage & Norcross, 1990).

These factors are not necessarily inherent to every situation. In a problem-solving process, some factors would be skillfully activated by the social worker to move the process positively and individualize it to the situation, the persons, and the relationship. The last factor, *practice strategies*, would be tools which guide practice activities, *skills* being the discrete actions used to enact strategies. Thus Cameron and Keenan (2010, p. 65) are arguing not for a generic practice, but rather for a skillful and differentiated use, according to the person(s), the process, and the situation of all five factors, of what is known to enhance effectiveness. These change processes, taking place between client and worker, are very consistent with much of the content of basic social work texts.[1]

The critique of the common factors discussion was that these common factors were useful, but insufficient in themselves to describe or to account for effective practice (Smith, 2012). As we have seen, focusing on an individual, such as Gloria and Roberta, or on the couples or on the families in our sample are quite different processes demanding somewhat different skills and techniques. Thus there was individual work with Gloria and eventually with Roberta. There was couples' work with Brian and Lisa, Joseph and Paula, and Ashford and Louise and some family work with Becky's family, the J. family, the Maxwell family, and Alyson's family. Whether it was couples' work, family work, or individual work, each focus would still have a somewhat different theory base and use of skills. Practitioners would be better at some than others, but from the case examples it was useful to know all three. Our book presupposes a general understanding of these common-factor, change processes. It connects these with family development processes and family therapy research and practice and applies these understandings to the architecture and process of couple and family intervention.

The Research Effectiveness of Couples' Work and Family Work

The remaining question is the general research effectiveness of couples work and family work. A short answer for this question is that there is now a well-established literature regarding the efficacy and effectiveness of couple and family-based interventions (Sexton, Alexander, & Mease, 2004; Sexton, Coop Gordon, Gurman, Lebow, Holtzworth-Monroe, & Johnson, 2011, p. 379). We can explore some of this literature.

Couples' Work   Similar to the approach of this book, couple therapy focuses on the couple relationship and is considered the treatment of choice for couple distress or improving couple relationship satisfaction. In this context, a focus on the individual apart from the relationship may be risky to the couple relationship (Gurman & Knishkern, 1986; Lebow, 2013). Couple therapy largely takes from integrative theory, drawing on generic and overlapping theories to serve the common task of helping couples more fully experience in their relationships and alter the patterns that erode connection. There is a common base of ways of understanding couple processes and working with couples that provide a foundation for practice (Lebow, 2013, p. 2). Despite continuing discussion of some particular efficacy issues, general couples therapy is empirically supported. Positive outcomes are realized in about two-thirds of couples, and this overall improvement rate affirms

---

[1]Within the family field, it is also commonplace for particular family or couple intervention strategies to account only for a small percentage of the variance in change that occurs in treatment (Sprenkle, Davis, & Lebow, 2009).

that the average treated couple is better off at termination than about 70 percent to 80 percent of untreated couples, paralleling the rates for most individual psychotherapy. Every Random Clinical Trial (RCT) has been found superior to no treatment. Also as in the case examples, couple therapy has been shown to have a positive effect on a number of common adult disorders that co-occur with couple conflict—for example, anxiety, depression, and alcoholism. (Gurman, 2011, pp. 281–283). One model of couple therapy quite similar to what is developed in this book, emotionally focused therapy (EFT), has developed its own practice manual to standardize interventions (Greenman & Johnson, 2013; Johnson, 2004). It has been tested using RCTs and has been proven effective. General couple therapy, with strong, general evidence of effectiveness but without a manual to standardize interventions more precisely, is considered *evidence-informed* rather than *evidence-based* (Sexton, Coop Gordon, Gurman, Lebow, Holtzworth-Monroe, & Johnson, 2011). For many reasons, it is important for measurement and comparability that an effective process be described.

Family Work   *Systemic* (family) *therapy* is a general term for a therapeutic orientation similar to the approach taken by this book. It (1) perceives behavior and mental symptoms within the context of the social systems people live in, (2) focuses on interpersonal relations and interactions and on social constructions of realities, (3) includes family members and other important persons, and (4) appreciates and uses clients' perspectives on problems, resources, and preferred solutions (Retzlaff, Sydow, Beher, Haun, & Schweitzer, 2013; Sydow, Beher, Schweitzer, & Retzlaff, 2010; Sydow, Retzlaff, Beher, Haun, & Schweitzer, 2013). Using these criteria, the three studies cited above reviewed random controlled trials of systemic therapy from studies in the United States, Europe, and China that met the above criteria. Sydow, Retzlaff, Beher, Haun, and Schweitzer (2013) studied the effectiveness of systemic therapy with externalizing disorders (ADHD, conduct disorders, substance use disorders) of children and adolescents. Of the forty-seven studies meeting criteria, forty-two showed systemic therapy to be either significantly more efficacious than control groups without a psychosocial intervention or equally efficacious as (or more efficacious than) other evidence-based interventions, such as individual and group cognitive behavioral (CBT) or family psychoeducation (Sydow, Retzlaff, Beher, Haun, & Schweitzer, 2013, p. 608). Retzlaff, Sydow, Beher, Haun, and Schweitzer (2013) did parallel studies from international sources on children and adolescents' internalizing behavior (mood disorders, anxiety disorders, eating disorders, suicidality and child abuse and neglect). In thirty-three of the thirty-eight studies in the group, systemic therapy was either significantly more efficacious than control groups without a systems-oriented intervention, or systemic therapy was more efficacious than other evidence-based interventions (CBT, psychodynamic therapy, behavioral family therapy/parent training, family psychoeducation, group therapy or inpatient treatment) (Retzlaff, Sydow, Beher, Haun, & Schweitzer, 2013, p. 642). Sydow, Beher, Schweitzer, and Retzlaff (2010) did parallel studies on systemic treatment for adult DSM categories (mood disorders, anxiety disorders, somatoform disorders, eating disorders, substance use disorders, psychotic disorders and psychosocial factors related to medical conditions in thirty-eight random controlled trials. In thirty-four of thirty-eight RCTs, either systemic therapy was significantly more efficacious than control groups without a psychosocial intervention, or systemic therapy was equally efficacious as, or more efficacious than, other evidence-based interventions (CBT, family psychoeducation, solution-focused group therapy or antidepressant/ neuroleptic medication) (Sydow, Beher, Schweitzer, & Retzlaff, 2010, p. 477). Of this general population, there are at least two studies that have developed a clear description of their intervention. In most respects, they are remarkably similar to the multisystemic family systems-based intervention we describe in the book and that is a hallmark of social work intervention. They are broad-based, dealing with the range of internal and external complexities found in communities and in families. These are functional family therapy (Sexton, 2010; Sexton & Alexander, 2003) and multi-systemic therapy (Henggeler, Melton, & Smith, 1992; National Institutes of Health, 2005; Sheidow, Henggeler, & Schoenwald, 2003).

CONCLUSION AND IMPLICATIONS

The river flows on into the sea. In some seasons, it may overflow its borders, causing floods. Nevertheless, the energy of the river can be partially diverted and directed to the common good.

Social workers help family members restructure their relationships through communication and interaction. There are many worlds of families: families at different life stages and families in different cultures. Family exists in a multicultural world. This world, however, is not static. It is in constant motion as families form themselves out of differences and as cultures themselves are in dynamic movement in the postmodern world. Living in a larger cultural complex, family creates its own culture of relationships. Applying an essential social work orientation to practice with families, we have drawn from a rich variety of theoretical approaches. Studying actual practice with families, we have made connections between theory, family development, emergent family structure, multicultural realities, institutional and environmental realities, and the work of the social worker. This is only the beginning of the connections that social workers can make in even more complex situations, with many different types of family structure, when the basic social work model with families is well understood.

The content and process of social work with families builds on persons who construct family units. These units are constructed to satisfy needs that only a unit of persons, a relational structure, a family can provide. Family members act together to secure certain basic needs proper to persons. Among these needs, which make us human, are the needs for interpersonal safety, belonging, the capacity to communicate, to choose what is good, to grow, and to interact and take care of self and others. Persons can grow in this interactional climate. Indeed, they require it. Rooted in a greater complex of cultural meanings and institutions, the family develops its own culture.

Family should be one place where one can be accepted as a human being and as a person. Despite severe contradictions inherent in postmodern life, the expectation that family culture should accommodate the needs of persons moves forward as inexorably as a river toward the sea. Even as they are violated, there remain expectations based on trust and permanence of commitment. Relationships are expected to be based less on a utilitarian calculus of contribution, as in a workplace, and more on status, membership, and personal bonds. Fractured norms and relationships can be reconstructed, though not easily or surely. Persons interact to form families to construct relationships, seeking in their own way basic human values of respect, belonging, acceptance, communication, choice and care. The family interacts with a social institutional world that can support or undermine this delicate complex of patterns and relationships—what could otherwise be called structure.

Social workers work with families that are in the process of reconstructing themselves. They work with the needed outside community and institutional world so that families and individual persons are able to survive and flourish in a world of risks, uncertainties, and external stresses with their accompanying felt effects on family life. Social work is value-based activity based on an understanding of the constant worth and needs of human beings. This understanding provides an ethical basis for family intervention, even if a particular family member or social institution may not recognize these facts and values. Social workers help persons in families and family units in which these possible relationships are at risk. They deal with the family as a whole, as well as with its members and its environment. They can draw from theories of family functioning and from intervention theory corresponding to these levels of functioning to assist family members to carry out their tasks of securing human need.

Understanding this logic, it is possible to help family members (and the family itself as a collective unit) alter patterns and recompose meanings and, thus, in a qualified way, to become agents of their own development. Events themselves, happening outside of the family, also may alter these structures and meanings. In practice with families we inevitably deal with the entire complexity of circumstances and persons, the inside and the outside of the family. We now have some understanding cross-nationally and cross-culturally of what goes into effective practice with families. Developments in theory, research, and our understanding of practice itself will certainly allow for greater prediction and control. However, ultimately the outcome of work with families remains somewhat unpredictable and uncontrollable. There is too much involved; it is too complex to be approached from only one direction. And this is the rationale for our organizing framework.

There are a number of implications of this organizing framework for social work with families. First, the normal relational work of persons with each other and with social institutions provides the natural basis for social work. There is a constant reality that persons normally interact with each other. They establish family structures to satisfy profound human needs: to solve problems, to support each other, and to enjoy relationships. The meanings and the relational structures emerge from social interaction. This constant reality provides a rationale to find the best way to understand these complex interactions and the most effective way to intervene in them. Social institutions assist family members in this endeavor. A variety of methods become possible, including working with individual family members, with subsets of the family, with social institutions, and with community networks of services according to the problem and need. Effective methods evolve from an understanding of their functions, of what they are supposed to do to assist family members.

Neither theory nor practice is an imposition on the natural order of people's forming families and living in them. It is a natural order, because persons do need families, do seek certain values in family life, and do act to form their families. It is complex, because there are always differences within and between families. People interpret, respond to, and support (or hide) differences in their own way. Family can never be one-dimensional or reduced to one member's process. Family units are formed out of multiple differences. Different relational structures necessarily appear at different phases of the family's developmental process. Among these differences in postmodern society are cultural differences, experienced in relation to a host culture and experienced within the family itself. Social work practice with families is built upon values that persons seek from families. How may one calculate an affirmation of the other's (and reciprocally one's own) worth and dignity as a person? Social work practice helps these processes take place optimally. Building on differences in a multicultural world, it must by definition become transcultural.

The second implication of this framework is that the variety of cultural and situational meanings make social work practice both a science and an art. Family may compose itself in a variety of ways in different cultures according to external and internal circumstances. Within different situations and consistent with cultural meanings and patterns, there are many different approaches to doing relatively similar things. Some forms of family can be more vulnerable to dissolution or dysfunction than others. The members' understanding of the structure may differ by culture and by internal and external circumstances, so approaches to intervention may vary. Within some cultures, there may be only a limited ability to communicate and connect a person's internal state with family interaction. In one culture the focus for intervention may rest on interaction itself, on helping family members create a workable structure rather than extensively talking about it. In other cultures and circumstances, a good deal of talk is a prerequisite to action. These families need to establish meanings clearly before they interact. Social workers need to make a distinction in cultural meanings and pathways in their assessment and planning for intervention, but what needs accomplishment is often quite similar.

The third implication is that it follows necessarily that there is a gap between present theory, which can explain and direct the social worker's actions and actual and concrete relational realities. Ultimately, the family writes its own story. Despite enormous progress, theory itself is still a somewhat limited help to the social worker in assisting families to recompose their realities. Family therapy has made enormous progress in developing techniques for working with families and is moving toward synthesis. It is still composed of a variety of competing schools, all dealing with the same reality. Social work with families demands an organizing framework. Even with such a framework, there is no accurate prediction, only a recognition of what is happening and an approximation of what may happen. In the same way, in the far more developed science of weather, a forecast and an understanding of certain principles may help a navigator deal with a storm, but even this does not pretend to predict the outcome of flying through that storm. Indeed the navigator and the pilot are equipped with different ways of responding, knowing the capability of their plane to deal with emerging realities.

The theories about work with families in general are translated into practice through the case or, better still, the situation. The case is an individual narrative or story of interactive help provided to the family. Story is the particular outcome of a complex of realities, of which only a few are predictable or well understood. This book has been filled with stories intended to teach—to accustom the social worker to the content and process of helping families. These stories are linked to theory with further links suggested in the footnotes. They are meant for reflection and discussion, and some of their interpretations are open-ended.

Finally, principles of effective practice are also values placed into action. The work of the social worker cannot simply be reduced to techniques. Social workers are part of a living, recursive, and responsive interaction with family members. The social worker is a coach for what family members need to do if they are to satisfy any of their needs through family structure and interaction. In this sense, practice principles are not abstract techniques, but they eventually become human qualities of the practitioner responding to family realities. In different situations, navigators and pilots also develop their own ways of responding to uncertain conditions. The practitioner develops the ability to respond to the infinite variations of the same themes. Identifying the themes is an important beginning step.

There are deep roots to social work practice theory. Many different rivers flow into more than a century of practice of social workers and social institutions with families, the ongoing source of meaning and support in a complex society. One purpose of these chapters has been to rediscover what has always been inherent, implicit, and somehow inchoate in social work practice and in its theoretical base. At the same time, a framework for practice needed to be connected with other approaches and to actual social work practice with families. We hope that the rediscovery of who we are as social work practitioners will help us become more fully what we are.

REFERENCES

Cameron, M., & Keenan, E. K. (2010). The common factors model: Implications for transtheoretical social work practice. *Social Work*, 55(1), 63–73.

Corcoran, J. (2000). *Evidence-based social work practice with families*. New York, NY: Springer.

Drisko, J. W. (2004). Common factors in psychotherapy outcome: Meta-analytic findings and their implications for practice and research. *Families in Society*, 83, 81–90.

Greenman, P. S., & Johnson, S. M. (2013). Process research on emotionally focused therapy (EFT) for couples: Linking theory to practice. *Family Process*, 52(1), 46–61.

Grencavage, L. M., & Norcross, J. C. (1990). Where are the commonalities among the therapeutic common factors? *Professional Psychology: Research and Practice*, 21, 372–378.

Gurman, A. S. (2011). Couple therapy research and the practice of couple therapy: Can we talk? *Family Process*, 50(3), 280–292.

Gurman, A. S., & Knishkern, D. P. (1978). Research on marital and family therapy: Progress, perspective and prospect. In S. L. Garfield & A. E. Bergin (Eds.), *Handbook of psychotherapy and behavior change* (2nd ed., pp. 817–902). New York, NY: Wiley.

Gurman, A. S., & Knishkern, D. P. (1986). Commentary: Individual marital therapy: Have reports of your death been somewhat exaggerated? *Family Process*, 25(1), 51–62.

Henggeler, S., Melton, G., & Smith, L. (1992). Family preservation using multisystemic therapy: An effective alternative to incarcerating serious juvenile offenders. *Journal of Consulting and Clinical Psychology*, 60, 953–961.

Hepworth, D. H., Rooney, R. H., & Larson, J. A. (1997). *Direct social work practice: Theory and skills* (5th ed.). Pacific Grove, CA: Brooks-Cole.

Hubble, D., Duncan, B., and Miller, S. (1999). *The heart and soul of change*. Washington, DC: American Psychological Association.

Johnson, S. M. (2004). *The practice of emotionally focused couple therapy* (2nd ed.). New York, NY: Brunner Routledge.

Lebow, J. (2013). Editorial: Couple therapy and family therapy. *Family Process*, 52(1), 1–4.

National Institutes of Health. (2005). *State of the science conference statement: Preventing violence and related health-risking social behaviors in adolescents.* Accessed at http://consensus.nih.gov/ta/023/YouthViolenceFinalStatement 011805.htm.

Retzlaff, R., Sydow, K. v., Beher, S., Haun, M. W., & Schweitzer, J. (2013). The efficacy of systemic therapy for internalizing and other disorders of childhood and adolescence: A systematic review of 38 randomized trials. *Family Process*, 52(4), 619–652.

Rogers, C. (1957). The necessary and sufficient conditions of therapeutic personality change. *Journal of Consulting Psychology*, 21, 95–103.

Sexton, T. L. (2010). *Functional family therapy in clinical practice: An evidence-based clinical model for at-risk adolescents.* New York, NY: Routledge.

Sexton, T., Coop Gordon, K., Gurman, A., Lebow, J., Holtzworth-Monroe, A., & Johnson, S. (2011). Guidelines for classifying evidence-based treatments in couple and family therapy. *Family Process*, 50(3), 377–392.

Sexton, T. L., Alexander, J. F., & Mease, A. L. (2004). Levels of evidence for the models and mechanisms of therapeutic change in family and couple therapy. In M. J. Lambert, A. E. Bergin, & S. L. Garfield (Eds.), *Handbook of psychotherapy and behavior change* (5th ed., pp. 590–646). New York, NY: Wiley.

Sexton, T. L., & Alexander, J. (2003). Functional family therapy: A mature clinical model for working with at-risk adolescents and their families. In T. L. Sexton, G. R. Weeks, & M. S. Robbins (Eds.), *Handbook of family therapy* (pp. 323–350). New York, NY: Brunner-Routledge.

Sheidow, A. J., Henggeler, S. W., & Schoenwald S. K. (2003). Multisystemic therapy. In T. L. Sexton, G. R. Weeks, & M. S. Robbins (Eds.), *Handbook of family therapy* (pp. 303–322). New York, NY: Brunner-Routledge.

Shulman, L. (1992). *The skills of helping: Individuals, families and groups* (3rd ed.). Itasca, IL: Peacock.

Smith, D. (2012). Jacquelines of all trades or masters of some? Negative implications of focusing on common factors. *Social Work, 57*(3), 283–287.

Snyder, C., Michael, S., & Cheavens, J. (1999). Hope as a psychotherapeutic foundation of common factors, placebos and expectancies. In D. Hubble, B. Duncan, & S. Miller (Eds.), *The heart and soul of change* (pp. 179–200). Washington, DC: American Psychological Association.

Sprenkle, D. H., Davis, S. D., & Lebow, J. L. (2009). *Common factors in couple and family therapy: The overlooked foundation for effective practice.* New York, NY: Guilford Press.

Sydow, K. v., Beher, S., Schweitzer, J., & Retzlaff, R. (2010). The efficacy of systemic therapy with adult patients: A meta-content analysis in 38 randomized controlled trials. *Family Process, 49*(4), 457–485.

Sydow, K. v., Retzlaff, R., Beher, S., Haun, M. W., & Schweitzer, J. (2013). The efficacy of systemic therapy for child and adolescent externalizing disorders: A systematic review of 47 RCT. *Family Process, 52*(4), 576–618.

Taft, J. (1949). Time as the medium of the helping process. *Jewish Social Service Quarterly, 24*, 2.

Tomm, K., & Wright, L. M. (1979). Training in family therapy: Perceptual, cognitive and executive skills. *Family Process, 18*(3), 227–250.

Walsh, J. (2003). *Endings in clinical practice.* Chicago, IL: Lyceum.

Questions for Discussion

These questions are useful for class discussion or simply to get a conceptual outline of the chapters.

CHAPTER 1

1. Describing family resilience, discuss how strengths-based family practice builds on it. How might this affect the way social workers assess and intervene with families?
2. Describe what is meant by social workers working on the "inside" and on the "outside" of families. Discuss the relation of the two in practice.
3. Describe the shift in emphasis of the charity organization societies (COSs) from charitable giving to helping people organize their worlds and cope with troubles. Discuss the implications of this shift.
4. Social workers were involved with families from the beginning. Discuss the implications of this focus on the family. What is the difference from a focus on helping individuals alone?
5. Describe the implications of working with a "situation" as defined in the chapter, rather than simply working with individuals. Discuss what developments in practice the focus on situations implied.
6. Describe the social work fields of practice that emerged in the first decades of the twentieth century. Discuss the role family would naturally play in each field.
7. How would casework be a common element in social work fields of practice? Discuss what might be some of the problems of a major focus on casework alone.
8. Defining the transactional and systems theory orientations to social work, discuss their contribution to a previous, predominant focus on casework. Discuss how family intervention might use transactional and systems theory orientations.
9. Describe in greater detail "family systemic therapy" as defined in the chapter. Discuss the extent to which this definition would resemble a traditional social work perspective on working with families.
10. Describe the human needs for which families uniquely provide. Discuss how this would provide a basis for working with families at multiple intervention points, including environmental systems.
11. Define relational justice. Discuss how questions of relational justice are embedded in the human needs for which families provide. Discuss the implications of this for social work practice with families.

12. Discuss the meaning of the feminist critique that family therapy practice had implicitly accepted gender dominance in families. Discuss how authority can be differentiated from from gender dominance in the family. What would be the implications of this differentiation for practice?
13. The transcultural perspective employs an active concept of family cultural adaptation for social work. Describe this perspective. Discuss its implications for social work practice.
14. Using the example of a family dealing with a member with special needs, describe and discuss four ways that family education might help the family.
15. Discuss the differences of family education from more individualized family interventions. Discuss the advantages and disadvantages of each.

CHAPTER 2

1. Describe and discuss the implications for family social work of the statement that every person is inherently relational.
2. Describe the qualities of the relational person. Describe the implications of family membership. In these contexts, discuss why the concept of an "autonomous" person would be somewhat of a myth.
3. Define the meanings of obligations and relational justice in the context of family membership. Discuss why these are important for social work with families.
4. Define and describe the relation of the "I" and the "me" in each person. How might one help a client such as Gloria (case study 2.1) to discover her "I," as well as understand her behavior as her boss might perceive it, and eventually deal with the implications of her obsessions about Dr. Smith?
5. Defining empathy, discuss how it is a powerful tool in the helping process. How would it contribute to a "holding system"?
6. Define "relational task," and give examples of such tasks. Discuss why the concept is important in family practice.
7. Discuss how one's self-differentiation (agency) and connectedness (communion) come to be defined in a relational task.
8. Discuss how one's attachment and membership patterns come to be defined in a relational task, giving a descriptive example of the task.
9. Using cultural examples other than British and Japanese family cultures illustrated in table 2.1, compare and discuss the different meanings of separateness and connectedness, differentiation, and integration in the cultures selected.
10. Define and discuss the relations of attachment theory to family membership.
11. Define the types of childhood attachment. Discuss how these types would apply to adult attachment.
12. Defining fidelity and commitment in family relational terms, discuss the relations of these learned, social sentiments to adult attachment and to the development of a secure relational base. Why might they be necessary?

13. Discuss the process of attachments being reworked at different developmental stages, as in the case of Marisa Antonelli.

CHAPTER 3

1. Taking one family life cycle stage outline on table 3.1, describe and illustrate the personal and relational tasks needed to cope with the demands of the stage.
2. Identify and discuss the implications for the family and for family members of "second-order changes in family status" required to move effectively to the next stage.
3. Identify and discuss the shifts in Sarah's and Phil's relationship that were needed when her back went out. Discuss the role of the social worker in helping them carry out these tasks with each other.
4. Using Walsh's chart on the resilient family (table 1.3), discuss the qualities of the resilient family, which would help families and family members deal with the stress and changes needed in any one stage of the family life cycle.
5. Taking the case of Miguel and Juana (case study 3.2), describe the personal and relational tasks both need to do. Discuss what might be the role of the social worker working with both of them.
6. Discuss what Brian and Lisa (case study 3.3) need to do with themselves (personal tasks) and with each other (relational tasks) (including dealing with some of the "myths of marriage") for the relationship to succeed.
7. Taking two principles of the systems perspective in the chapter, using examples from the case studies or from other sources, describe the implications of each for understanding family systems. Discuss why these would be important to social workers working with families.
8. Discuss why language and communication are important as the relationship of the newly married couple develops. Discuss what might be the role of the social worker helping couples develop language and communication.
9. Discuss how the development of language and communication worked in the case of Jim and Cheryl (case study 3.4).
10. Discuss the effect of outside, situational stress on family members dealing with personal and relational tasks at a particular stage. Discuss how the social worker would work with family members dealing with situational stress, as well as with personal and relational tasks.
11. Discuss how normalization of the stresses of personal, of relational, and of situational tasks might help family members cope better.

CHAPTER 4

1. Describe how family structures develop out of family members' subjective perceptions.
2. Discuss what difference might come from the social worker "entering" the family, as described in the chapter, rather than remaining an objective "expert" outside the family. Describe how this might take place.

3. Discuss the implications for social work with families of John Gottman's research on the way happily and unhappily married couples deal with differences.

4. Describe the interaction between Mark and Leslie, Amber, and Julie in case study 4.1, with particular focus on what went on between Mark and Leslie, including Amber's role in the interchange. Discuss why the episode is important for an understanding of Mark and Leslie's relationship.

5. Taking the chapter's discussion of the way criticism, defensiveness, contempt and stonewalling might have disturbed (but didn't really disturb) Mark and Leslie's communication, discuss the implications of the identification of these patterns for social work family assessment. Discuss the implications of the identification of these patterns for social work family intervention.

6. Defining identity bonds, discuss why they are so important in families. Discuss why identity bonds are fragile. Discuss how other bonds might shore up identity bonds in their processes of deterioration and reorganization over a family's relational history.

7. Describe a cross-generational coalition. Discuss how a very strong cross-generational coalition would potentially undermine the spousal coalition. What might a social worker do with the family in response to this situation?

8. Describe how roles are developed reciprocally with other family members. Since they are developed reciprocally, discuss how they might be altered.

9. Discuss why socialization of children demands unequal authority. Discuss how a cross-generational coalition might undermine this process.

10. Differentiate power from authority in the family, using the example of the infant. Discuss the desirable balances in families between power, boundaries, and alignment.

11. Discuss how recurring, self-reinforcing patterns in families eventually come to be perceived as "rules." Using some of the case studies, discuss what might bring about a shift in these "rules." How long might this shift take?

12. When the pursuer-distancer pattern becomes attack-withdraw, sometimes "softening" can shift the negative interactions and prevent an out-of-control episode. Using case study 4.2, discuss the possible positive and negative effects of a softening on either Maria's or Tom's part. Discuss why such a softening would be perceived by either as very difficult to do.

13. Discuss how Armand's repair process in case study 4.3 eventually brought Rosalind to relent. Discuss why she initially had difficulty accepting it. Discuss why Armand would have difficulty carrying out the relationship repair.

14. Discuss the reasons social workers deal with all of the levels of family functioning listed on table 4.1. Discuss the implications of this for an integrative, theoretical approach to family intervention that, when possible, would "assimilate" different family therapy approaches into a broader picture of social work with families.

CHAPTER 5

1. Compare the cases of the Hmong family (case study 5.1) and the hospital that provided a healing space (case study 5.2). Discuss what was missing in one and present in the other in terms of cultural and family implications. Discuss the implications of these differences for social work practice with families.

2. Taking the definition of transcultural practice in the first part of the chapter, discuss the common threads social workers with families need to look for in dealing with families from particular cultures. In the context of cultural diversity and diversity within cultures as well, discuss the meaning for social work practice with families of the metaphor "rivers flowing into the sea."

3. Discuss how the transcultural work of the family is embodied in relational work, using examples of cultural implications of this work.

4. Using examples from different cultures, discuss the relation of multicultural perspectives to a transcultural perspective.

5. Using examples, describe the differences between assessment with individuals and assessment with families. Discuss the cultural component of each.

6. Discuss why assessment demands a purpose and a time focus on the present, with consideration for past and future realities.

7. Discuss why assessment with families would need to focus on the family's internal and external balances in relation to present tasks and realities.

8. Recent findings point out that there is diversity within one cultural theme, such as *machismo* for Hispanic males. Identify and discuss the implications for social work practice of this diversity within one cultural theme. Discuss the differences it would make for assessment and intervention.

9. Using Lee's (1996) chart (table 5.1) as a context, discuss the importance for social work practice of the concept of cultural transition.

10. Discuss the implications for social work practice with families of the idea that different family members have very different interpretations of cultural themes within a common set of meanings in the dynamic contexts of today's societies. Using one of the case studies in the chapter, such as that of Catherine and Dwain (case study 5.3), discuss how the social worker might help family members develop a constructive conversation around these differences.

11. Using one of the cases in the chapter, discuss how the list of strategies for transcultural assessment would provide guideposts to discern both differences and commonalities across cultures.

12. Taking one of the first five principles of transcultural practice, discuss its implications for working with one of the cases in the chapter. Give a detailed description of how you think this principle might influence practice.

13. Taking one of the second five principles of transcultural practice, discuss its implications for working with one of the cases in the chapter. Give a detailed description of how you think this principle might influence practice.
14. Taking the Hong family case, discuss the family implications and the implications for Myong of their move to a new neighborhood and a new school. Discuss how the social worker helped the family, Myong, and the school cope with the situation. Discuss the transcultural implications of the case.
15. Discuss the bicultural tasks of Jack and Jung's family (case study 5.6). Discuss how both seem initially oblivious to these tasks. Discuss the work of the social worker to assist them with these tasks. Discuss how the Christmas tree becomes a metaphor for larger family realities and for their personal and relational tasks.
16. Discuss the use of the genogram with the J. family. What emerges from the genogram about family relations as they affect the father's relational tasks with Kwak and the others in the family and the court. Discuss Kwak's personal and relational tasks in response to his father's efforts to rebalance their relationship.
17. Discuss the contribution of the ecomap to understanding the J. family's relations and surroundings.
18. Reviewing goal setting and intervention, discuss the work with the J. family to create safety and relational justice and help the family develop its relational structure.

CHAPTER 6

1. How is the couple the executive subsystem of an elaborated family (two or more generations)? Discuss the implications of this for social work practice.
2. Identify and discuss the further relational tasks and implicit issues when marriage is considered as a covenant (such as in table 6.1). Taking one of the case studies in the chapter, discuss the ways that such commitment could be processed positively or negatively by the couple.
3. Using one of the case studies in the chapter, describe and discuss the concept of projective identification in the early history of a couple, including its influence on their communication.
4. Identify and discuss the personal tasks and couple tasks implicit in case studies 6.1 and 6.2. Identify and discuss the tasks for *ego* and for *alter* as the couple seeks to resolve the problems that the personal patterns create for the relationship.
5. Identify and discuss the family-of-origin issues that both Rafael and Angie (case study 6.3) need to deal with to move their marriage beyond its four-year holding pattern. Discuss the personal and relational tasks implicit in this work.

6. Identify and discuss the tasks the social worker would have in helping Sherry and Bill (case study 6.4) make a beginning. Discuss the difficulties you might anticipate. Why would it take at least two sessions to make a beginning?

7. In the case of Sherry and Bill, the social worker might centralize herself as the therapist and take charge of their interaction, or she might let the couple begin in their own way, providing a minimal amount of structure. Discuss the positives and negatives of each approach to creating a holding environment and helping the couple begin. Based on this discussion, discuss what should be your approach.

8. Using any one of the case studies in chapter 6, discuss the importance of the holding environment to their beginning. How might the worker structure this holding environment? What might be the implicit hang-ups to avoid in this particular case?

9. Discuss why it might be risky to centralize yourself and your problem solving suggestions as your couple attempts to begin. Use any case study in chapter 6.

10. Using any case study in chapter 6 other than Rafael and Angie's, discuss how the social worker might help the couple do an *enactment* of their relationship. Create an imaginary scenario for this enactment. When they do enact, discuss how you might help them to use their enactment.

11. Let us assume that one of the couples in chapter 6 (other than Rafael and Angie) gets stuck and has difficulty beginning. Discuss the use of the miracle question, or the exception question, to help them move along. Create an imaginary scenario with the case you have chosen.

12. Taking a case in chapter 6, other than Rafael and Angie's, you discover that the couple has an extremely unequal and unbalanced relationship. Discuss the possible effects on the couple of your asking how each of them perceives the fairness of the relationship. How would you manage the risk that one partner might become explosive when asked this question?

13. Using the case of John and Eileen (case study 6.5), discuss how you might assist both to deal with issues of commitment in the relationship when Eileen would implicitly prefer you to pronounce the relationship as unworkable and John would prefer you to create a quick, painless fix so that he might rejoin his wife. What personal and relational tasks for both would you expect to emerge from their discussion? What would be your role in assisting them?

14. Using the two communication vignettes, let us assume for the moment that the Asian couples are interested in working with you and that this is their initial conversation. Discuss what you would need to do with this conversation and with them to help the conversation become a useful beginning enactment.

15. Discuss the possible use of MRE with the two Asian couples in the communication vignettes. Identify and discuss what might be the possible advantages and disadvantages of MRE with them over a more individualized couples' counseling approach.
16. Using the approaches to marriage and relationship education (MRE) suggested by the research of Halford and Moore, discuss the advantages and disadvantages of MRE in comparison with the more individualized family intervention described in the other parts of chapter 6.

CHAPTER 7

1. Using one of the cases in chapter 7, discuss the distinct tasks of the middle phase with couples continuing from the beginnings they have established. Using the same case, discuss why the middle phase would also be considered the "work phase."
2. Using the case of Nicholas and Johanna (case study 7.1), discuss the use of communication to shift the discussion from a concrete discussion of the couples' division of labor (Who will do the checks?) to deeper relationship issues.
3. From the sample of their communication in case study 7.1, discuss what tasks lie ahead of Nicholas and Johanna. Discuss what you would expect to be the future role of the social worker during their middle phase.
4. Using a case in chapter 7 other than case study 7.1, discuss the use of communication in relation to the couple's difficult issues of relational closeness and boundaries.
5. Discuss how "taking the attitude of the other" in the empathic mode could be a tool to move communication along. Use one of the cases in the chapter or a case with which you are familiar to describe this process.
6. Describe and discuss the use of task prescriptions to move the couple process along. What might be the benefits in using task prescriptions? What might be the dangers of using task prescriptions? What might the social worker do to counter these dangers?
7. What were the factors in the dynamics of their relationship and in the situation, that made it difficult for Rita and Joav Green (case study 7.2) to make a decision together? Analyze what the worker did to move the process along. What do you think of it?
8. Describe and discuss the implications for Joseph and Paula (case study 7.3) of the worker's prescribing a partial shutdown of communication. How would it move the process along? What might be the dangers of doing this? What might counter these dangers?
9. Taking Haley's framework for directives and using case studies 7.3, 7.4, and 7.5, discuss and compare the use of directives and the way the couples responded to them.

10. Ashford and Louise Caldwell (case study 7.7) and Bonnie and Andy Kowalski (case study 7.6) rediscovered a certain closeness in their relationships with each other after a difficult process. Compare these cases and discuss what similar or different factors might have brought both couples to cycle back into a closer relationship with each other.
11. Describe and discuss the role of the social worker in these two cases.

CHAPTER 8

1. Using the family structural theory developed in this book, identify and discuss the reasons why even in a family with a very centralizing, acting-out child, it is important for the social worker first to focus on the way the parents are processing the child's behavior, rather than on the child's issues or the child himself or herself.
2. Analyze the beginning process of the Kim case (case study 8.2) with particular focus on what took place and why the social worker did not ask Justin to come to the first meeting.
3. Using some of the chapter's cases as examples, discuss the differences involved in working with the family as an outside "expert" or "joining" the family temporarily while remaining a professional. Within the complexity of possible alliances in the family, discuss the implications for the helping process of maintaining this position.
4. Identify and discuss what reasons might lead a social worker to work only with the parents (a one-step beginning) rather than seeing the parents and then the family as a whole (a two-step beginning). Discuss why it would not be advisable to begin with the whole family without first seeing the parents.
5. In the Antonelli case (case study 8.4), identify and discuss the family relational shifts that had to take place for Marisa eventually to appropriately emancipate. Discuss what the social worker did with the family.
6. In the Peterson case (case study 8.5), identify and discuss the relational and personal shifts that happened for Jerry to learn to control his tantrums. What did the social worker do to help this take place? Discuss why the social worker immediately put Jerry in charge of his tantrums.
7. In the case of George, Miriam, and Sean (case study 8.6), discuss the meanings of the shift from power themes to attachment themes.
8. In the O'Conner case (case study 8.9), analyzing family structure, discuss why the family was unable to respond to Peter's disability and Maura's Parkinson disease—indeed, seeming relationally paralyzed. Identify and discuss the family structural shifts optimally needing to take place within the whole (three-generation) family as Peter's and Maura's functioning declines.
9. In the O'Conner case (case study 8.9), discuss what might be the social worker's role in facilitating a better adjustment. Where should he or she start? Who should be the units of attention? What could they do together?

CHAPTER 9

1. Using the case of Tom Fields's family (case study 9.1), identify and discuss the structural shifts between Tom, Ashley, and Meg as Meg went through a dying process and then after Meg's death. Discuss what the social worker would need to do with family members to help them find an appropriate structure and balance.

2. Identify and discuss the family structural and attachment theory reasons why divorce needs to be seen as a family transaction and a process, rather than an event.

3. When parents are divorcing, identify and discuss the reasons why the social worker would need to avoid triangulation into the family system. Discuss the most appropriate role for the social worker to maintain, explaining how this would be done.

4. Identify and discuss the family practice implications of E. W. Beals's list of five dysfunctional beliefs and cognitions about divorce.

5. Identify and discuss the structural issues of relational vacuums and the realignment of relational architecture that takes place, often with great difficulty, during the process of divorce. Using the case of Edna Friedman and Renee (case study 9.2), discuss the implications of these structural shifts for the social worker working with parents, and their children, in the process of divorce.

6. Using the case of Rich and Maria (case study 9.3), identify and discuss what relationships need to be maintained and what structural shifts need to take place between Rich, Maria, and Julia. Using this case, discuss the role of the social worker responding to the needs of a family in process of "blending."

7. Bereaved families, divorcing families, postdivorce families, and families in process of "blending" all have very different needs for family education. Taking one of these, discuss what particular themes would be important to emphasize in a family education program designed for them.

8. Discuss what makes many underorganized families different from the above families. In what ways might they be similar? Discuss the roles that social institutions often play with underorganized families, and the implications of this for social workers.

9. Using the Hannon family case (case study 9.4), analyze the interaction of the family and the social worker with the family as the interview process shifts through eight phases. Discuss the changes which take place. Discuss what longer-term work with the Hannon family would be necessary after the initial session.

CHAPTER 10

1. Taking one social institution, identify and discuss the role of the social worker between family and institution. Using your example, discuss how,

working inside the family, the social worker is also doing institutional work, and, working within the institution, the social worker is doing family work.

2. Identify and discuss the rationale for a family component in the school social worker's role. What school focus should the school social worker bring to work with the family? How would that give direction to the process with the family? What family focus would the school social worker bring to her work with teachers and the principal in school?

3. Using the case of Alan (case study 10.1), analyze and discuss the social worker's intervention with Alan, with the school as a system, and with family members during a difficult stage of the divorce, during the postdivorce, and during the remarriage process. Discuss how each stage of the process affected Alan. Discuss the school social worker's intervention with Alan and between home and school.

4. Using your understanding of family preservation practice in child welfare, as well as work with underorganized families, analyze and discuss the social worker's work with the Clark family (case study 10.2), stage by stage of the intervention. What do you think should (and could) be achieved in this necessarily short-term, but intensive, work over a few months?

5. Continuing with the Clark family, discuss and evaluate what the worker's goals with the family seemed to be. Discuss what problems might arise if the worker's involvement were open-ended and long-term. Why is the referral process so important? Evaluate what seemed to have been achieved in the short-term contact with the Clark family.

6. Foster care is a temporary placement with a substitute-care home with the intent of eventually returning the child(ren) to the family of origin within a time frame set by the court, but when the home situation is suitable. Applying what you know about attachment and family structure, discuss what family issues are likely in this situation between the foster family, the court and the family of origin. Using the case of Alice and Michael (case study 10.3), identify and discuss the type of family-oriented practice needed to work between the court and the family units.

7. The probation officer in the juvenile court works with the youth on probation as the identified client with the objective of assisting the youth to meet the court's expectations. The officer will report to the court whether these expectations have been met. However, invariably, as in the three case studies in the chapter, there is family involvement. Because of this, many professional courts have included the family as a unit of necessary attention, through contract or arrangement with other services, although the practice is not universal. In the three cases, discuss the family involvement needed if the youths are to meet the court's expectations. Discuss the roles the social worker, as a probation officer, should take with the youth(s) and the family. Discuss possible relations with other services, as in the Pollack case.

CHAPTER 11

1. Taking John Rolland's psychosocial model for illness and disability, embodied in his three principles, discuss the principles' implications for the social work assessment of the O'Conner family (case study 8.9) as it struggles with the illnesses and disability of Peter and Maura, its first generation.

2. Continuing with the O'Conner family, the social worker is working for a special senior citizens unit of a family service-mental health center. Discuss what might be feasible goals to help this family discover some of its own resilience and to help Peter and Maura be less isolated. Discuss who would be in the unit of attention and what might be the process of working with this family.

3. The social worker is working with the O'Conner case in a nursing home, and nursing home care seems to be the only possibility. Discuss what might be feasible goals to help this family discover some of its own resilience and to help Peter and Maura be less isolated. Discuss who would be in the unit of attention and what might be the process of working with this family.

4. Describe and discuss how the combination of Victoria and Manuel Jimenez's (case study 11.1) undocumented status in a different culture and marital issues paralyzed their efforts to get medical and dietary help for Teresa, also paralyzing their ability to deal with the marital issues.

5. Continuing with the Jimenez family, describe and discuss the marital issues that prevented their taking action together. Laura is a medical social worker from their clinic. Describe and discuss Laura's multifaceted approach to working with the Jimenez family, which brought them eventually to get nutrition assistance for Teresa and to begin marriage counseling with a Spanish-speaking counselor from Catholic Charities.

6. Discuss the possible use of the multiple family group (MFG) modality in dealing with issues of family health information and health stress around serious illness that will affect family functioning. Discuss the social worker's responsibilities moderating the "group within a group." How would this be different from classical group work?

7. Discuss how a psychoeducational approach might be useful for families experiencing intense emotional outbursts directed toward a schizophrenic member. Taking the particulars of the MFG approach described in the chapter, how might the group be structured and the group process proceed?

8. In the case of Jack and Barbara (case study 11.2), discuss the overlapping family issues connected with Jack's leaving for the hospital and his return home. In light of this assessment, discuss why George would focus on Jack and Barbara rather than on the girls, who have experienced the most immediate conflict. Discuss the personal and relational work the parents and the two girls need to do for the family to settle into Jack's being home. Discuss what needs to take place in the family group sessions for this to happen.

9. Examining the case of Charlotte des Jardins, discuss the personal and family life cycle issues connected with her depression and her suicide attempt. Outline and discuss the steps the social worker took with Charlotte and her family over the two-year history of her working with the family.
10. Often multiproblem families with complex needs (or underorganized families) are serviced by many agencies, fragmenting what is offered and confusing the family. Case studies 11.4, 11.5, and 11.6 present three wrap-around team situations. Examining all three cases, discuss what team members and the team as a whole had to do to empower, but not overwhelm, the family.

CHAPTER 12

1. Discuss the relational "work" of ending. Discuss why ending a professional relationship is necessary if life goes on in any case.
2. Discuss the differences between (a) the social worker ending with the client(s) and (b) the social worker primarily helping the client end and secondarily making his or her ending.
3. Discuss differences between ending with a single client and ending with a family network.
4. In the case of Becky (case study 12.1), identify and discuss the relational shifts that took place. Discuss how they should be handled in relation to ending and in relation to Becky's new beginnings in high school.
5. Identify and discuss your thinking about why the ending with Michael and Alyson took three months. Discuss the work of ending in this case.
6. Often institutional time dictates the ending, as in a school or a ninety-day intensive family preservation process. Discuss what additional components, such an external limit, provide to the ending process. Discuss how it would influence and make a difference in ongoing work from the beginning of the process with the family.
7. In Roberta and Sam Piotrowski's case (case study 12.3), discuss the dual ending and the shift that occurred when Sam admitted to his affair and intent to divorce Roberta. Discuss the implications of this for each partner. Discuss how the endings might be best managed.
8. Discuss the research and practice issues that arise when the measure of effectiveness is derived from the expectation that the clients' expected outcome in the first interview will be achieved by the end of the process. If this is the only way that effectiveness can be measured, discuss why the findings, although useful, may need some qualification.
9. Discuss the implications for research and for the theory of Hubble, Duncan, and Miller's findings that the beneficial effects of intervention rest largely on a combination of four (common) therapeutic factors.
10. Discuss the research and practice implications of the critique of Hubble, Duncan, and Miller's common factors effectiveness approach.

Index

About the Authors

Robert Constable has been a social work practitioner with couples and families for more than forty years, working in a family service agency, in an inner-city parish, in family life education, in private practice, and in school social work. He is professor emeritus in the School of Social Work at Loyola University Chicago and has published extensively in social work, including the widely used *School Social Work: Practice, Policy, and Research Perspectives*, now in its eighth edition.

Daniel B. Lee is professor at Soongsil University, Graduate School of Social Work in Seoul, Korea. He is professor emeritus in the School of Social Work at Loyola University Chicago. He has also taught at Doshisa University in Kyoto, Japan, and Hallym University in Chooncheon, Korea. He has been a clinical member of the American Association for Marriage and Family Therapy since 1972. He is founder of the Transcultural Family Institute and cofounder and former president of the Global Awareness Society International. Professor Lee was educated in Korea and in the United States. He served as a commissioned officer and a social worker in the US Army, overseas and in the United States. He has been a consultant on cross-cultural family life and family advocacy to the Department of Defense. He is also an ordained minister in the United Methodist Church and has been in private practice since 1987. He is the author of several books and more than one hundred journal articles.